THE WORLD ALMANAC FOR KIDS 2007

WORLD ALMANAC BOOKS
A Division of World Almanac Education Group, Inc.
A WRC Media Company

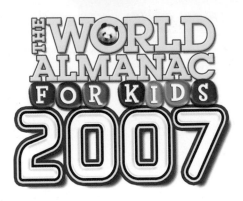

THE WORLD ALMANAC FOR KIDS 2007

EDITOR: Zoë Kashner

CONSULTANTS: Margaret Altoff, Supervisor of Social Studies K-12, School District 11, Colorado Springs, Colorado; Richard Hogen, Director of Preschool/Elementary Division, National Science Teachers Association

CONTRIBUTORS: Ryan Bartelmay, Maria Brock Schulman, Emily Keyes, Chris Larson, Sara Levin, William A. McGeveran, Jr., Caroline Milne, Maureen Ryan, Aram Schvey, Evan Schwartz, Charu Suri

KID ADVISORS: Camille Boushey, Yakima, Washington; Leonard and Andrea Chen, Kent, Washington; Abigail Cline, Fort Lauderdale, Florida; Vanessa Cole, Killeen, Texas; Sariah Dilka, Castle Rock, Colorado; Kevin Finn, Arlington, Virginia; Natasha Hallam, Tye, Texas; Elyse Stephens, Emmaus, Pennsylvania; Cheney Ravitz, Takoma Park, Maryland; Carly Lee and Jordanna Roman, Larchmont, New York; Tony Sanchez, Phoenix, Arizona

DESIGN: BILL SMITH STUDIO

Creative Director: Brian Kobberger **Project Director:** David Borkman
Design: Geron Hoy, Ron Leighton, Eric Hoffsten, Marina Terletsky, Mie Tsuchida
Production: Eric Murray, Steven Scheluchin, Mie Tsuchida

WORLD ALMANAC BOOKS

Managing Editor: Lisa Lazzara; **Senior Editor:** Erik C. Gopel; **Editors:** Sarah Janssen, Vincent G. Spadafora; **Associate Editors:** M. L. Liu, Andy Steinitz;
Desktop Production Staff: Michael Meyerhofer, Sean Westmoreland

WORLD ALMANAC EDUCATION GROUP

Chief Executive Officer, WRC Media Inc.: Ann Jackson
COO, EVP WRC Media, Inc.: Rick Nota
President, World Almanac Education Group: Peter M. Esposito
General Manager/Publisher: Ken Park
Vice President – Sales and Marketing: Lola A. Valenciano
Associate Publisher/Photo Research: Edward A. Thomas
Sales & Marketing Associates: Julia Suarez, Sheena Scott

CONTENTS

Faces and Places
6

Animals
20

Art
32

Birthdays
36

Books
42

Buildings
48

Camping
54

Disasters
56

Environment
62

Fashion
74

Games and Toys
76

Geography
80

Health
88

Holidays
98

Homework Help
102

Inventions
108

Language
110

Magic
116

Military
118

Money
122

Movies and TV
126

Museums
130

Music and Dance
132

Mythology
136

Nations

Governments
140

Maps
142

Nations of the World
154

Kids Around the World
178

Native Americans
180

Numbers
184

Population
190

Prizes and Contests
196

Religion
202

Science
206

Space
218

Sports
228

Olympics
230

Auto Racing
232

Baseball
234

Basketball
236

Football
238

Hockey
242

Soccer
243

Tennis
244

X Games
245

Technology and Computers
246

Transportation
250

Travel
254

United States
260

Presidents
270

Time Line
277

They Made History
285

Map of the U.S.
286

States
288

Washington, DC
307

World History

Middle East
318

Africa
320

Asia
322

Europe
324

The Americas
328

Looking Back
330

Women in History
332

Answers
334

Index
338

Photo Credits
351

Volunteering
308

Weather
310

Weights and Measures
314

family tv

Life Is Suite

Dylan and Cole Sprouse star in *The Suite Life of Zack and Cody*. The twins have a little too much fun living it up at a swanky Boston hotel.

Don't Be a Hater

Everybody Hates Chris shows what it was like growing up for comedian Chris Rock. Tyler James Williams plays Chris at age 13.

The Amazing Linz Family

The Amazing Race: Family Edition "saw" the winning Linz family cutting it up in New Orleans, Louisiana.

Idolicious

One member of this "family of finalists" became your 2006 American Idol. Can you spot the winner?

big screen hits

Wallace, Gromit, and Oscar

Wallace & Gromit: The Curse of the Were-Rabbit takes vegetables seriously, and that paid off with a 2005 Oscar for Best Animated Feature Film.

Yo-ho-ho!

Orlando Bloom and Keira Knightley star in *Pirates of the Caribbean: Dead Man's Chest*.

Reese Witherspoon

Born: March 22, 1976, New Orleans, Louisiana

Claim to Fame: Won the 2005 Oscar for Best Actress

Fun Facts:
- Her full name is Laura Jeanne Reese Witherspoon.
- Her ancestor John Witherspoon signed the Declaration of Independence.
- Reese also won a 2001 MTV Movie Award for Best Comedic Performance, for *Legally Blonde*.

CUT-OUT
Mini-Poster
THE WORLD
ALMANAC
FOR KIDS

LeBron James

Born: December 30, 1984, Akron, Ohio

Claim to Fame: Youngest-ever NBA All-Star MVP in 2006

Fun Facts:
▶ Was the top draft pick in 2003 out of St. Vincent–St. Mary High School in Akron, Ohio.
▶ Wears the same number, 23, as his role model, Michael Jordan.

CUT-OUT Mini-Poster
THE WORLD ALMANAC FOR KIDS

Jeff Gordon

Born: August 4, 1971, Vallejo, California

Claim to Fame: Four-time NASCAR Cup Series champion

Fun Facts:

▶ He won his first quarter-midget car championship by the time he was eight years old.

▶ At 16 he became the youngest person ever granted a racing license by the United States Auto Club (USAC).

Black Eyed Peas

Members: Taboo, Fergie, will.i.am, and apl.de.ap

Claim to Fame: Triple-platinum *Monkey Business* (2005), double-platinum *Elephunk* (2003)

Facts:
▶ will.i.am and apl.de.ap have been friends since eighth grade.
▶ Fergie is the newest group member. She joined the Black Eyed Peas to record *Elephunk.*

CUT-OUT
Mini-Poster
THE
WORLD
ALMANAC
FOR KIDS

HIGH SCHOOL MUSICAL

Soundtrack of the year

High School Hit

Zac Efron and Vanessa Anne Hutchinson star as two teens with little in common who discover their love of singing in *High School Musical*.

Carrie Up the Charts

She won the 2005 American Idol competition, and that was just the beginning. Carrie Underwood's album *Some Hearts* reached #1 on the Billboard Top Country Album chart.

Young Originals

Aly turned 17 in 2006, and her sister A.J. turned 15. These talented teens—with the last name Michalka—sing their own songs, play their own instruments, and are writing their own one-way ticket to success.

13

winter olympic winners

Giant Gold

Julia Mancuso earned gold for the U.S. in the Women's Giant Slalom for the first time in 22 years.

Black Gold

Shani Davis of Evanston, Illinois, won the 1,000-meter Speedskating to become the first black gold medalist in Winter Olympic history.

The Flying Tomato

Shaun White (right, with Daniel Kass) burned through the Men's Snowboard Half-Pipe competition to take home the gold.

Cindy, Champion of Canada

Cindy Klassen took home five medals, the most in the games, including gold in the Women's 1,500-meter Speedskating.

15

Sports of the year

Quest for the Cup

Landon Donovan hopes to help lead the United States soccer team to glory at the 2006 FIFA World Cup in Germany.

The Start of a Classic

Japan beat Cuba, 10-6, to become the first World Baseball Classic champions. Here the players salute their manager, Japanese home-run king Sadaharu Oh.

Big Ben's Big Game

Ben Roethlisberger at 23 years old became the youngest quarterback ever to lead a team to a Super Bowl championship when his Pittsburgh Steelers won a record-tying fifth Super Bowl, 21-10, over the Seattle Seahawks.

No Way

In summer 2005, pro skateboarder Danny Way got huge air by riding down his nine-story "MegaRamp" and over the Great Wall of China. He also won the X-Games Big Air competition despite a sprained ankle.

17

news of the year

Panda-monium

In summer 2005, giant panda cub Tai Shan (tie-SHON) was born at the National Zoo in Washington, D.C. Here, he plays with his mother Mei Xiang.

Olympic Charity Champion

Speedskating gold and silver medalist Joey Cheek (left) put his bonus money where his heart is—donating his $40,000 bonus to Right to Play. That organization, founded by former Norwegian Olympic athlete Johann Olav Koss, helps disadvantaged kids get involved in sports.

Supreme Court

Associate Justice Samuel Alito is sworn in by Chief Justice John Roberts (right), as Alito's family and President George W. Bush (left) look on.

Hero Laid To Rest

Civil rights pioneer Rosa Parks died on October 24, 2005. She was the first woman to lie in honor in the Capitol Rotunda. More than 30,000 people came to pay their respects.

Parks was arrested in 1955 for refusing to give up her bus seat to a white passenger in Montgomery, Alabama. Her act inspired a 381-day boycott that helped end segregation on the city's buses.

7053

Americans and Iraqis

As Operation Iraqi Freedom entered its fourth year in spring 2006, more than 100,000 American troops continued efforts to bring peace and order to the new Iraqi nation.

Animals

Who is Python Pete? ➡ page 30

Furry or scaly, creepy or crawly, schoolbus-sized or microscopic—animals fascinate people of all stripes. Here's some news from the Animal Kingdom.

Animal News

The Odd Couple

Usually when a hamster and a snake are in the same cage, it's because the first is dinner for the second. Not so for Gohan, a hamster, and Aochan, a four-foot-long rat snake. Both live in the same cage at Mutsugoro Okoku Zoo, outside of Tokyo, Japan. Actually, Gohan's name is the Japanese word for "meal," which is what he was put into the snake's cage to be. But Aochan decided to befriend the furry critter rather than eat him. Sometimes Gohan even climbs onto Aochan for a snooze on his back.

Pet Project

Pet owners who feel guilty for leaving Fido and Spot alone all day while they go to work or school should listen up. Adrian Martinez (owner of six cats and two dogs) started an Internet radio station especially for pets called DogCatRadio.com. The station has 4 DJs streaming live, animal-themed programs 17 hours each day—including a "Spanish Hour" for "bilingual" animals. Popular song requests include the Baha Men's "Who Let the Dogs Out" and Elvis Presley's "Hound Dog." DJs also offer advice to four-legged friends everywhere: "Remember, be kind to your mailman. He only wants to deliver the mail."

Life on Earth

This time line shows how life developed on Earth. The earliest animals are at the bottom of the chart. The most recent are at the top of the chart.

Years Ago		Animal Life on Earth
Cenozoic	**10,000– present** 	Human civilization develops.
	1.8 million to 10,000 	Large mammals like mammoths, sabre-toothed cats, and giant ground sloths develop. Modern human beings evolve. This era ends with an ice age.
	65 to 1.8 million 	Ancestors of modern-day horses, zebras, rhinos, sheep, goats, camels, pigs, cows, deer, giraffes, camels, elephants, cats, dogs, and primates begin to develop.
Mesozoic	**144 to 65 million** 	In the Cretaceous period, new dinosaurs appear. Many insect groups, modern mammal and bird groups also develop. A global extinction of most dinosaurs occurs at the end of this period.
	206 to 144 million 	The Jurassic is dominated by giant dinosaurs. In the late Jurassic, birds evolve.
	248 to 206 million 	In the Triassic period, marine life develops again. Reptiles also move into the water. Reptiles begin to dominate the land areas. Dinosaurs and mammals develop.
Paleozoic	**290 to 248 million** 	A mass extinction wipes out 95% of all marine life.
	354 to 290 million 	Reptiles develop. Much of the land is covered by swamps.
	417 to 354 million 	The first trees and forests appear. The first land-living vertebrates, amphibians, and wingless insects appear. Many new sea creatures also appear.
	443 to 417 million 	Coral reefs form. Other animals, such as the first known freshwater fish develop. Relatives of spiders and centipedes develop.
	542 to 443 million 	Animals with shells (called trilobites) and some mollusks form. Primitive fish and corals develop. There is also evidence of the first primitive land plants.
Precambrian	**3.8 billion to 542 million** 	First evidence of life on Earth. All life is in water. Early single-celled bacteria and achaea appear, followed by multi-celled organisms, including early animals.
	4.6 billion	Formation of the Earth.

Animal Kingdom

The world has so many animals that scientists looked for a way to organize them into groups. A Swedish scientist named Carolus Linnaeus (1707–1778) worked out a system for classifying both animals and plants. We still use it today.

The Animal Kingdom is separated into two large groups—animals with backbones, called **vertebrates**, and animals without backbones, called **invertebrates**.

These large groups are divided into smaller groups called **phyla**. And phyla are divided into even smaller groups called **classes**. The animals in each group are classified together when their bodies are similar in certain ways.

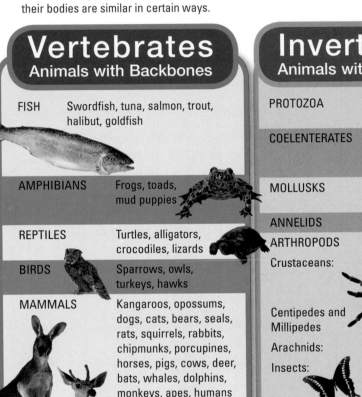

Vertebrates
Animals with Backbones

FISH	Swordfish, tuna, salmon, trout, halibut, goldfish
AMPHIBIANS	Frogs, toads, mud puppies
REPTILES	Turtles, alligators, crocodiles, lizards
BIRDS	Sparrows, owls, turkeys, hawks
MAMMALS	Kangaroos, opossums, dogs, cats, bears, seals, rats, squirrels, rabbits, chipmunks, porcupines, horses, pigs, cows, deer, bats, whales, dolphins, monkeys, apes, humans

Invertebrates
Animals without Backbones

PROTOZOA	The simplest form of animals
COELENTERATES	Jellyfish, hydra, sea anemones, coral
MOLLUSKS	Clams, snails, squid, oysters
ANNELIDS	Earthworms
ARTHROPODS	
Crustaceans:	Lobsters, crayfish
Centipedes and Millipedes	
Arachnids:	Spiders, scorpions
Insects:	Butterflies, grasshoppers, bees, termites, cockroaches
ECHINODERMS	Starfish, sea urchins, sea cucumbers

How can you remember the animal classifications from most general to most specific? Try this sentence:

King **P**hilip **C**ame **O**ver **F**rom **G**reat **S**pain.
K = Kingdom; **P** = Phylum; **C** = Class; **O** = Order; **F** = Family; **G** = Genus; **S** = Species

What Is Biodiversity?

The Earth is shared by millions of species of living things. The wide variety of life on Earth, as shown by the many species, is called "biodiversity" (bio means "life" and diversity means "variety"). Human beings of all colors, races, and nationalities make up just one species, *Homo sapiens*.

Species, Species Everywhere

Here is just a sampling of how diverse life on Earth is. The numbers are only estimates, and more species are being discovered all the time!

ARTHROPODS (1.1 million species)

insects: 750,000 species
moths & butterflies: 165,000 species
flies: about 122,000 species
cockroaches: about 4,000 species
crustaceans: 44,000 species
spiders: 35,000 species

FISH (24,500 species)

bony fish: 23,000 species
skates & rays: 450 species
sharks: 350 species
seahorses: 32 species

BIRDS (9,000 species)

perching birds: 5,200-5,500 species
parrots: 353 species
pigeons: 309 species
raptors (eagles, hawks, etc.): 307 species
penguins: 17 species
ostrich: 1 species

MAMMALS (9,000 species)

rodents: 1,700 species
bats: 1,000 species
monkeys: 242 species
whales & dolphins: 83 species
cats: 38 species
apes: 21 species
pigs: 14 species
bears: 8 species

REPTILES (8,000 species)

lizards: 4,500 species
snakes: 2,900 species
tortoises & turtles: about 294 species
crocodiles & alligators: 23 species

AMPHIBIANS (5,000 species)

frogs & toads: 4,500 species
newts & salamanders: 470 species

PLANTS (260,000 species)

flowering plants: 250,000 species
bamboo: about 1,000 species
evergreens: 550 species

Fascinating Bio Facts

- There are 17 different species of penguins. All of them live in the southern hemisphere.

- Modern-day birds do not have teeth. But a baby bird hatches from an egg by using its "egg tooth," a small bump on its beak or bill, to break through the shell. A few days later, the egg tooth falls off.

- Australia's platypus and the echidna, found in both Australia and New Guinea, are the only two mammal species that lay eggs. All other mammals bear live young.

- There are 30,000 species of edible plants in the world. But just 20 of them, including corn, rice, and wheat, provide 90% of the world's food.

BIGGEST, SMALLEST, FASTEST

IN THE WORLD

WORLD'S BIGGEST ANIMALS

Marine mammal: blue whale (100 feet long, 200 tons)

Land mammal: African bush elephant (12 feet high, 4–7 tons)
  Tallest mammal: giraffe (18 feet tall)

Reptile: saltwater crocodile (20 feet long, 1,150 pounds)

Snake: anaconda (27 feet, 9 inches long, 500 pounds)
  longest snake: reticulated python (26–32 feet long)

Fish: whale shark (45 feet long, 10 tons)

Bird: ostrich (9 feet tall, 345 pounds)

Insect: stick insect (15 inches long)

WORLD'S SMALLEST ANIMALS

Mammal: bumblebee bat
  (1.1 to 1.3 inches)

Fish: stout infantfish (0.25 inches)

Bird: bee hummingbird
  (2.2 inches)

Snake: thread snake and brahminy
  blind snake (4.25 inches)

Lizard: Jaragua sphaero lizard
  (0.63 inches)

Insect: fairy fly (0.01 inches)

WORLD'S FASTEST ANIMALS

Marine mammal: killer whale
  (35 miles per hour)

Land mammal: cheetah (70 miles per hour)

Fish: sailfish (68 miles per hour)

Bird: peregrine falcon
  (150 miles per hour)

Insect: dragonfly (36 miles per
  hour)

Snake: black mamba (14 mph)

How Fast Do Animals Run?

Some animals can run as fast as a car. But a snail needs more than 30 hours just to go 1 mile. If you look at this table, you will see how fast some land animals can go. Humans at their fastest are still slower than many animals. The record for fastest speed for a human for a recognized race distance is held by Michael Johnson, who won the 1996 Olympic 200 meter dash in 19.32 seconds for an average speed of 23.16 mph.

	MILES PER HOUR
Cheetah	70
Antelope	60
Lion	50
Elk	45
Zebra	40
Rabbit	35
Reindeer	32
Cat	30
Elephant	25
Wild turkey	15
Squirrel	12
Snail	0.03

HOW LONG DO
ANIMALS LIVE?

Most animals do not live as long as human beings do. A monkey that's 14-years-old is thought to be old, while a person at that age is still considered young. The average life spans of some animals are shown here. The average life span of a human in the United States today is about 75 to 80 years.

Animal	Life Span
Galapagos tortoise	200+ years
Box turtle	100 years
Gray whale	70 years
Alligator	50 years
Chimpanzee	50 years
Humpback whale	50 years
African elephant	35 years
Bottlenose dolphin	30 years
Gorilla	30 years
Horse	20 years
Black bear	18 years
Tiger	16 years
Lion	15 years
Lobster	15 years
Cat (domestic)	15 years
Cow	15 years
Tarantula	15 years
Dog (domestic)	13 years
Camel (bactrian)	12 years
Moose	12 years
Pig	10 years
Squirrel	10 years
Deer (white-tailed)	8 years
Goat	8 years
Kangaroo	7 years
Chipmunk	6 years
Beaver	5 years
Rabbit (domestic)	5 years
Guinea pig	4 years
Mouse	3 years
Opossum	1 year
Worker bee	4-5 weeks
Adult housefly	3-4 weeks

Animal Words

Animal	Male	Female	Young
bear	boar	sow	cub
cattle, giraffe, whale, hippo, elephant	bull	cow	calf
deer	buck, stag	doe	fawn
duck	drake	duck	duckling
ferret	hob	jill	kit
fox	reynard	vixen	kit, cub, pup
goat	buck	doe	kid
goose	gander	goose	gosling
gorilla	male	female	infant
hawk	tiercel	hen	eyas
horse	stallion	mare	foal, filly (female), colt (male)
kangaroo	buck	doe	joey
pig	boar	sow	piglet
rabbit	buck	doe	kit, bunny
swan	cob	pen	cygnet
tiger	tiger	tigress	cub
turkey	gobbler, tom	hen	chick, poult
woodchuck	he-chuck	she-chuck	kit, cub

What Are Groups of Animals Called?

Here are some (often odd) names for animal groups:

BEARS: *sleuth* of bears	**LIONS**: *pride* of lions
CATTLE: *drove* of cattle	**MINNOWS**: *shoal* of minnows
CROCODILES: *bask* of crocodiles	**MONKEYS**: *troop* of monkeys
CROWS: *murder* of crows	**MULES**: *span* of mules
ELKS: *gang* of elks	**NIGHTINGALES**: *watch* of nightingales
FISH: *school* of fish	**OYSTERS**: *bed* of oysters
FOXES: *skulk* of foxes	**OWLS**: *parliament* of owls
GEESE: *flock* or *gaggle* of geese	**PEACOCKS**: *muster* of peacocks
GNATS: *cloud* of gnats	**SHARKS**: *shiver* of sharks
HARES: *down* of hares	**TURTLES**: *bale* of turtles
HAWKS: *cast* of hawks	**RAVENS**: *unkindness* of ravens
KITTENS: *kindle* or *kendle* of kittens	**WHALES**: *pod* of whales
LEOPARDS: *leap* of leopards	**WOLVES**: *pack* of wolves

Pets At The Top

Here are the 10 most popular pets in the United States and the approximate number of each pet:

1.	Cats	70,796,000	6.	Rabbits	4,813,000
2.	Dogs	61,572,000	7.	Turtles	1,070,000
3.	Fish	49,251,000	8.	Ferrets	991,000
4.	Birds	12,999,000	9.	Hamsters	881,000
5.	Horses	5,107,000	10.	Snakes	661,000

Source: 2002 U.S. Pet Ownership and Demographic Sourcebook

did you know?

It is estimated at least half of the people in the world include insects in their diet. Shoppers in Thailand can buy water bugs and grasshoppers at the market. Moviegoers in some parts of South America can snack on roasted ants instead of popcorn at the theater. In the U.S., each person unintentionally eats up to one pound of insects per year. Common foods such as tomato sauce, hot dogs, and chocolate all may contain insect eggs and parts. But don't worry: health codes allow only very low levels of these ingredients.

Endangered Species

When a species becomes extinct, it reduces the variety of life on Earth. In the world today, 7,180 known species of animals (and even more plant species) are threatened with extinction, according to the International Union for Conservation of Nature and Natural Resources. Humans have been able to save some endangered animals and are working to save more.

Some Endangered Animals

Giant Pandas Giant pandas need to spend up to 16 hours a day foraging for the 20-40 pounds of bamboo they eat each day. But the forests in China where they live are disappearing. There are only about 1,600 giant pandas left in the wild. Zookeepers and biologists are working to protect pandas, though. In 2005, a record 25 giant pandas were born in captivity, including Tai Shan at the National Zoo in Washington, D.C., and Su Lin at the San Diego Zoo in California. Chinese scientists are working with environmentalists to create new nature reserves to protect panda habitats. And that means that other endangered species within the reserves will be protected too!

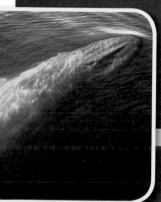

Blue Whales There are only about 1,300-2,000 blue whales left in the world. They can live up to 80 years in the wild, but their lives are often cut short by illegal whaling, pollution, and fishing nets. The blue whale is the biggest animal that has ever lived on Earth—even bigger than the biggest dinosaur—averaging about 80 feet long and 240,000 pounds.

FACTORS THAT CAN MAKE A SPECIES ENDANGERED:

HABITAT DESTRUCTION. As human populations grow, they need places to live and work. People build houses and factories in areas where plants and animals live. Filling in wetlands and clearing forests (**deforestation**) are examples of this threat.

OVERHARVESTING. People may catch a kind of fish or hunt an animal until its numbers are too low to reproduce fast enough. Bison or buffalo once roamed over the entire Great Plains until they were almost hunted into extinction in the 19th century. They are now protected by law, and their numbers are increasing.

ALIEN SPECIES are plants and animals that have been moved by humans into areas where they are not naturally found. They may have no natural enemies there and can push out native species. Red fire ants, zebra mussels, and kudzu are examples of alien species.

POLLUTION in the air, water, and land can affect plants and animals. It can poison them or make it hard for them to grow or reproduce. Factories are not the only source. Oil, salt, and other substances sprayed or spilled on roads can wash into streams, rivers, and lakes. Acid rain damages and kills trees, especially in the mountains where acidic clouds and fog often surround them.

POLAR BEARS

Polar bears are large, powerful animals that live in the Arctic Circle, the icy cold area around the North Pole. Winter temperatures there can hover around 40-50 degrees below zero for weeks at a time. But polar bears are well-suited for the cold, with up to 4 ½ inches of blubber under a thick, two-layer fur coat. The "Kings of the North" are actually more likely to overheat than to freeze. They can run up to 25 miles per hour, but because they get hot so quickly, they mostly walk at a leisurely pace.

Polar bears are the world's largest land predators, with males ranging from 775-1,500 pounds (females are much smaller). The ice bears spend most of their time hunting the seals that make up most of their diets.

WEEKLY (WR) READER®

From *Weekly Reader*

Polar Bear Patrol

A polar bear's body is made for hunting. Here's how:

Fur that looks white helps the bear blend in with the ice and snow.

A long **nose** helps a polar bear smell things from far away.

Long **teeth** and powerful **jaws** help the bear drag its food out of the water.

Pads on the bottom of its paws keep it from slipping on the ice.

Strong **legs** help the polar bear run and swim to catch its food.

Sharp **claws** on its front paws help a polar bear hold onto its food.

— Teeth: Dan Guravich/Corbis

— Bear: Fritz Polking/Peter Arnold, Inc.; Paw: Flip Nicklin/Minden Pictures

All About GILA MONSTERS

Gila monsters are one of only two kinds of venomous lizards in the world. Their venom is about as toxic as diamondback rattlesnake venom, but the Gila can only inject a small amount at one time. Their bite is fast and very strong. Venom flows through grooved bottom teeth into the wound. People are not usually killed by Gila monster bites, but the wound is really painful. It is also very hard to get the creature to unclench its jaws and release its victim.

Even the largest "monsters" are only about two feet long and weigh about 5 pounds. They have thick tails that grow thicker after meals because that's where they store fat. **These lizards have been known to eat up to one-third of their body weight in one meal! That's like a 60-pound kid eating 80 quarter-pound hamburgers.** Food isn't always easy to find in their Southwestern U.S. desert habitat, even though Gilas aren't picky eaters. They eat mostly small birds and mammals, eggs, lizards, frogs, and insects. A Gila monster tracks its prey by picking up a scent, then following a "taste trail" by flicking its tongue. Gila monsters also sometimes eat carrion, which is an animal that is already dead.

Gila monsters have distinctive coloring: they are black with either bands or blotches of pink or orange. Their coloring helps them to blend into their desert habitat, but Gila monsters spend most of their time in underground burrows. They emerge only to eat or bask in the sun, because—like all reptiles—they are cold-blooded.

All About TASMANIAN DEVILS

They don't look much like the cartoon character named after them, but Tasmanian devils are actual creatures. Tasmanian devils are marsupials—the same group of mammals as koalas and kangaroos—meaning they carry their young in a pouch for a while after birth. The "devil" got its name when Europeans exploring Australia heard the spine-chilling growls and screeches a devil makes in search of food.

Today the real-life Tasmanian devil only lives in Tasmania, an island off the coast of Australia. They look a little bit like badgers, with shiny black fur, large flat heads, and stocky builds. Devils are about the size of small dogs—a size that varies depending on their diet and habitat. The largest weigh more than 25 pounds.

Tasmanian devils are scavengers, often eating smaller animals that are already dead. It might seem gross, but it's actually an important job. By eating the carcasses of dead animals, Tasmanian devils help to balance and clean up their environment. The way they eat is another matter, though. Devils are famous for their terrible table manners and will gather around a meal screeching and growling at each other. They have powerful teeth and jaws and will devour a whole creature, including its bones and fur.

ANIMALS ON THE JOB

Some kinds of animals make great pets. Others are fun to look at when you visit the zoo. But many creatures also do a lot for people. In fact, many animals can do jobs that people can't! Work animals, like oxen and horses, have been used on farms for thousands of years. Animals have also played a big role in many scientific discoveries. Scientists and researchers use animals every day to learn more about how DNA works and new ways to treat diseases. Below are a few of the more unusual animal occupations.

SNAKE DETECTIVE

For centuries, hunters and police officers have been using dogs' fantastic sense of smell to follow a trail and find things. In a new twist on an old tradition, Everglades National Park rangers in Florida are training "Python Pete," a beagle puppy, to use his sniffer to track down 15-foot-long Burmese pythons. The giant snakes, which are abandoned in the park by irresponsible pet owners, upset the natural balance of the habitat. Park rangers have removed over 150 of the scaly reptiles from the Everglades since 2003. Now officials hope to install a "Python Hotline," so that visitors who spot the giant snakes can report where they saw them. When he is fully trained, Pete will be able to pick up on the python's scent from the reported location and track it down so that park officials can remove it.

DOLPHIN BOMB SQUAD

In 2003, the U.S. Navy used a squad of highly-trained dolphins in wartime for the first time. They were using their natural sonar (called "echolocation") to find explosives and booby traps underwater. Echolocation means that dolphins can hear differences in the ways that noises they make bounce off the sea floor and underwater objects. The Navy trained them to use this skill to find threatening devices and report the location to military trainers waiting at the surface. Sometimes the dolphins returned to the object below to attach a transmitter. That way, the military could disarm it later when all the dolphins (and people) were out of harm's way. Not much risk to the dolphins was involved, because the explosives are set to go off only for heavy, metal objects, like big ships. In March 2003 alone, a team of nine dolphins—with the help of military trainers and divers—got rid of over 100 anti-ship mines and underwater booby traps in one Iraqi port. While dolphins can help save people's lives, some critics argue that it is not ethical to use dolphins for military purposes.

On the Job

Jane EckesEtzel, Service Dog Trainer for Helping Paws

Helping Paws' Mission: to further the independence of people with physical disabilities through the use of service dogs.

How do you train Cedar, the dog you work with?

While I'm at work, Cedar retrieves things, opens doors, turns lights on and off, and carries small items for me. After we get home she takes off her pack and runs and plays like a normal dog. Once a week we formally train at Helping Paws' training center. Throughout the week we train at places like grocery stores, malls, movie theaters, and restaurants. Cedar is allowed to go into any public place.

Are there any difficult tasks a dog can perform that might surprise people?

Cedar is trained to open and close doors, turn lights on and off, bark for help, retrieve objects, assist walking, aid undressing, and perform many other tasks. Another difficult skill that Cedar has learned is to pick up a quarter, dime, or nickel and put it on a counter or table.

Can you give an example of how a service dog has helped someone?

Service dogs help people to be more independent. Their skills and training can even save lives. A golden retriever that had graduated from Helping Paws was teamed with a young woman. They had only been together for about four months when her wheelchair got too close to the edge of the sidewalk outside her home and tipped over in the snow. She unclipped her dog and commanded him to "Get help." He jumped a three-foot fence and got her neighbor by barking outside of a patio door. The story reminded all of us at the agency how important the work we do is and that in the end having to let a dog go is worth it.

Is there anything else kids should know about service dogs?

When you see a dog with a service vest on, it is important that you remember it is a working dog. It has to stay focused and pay attention to the person it is serving. If you want to pet the dog, always ask the person if it is a good time. Don't be offended if they say no. Sometimes it could be a matter of life or death for the person the dog is serving.

WEB SITE *www.helpingpaws.org*

Art

What is a line of symmetry? ➡ page 35

Artists look at the world in new ways. Their work can be funny or sad, beautiful or disturbing, realistic or strange.

Throughout history, artists have painted pictures of nature (called landscapes), pictures of people (called portraits), and pictures of flowers in vases, food, and other objects (known as still lifes). Today many artists create pictures that do not look like anything in the real world. These are examples of abstract art.

▶ Photography, too, is a form of art. Photos record both the commonplace and the exotic and help us look at events in new ways.

▶ Sculpture is a three-dimensional form made from clay, stone, metal, or other material. Sculptures can be large, like the Statue of Liberty, or small. Some are realistic. Others have no form you can recognize.

▶ Contemporary artists today often use computers and video screens to create art. Some video art uses 20 or 30 video screens that show different colors or images to create one big work of art.

ALL ABOUT...
KING TUT

Coffin of Tutankhamen

Over 3,000 years ago, Tutankhamen was one of the world's most powerful kids when he became the pharaoh of Egypt around the age of nine. He died at the age of 18 and was not really an important ruler but became very famous after his tomb was discovered in 1922. Although many royal tombs in Egypt had been robbed, the tomb of the "boy king" was nearly untouched. It contained his gold sarcophagus (an ancient coffin) along with much of its treasure. Usually on display at the Egyptian Museum of Cairo, Egypt, his treasures have been traveling in the U.S. for the first time in 30 years! The exhibit was being shown at the Field Museum in Chicago from May 26, 2006, until January 1, 2007, and at The Franklin Institute in Philadelphia from February 3 to September 30, 2007.

Art All-Stars

Check out famous works by these brilliant artists.

LEONARDO DA VINCI (1452-1519)
MONA LISA (1503-06)

Leonardo da Vinci was a great engineer, inventor, painter, and sculptor from the High Renaissance in Italy. *Mona Lisa* is a portrait of a woman in front of a dark, rocky landscape. Her smile has been interpreted in many different ways. The *Mona Lisa* remains the most famous and copied image in the world.

VINCENT VAN GOGH (1853-1890)
THE STARRY NIGHT (1889)

Van Gogh was a Dutch-born painter who lived in France for many years. With his masterpiece *The Starry Night*, expressionism was born. Expressionism stresses expressing the emotion and inner vision of the artist, instead of depicting the subject matter accurately. This is done through distorted lines and shapes and the use of intense color. *The Starry Night* shows a night sky filled with exploding stars.

JACOB LAWRENCE (1917-2000)
BROWNSTONES (1958)

Lawrence, an American painter, was known for depicting real-life subjects from the world around him. *Brownstones* depicts a typical scene in Harlem, a neighborhood in New York City. It shows everyday activities such as young girls jumping rope, neighbors talking on their front steps, a mother pushing a baby carriage, and the brownstone buildings that are common in Harlem.

MAYA LIN (1959-) *VIETNAM VETERANS MEMORIAL* (1982)

Lin's Vietnam Veterans Memorial is both a sculpture and a monument to American soldiers who lost their lives in the Vietnam War. Its success is in the simplicity of its form. It is a highly polished black granite wall; carved on it are the names of soldiers killed in the war. Many war memorials show images of soldiers. With her design, Lin created a monument that is very plain but conveys great emotion.

Color Wheel

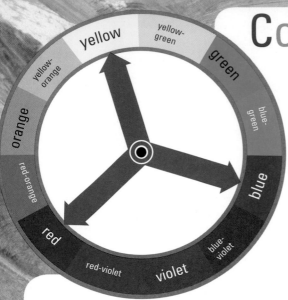

This color wheel shows how colors are related to each other.

Primary colors The most basic colors are **RED**, **YELLOW**, and **BLUE**. They're called primary because you can't get them by mixing any other colors. In fact, the other colors are made by mixing red, blue, or yellow. Arrows on this wheel show the primary colors.

Secondary colors ORANGE, GREEN, and **VIOLET** are the secondary colors. They are made by mixing two primary colors. You make orange by mixing yellow and red, or green by mixing yellow and blue. On the color wheel, GREEN appears between **BLUE** and YELLOW.

Tertiary colors When you mix a primary and a secondary color, you get a tertiary, or intermediate, color. **BLUE-GREEN** and YELLOW-GREEN are intermediate colors.

More Color Terms

VALUES The lightness or darkness of a color is its value.

Tints are light values made by mixing a color with white. Pink is a tint of red.

Shades are dark values made by mixing a color with black. **Maroon** is a shade of red.

COMPLEMENTARY COLORS

are contrasting colors that please the eye when used together. These colors appear opposite each other on the wheel and don't have any colors in common. RED is a complement to GREEN, which is made by mixing YELLOW and BLUE.

COOL COLORS

are mostly GREEN, BLUE, and PURPLE. They make you think of cool things like water and can even make you feel cooler.

WARM COLORS

are mostly RED, ORANGE, and YELLOW. They suggest heat and can actually make you feel warmer.

ANALOGOUS COLORS

The colors next to each other on the wheel are from the same "family." BLUE, BLUE-GREEN, and GREEN all have BLUE in them and are analogous colors.

Art Project: **PORTRAIT**

Materials: Paper, Pencil, Eraser

Step 1: Draw the head.

Draw an oval or egg shape. Halfway down the oval draw a horizontal line. This is the eye line, which is where the eyes will be placed. Next, draw a vertical line down the middle of the oval. This is the line of symmetry.

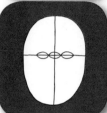

Step 2: Draw the eyes.

The face is "five eyes" wide, and the distance between the two eyes is equal to the width of one eye. Find the intersection of the vertical and horizontal lines. There, draw a shape like a football. Next, draw an eye on both the left and right side of this football shape. There should be enough space to fit one more eye on both the left and right side of the face. Erase the middle shape.

Step 3: Find the mouth.

About 1/3 of the way from the bottom of the oval, make a mark on both sides of the oval. Draw a horizontal half-circle using these marks as a guide. Finally, draw a light line from the middle of both eyes down to the half-circle you have just drawn.

Step 4: Find the nose.

Draw a small half-circle on top of the larger half-circle, between the two lines that you drew from the middle of the eyes down. This is the top of the mouth. Next, draw a triangle that connects the two corners of the mouth to the point formed by the intersection of the eye line and the line of symmetry. Above the mouth, draw a light line from one side of the triangle to the other. This is where the bottom of the nose will be. The triangle is how wide the nose will be.

Step 5: Draw the features.

Erase the eye line, the line of symmetry, the large half-circle that the mouth rests on, and the triangle that the nose is inside of. Look at the person you want to draw and adjust your sketch. You might want to move the chin up or down or have more or less space between the eyes and the sides of the head. Draw a new shape for the face that looks more like who you are trying to draw. Then, draw the features: eyelids, eyeballs, eyebrows, a nose, an upper and lower lip, and cheekbones.

Step 6: Draw details.

Erase any extra lines. Add hair, eyelashes, and the features of the ears and eyes. Keep erasing and drawing until you like the way your portrait looks.

Birthdays

Who shares your birthday?

JANUARY

READ
ROOKIE
ON TRIAL!

Jackie Robinson

Birthstone: Garnet

1 J.D. Salinger, author, 1919
2 Kate Bosworth, actress, 1983
3 Eli Manning, football player, 1981
4 Isaac Newton, physicist/mathematician, 1643
5 Diane Keaton, actress, 1946
6 Early Wynn, baseball player, 1920
7 Liam Aiken, actor, 1990
8 Stephen Hawking, physicist, 1942
9 Dave Matthews, musician, 1967
10 Jake Delhomme, football player, 1975
11 Mary J. Blige, singer, 1971
12 Christiane Amanpour, journalist, 1958
13 Orlando Bloom, actor, 1977
14 Dave Grohl, musician, 1969
15 Rev. Martin Luther King Jr., civil rights leader, 1929
16 Dizzy Dean, baseball player, 1910
17 Jim Carrey, actor, 1962
18 A.A. Milne, author, 1882
19 Katey Sagal, actress, 1957
20 Buzz Aldrin, astronaut, 1930
21 Geena Davis, actress, 1956
22 George Balanchine, choreographer, 1904
23 John Hancock, revolutionary leader, 1737
24 Mischa Barton, actress, 1986
25 Alicia Keys, singer, 1981
26 Ellen DeGeneres, comedian/TV personality, 1958
27 Wolfgang Amadeus Mozart, composer, 1756
28 Elijah Wood, actor, 1981
29 Heather Graham, actress, 1970
30 Christian Bale, actor, 1974
31 Jackie Robinson, baseball player, 1919

FEBRUARY

Birthstone: Amethyst

1 Langston Hughes, poet, 1902
2 Jordin Tootoo, hockey player, 1983
3 Elizabeth Blackwell, first woman physician, 1821
4 Rosa Parks, civil rights activist, 1913
5 Sara Evans, singer, 1971
6 Ronald Reagan, 40th president, 1911
7 Frederick Douglass, abolitionist, 1817
8 Alonzo Mourning, basketball player, 1970
9 Travis Tritt, singer, 1963
10 Emma Roberts, actress, 1991
11 Jennifer Aniston, actress, 1969
12 Charles Darwin, scientist, 1809
13 Grant Wood, artist, 1891
14 Rob Thomas, musician, 1972
15 Susan B. Anthony, women's rights activist, 1820
16 Jerome Bettis, football player, 1972
17 Michael Jordan, basketball player, 1963
18 Toni Morrison, author, 1931
19 Nicolaus Copernicus, astronomer, 1473
20 Ansel Adams, photographer, 1902
21 Jennifer Love Hewitt, actress, 1979
22 Edna St. Vincent Millay, poet, 1892
23 Dakota Fanning, actress, 1994
24 Steve Jobs, computer innovator, 1955
25 Sean Astin, actor, 1971
26 Marshall Faulk, football player, 1973
27 Josh Groban, singer, 1981
28 Lemony Snicket (Daniel Handler), author, 1970
29 Ja Rule, rapper, 1976

Charles Darwin

MARCH

Birthstone: Aquamarine

1 Frederic Chopin, composer, 1810
2 Dr. Seuss, author, 1904
3 Jessica Biel, actress, 1982
4 Landon Donovan, soccer player, 1982
5 Jake Lloyd, actor, 1989
6 D.L. Hughley, actor/comedian, 1964
7 Laura Prepon, actress, 1980
8 Marcia Newby, gymnast, 1988
9 Bow Wow, actor/rapper, 1987
10 Carrie Underwood, singer, 1983
11 Benji and Joel Madden, musicians, 1979
12 Edward Albee, playwright, 1928
13 Percival Lowell, astronomer, 1855
14 Albert Einstein, physicist, 1879
15 Ruth Bader Ginsburg, U.S. Supreme Court justice, 1933
16 Lauren Graham, actress, 1967
17 Mia Hamm, soccer player, 1972
18 Queen Latifah, rapper/actress, 1970
19 Bruce Willis, actor, 1955
20 Spike Lee, filmmaker, 1957
21 Matthew Broderick, actor, 1962
22 Reese Witherspoon, actress, 1976
23 Jason Kidd, basketball player, 1973
24 Peyton Manning, football player, 1976
25 Sheryl Swoopes, basketball player, 1971
26 Keira Knightley, actress, 1985
27 Mariah Carey, singer, 1970
28 Vince Vaughn, actor, 1970
29 Sam Walton, Wal-Mart founder, 1918
30 Vincent Van Gogh, artist, 1853
31 Christopher Walken, actor, 1943

APRIL

Birthstone: Diamond

1 Sergey Rachmaninoff, composer, 1873
2 Hans Christian Anderson, author, 1805
3 Amanda Bynes, actress, 1986
4 Heath Ledger, actor, 1979
5 Booker T. Washington, educator, 1856
6 Zach Braff, actor, 1975
7 Jackie Chan, actor, 1954
8 Kofi Annan, UN secretary-general, 1938
9 Jesse McCartney, actor/singer, 1987
10 John Madden, sportscaster, 1936
11 Jason Varitek, baseball player, 1972
12 Beverly Cleary, author, 1916
13 Thomas Jefferson, 3rd president, 1743
14 Vivien Cardone, actress, 1993
15 Emma Watson, actress, 1990
16 Kareem Abdul-Jabar, basketball player, 1947
17 Jennifer Garner, actress, 1972
18 Alia Shawkat, actress, 1989
19 Kate Hudson, actress, 1979
20 Tito Puente, musician, 1923
21 Queen Elizabeth II, British monarch, 1926
22 Robert J. Oppenheimer, physicist, 1904
23 Andruw Jones, baseball player, 1977
24 Kelly Clarkson, singer, 1982
25 Jason Lee, actor, 1970
26 Tom Welling, actor, 1977
27 August Wilson, playwright, 1945
28 Harper Lee, author, 1926
29 Uma Thurman, actress, 1970
30 Kirsten Dunst, actress, 1982

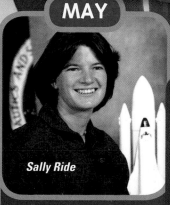
Sally Ride

MAY

Birthstone: Emerald

1 Tim McGraw, musician, 1967
2 Dwayne "The Rock" Johnson, actor/wrestler, 1972
3 Sugar Ray Robinson, boxer, 1921
4 Dawn Staley, basketball player, 1970
5 Brian Williams, journalist, 1959
6 Martin Brodeur, hockey player, 1972
7 Johannes Brahms, composer, 1833
8 Enrique Iglesias, singer, 1975
9 Rosario Dawson, actress, 1979
10 Bono, musician/activist, 1960
11 Salvador Dali, artist, 1904
12 Tony Hawk, skateboarder, 1968
13 Stevie Wonder, singer, 1950
14 Amber Tamblyn, actress, 1983
15 L. Frank Baum, author, 1856
16 Janet Jackson, singer, 1966
17 Sugar Ray Leonard, boxer, 1956
18 Tina Fey, actress/comedian, 1970
19 Kevin Garnett, basketball player, 1976
20 Stan Mikita, hockey player, 1940
21 Al Franken, author/comedian/radio personality, 1951
22 Sir Arthur Conan Doyle, author, 1859
23 Margaret Wise Brown, author, 1910
24 Tracy McGrady, basketball player, 1979
25 Mike Myers, actor, 1963
26 Sally Ride, astronaut, 1951
27 André 3000, musician, 1975
28 Jim Thorpe, Olympic champion, 1888
29 John F. Kennedy, 35th president, 1917
30 Manny Ramirez, baseball player, 1972
31 Walt Whitman, poet, 1819

JUNE

Birthstone: Pearl

1 Justine Henin-Hardenne, tennis player, 1982
2 Freddy Adu, soccer player, 1989
3 Carl Everett, baseball player, 1971
4 Angelina Jolie, actress, 1975
5 Richard Scarry, author/illustrator, 1919
6 Cynthia Rylant, author, 1954
7 Anna Kournikova, tennis player, 1981
8 Kanye West, musician, 1977
9 Natalie Portman, actress, 1981
10 Maurice Sendak, author/illustrator, 1928
11 Diana Taurasi, basketball player, 1982
12 Anne Frank, diary writer, 1929
13 Ashley and Mary-Kate Olsen, actresses, 1986
14 Harriet Beecher Stowe, author, 1811
15 Neil Patrick Harris, actor, 1973
16 Kerry Wood, baseball player, 1977
17 Venus Williams, tennis player, 1980
18 Paul McCartney, musician, 1942
19 Paula Abdul, singer/TV personality, 1962
20 Nicole Kidman, actress, 1967
21 Prince William of Great Britain, 1982
22 Donald Faison, actor, 1974
23 Clarence Thomas, U.S. Supreme Court justice, 1948
24 Solange Knowles, singer/actress, 1986
25 Carlos Delgado, baseball player, 1972
26 Jason Schwartzman, actor/musician, 1980
27 Tobey Maguire, actor, 1975
28 John Cusack, actor, 1966
29 Theo Fleury, hockey player, 1968
30 Michael Phelps, Olympic champion, 1985

Thomas Jefferson

Venus Williams

JULY

Daniel Radcliffe

Birthstone: Ruby

1 Missy Elliott, rapper, 1971
2 Lindsay Lohan, actress, 1986
3 Tom Cruise, actor, 1962
4 Neil Simon, playwright, 1927
5 P.T. Barnum, showman/circus founder, 1810
6 George W. Bush, 43rd president, 1946
7 Michelle Kwan, figure skater, 1980
8 Toby Keith, musician, 1961
9 Tom Hanks, actor, 1956
10 Jessica Simpson, singer, 1980
11 E.B. White, author, 1899
12 Topher Grace, actor, 1978
13 Harrison Ford, actor, 1942
14 Matthew Fox, actor, 1966
15 Rembrandt van Rijn, artist, 1606
16 Will Farrell, actor, 1967
17 Donald Sutherland, actor, 1935
18 Kristin Bell, actress, 1980
19 Edgar Degas, artist, 1834
20 Sir Edmund Hillary, Everest climber, 1919
21 Ernest Hemingway, author, 1899
22 Keyshawn Johnson, football player, 1972
23 Daniel Radcliffe, actor, 1989
24 Jennifer Lopez, actress/singer, 1969
25 Ray Billingsley, cartoonist, 1957
26 Sandra Bullock, actress, 1964
27 Alex Rodriguez, baseball player, 1975
28 Beatrix Potter, author, 1866
29 Allison Mack, actress, 1982
30 Jaime Pressley, actress, 1977
31 J.K. Rowling, author, 1965

AUGUST

Birthstone: Peridot

1 Francis Scott Key, composer/lawyer, 1779
2 Hallie Eisenberg, actress, 1992
3 Tom Brady, football player, 1977
4 Jeff Gordon, racecar driver, 1971
5 Neil Armstrong, astronaut, 1930
6 Andy Warhol, artist, 1928
7 Charlize Theron, actress, 1975
8 Roger Federer, tennis player, 1981
9 Eric Bana, actor, 1968
10 Antonio Banderas, actor, 1960
11 Stephen Wozniak, computer pioneer, 1950
12 Ann M. Martin, author, 1955
13 Alfred Hitchcock, filmmaker, 1899
14 Halle Berry, actress, 1966
15 Ben Affleck, actor, 1972
16 Steve Carell, actor, 1963
17 Robert De Niro, actor, 1943
18 Meriwether Lewis, explorer, 1774
19 Bill Clinton, 42nd president, 1946
20 Fred Durst, musician, 1970
21 Stephen Hillenburg, SpongeBob creator, 1961
22 Bill Parcells, football coach, 1941
23 Julian Casablancas, singer, 1978
24 Rupert Grint, actor, 1988
25 Tim Burton, filmmaker, 1958
26 Mother Teresa, Nobel laureate, 1910
27 Alexa Vega, actress, 1988
28 Jack Black, actor, 1969
29 John McCain, U.S. senator, 1936
30 Andy Roddick, tennis player, 1982
31 Chris Tucker, actor, 1972

Neil Armstrong

Hilary Duff

SEPTEMBER

Birthstone: Sapphire

1 Dr. Phil McGraw, psychologist/TV personality, 1950
2 Keanu Reeves, actor, 1964
3 Shaun White, Olympic snowboarder, 1986
4 Beyoncé Knowles, singer/actress, 1981
5 Michael Keaton, actor, 1951
6 Mark Chesnutt, singer, 1963
7 Shannon Elizabeth, actress, 1973
8 Latrell Sprewell, basketball player, 1970
9 Adam Sandler, actor, 1966
10 Bill O'Reilly, TV personality, 1949
11 Ludacris, rapper, 1977
12 Benjamin McKenzie, actor, 1978
13 Roald Dahl, author, 1916
14 Nas, rapper, 1973
15 Prince Harry of Great Britain, 1984
16 Alexis Bledel, actress, 1981
17 Rasheed Wallace, basketball player, 1974
18 Lance Armstrong, cyclist, 1971
19 Ryan Dusick, musician, 1977
20 Red Auerbach, basketball coach, 1917
21 Luke Wilson, actor, 1971
22 Tom Felton, actor, 1987
23 Ray Charles, musician, 1930
24 Paul Hamm, gymnast, 1982
25 Will Smith, actor/rapper, 1968
26 Serena Williams, tennis player, 1981
27 Avril Lavigne, singer, 1984
28 Hilary Duff, actress/singer, 1987
29 Enrico Fermi, physicist/Nobel laureate, 1901
30 Lacey Chabert, actress, 1982

OCTOBER

Birthstone: Opal

1 Julie Andrews, actress, 1935
2 Mohandas Gandhi, activist, 1869
3 Ashlee Simpson, singer, 1984
4 Rachael Leigh Cook, actress, 1979
5 Parminder Nagra, actress, 1975
6 Elisabeth Shue, actress, 1963
7 Rachel McAdams, actress, 1976
8 R. L. Stine, author, 1943
9 Brandon Routh, actor, 1979
10 Dale Earnhardt Jr., racecar driver, 1974
11 Michelle Trachtenberg, actress, 1985
12 Hugh Jackman, actor, 1968
13 Ashanti, singer, 1980
14 Usher, singer, 1978
15 Elena Dementieva, tennis player, 1981
16 John Mayer, musician, 1977
17 Mae Jemison, astronaut, 1956
18 Wynton Marsalis, musician, 1961
19 Ty Pennington, TV personality, 1965
20 Snoop Dogg, rapper/actor, 1971
21 Carrie Fisher, actress, 1956
22 Ichiro Suzuki, baseball player, 1973
23 Tiffeny Millbrett, soccer player, 1972
24 Kevin Kline, actor, 1947
25 Ciara, singer, 1985
26 Jon Heder, actor, 1977
27 Teddy Roosevelt, 26th president, 1858
28 Bill Gates, computer pioneer, 1955
29 Winona Ryder, actress, 1971
30 Henry Winkler, actor, 1945
31 Juliette Gordon Low, Girl Scouts' founder, 1860

NOVEMBER

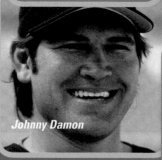

Johnny Damon

Birthstone: Topaz

1 Toni Collette, actress, 1972
2 Nelly, rapper, 1974
3 Walker Evans, photographer, 1903
4 Laura Bush, First Lady, 1946
5 Johnny Damon, baseball player, 1973
6 John Philip Sousa, composer, 1854
7 Marie Curie, scientist, 1867
8 Parker Posey, actress, 1968
9 Nick Lachey, singer, 1973
10 Brittany Murphy, actress, 1977
11 Leonardo DiCaprio, actor, 1974
12 Ryan Gosling, actor, 1980
13 Rachel Bilson, actress, 1981
14 Claude Monet, artist, 1840
15 Zena Grey, actress, 1988
16 Marg Helgenberger, actress, 1958
17 Reggie Wayne, football player, 1978
18 Owen Wilson, actor, 1968
19 Larry Johnson, football player, 1979
20 John R. Bolton, U.N. ambassador, 1948
21 Jena Malone, actress, 1984
22 Jamie Lee Curtis, actress, 1958
23 Billy the Kid, outlaw, 1859
24 Katherine Heigl, actress, 1978
25 Jenna and Barbara Bush, Pres. Bush's daughters, 1981
26 Charles Schulz, cartoonist, 1912
27 Bill Nye, "The Science Guy," 1955
28 Jon Stewart, TV host, 1962
29 Louisa May Alcott, author, 1832
30 Ben Stiller, actor, 1965

DECEMBER

Birthstone: Turquoise

1 Woody Allen, writer/director, 1935
2 Sarah Silverman, actress/comedian, 1970
3 Brendan Fraser, actor, 1967
4 Tyra Banks, model/TV personality, 1973
5 Cliff Floyd, baseball player, 1972
6 Otto Graham, football player/coach, 1921
7 Aaron Carter, actor/singer, 1987
8 Annasophia Robb, actress, 1993
9 Felicity Huffman, actress, 1962
10 Raven, actress, 1985
11 Mos Def, actor/rapper, 1973
12 Edvard Munch, artist, 1863
13 Jamie Foxx, actor, 1967
14 Craig Biggio, baseball player, 1965
15 Adam Brody, actor, 1979
16 Ludwig van Beethoven, composer, 1770
17 Sean Patrick Thomas, actor, 1970
18 Brad Pitt, actor, 1963
19 Jake Gyllenhaal, actor, 1980
20 Rich Gannon, football player, 1965
21 Ray Romano, actor/comedian, 1957
22 Diane Sawyer, journalist, 1945
23 Alge Crumpler, football player, 1977
24 Ryan Seacrest, DJ/TV personality, 1974
25 Clara Barton, American Red Cross founder, 1821
26 Jared Leto, actor, 1971
27 Carson Palmer, football player, 1979
28 Denzel Washington, actor, 1954
29 Jude Law, actor, 1972
30 LeBron James, basketball player, 1984
31 Henri Matisse, artist, 1869

Ludwig van Beethoven

Parminder Nagra

39

Talkin' 'Bout Your Generation

Do you ever feel like your parents don't really get your slang or the clothes and music you like? Ever feel like you don't really get the stuff they like either? Maybe it's because you're from different generations.

A generation usually spans about 20 years. Not everyone agrees on which years each generation covers, but the labels can be helpful in describing the shared experiences and popular culture of a group of the population.

Generation Y (born about 1980-2000)
- Also known as "Millennials," "Echo Boomers," or "the Internet Generation"
- About 27.8% of the U.S. population, or around 79 million people in 2004
- First generation to grow up fluent in—and some say too reliant on—digital technology
- Seen as confident and cooperative, eager to "fix" the world by solving its problems

Generation X (born about 1965-79)
- About 21.0% of the U.S. population, or around 59 million people in 2004
- Born during the so-called "Baby Bust," a drop in birthrates after the Baby Boom
- A generation with many "latchkey kids" due to the growing number of divorces and families with two working parents
- Seen as unmotivated and intimidated by world problems that they didn't create
- Independent-minded and obsessed with pop culture

Baby Boomers (born about 1946-64)
- About 28.2% of the population, or around 81 million people in 2004
- The "Baby Boom" began right after World War II, as millions of soldiers returned home
- Baby boomers witnessed the civil rights and women's rights movements, as well as the Vietnam War
- Seen as idealistic and spoiled, used to getting what they want, and denying they are aging.

MOST POPULAR NAMES

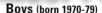

Boys (born 1970-79)	Girls (born 1970-79)	Boys (born 1990-99)	Girls (born 1990-99)
1. Michael	1. Jennifer	1. Michael	1. Jessica
2. Christopher	2. Amy	2. Christopher	2. Ashley
3. Jason	3. Melissa	3. Matthew	3. Emily
4. David	4. Michelle	4. Joshua	4. Samantha
5. James	5. Kimberly	5. Jacob	5. Sarah

In 2007, the world's first surviving septuplets (that's SEVEN siblings born at the same time) will turn 10 years old. Kenneth, Alexis, Natalie, Kelsey, Brandon, Nathan, and Joel McCaughey were born on November 19, 1997, making Mikayla, then an only child, a big sister of seven in one hour's time. The McCaughey family lives in Carlisle, Iowa, in a seven-bedroom house. But aside from a little more attention from reporters, the McCaugheys say they aren't much different from any other family.

Genealogy Tracing Your Family Tree

Genealogy is the study of one's family, tracing back through generations of relatives. The first place to start in your family genealogy is with yourself. Write down the answers to the following questions:

- What is your full name (include middle name)?
- When and where were you born (town, city, state, country)?

Next, write down the name, birth date, and place of birth for each of your parents (ask them or the adult who takes care of you). Then, interview your grandparents and other relatives. Get their birthdates and places of birth as well. If any of these people have died, record their date of death. You might also ask about interesting events in their lives.

Now, you have the beginnings of a family tree. Fill out as much of this chart as you can.

GRANDPARENT
Name _____
Birth _____
Death _____

PARENT
Name _____
Birth _____
Death _____

GRANDPARENT
Name _____
Birth _____
Death _____

ME
Your Name _____
Birth _____

GRANDPARENT
Name _____
Birth _____
Death _____

PARENT
Name _____
Birth _____
Death _____

GRANDPARENT
Name _____
Birth _____
Death _____

When you find out more about a relative, you may get access to photographs and photocopies of important documents. Documents might include birth certificates, marriage licenses, or immigration papers.

To find out where you can get official copies of "vital records" such as birth, death, and marriage certificates for a particular state, check the website of the U.S. National Center for Health Statistics (www.cdc.gov/nchs). Baptism, marriage, and burial records can often be found at family churches. Also, many libraries have U.S. Census records for 1790-1930. Make sure to keep copies of the documents you find.

Additional Sources

A good book for children to read is *Climbing Your Family Tree: Online and Off-Line Genealogy for Kids*, by Ira Wolfman. (*www.workman.com/familytree*)

Websites that can help you find out more information about your family and lead you further on your trail of discovery are *www.ancestry.com* and *www.familysearch.com*.

The Church of Jesus Christ of Latter Day Saints (the Mormons) has Family History Centers throughout the world. There you can access their databases and programs, and possibly find members of your family.

Old family photos are a great way to explore your family history.

Books

Who wrote *The Chronicles of Narnia?* ➡ page 44

Book Awards, 2006

NEWBERY MEDAL

For the author of the best children's book
2006 winner: *Criss Cross,* by Lynne Rae Perkins

CALDECOTT MEDAL

For the artist of the best children's picture book
2006 winner: *The Hello, Goodbye Window*, illustrated by
Chris Raschka and written by Norton Juster

MICHAEL L. PRINTZ AWARD

For excellence in literature written for young adults
2006 winner: *Looking for Alaska,* written by John Green

CORETTA SCOTT KING AWARD

For artists and authors whose works encourage
expression of the African American experience

2006 winners:
Author Award: *Day of Tears: A Novel in Dialogue*, written by Julius Lester
Illustrator Award: *Rosa*, illustrated by Bryan Collier (written by Nikki Giovanni)

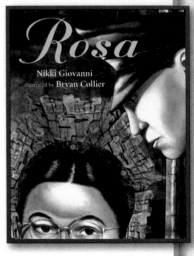

NEW BOOK SPOTLIGHT

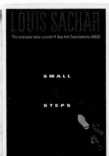

Have you ever read the Newbery-medal winning book
Holes by Louis Sachar? That popular book was also made
into a movie. Check out Sachar's new book for 2006,
Small Steps. Armpit, one of the characters from *Holes*,
continues his story in this new novel.

RECORD-BREAKING BOOKS

Which books get readers' seal of approval—by making record-breaking sales?
Find out these record-breakers by unscrambling the letters of each book.

Book with Most One-Day Sales...	Try Hero Part and the Bacon-Fed Hill Pro
Bestselling Book of All Time...	Be Blithe
Biggest Library in the World...	Crayon for Girl, Bess

To learn about 5,000 different records,
check out the *World Almanac
Book of Records*. See p. 45.

**ANSWERS ON PAGES 334-337.
FOR MORE PUZZLES GO TO
WWW.WORLDALMANACFORKIDS.COM**

Reading the News

Newspaper stories are factual accounts written by reporters about events that have happened since the last issue. They provide what people call **hard news**. The most important news stories start on the front page.

A news story begins with a headline that says what happened in very few words. Sometimes there's a byline, saying who wrote the story, and there usually is a dateline, showing where and when it was written. Then comes the lead, a sentence that reveals all or most of the "five Ws" of news—who was involved, what happened, and where, when, and why it happened. The rest of the story gives further details, starting with the most important ones. Newspapers often have separate sections covering particular areas of interest, such as sports or business.

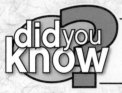

The most popular U.S. newspaper is USA Today, *which is read every day by more than 2 million people around the country. Other well known papers include the* New York Times *and the* Washington Post.

THE WEB

The Internet is a great source for news and information of current interest. Because anyone can put up a Web site and say anything they want, you need to stick to sites that you know are reliable. Sites to look for include those put out by government agencies such as NASA, news organizations or broadcasters such as CNN, and newspapers and magazines.
For more ideas, try going to:
www.ala.org/greatsites
www.cybrary.org/news.htm
www.writesite.org/html/tapping.html
www.monroe.lib.in.us/childrens/kidsmags.html

QUIZ: HOW WELL DO YOU KNOW HARRY POTTER?

1. The Mirror of Erised shows your heart's desire. What does Harry see when he first looks into the mirror?
2. Where is the entrance to the Chamber of Secrets?
3. What does Harry's patronus look like?
4. Which team won the Quidditch World Cup in *Goblet of Fire*?
5. According to prophecy, who else besides Harry Potter could be the boy destined to fight Lord Voldemort?
6. Which character is the "Half-Blood Prince"?

ANSWERS ON PAGES 334-337.
FOR MORE PUZZLES GO TO
WWW.WORLDALMANACFORKIDS.COM

Books to Read

There are two major types of literature: fiction and nonfiction. A **fiction** book includes people, places, and events that are often inspired by reality, but are mainly from an author's imagination. **Nonfiction** is about real things that actually happened and should be totally accurate. Nonfiction may be about how something works or the history of an event or a person's life.

Within these two groups there are smaller subgroups called **genres** (ZHAN-ruz).

FICTION

▶ **Mysteries and Thrillers**

These adventure stories will keep you up late, as you follow a main character who must uncover a secret.

Try These *Flush*, by Carl Hiaasen; *Eye of Eternity*, by Chris Archer

▶ **Fantasy and Science Fiction**

This genre is one of the most popular for teen readers. You've heard of the Harry Potter books, but there are thousands of books for kids and teens in this genre.

Try These *The Chronicles of Narnia*, by C.S. Lewis; *The Book Without Words: A Fable of Medieval Magic*, by Avi

▶ **Myths and Legends**

These made-up stories go way back. Some are from nineteenth century America, others are from ancient Greece and Africa.

Try These *Spider Spins a Story: Fourteen Legends from Native America*, edited by Jill Max; *The Magical Monkey King: Mischief in Heaven*, by Ji-Li Jiang

▶ **Historical Fiction**

If you think history is just about facts, this is the genre for you. Authors take exciting historical events and put the most interesting fictional characters right in the middle of them.

Try These *Shadows on the Sea*, by Joan Hiatt Harlow; *Al Capone Does My Shirts*, by Gennifer Choldenko

▶ Realistic Fiction

Do you like stories that might have happened to you? Realistic fiction is about real-life situations that teens and kids deal with every day.

Try These *The Penderwicks: A Summer Tale of Four Sisters, Two Rabbits, and a Very Interesting Boy*, by Jeanne Birdsall; *Surviving the Applewhites*, by Stephanie S. Tolan

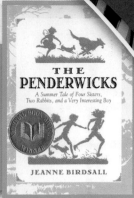

THE PENDERWICKS
A Summer Tale of Four Sisters, Two Rabbits, and a Very Interesting Boy

JEANNE BIRDSALL

Graphic Novels, Comics, and Manga

Check out these adventure series that use drawings and text to tell complicated adventure stories.

Try These *Fruits Basket*, a series by Natsuki Takaya; *The Adventures of Tintin*, a series by Hergé

NONFICTION

▶ Biographies, Autobiographies, and Memoirs

Do you like reading all about the details of a real person's life? This genre is for you.

Try These *Farewell to Manzanar: A True Story of Japanese American Experience During and After the World War II Internment*, by Jeanne Wakatsuki Houston and James D. Houston; *A Girl from Yamhill: A Memoir*, by Beverly Cleary

Farewell to Manzanar
Jeanne Wakatsuki Houston and James D. Houston

▶ History

Books in this genre can be about an event, an era, a country, or even a war.

Try These *Egyptology*, by Dugald A. Steer; *Hitler Youth*, by Susan Campbell Bartoletti

▶ Reference

Books that supply facts and practical information on one topic or many, including almanacs, atlases, dictionaries, and encyclopedias.

Try This *The World Almanac Book of Records*

THE WORLD ALMANAC BOOK OF RECORDS

FIRSTS, FEATS, **FACTS** & PHENOMENA

Famous Authors FOR KIDS

Author	Try the Book...
The writer known as **Avi** was born in New York in 1937, and "Avi" is a nickname given to him by his twin sister. Avi was able to overcome a learning disability called dysgraphia to become the successful author of dozens of books.	*The True Confessions of Charlotte Doyle*
Irish author **C.S. Lewis** was a soldier (during World War I) and a teacher. He was a member of the famous literary group "The Inklings" with J.R.R. Tolkien, author of *The Lord of the Rings*.	*The Lion, the Witch, and the Wardrobe*
Lemony Snicket is really a man called Daniel Handler whose life is far less unfortunate than Snicket's. He lives in San Francisco and loves opera.	*The Bad Beginning*
Lois Lowry was in Antarctica when her book, *The Giver*, won the Newbery Medal. She now resides in Massachusetts and Maine.	*The Giver*
Katherine Paterson says she loves to write because it is a job where she can wear what she likes. Though her parents were American, she was born in China. She also lived in Japan and says she has great respect for other cultures.	*Bridge to Terabithia*
Christopher Paolini first started writing *Eragon* when he was 15 and by the time he was 21, it was a bestseller. He and his sister were home-schooled by their parents. The family originally published and promoted *Eragon* by themselves.	*Eragon*

Katherine Paterson

Christopher Paolini

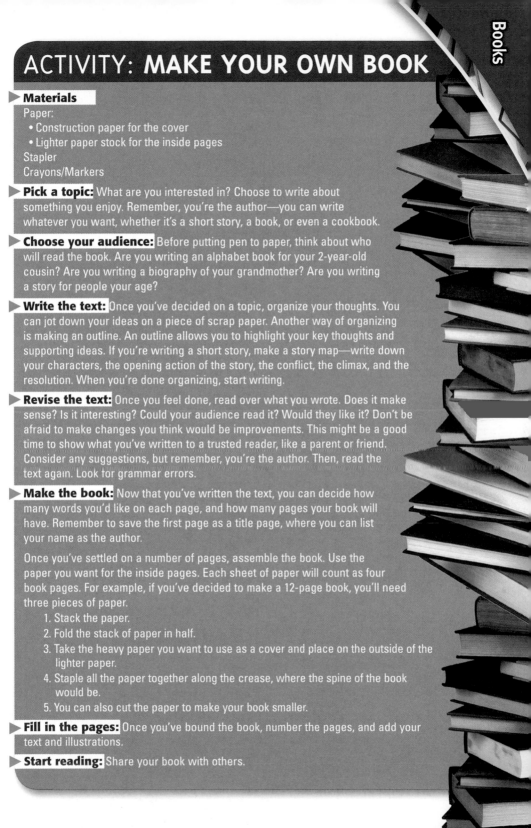

ACTIVITY: **MAKE YOUR OWN BOOK**

▶ **Materials**

Paper:
- • Construction paper for the cover
- • Lighter paper stock for the inside pages

Stapler

Crayons/Markers

▶ **Pick a topic:** What are you interested in? Choose to write about something you enjoy. Remember, you're the author—you can write whatever you want, whether it's a short story, a book, or even a cookbook.

▶ **Choose your audience:** Before putting pen to paper, think about who will read the book. Are you writing an alphabet book for your 2-year-old cousin? Are you writing a biography of your grandmother? Are you writing a story for people your age?

▶ **Write the text:** Once you've decided on a topic, organize your thoughts. You can jot down your ideas on a piece of scrap paper. Another way of organizing is making an outline. An outline allows you to highlight your key thoughts and supporting ideas. If you're writing a short story, make a story map—write down your characters, the opening action of the story, the conflict, the climax, and the resolution. When you're done organizing, start writing.

▶ **Revise the text:** Once you feel done, read over what you wrote. Does it make sense? Is it interesting? Could your audience read it? Would they like it? Don't be afraid to make changes you think would be improvements. This might be a good time to show what you've written to a trusted reader, like a parent or friend. Consider any suggestions, but remember, you're the author. Then, read the text again. Look for grammar errors.

▶ **Make the book:** Now that you've written the text, you can decide how many words you'd like on each page, and how many pages your book will have. Remember to save the first page as a title page, where you can list your name as the author.

Once you've settled on a number of pages, assemble the book. Use the paper you want for the inside pages. Each sheet of paper will count as four book pages. For example, if you've decided to make a 12-page book, you'll need three pieces of paper.

1. Stack the paper.
2. Fold the stack of paper in half.
3. Take the heavy paper you want to use as a cover and place on the outside of the lighter paper.
4. Staple all the paper together along the crease, where the spine of the book would be.
5. You can also cut the paper to make your book smaller.

▶ **Fill in the pages:** Once you've bound the book, number the pages, and add your text and illustrations.

▶ **Start reading:** Share your book with others.

Buildings

What is the largest hydroelectric dam in the U.S.? → page 53

Buildings are an essential part of our lives. Houses and apartment buildings are used for shelter from the elements, like cold and rain. Other buildings are used for work or school. Some are simple in form while others are impressive works of art or memorials. Structures such as bridges and dams have special functions. From the pyramids of ancient Egypt to the modern skyscraper, humans have used buildings to seek greater and greater heights.

News

Three Gorges Dam

When completed in 2009, this will be the world's largest dam, made of 989 million cubic feet of concrete. It will span 1.3 miles across the Yangtze (Chang) River in China and create a reservoir about 360 miles long. The reservoir will hold some 1.39 trillion cubic feet of water, so much that it will take 6 years to fill. The dam's 18,200-megawatt hydroelectric plant will also be the world's largest, generating as much energy as 15 nuclear power plants. To make room for the reservoir, over 1 million people are being relocated.

Freedom Tower

Designed to replace the World Trade Center in New York City that was destroyed on September 11, 2001, the Freedom Tower will stand 1,776 feet tall. Its height—matching the year of America's independence—was chosen to honor freedom in reponse to the terrorist attacks. An observation deck will be located at 1,362 feet, with a glass walkway at 1,368 feet, the heights of the original Twin Towers. A 414-foot spire at the top of the building will be lit at night. The building is expected to be finished in 2010.

Arthur Ravenel Jr. Bridge

Completed in 2005, this new bridge spans the Cooper River in Charleston, South Carolina, and is now the longest cable-stayed bridge in the U.S., with a main span of 1,546 feet. It replaced two truss bridges.

A cable-stayed bridge is similar to a suspension bridge, except that the cables are attached directly from the main towers to the bridge's deck (see page 52).

Tallest
Buildings
IN THE World

Here are the world's tallest buildings, with the year each was completed. Heights listed here don't include antennas or other outside structures.

◄ **Taipei 101,** Taipei, Taiwan (2004) Height: 101 stories, 1,671 feet

Petronas Towers 1 & 2, Kuala Lumpur, Malaysia (1998) Height: each building is 88 stories, 1,483 feet

Sears Tower, Chicago, Illinois (1974) Height: 110 stories, 1,450 feet

Jin Mao Tower, Shanghai, China (1998) Height: 88 stories, 1,380 feet

Two International Finance Centre, Hong Kong, China (2003) Height: 88 stories, 1,362 feet

Citic Plaza, Guangzhou, China (1997) Height: 80 stories, 1,283 feet

WORLD'S TALLEST WHEN BUILT

(all in New York City)

The New York World Building Built 1890. Height: 309 feet. Torn down 1955.
• Home of the **New York World** newspaper, which started **The World Almanac** in 1868.

Metropolitan Life Insurance Tower Built 1909. Height: 700 feet.

Woolworth Building Built 1913. Height: 792 feet.

Chrysler Building Built 1930. Height: 1,046 feet.

Empire State Building Built 1931. Height: 1,250 feet.

World Trade Center Towers 1 & 2 Built 1973. Height: 1,368 feet and 1,362 feet. Destroyed in September 2001.

The Tallest Towers

The world's **tallest structure** is the **KVLY-TV tower** in Fargo, North Dakota. It's 2,063 feet tall (including the 113-foot antenna) and made of steel. The tower is anchored and supported by more than 7.5 miles of steel wires.

The world's **tallest free-standing structure** is the 1,815-foot **CN Tower** in Toronto, Canada. It is not exactly a building since it does not have stories. "Free-standing" means it supports its own weight and is not attached to anything. Brave visitors can walk across the glass floor at the 1,122-foot level!

◄ *CN Tower*

A Short History of Tall Buildings

For over 4,000 years, the world's tallest structure was the 480-foot-tall Great Pyramid at Giza. Next to top the list was the cathedral spire in Cologne, Germany (513 ft., built in 1880), then the Washington Monument in Washington, D.C. (555 ft., 1884). These buildings all had thick stone walls, with not much space inside.

The biggest challenge to building tall was gravity. Whether made of mud, stone, brick, timber, or concrete, most buildings had load-bearing walls. This meant that the walls had to support their own weight, the roof, the floors, and everything in the building. The higher the walls, the thicker they needed to be, and too many windows would weaken the building.

By the 1880s, three **key factors in the evolution of tall buildings** were in place:

1 A NEED FOR SPACE Crowded cities had less space for building, and land got expensive. To create more space, buildings had to go up instead of out.

2 BETTER STEEL PRODUCTION Mass-producing steel made more of it available for construction. Long beams could be connected to make **columns**. These were braced with horizontal beams called girders. The columns and **girders** formed a strong three-dimensional grid called a **superstructure**. This type of building was lighter than a similar one made of stone or brick and its weight was directed down the columns, which were supported by a solid **foundation**.

3 THE ELEVATOR Tall buildings need elevators! The first elevator, powered by steam, was installed in a New York store in 1857. Electric elevators came along in 1880.

The first American "skyscraper" was built in Chicago in 1885. Though it was only 10 stories and 138 feet tall, the Home Insurance Building was the first tall building to have a metal superstructure and many windows.

As buildings got taller, a new problem sprang up—**wind**. Too much movement could damage buildings or make the people inside uncomfortable. Some tall buildings, like New York's Citicorp Center, actually have a counter-weight near the top. A computer controls a 400-ton weight, moving it back and forth to lessen the building's sway.

In California and Japan, **earthquakes** are a big problem and special techniques are needed to make tall buildings safer from quakes.

Race for the Sky In 1929, two buildings in New York City—the Bank of Manhattan Trust Building (now the Trump Building) and the Chrysler Building—competed to become the world's tallest. The Bank of Manhattan building was finished first at 927 feet high, just slightly higher than the expected height of its rival. Not to be outdone, the Chrysler Building's architect, William Van Alen, had hidden a 27-ton, 185-foot steel spire inside the structure. When it was raised, the total height was 1,046 feet, more than 100 feet taller than the Bank of Manhattan Building. Less than a year later, the Empire State Building rose above both to claim the title.

It's Not All About... TALL!

When it comes to buildings, the tall ones grab people's attention. But many other buildings are interesting and fun to look at. Here are a few really cool buildings.

SYDNEY OPERA HOUSE,
Sydney, Australia

Though it looks like a giant sea creature rising out of Sydney Harbor, architect Joern Utzon had the sections of an orange in mind when he designed this building. Finished in 1973, the shells were made of over 2,000 concrete sections held together by 217 miles of steel cable. The roof cover—bolted on in 4,240 sections—is covered with 1.5 million ceramic tiles.

THE GUGGENHEIM MUSEUM,
Bilbao, Spain

People from all over visit this building by the architect Frank O. Gehry—maybe as much to see the outside as for the art that's inside! Completed in 1997, it's made of steel, glass, and titanium, in a design that was inspired by fish and boats. This wild, curvy wonder is a good example of the power of imagination.

THE GLASS HOUSE,
New Canaan, Connecticut

When architect Philip Johnson designed his own home in 1949, he created something beautiful and unique. What makes this house special is the structure: it is a steel frame with outside walls made of clear glass. This makes the house totally see-through. (Johnson did enclose the bathroom in brick!) In an interview, Johnson said, "It's the only house in the world where you can watch the sun set and the moon rise at the same time."

BURJ AL ARAB HOTEL, Dubai, United Arab Emirates

If you think the unusual design of this luxury hotel looks like a ship under full sail—you're right. British architect Tom Wills-Wright started with the idea of a dhow (an ancient Arab sailing vessel) and transformed it into this modern image. Built in 1999, the Burj al Arab (meaning "Tower of the Arabs") sits on an artificial island just off shore in the Persian Gulf.

Bridges

There are four main bridge designs: beam, arch, truss, and suspension or cable-stayed.

BEAM

The beam bridge is the most basic kind. A log across a stream is a simple style of beam bridge. Highway bridges are often beam bridges. The span of a beam bridge, or the length of the bridge without any support under it, needs to be fairly short. Long beam bridges need many supporting poles, called piers.

ARCH

You can easily recognize an arch bridge, because it has arches holding it up from the bottom. The columns that support the arches are called abutments. Arch bridges were invented by the ancient Greeks.

TRUSS

The truss bridge uses mainly steel beams, connected in triangles to increase strength and span greater distances.

SUSPENSION

On suspension bridges, the roadway hangs from smaller cables attached to a pair of huge cables running over two massive towers. The ends of the giant cables are anchored firmly into solid rock or huge concrete blocks at each end of the bridge. The weight of the roadway is transferred through the cables to the anchors.

CABLE-STAYED

Magnifique!

Cable-stayed bridges are similar to suspension bridges, but the cables are attached directly from the towers to the deck. All of the bridge's weight is carried by the towers. The Millau Bridge in France (left), is a cable-stayed bridge. With its roadway 885 feet above the River Tarn, it became the world's highest road bridge when it opened in 2004. The top of its highest tower reaches a height of 1,125 feet, higher than the Eiffel Tower.

Dams

Here are the facts on two of the most famous dams in the U.S.

GRAND COULEE DAM

- spans the Columbia River in northern Washington state
- built from 1933 to 1942
- 550 feet high and 5,223 feet long
- made up of nearly 12 million cubic yards of concrete
- biggest hydroelectric dam in the U.S. and one of the largest in the world
- reservoir is Franklin D. Roosevelt Lake, which covers about 130 square miles
- contains 33 generators that can produce 6,480,000 kilowatts of power—the most of any hydroelectric dam in the U.S.

HOOVER DAM

- spans the Colorado River at the Arizona-Nevada border
- built between 1930 and 1936
- originally called Boulder Dam; renamed for former President Herbert Hoover in 1947
- 726 feet high and 1,244 feet long
- reservoir is Lake Mead, which covers 247 square miles and is the largest reservoir in the U.S. and one of the largest man-made lakes in the world
- One of the best ways to see Hoover Dam is to drive across it!

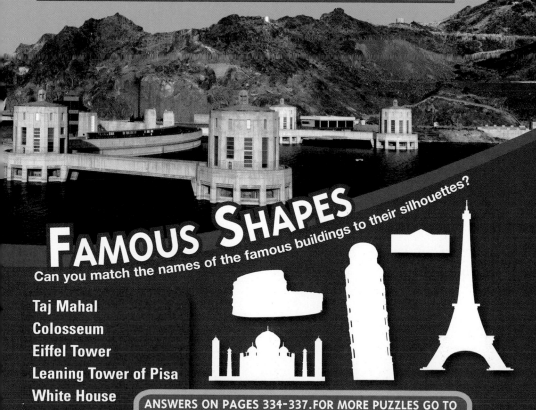

FAMOUS SHAPES

Can you match the names of the famous buildings to their silhouettes?

Taj Mahal
Colosseum
Eiffel Tower
Leaning Tower of Pisa
White House

ANSWERS ON PAGES 334-337. FOR MORE PUZZLES GO TO
WWW.WORLDALMANACFORKIDS.COM

53

Camping

At which camp might a clown be your counselor? ➡ page 55

Let's Go to Camp!

Do you want to learn how to do something completely new? Or maybe you want to improve at something you already know how to do in sports, art, music, dance, or drama. Or, maybe you just want to spend time outdoors and make new friends!

These are a few of the reasons why more than 10 million kids and adults in the U.S. go to camp each year.

Camp Is for Everyone

Resident Camp: Usually for kids age 7 or older. Campers stay overnight, usually in cabins, tents, or tepees. Stays can last a few days, a week, or more.

Day Camp: For kids as young as 4. Many of the same activities as a resident camp, but everyone goes home at the end of the day.

Specialty Camp: Helps kids learn a special skill, like horseback riding, water skiing, or dancing, to name just a few.

Special Needs Camp: Each year, more than a million kids with special needs go to summer camp.

THE AMERICAN CAMP ASSOCIATION®

The American Camp Association is a resource for parents and kids to help them find the right camp to fit any need and budget. For more information, visit

WEB SITE www.CAMPParents.org

Four Fun Camps

Would you like to do something a little different next summer? Try one of these unusual camps.

GIRLS ROCK!

Are you a girl who wants to be a rock star? The Rock 'n' Roll Camp for Girls, in Portland, Oregon, is the camp for you. A typical day at this camp includes instrument instruction, visiting band performances, songwriting, and amplified band practice.

WEB SITE *www.girlsrockcamp.org*

CLOWN AROUND

During the summers at Smirkus Camp in Greensboro, Vermont, kids learn how to tumble, ride unicycles, ride on a wire—and fall down—without getting hurt. Taught by real circus clowns and acrobats, kids train for five hours a day, and then enjoy movies and games in the evenings.

WEB SITE *www.circussmirkus.org*

TECH CAMP

Think you'll miss your computer too much to leave home for summer camp? Don't worry, you can go to an iD Tech Camp, hosted at 40 universities around the country. iD stands for "internalDrive"—that's your brain! At iD, kids use the newest computers and programs to have fun exploring, building video games, producing digital videos, and more.

WEB SITE *www.internaldrive.com*

BREATHE EASY

Do you wish you could go to camp, but can't because you have difficulty with asthma? There is a special camp designed just for you. Plus, other than a $25 registration fee—it's free! At Camp Breathe Easy in Livermore, California, doctors and camp counselors make sure that you can have a safe—and totally fun—camping experience. **WEB SITE** *www.alaebay.org*

FIND A CAMP FOR YOU!

These are only a few of the more than 12,000 day and sleepaway camps in the U.S. Many camps offer help with camp fees. Check out the directory online at American Camp Association to find the perfect camp for you. **WEB SITE** *www.acacamps.org*

Disasters

What was the worst single-airplane crash in history? ➡ page 60

HURRICANES

Hurricanes—called typhoons or cyclones in the Pacific—are Earth's biggest storms. They form over warm oceans. As warm seawater evaporates, the pressure drops, and winds begin to circulate, creating a wall of clouds and rain wrapped around a calm center called the **eye**. The storm strengthens as warm, moist air feeds into it and can cover an area 300 miles wide.

Hurricanes are classified by wind speed. When steady winds from a tropical storm reach 39 mph, the storm is named. At 74 mph, the storm is called a hurricane.

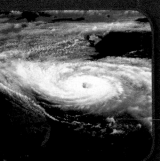

Hurricanes can knock down trees and tear roofs apart. Strong winds blowing toward shore can create a rise in the ocean water called a **storm surge**. It can combine with heavy rains to cause flooding and massive damage.

For the Atlantic Ocean, Caribbean Sea, and Gulf of Mexico, hurricane season traditionally runs from June 1 to November 30. Most hurricanes happen in August, September, or October, when the oceans are warmest. Hurricanes only form when water at the ocean's surface is above 80 degrees.

Hurricane Categories:
1: 74-95 mph
2: 96-110 mph
3: 111-130 mph
4: 131-155 mph
5: over 155 mph

RECORD YEAR

In 2005, there were 27 named storms in the Atlantic region, 15 of which were hurricanes. That makes 2005 the busiest Atlantic hurricane season since record keeping began in 1851. Four major hurricanes hit the U.S. Of those, a record three storms reached Category 5 (Katrina, Rita, and Wilma). The previous record was set in 1961, when the U.S. was affected by two Category 5 hurricanes.

FACTS ABOUT HURRICANE KATRINA

- Hurricane Katrina struck Florida on August 25, 2005. It gained strength over the Gulf of Mexico before moving through Louisiana, Mississippi, and Alabama on August 29.
- Hurricane Katrina had weakened from a Category 5 to a Category 3 storm when it reached New Orleans. But some of the levees–structures built to protect the city from flooding–gave way. Soon 80% of the city was under water. The flooding trapped up to 100,000 people in the city for several days. More than 1,300 people died as a result of the storm.
- The storm caused a record-setting $80 billion worth of damage.

HURRICANE NAMES

The U.S. government began using women's names for hurricanes in 1953 and added men's names in 1978. (When all letters except Q, U, X, Y, and Z are used in one season, any additional storms are named with Greek letters.) Six Greek letters were needed to name 2005 storms.

2006 names: Alberto, Beryl, Chris, Debby, Ernesto, Florence, Gordon, Helene, Isaac, Joyce, Kirk, Leslie, Michael, Nadine, Oscar, Patty, Rafael, Sandy, Tony, Valerie, William

TORNADOES

Also called **twisters** and **whirlwinds**, tornadoes are the most violent storms on Earth. These rapidly spinning columns of air are often described as **funnel clouds**.

Tornadoes form when winds change direction, speed up, and spin around in or near a thunderstorm. They can also spin off from hurricanes. The high winds can cause massive destruction, especially from flying debris such as cars!

Tornadoes can come in any month, but are more likely to happen between March and July. They occur most often in Oklahoma, Texas, and Florida, but they can happen in any state. Many strong tornadoes touch down in the U.S central plains. This 10-state area, which stretches from north Texas to Nebraska, is called **Tornado Alley**.

According to the National Oceanic and Atmospheric Administration's (NOAA) Storm Prediction Center in Norman, Oklahoma, an average of 1,200 tornadoes occur in the U.S. each year. They cause an average of 55 deaths and 1,500 injuries a year and over $400 million in damage.

Tornado categories:

WEAK
EF0: 65-85 mph

EF1: 86-110 mph

STRONG
EF2: 111-135 mph

EF3: 136-165 mph

VIOLENT
EF4: 166-200 mph

EF5: over 200 mph

Tornadoes are measured by how much damage they cause. In Feb. 2007, the U.S. will begin using the Enhanced Fujita (EF) Scale (at left) to measure tornadoes. The EF Scale, like the older Fujita Scale, provides an estimate of a tornado's wind speed. But the new scale is based on more tornado details. If a tornado doesn't hit any buildings, it may not be possible to classify it. Wind speeds have been recorded in weak tornadoes, but the measuring instruments are destroyed in more violent winds. The highest wind speed ever recorded—318 mph—was taken in May 1999 in an Oklahoma tornado.

U.S. TORNADO RECORDS (since record keeping began in 1950)

YEAR: The 1,717 tornadoes reported in 2004 topped the previous record of 1,424 in 1998.

MONTH: In May 2003, there were a total of 516 tornadoes, easily passing the old record of 399 set in June 1992.

TWO-DAY PERIOD: On April 3 and 4, 1974, 147 tornadoes touched down in 13 states.

WEB SITE For more information on storms and weather, go to the NOAA Education page: *www.education.noaa.gov/cweather.html*

EARTHQUAKES

Earthquakes may be so weak that they are hardly felt, or strong enough to do great damage. There are thousands of earthquakes each year, but most are too small to be noticed. About 1 in 5 can be felt, and about 1 in 500 causes damage.

North America · Europe · Asia · Africa · Pacific Ocean · Pacific Ocean · South America · Australia · Antarctica

WHAT CAUSES EARTHQUAKES?

To understand earthquakes, think of the Earth as a big round egg and imagine that the shell has been cracked. This cracked outer layer of the Earth (the eggshell) is called the **lithosphere**, and it is divided into huge pieces called **plates** (see map above). Underneath the lithosphere is a softer layer called the **asthenosphere**. The plates of the cracked lithosphere are constantly gliding over this softer layer, moving away from one another, toward one another, or past one another. These plates average about 60 miles thick. Earthquakes result when plates collide.

The cracks in the lithosphere are called **faults**. Many quakes occur along these fault lines.

MAJOR EARTHQUAKES

The earthquakes listed here are among the largest and most destructive recorded in the past 50 years. (See also "Tsunami," page 59.)

Year	Location	Magnitude	Deaths (approximate)
1960	near Chile	9.5	5,000
1970	Peru (northern)	7.8	66,000
1976	China (Tangshan)	8.0	255,000
1988	Soviet Armenia	7.0	55,000
1989	United States (San Francisco area)	7.1	62
1990	Iran (western)	7.7	40,000+
1994	United States (Los Angeles area)	6.8	61
1995	Japan (Kobe)	6.9	5,502
1998	Afghanistan (northeastern)	6.9	4,700+
1999	Turkey (western)	7.4	17,200+
2001	India (western)	7.9	30,000+
2003	Iran (southeastern)	6.5	41,000+
2005	Pakistan and India	7.6	87,000+

VOLCANOES

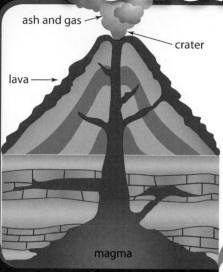

ash and gas
crater
lava
magma

A volcano is a mountain or hill (**cone**) with an opening on top known as a **crater**. Hot melted rock (**magma**), gases, and other material from inside the Earth mix together miles underground and rise up through cracks and weak spots. When enough pressure builds up, the magma may blast out, or erupt, through the crater. The magma is called **lava** when it reaches the air. This lava may be hotter than 2,000 degrees Fahrenheit. The cone of a volcano can comprise layers of lava and ash that have erupted, then cooled.

Some islands, like the Hawaiian islands, are really the tops of undersea volcanoes.

Where *is the* **Ring of Fire?**

The hundreds of active volcanoes found on the land near the edges of the Pacific Ocean make up what is called the **Ring of Fire**. They mark the boundary between the plates under the Pacific Ocean and the plates under the continents around the ocean. (Earth's plates are explained on page 58, with the help of a map.) The Ring of Fire runs all along the west coast of South and North America, from the southern tip of Chile to Alaska. The ring also runs down the east coast of Asia, starting in the far north in Kamchatka. It continues down past Australia.

SOME FAMOUS VOLCANIC ERUPTIONS

Year	Volcano (place)	Deaths (approximate)
79	Mount Vesuvius (Italy)	16,000
1586	Kelut (Indonesia)	10,000
1792	Mount Unzen (Japan)	14,500
1815	Tambora (Indonesia)	10,000
1883	Krakatau, or Krakatoa (Indonesia)	36,000
1902	Mount Pelée (Martinique)	28,000
1980	Mount St. Helens (U.S.)	57
1982	El Chichón (Mexico)	1,880
1985	Nevado del Ruiz (Colombia)	23,000
1986	Lake Nyos (Cameroon)	1,700
1991	Mount Pinatubo (Philippines)	800

TSUNAMI (pronounced *tsoo-NAH-mee*) comes from two Japanese words: "tsu" (harbor) and "nami" (wave). These huge waves are sometimes called tidal waves, but they have nothing to do with the tides.

The strongest tsunamis happen when a big part of the sea floor lifts along a fault (see page 58), pushing up a huge volume of water. The resulting waves are long and low, and might not even be noticed in deep water. They move at speeds of up to 500 miles per hour. As they near shore, they slow down and the great energy forces the water upward into big waves.

On December 26, 2004, a magnitude-9.0 earthquake off the Indonesian island of Sumatra triggered a tsunami in the Indian Ocean. The tsunami hit 12 countries. An estimated 300,000 people were killed, and 1.6 million were left homeless.

MAJOR Disasters

AIRCRAFT DISASTERS

Date	Location	What Happened?	Deaths
May 6, 1937	Lakehurst, NJ	German zeppelin (blimp) *Hindenburg* caught fire as it prepared to land	36
Aug. 12, 1985	Japan	Boeing 747 jet collided with Mt. Osutaka. Japan's worst single-aircraft disaster in history	520
March 27, 1977	Tenerife, Canary Islands	Two Boeing 747s collide in worst airline disaster ever	582
Nov. 12, 2001	New York City	Airbus A-300 crashed just after takeoff from JFK Airport	265

EXPLOSIONS AND FIRES

Date	Location	What Happened?	Deaths
June 15, 1904	New York City	*General Slocum*, wooden ship carrying church members across East River, caught fire	1,021
March 25, 1911	New York City	Triangle Shirtwaist Factory caught fire, workers were trapped inside	146
Nov. 28, 1942	Boston, MA	Fire swept through the Coconut Grove nightclub; patrons panicked. Deadliest nightclub fire in U.S. history	491
Dec. 3, 1984	Bhopal, India	A pesticide factory explosion spread toxic gas; worst industrial accident in history	15,000+

RAIL DISASTERS

Date	Location	What Happened?	Deaths
Jan. 16, 1944	León Prov., Spain	Train crashed in the Torro Tunnel	500
March 2, 1944	Salerno, Italy	Passengers suffocated when train stalled in tunnel	521
Feb. 6, 1951	Woodbridge, NJ	Commuter train fell through a temporary overpass	84
June 6, 1981	Bihar, India	Train plunged off of a bridge into the river. India's deadliest rail disaster ever	800+

WORST NUCLEAR POWER ACCIDENT. *On April 26, 1986, an explosion occurred at one of the reactors at a nuclear power plant near Chernobyl, USSR (now Ukraine). The explosion destroyed the reactor's protective covering, and radioactive material leaked into the air for the next 10 days. High levels of radiation were detected as far away as Italy and Norway. At least 31 people died immediately after the disaster, and thousands more may eventually die from illnesses caused by radiation exposure. More than 135,000 people had to be evacuated from the area within 1,000 miles of the plant.*

SHIP DISASTERS

Date	Location	What Happened?	Deaths
April 14, 1912	near Newfoundland	Luxury liner *Titanic* collided with iceberg	1,503
May 7, 1915	Atlantic Ocean, near Ireland	British steamer *Lusitania* torpedoed and sunk by German submarine	1,198
Jan. 30, 1945	Baltic Sea	Liner *Wilhelm Gustloff* carrying German refugees and soldiers sunk by Soviet sub. Highest death toll for a single ship	6,000-7,000
Aug. 12, 2000	Barents Sea	Explosions sank Russian submarine *Kursk*; multiple rescue attempts failed	118
Sept. 26, 2002	Atlantic Ocean near The Gambia	Senegalese ferry capsized	1,863
Feb. 3, 2006	Red Sea	Egyptian ferry returning from Saudi Arabia sank after fire broke out onboard	1,013

OTHER DISASTERS

Date	Location	What Happened?	Deaths
March 11-14, 1888	Eastern U.S.	20-50 inches of snow buried the eastern U.S. in a famous blizzard	400
Aug. 1931	China	Vast flooding on the Huang He River. Highest known death toll from a flood	3,700,000
Dec. 1999	Venezuela	Flooding and mudslides devastated the capital (Caracas) and surrounding areas	9,000+
Aug. 2005	Southeast U.S.	Hurricane Katrina struck Florida, Louisiana, Mississippi, and Alabama. Levee failure in New Orleans flooded 80% of city	1,300+
Feb. 2006	The Philippines	Landslide on Leyte Island buries a village	1,000

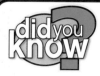

MASSIVE FLOOD. *The worst U.S. flood happened on June 1, 1889, in Johnstown, Pennsylvania. At about four in the afternoon, people in this small city heard a rumble and then a "roar like thunder." Fourteen miles upriver, the old South Fork Dam had broken and a huge wall of water— sometimes as high as 60 feet—came crashing down on the city at 40 miles per hour. The official death toll reached nearly 2,200, but many victims were never found.*

Johnstown, PA

Environment

What was the warmest year? ➡ page 67

The World's ENERGY

One important way we interact with our environment is by extracting energy from natural resources and putting it to use in industry and everyday life.

Who Produces and Uses the MOST ENERGY?

The United States produces about 17% of the world's energy—more than any other country—but it also uses 24% of the world's supply. The table below on the left lists the world's top ten energy producers and the percent of the world's production that each nation was responsible for in 2003. The table on the right lists the world's top energy users and the percent of the world's energy that each nation consumed.

Top Energy Producers	
United States	17%
Russia	12%
China	11%
Saudi Arabia	6%
Canada	4%
Iran	3%
United Kingdom	3%
Norway	3%
Australia	3%
Mexico	2%

Top Energy Users	
United States	24%
China	11%
Russia	7%
Japan	5%
Germany	3%
India	3%
Canada	3%
France	3%
United Kingdom	2%
Brazil	2%

WHERE DOES U.S. ENERGY COME FROM?

In 2004, nearly 86% of the energy used in the U.S. came from fossil fuels, mainly petroleum, natural gas, or coal. The rest came mostly from nuclear power, hydropower (water power), and renewable resources such as geothermal, solar, and wind energy, and from burning materials such as wood and animal waste.

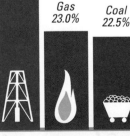

Petroleum 40.2%
Natural Gas 23.0%
Coal 22.5%
Nuclear power 8.3%
Hydro-power 2.7%
Other 3.4%

New Ways to Get Energy

Energy from Animal Droppings

Pig dung has long been a source of methane gas, which could be burned for heat or to power a generator. But in recent years, American cities and states have been seeking new ways to use animal waste. San Francisco, one of the leading recycling cities in the U.S., announced that in 2006 it will start using dog and cat droppings to generate electricity. Pet owners will put their pet's waste in special bags that will be picked up by trash collectors and brought to a special facility. The droppings will be put into something called a "methane digester." There, microbes will feed on the waste and release methane gas that can power a generator.

In Minnesota, a power plant that runs on clean-burning turkey droppings is in the works. In addition, the Minnesota plant will produce fertilizer as a byproduct.

Mowed Grass Burned for Heat

Shelburne Farms in Vermont is going to use the grass it mows on its property to heat its massive barn. The plan is to take the cut grass, run it through a special machine that turns grass into pellets, and burn the pellets in the barn's boiler. Since the grass was going to be thrown away anyway, the farm owners figured they might as well use it. Actually, burning grass for heat isn't new. People have been doing it for years. But grass pellets burn more like wood, which is more efficient. Even better, this method costs less than using oil or regular wood to heat the boiler. The farm hopes to be fully powered by renewable energy by the year 2020.

Cars That Smell Like French Fries

Biodiesel is a type of renewable biomass energy (see page 65) that works like regular diesel fuel from oil. Made from vegetable (mostly soybean) and recycled cooking oil, biodiesel is less polluting than regular diesel. Its exhaust, instead of smelling like regular car exhaust, smells like French fries or fried food!

Another great thing about biodiesel is that it can be used in cars and trucks that have regular diesel (but not gasoline) engines. Most alternative fuels for cars, like ethanol, require special engine modifications to work. But biodiesel doesn't.

The main drawback to biodiesel is that it doesn't have as much energy as regular diesel. However, car makers are working to make engines that are more efficient, so that the energy difference between diesel and biodiesel isn't so great.

Can you figure out which alternative energy source would work best in each place?

Type of place:

1. Very hot and sunny desert
2. Town near a waterfall
3. Cliffside village on an ocean coast
4. Area with lots of geysers and volcanic activity

Energy source:

A. Wind power
B. Solar power
C. Geothermal energy
D. Hydroelectric power

ANSWERS ON PAGES 334-337. FOR MORE PUZZLES GO TO WWW.WORLDALMANACFORKIDS.COM

Sources of Energy

FOSSIL FUELS

Fuels are called "fossil fuels" because they were formed from ancient plants and animals.

The three basic fossil fuels are **coal**, **oil**, and **natural gas**. Most of the energy we use today comes from these sources. **Coal** is mined, either at the Earth's surface or deep underground. Pumpjacks pump **oil**, or petroleum, from wells drilled in the ground. **Natural gas**, which is made up mostly of a gas called methane, also comes from wells. Natural gas is a clean-burning fuel, and it has been used more and more. Oil and coal create more air pollution.

All fossil fuels have one problem: they are gradually getting used up. In the case of oil, many industrial and other countries lack oil resources or need much more oil than they have, so they depend on importing large amounts from oil-rich countries.

▽ A pumpjack

Hoover Dam, on the Colorado River about 30 miles southeast of Las Vegas, Nevada, provides power for 1.3 million people.

NUCLEAR ENERGY

A nuclear power plant

Nuclear power is created by releasing energy stored in the nucleus of an atom. This process is nuclear **fission**, which is known as "splitting" an atom. Fission takes place in a **reactor**, which allows the nuclear reaction to be controlled. Nuclear power plants release almost no air pollution, but they do have some radioactive waste that needs to be stored somewhere. Many countries today use nuclear energy. There are some big safety concerns with nuclear power. In 1979 a nuclear accident at Three Mile Island in Pennsylvania led to the release of some radiation. A much worse accident at Chernobyl in Ukraine in 1986 threatened thousands of lives over a wide area (see page 60 for more information).

WATER POWER

Water power is energy that comes from the force of falling or fast-flowing water. It was put to use early in human history. **Water wheels**, turned by rivers or streams, were common in the Middle Ages. They were used for tasks like grinding grain and sawing lumber.

Today water power comes from waterfalls or from dams. As water flows from a higher to a lower level, it runs a turbine—a device that turns an electric generator. This is called **hydroelectric power** (hydro = water). Today, over half of the world's hydroelectric power is produced in five countries: Brazil, Russia, Canada, China, and the United States.

A "farm" of wind turbines

WIND ENERGY

People have used the wind's energy for a long time. **Windmills** were popular in Europe during the Middle Ages. Later, windmills became common on U.S. farms. Today, huge high-tech windmills with propeller-like blades are grouped together in **"wind farms."** Dozens of wind turbines are spaced well apart (so they don't block each other's wind). Even on big wind farms, the windmills usually take up less than 1% of the ground space. The rest of the land can still be used for farming or for grazing animals.

Wind power is a rapidly growing technology that doesn't pollute or get used up like fossil fuels. Unfortunately, the generators only work when the wind blows. Some people think they are noisy or spoil scenery. There is also some concern that they can harm birds.

BIOMASS ENERGY

Burning wood and straw (materials known as **biomass**) is probably the oldest way of producing energy. It's an old idea, but it still has value. Researchers are growing crops to use as fuel. Biomass fuels can be burned, like coal, in a power plant. They can also be used to make **ethanol**, which is similar to gasoline. Most ethanol comes from corn, which can make it expensive. Natural oils from crops or waste oil from restaurants can be used to make biodiesel which is like regular diesel fuel currently used in some cars and trucks. Researchers are experimenting with other potentially useful crops, like "switchgrass" and alfalfa.

A biomass power plant provides energy for Burlington, Vermont. It turns wood chips, solid waste, and switchgrass into a substance similar to natural gas.

GEOTHERMAL ENERGY

Geothermal energy comes from the heat deep inside the Earth. About 30 miles below the surface is a layer called the **mantle**. This is the source of the gas and lava that erupt from volcanoes. Hot springs and geysers, with temperatures as high as 700 degrees, are also heated by the mantle. Because it's so hot, the mantle holds great promise as an energy source, especially in areas where the hot water is close to the surface. Iceland, which has many active volcanoes and hot springs, uses lots of geothermal energy. About 85% of homes there are heated this way.

SOLAR POWER

Energy directly from sunlight is a promising new technology. Vast amounts of this energy fall upon the Earth every day—and it is not running out. Energy from the Sun is

A solar power plant

expected to run for some 5 billion years. Solar energy is also friendly to the environment. One drawback is the need for space for the solar panels, which are large. Also, energy can't be gathered when the Sun isn't shining.

A solar cell is usually made of silicon, a semiconductor. It can change sunlight into electricity. The cost of solar cells has been dropping in recent years. Large plants using solar cell systems have been built in several countries, including Japan, Saudi Arabia, the United States, and Germany.

The Air We Breathe

T he Earth's air is made up of different gases: about 78% nitrogen, 21% oxygen, and 1% carbon dioxide, water vapor, and other gases. All humans and animals need air to survive. Plants also need it. They use sunlight and the carbon dioxide in air to make food, and then give off oxygen.

Humans breathe more than 3,000 gallons of air a day. Because air is so basic to life, it is important to keep it clean. Air pollution causes health problems and may bring about acid rain, smog, global warming, and a breakdown of the ozone layer.

What is **Acid Rain**?

Acid rain is a kind of air pollution caused by chemicals in the air. Eventually these chemicals can make rain, snow, or fog more acidic than normal. The main source of these chemicals is exhaust from cars, trucks, buses, waste incinerators, factories, and some electric power plants, especially those that burn fossil fuels, such as coal. When these chemicals mix with moisture and other particles, they create sulfuric acid and nitric acid. The wind often carries these acids many miles before they fall to the ground in rain, snow, and fog, or even as dry particles.

Acid rain can harm people, animals, and plants. It is especially harmful to lakes. Thousands of lakes in Canada, Finland, Norway, and Sweden have been declared "dead." Not even algae can live in them. Birds and other species that depend on the lakes for food are also affected. Acid rain can also affect crops and trees. Buildings, statues, and cars are also damaged when acid rain destroys metal, stone, and paint.

What is the **Ozone Layer**?

Our atmosphere is made up of different layers. One layer, between 6 and 30 miles above the Earth, is made up of ozone gas. This **ozone layer** protects us from the Sun's harshest rays, called **ultraviolet** or **UV rays.** These rays can cause sunburn and skin cancer.

When old refrigerators, air conditioners, and similar items are thrown away, gases from them (called **chlorofluorocarbons,** or CFCs) rise into the air and destroy some of the ozone in this layer. Most countries no longer produce CFCs, but the gas can stay in the atmosphere for years—destroying ozone and adding to the greenhouse effect.

Each August, a **hole in the ozone layer** forms over Antarctica (it usually closes by December). Since it was discovered in the 1980s, it has doubled to about the size of North America. It sometimes extends over southern Chile and Argentina. On some days, people in Punta Arenas, Chile (the world's southernmost city), may limit their sun exposure to no more than 20 minutes between noon and 3 P.M. Other days, they don't go out at all!

WHAT IS SMOG?

The brownish haze seen mostly in the summer and especially around big cities is smog. The main ingredient in smog is ozone. When ozone is high up in the atmosphere, it helps protect us from the Sun's stronger rays. But near the ground, ozone forms smog when sunlight and heat interact with oxygen and particles produced by the burning of fossil fuels. Smog makes it hard for some people to breathe, especially those with asthma. "Ozone Alerts" are not just for Los Angeles (famous for its smog). Many cities in the U.S. issue them through newspapers, TV, and radio stations to let people know when the air can be unhealthy for outdoor activities.

WEB SITE For more information visit *www.epa.gov/airnow/aqikids*

What is Global Warming?

Heat from the Sun

Most heat is trapped in the atmosphere

Carbon dioxide, other gases from cars and factories trap extra heat.

Some heat escapes

The average surface temperature on Earth was 58.02°F in 2005, which makes it the warmest year since accurate record keeping began in 1880. It just barely beat out 1998, when global temperature averaged 58.00°F. Historical climate data shows us that the global temperature is about 1°F higher than it was 100 years ago. The 10 hottest years on record have all been since 1990. (For the U.S. only, 2005 was the 49th wettest year and the 13th hottest on record, with an average temperature of 54.0°F). This gradual rise is called global warming. On that much, scientists agree. What they can't agree on is the cause. Some think it is just part of a natural cycle of warming and cooling. But most scientists believe that an increase in certain gases in the air generated by human activity plays a big role.

The **greenhouse effect** is a natural process, needed for life to exist on Earth. Certain gases in the atmosphere act like the glass walls of a greenhouse: they let the rays of the Sun pass through to the Earth's surface but hold in some of the heat that radiates from the Sun-warmed Earth.

These naturally occurring greenhouse gases include water vapor, carbon dioxide, methane, nitrous oxide, and ozone. Without these gases, Earth's average temperature would be much colder.

Human activity is putting more of these "greenhouse gases" into the air. As cities have grown in size and population, people have needed more and more electricity, cars, and manufactured things of all kinds. As industries have grown, more greenhouse gases have been produced by the burning of fossil fuels such as oil, coal, and natural gas. The increases in these gases make the greenhouse "glass" thicker, causing more heat to be trapped than in the past.

It doesn't seem like much, but a slight warming could cause changes in the climate of many regions. If the climate changed enough, plants and animals would not be able to survive in their native habitats. Many scientists think average temperatures could rise as much as 6°F over the next 100 years. This warming could cause a lot of ice near the North and South Poles to melt, making more water go into the oceans and causing flooding along coasts.

WATER, WATER EVERYWHERE

Earth is the water planet. More than two-thirds of its surface is covered with water, and every living thing on it needs water to live. Water is not only part of our life (drinking, cooking, cleaning, bathing); it makes up 75% of our brains and 60% of our whole bodies! Humans can survive for about a month without food, but only for about a week without water. People also use water to cool machines in factories, to produce power, and to irrigate farmland.

HOW MUCH IS THERE TO DRINK?
Seawater makes up 97% of the world's water. Another 2% of the water is frozen in ice caps, icebergs, glaciers, and sea ice. Half of the 1% left is too far underground to be reached. That leaves only 0.5% of freshwater for all the people, plants, and animals on Earth. This supply is renewable only by rainfall.

WHERE DOES DRINKING WATER COME FROM?
Most smaller cities and towns get their freshwater from **groundwater**—melted snow and rain that seeps deep into the ground and is drawn out from wells. Larger cities usually rely on lakes or reservoirs for their water. Some areas of the world with little fresh water are turning to a process called desalinization (removing salt from seawater) as a solution. But this process is slow and expensive.

THE HYDROLOGICAL CYCLE:
Water's Endless Journey Water is special. It's the only thing on Earth that exists naturally in **all three physical states**: solid (ice), liquid, and gas (water vapor). It never boils naturally (except around volcanoes), but it evaporates (turns into a gas) easily into the air. These unique properties send water on a cycle of repeating events.

HOW DOES WATER GET INTO THE AIR?
Heat from the sun causes surface water in oceans, lakes, swamps, and rivers to turn into water vapor. This is called **evaporation**. Plants release water vapor into the air as part of the process called **transpiration**. Animals also release a little bit when they breathe.

HOW DOES WATER COME OUT OF THE AIR?
Warm air holds more water vapor than cold air. As the air rises into the atmosphere, it cools and the water vapor **condenses**—changes back into tiny water droplets. These droplets form clouds. As the drops get bigger, gravity pulls them down as **precipitation** (rain, snow, sleet, fog, and dew are all types of precipitation).

WHERE DOES THE WATER GO?
Depending on where the precipitation lands, it can: **1.** evaporate back into the atmosphere **2.** run off into streams and rivers **3.** be absorbed by plants **4.** soak down into the soil as ground water **5.** fall as snow on a glacier and be trapped as ice for thousands of years.

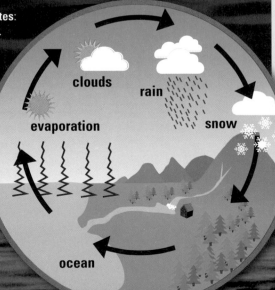

clouds

rain

evaporation

snow

ocean

Why We Need Wetlands

Wetlands are—you guessed it—wet lands. They are wet (covered with water, or with water at or near the surface) at least part of every year. Bogs, swamps, and marshes are all kinds of wetlands.

Wetlands have at least three important functions:

▶ **Storing water.** They absorb water like giant sponges and hold it in, releasing it slowly. During floods an acre of wetland can hold in 1.5 million gallons of water.

▶ **Cleaning up water.** They slow down water flow and let harmful sediments drop to the bottom. Plant roots and tiny organisms remove human and animal waste.

▶ **Providing habitats.** They are home to huge numbers of plants, fish, and wildlife. More than one-third of all threatened and endangered species in the U.S. live only in wetlands.

Wetlands, Everglades National Park

There are about 100 million acres of wetlands left in the lower 48 states, less than half of what there were in 1600. Wetlands are lost when people drain and fill them in for farmland, dam them up to form ponds and lakes, or pave and build up surrounding areas.

WATER WOES

Pollution: Polluted water can't be used for drinking, swimming, or watering crops, or provide a habitat for plants and animals. Major sources of water pollutants are sewage, chemicals from factories, fertilizers and weed killers, and landfills that leak. In general, anything that anyone dumps on the ground finds its way into the water cycle. Each year, the United Nations promotes March 22 as "World Water Day" to remind people how important it is to protect precious freshwater.

Overuse: Using water faster than nature can pass it through the hydrological cycle can create other problems. When more water is taken out of lakes and reservoirs (for drinking, bathing, and other uses) than is put back in, the water levels begin to drop. Combined with lower than normal rainfall, this can be devastating. In some cases, lakes become salty or dry up completely.

The Dreaded Dripping Faucet: Just one faucet, dripping very slowly (once a minute), can waste 38 gallons of water a year. Multiply that by several million houses and apartments, and you see a lot of water going down the drain!

HOME SWEET BIOME

A "biome" is a large natural area that is home to a certain type of plant. The animals, climate, soil, and even the amount of water in the region also help distinguish a biome. There are more than 30 kinds of biomes in the world. But the following types cover most of Earth's surface.

Forests

Forests cover about one-third of Earth's land surface. Pines, hemlocks, firs, and spruces grow in the cool **evergreen forests** farthest from the equator. These trees are called **conifers** because they produce cones.

Temperate forests have warm, rainy summers and cold, snowy winters. Here **deciduous trees** (which lose their leaves in the fall and grow new ones in the spring) join the evergreens. Temperate forests are home to maple, oak, beech, and poplar trees, and to wildflowers and shrubs. These forests are found in the eastern United States, southeastern Canada, northern Europe and Asia, and southern Australia.

Still closer to the equator are the **tropical rain forests**, home to the greatest variety of plants on Earth. About 60 to 100 inches of rain fall each year. Tropical trees stay green all year. They grow close together, shading the ground. There are several layers of trees. The top, **emergent layer** has trees that can reach 200 feet in height. The **canopy**, which gets lots of sun, comes next, followed by the **understory**. The **forest floor**, covered with roots, gets little sun. Many plants cannot grow there.

Tropical rain forests are found mainly in Central America, South America, Asia, and Africa. They once covered more than 8 million square miles.

Today, because of destruction by humans, fewer than 3.4 million square miles remain. More than half the plant and animal species in the world live there. Foods such as bananas and pineapples first grew there. Woods such as mahogany and teak also come from rain forests. Many kinds of plants there are used to make medicines.

When rain forests are burned, carbon dioxide is released into the air. This adds to the **greenhouse effect** (see page 67). As forests are destroyed, the precious soil is easily washed away by the heavy rains.

Emergent Layer

Canopy

Understory

Forest floor

Tundra & Alpine Region

In the northernmost regions of North America, Europe, and Asia surrounding the Arctic Ocean are plains called the **tundra**. The temperature rarely rises above 45 degrees Fahrenheit, and it is too cold for trees to grow there. Most tundra plants are mosses and lichens that hug the ground for warmth. A few wildflowers and small shrubs also grow where the soil thaws for about two months of the year. This kind of climate and plant life also exists in the **alpine** region, on top of the world's highest mountains (such as the Himalayas, Alps, Andes, and Rockies), where small flowers also grow.

What Is the Tree Line? On mountains in the north (such as the Rockies) and in the far south (such as the Andes), there is an altitude above which trees will not grow. This is the **tree line** or **timberline**. Above the tree line, you can see low shrubs and small plants.

Deserts

The driest areas of the world are the **deserts**. They can be hot or cold, but they also contain an amazing number of plants. Cacti and sagebrush are native to dry regions of North and South America. The deserts of Africa and Asia contain plants called euporbias. Date plants have grown in the deserts of the Middle East and North Africa for thousands of years. In the southwestern United States and northern Mexico, there are many types of cacti, including prickly pear, barrel, and saguaro.

Arizona desert

Grasslands

Grassland in Alberta, Canada

Areas that are too dry to have green forests, but not dry enough to be deserts, are called **grasslands**. The most common plants found there are grasses. Cooler grasslands are found in the Great Plains of the United States and Canada, in the steppes of Europe and Asia, and in the pampas of Argentina. The drier grasslands are used for grazing cattle and sheep. In the **prairies**, where there is a little more rain, wheat, rye, oats, and barley are grown. The warmer grasslands, called **savannas**, are found in central and southern Africa, Venezuela, southern Brazil, and Australia. Most savannas have moist summers and cool, dry winters.

Oceans

Covering two-thirds of the earth, the **ocean** is by far the largest biome. Within the ocean are smaller biomes that include **coastal areas**, **tidal zones**, and **coral reefs**. Found in relatively shallow warm waters, the reefs are called the "rain forests of the ocean." Australia's Great Barrier Reef is the largest in the world. It is home to thousands of species of plant and animal life.

Coral reef

WHERE GARBAGE GOES

Most of the things around you will be thrown away someday. Skates, clothes, the toaster, furniture—they can break or wear out, or you may get tired of them. Where will they go when they are thrown out? What kinds of waste will they create?

Look at What Is Now in U.S. Landfills

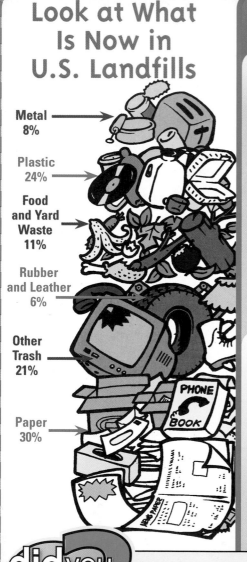

Metal 8%

Plastic 24%

Food and Yard Waste 11%

Rubber and Leather 6%

Other Trash 21%

Paper 30%

WHAT HAPPENS TO THINGS WE THROW AWAY?

Landfills

Most of our trash goes to places called landfills. A **landfill** (or dump) is a low area of land that is filled with garbage. Most modern landfills are lined with a layer of plastic or clay to try to keep dangerous liquids from seeping into the soil and ground water supply.

The Problem with **Landfills**

More than half of the states in this country are running out of places to dump their garbage. Because of the unhealthy materials many contain, landfills do not make good neighbors, and people don't want to live near them. But where can cities dispose of their waste? How can hazardous waste — material that can poison air, land, and water — be disposed of in a safe way?

Incinerators

One way to get rid of trash is to burn it. Trash is burned in a furnace-like device called an **incinerator.** Because incinerators can get rid of almost all of the bulk of the trash, some communities would rather use incinerators than landfills.

The Problem with **Incinerators**

Leftover ash and smoke from burning trash may contain harmful chemicals, called **pollutants**, and make it hard for some people to breathe. They can harm plants, animals, and people.

did you know?

Waste from pig farms is getting to be a big problem. One pig can create thousands of pounds of waste in a year. Hauling away the smelly sludge takes time and money. And this waste can't be used to fertilize crops meant for people. Researchers have an idea that may help: using hybrid poplar trees. One acre of these trees absorbs about 3,000 gallons of waste per day! After 10 years of sucking up pig waste, the trees can be harvested and used to make paper or burned as biomass fuel.

REDUCE, REUSE, RECYCLE

You can help reduce waste by reusing containers, batteries, and paper. You can also recycle newspaper, glass, and plastics to provide materials for making other products. Below are some of the things you can do.

	TO REDUCE WASTE	TO RECYCLE
Paper	Use both sides of the paper. Use cloth towels instead of paper towels.	Recycle newspapers, magazines, comic books, and junk mail.
Plastic	Wash food containers and store leftovers in them. Reuse plastic bags.	Return soda bottles to the store. Recycle other plastics.
Glass	Keep bottles and jars to store other things.	Recycle glass bottles and jars.
Clothes	Give clothes to younger relatives or friends. Donate clothes to thrift shops.	Cut unwearable clothing into rags to use instead of paper towels.
Metal	Keep leftovers in storage containers instead of wrapping them in foil. Use glass or stainless steel pans instead of disposable pans.	Recycle aluminum cans and foil trays. Return wire hangers to the dry cleaner.
Food/ Yard Waste	Cut the amount of food you throw out. Try saving leftovers for snacks or meals later on.	Make a compost heap using food scraps, leaves, grass clippings, and the like.
Batteries	Use rechargeable batteries for toys and games, radios, tape players, and flashlights	Find out about your town's rules for recycling or disposing of batteries.

What Is Made From RECYCLED MATERIALS?

- ▶ *From* RECYCLED PAPER we get newspapers, cereal boxes, wrapping paper, cardboard containers, and insulation.

- ▶ *From* RECYCLED PLASTIC we get soda bottles, tables, benches, bicycle racks, cameras, backpacks, carpeting, shoes, and clothes.

- ▶ *From* RECYCLED STEEL we get steel cans, cars, bicycles, nails, and refrigerators.

- ▶ *From* RECYCLED GLASS we get glass jars and tiles.

- ▶ *From* RECYCLED RUBBER we get bulletin boards, floor tiles, playground equipment, and speed bumps.

Fashion

When did women start wearing blue jeans? ➡ page 74

Take a trip through fashion history over the last 100 years. What style do you like the best? It's a modern trend for the fashion-forward, especially kids, to borrow from the decades and make their own special styles.

1900s:

THE EDWARDIAN ERA

Women: "Formal" females favored custom-made dresses, tight corsets, lots of lace, and feathered hats.
Men: "High society" gents wore tailored wool suits, straw "boater" hats, and narrow shoes.

1920s:

THE ROARING TWENTIES

Women: "Flappers" had short, sleek hair and wore drop-waist sequined dresses and fancy costume jewelry.
Men: Distinguished men wore pastel colored shirts, and silk ties that were secured with tiepins.

1940s:

MAKE DO AND MEND

Women: During World War II, "Rosie the Riveter" styles were practical and patriotic: blue jeans, baggy sweaters, and "drainpipe" trousers. Stockings were a luxury.
Men: Materials were scarce during the war. Pillow cases and parachutes were used to make clothing. Instead of wool, suits were made of wood pulp and had fake pockets.

1960s:

FLOWER POWER

Women: A "groovy chick" would look mod in a bright colored miniskirt, blue eye shadow, white go-go boots, and super-long hair.
Men: A "hippie" guy might wear bell-bottom jeans, a paisley shirt, and a leather vest. Funky peace signs and flower patches were popular.

1970s:

DISCO DAYS

Women: Girls were "staying alive" in "hot pants," polyester pantsuits, bell-bottoms, and platform shoes.

Men: "Mr. Disco" wore polyester bell-bottoms, brightly colored shirts, and gold chains on the dance floor.

1990s:

ANYTHING GOES

Women: Dr. Martens big black boots, hooded sweatshirts, and layered T-shirts for the neo-hippie chick.

Men: Grungy guys kept themselves warm in lumberjack flannels and their money secure with trucker chain wallets. The hip-hoppers, on the other hand, warmed up in puffy athletic jackets and sneakers.

2000s:

HIP-HOP STYLE

Women: Girls hang out in low-rise jeans, tight T-shirts with bare midriffs, and bell-bottoms. Peasant tops and chunky necklaces are also trendy.

Men: Guys keep a beat in baggy jeans, gold chains, and athletic gear.

Piercing Around the World

You've seen pierced ears, noses, or maybe even eyebrows. But did you know that piercing has been practiced around the world for thousands of years? Scientists found a 5,000-year-old mummy with pierced ears. Nose piercing was practiced in India as far back as the 16th century. And in Mexico, the Aztec and Mayan tribes used tongue piercing as part of a blood ritual to bring them close to their gods.

did you know?

Games & Toys

In what game is the right answer always "rhubarb"? ➜ page 79

WANT TO PLAY?

It's a safe bet that games and toys have been around as long as people have. The earliest toys were probably natural things kids found lying around: stones, clay, and sticks. Most of our clues about the earliest games come from things ancient peoples left behind. Baked clay marbles dating back to 3000 B.C. have been found in prehistoric caves.

Kids still play with simple things like blocks, clay, and sticks, but toys and games sure have come a long way in the age of machines and computers!

registered trademark of Binney & Smith.

TIMELESS TOYS

The Boomerang is actually an ancient weapon invented by Australian Aborigines that is thought to be about 100,000 years old. Today, the returning boomerang is sold as a toy all over the world.

Matchbox® Cars, invented in 1952, were first designed for a girl to play with! Jack Odell created a brass miniature of a Road Roller car and put it in a matchbox-size container so that his daughter could take it to school.

Etch A Sketch® began entertaining "arty" kids in 1960. When you turn the knobs, a stylus scrapes aluminum powder off the inside of the screen to draw a line.

Edwin Binney and C. Harold Smith made their first box of **Crayola crayons** in 1903. There were 8 colors—compared to 120 today. The Crayola factory in Easton, Pennsylvania, now turns out more than 3 billion crayons each year.

Plastic **LEGO** bricks were invented in Denmark by Ole Kirk Christiansen in 1949. The company, whose name comes from the Danish words "LEg GOdt" (play well) has since made more than 206 billion of them! Imagine if you had to clean up that many in your room.

OTHER CLASSIC TOYS

Teddy Bear	1902
Yo-Yo	1929
Silly Putty®	1949
Barbie® Doll	1959

VIDEO GAME NEWS 2006

▶ Sony PlayStation 3 and Microsoft Xbox 360—Microsoft unveiled its successor to the Xbox in late 2005, and Sony is expected to reveal its new console in 2006. Both consoles will feature high-definition graphics for incredibly lifelike gaming environments, surround sound, and wireless controllers.

▶ Nintendo Revolution—The new Nintendo console, also due out in 2006, will feature improved graphics and sound. But the real leap forward is the controller. Instead of just tapping a joystick and hitting buttons, players will actually move the controller itself to control the action onscreen. A player might swing the controller to control a batter in a baseball game or jab the joystick forward to control a swordsman.

VIDEO GAME TIME LINE

1962—Spacewar, played on an early microcomputer, is the first fully interactive video game.

1974—Atari's Pong, one of the first home video games, has "paddles" to hit a white dot back and forth on-screen.

1980—Pac-Man, Space Invaders, and Asteroids (first to let high scorers enter initials) invade arcades.

1985—Nintendo Entertainment System comes to the U.S. Super Mario Bros. is a huge hit!

1987—Legend of Zelda game released.

1989—Nintendo's handheld video game system, Game Boy, debuts.

1996—Nintendo 64 is released.

2000—Sony's PlayStation 2 arrives.

2001—Microsoft's Xbox and Nintendo's GameCube hit the shelves.

2005—Sony's PSP, a new handheld video game system, goes on sale.

VIDEO GAMES YOU SHOULD TRY

Civilization IV—The newest version of one of the most popular strategy games of all time. Players control a people, such as the Americans, Germans, Chinese, or Russians, and guide them from the Stone Age to the Space Age. Available for PC.

Mario Kart DS—This is a version of the popular Mario Kart game for the handheld Nintendo DS (Dual Screen). Players race each other on fantastical go-kart tracks. Available for Nintendo DS.

Legend of Zelda: Twilight Princess—The latest installment of Nintendo's Legend of Zelda is an adventure game in which the player assumes the role of Link, a humble farmhand. When monsters threaten the land, Link must come to the rescue. Available for Nintendo GameCube.

FIFA '06 Soccer—Soccer is the most popular game in the world, and now you can play it on your computer. FIFA '06 Soccer lets you control one of several hundred teams from around the world. The graphics are so realistic, it's hard to tell it's a video game and not a televised soccer match. Available for all platforms and PC.

Homework Help

Take a "Chance":
UNDERSTANDING PROBABILITY

Probability can be a fun subject, and it may be a little more fun and easier to learn about if you think of it in terms of the dice you use to play games with.

A single die has six different faces, numbered 1 through 6. Each has an equal chance of coming up. So the chance, or **probability,** of rolling any one of the numbers with one die is one in six. We write this as the ratio or fraction 1/6 because there are six possible **outcomes.**

What if you roll two dice? There are 36 possible outcomes, because each die can come out one of six ways: 6 x 6 = 36. The lowest possible outcome would be 2 (a 1 on each die). The highest possible outcome would be 12 (a 6 on each die).

With two dice, some totals are more likely to come up than others. Pretend that the dice are red and blue. The only way to roll a total of 2 (called "snake eyes") is for the red die to come up as a 1 and the blue die to come up as a 1. So the probability of shaking 2 is 1 in 36 (1/36). But there are two ways to shake a 3. The red die could have a 1 and the blue die could have a 2, or the red die could be a 2 and the blue die could be a 1. So the probability of shaking a 3 is 2 in 36 (2/36, which equals 1/18).

The total that has the most possible outcomes is 7. The red die can be any of the numbers from 1 to 6, and the blue die can be the number that makes seven when added to the number on the red die (1 and 6, 2 and 5, 3 and 4, 4 and 3, 5 and 2, 6 and 1). Because there are six possible combinations to total 7, the chances of rolling a 7 are 6 in 36 (6/36, which equals 1/6, or one out of six).

Look below for your chances of shaking each total with two dice.	
2	1 in 36
3	2 in 36
4	3 in 36
5	4 in 36
6	5 in 36
7	6 in 36
8	5 in 36
9	4 in 36
10	3 in 36
11	2 in 36
12	1 in 36

BUILDING BY CHANCE:
THE SETTLERS OF CATA

In the popular board game The Settlers of Catan, players control a budding civilization on the fictional island of Catan. Players build settlements and cities with resources like bricks, wood, and wheat. Every resource is given a number between 2 and 12. Players roll two dice, and if the number on the dice matches the number assigned to that resource, then the resource is created. The numbers 2 and 12 are the least likely to be rolled, because there is only one combination of dice rolls that produces each number (two 1s or two 6s). Other numbers are more likely because there are several ways to roll them (an 8 is rolled by getting 2 and 6, 3 and 5, 4 and 4, 5 and 3, or 6 and 2).

Four Fun Family Car Games

THE LICENSE PLATE GAME

When you spot a passing car's license plate, call out the letters on the plate. Using each letter, try to come up with a funny phrase. For example, if the letters are E-L-C, a possible phrase could be *Eat Lasagna Constantly* or *Everyone Loves Candy.* There's no winner or loser in this game, but there sure are a lot of laughs. Try these: R-F-C, M-E-S, T-P-D.

RHUBARB GAME

This is a question and answer game that only has one answer. Everyone takes a turn asking a random question like "What color is your swimsuit?" When it's your turn to answer, no matter the question, you have to answer "Rhubarb." But if you laugh, you're out. The last person to laugh wins the game.

ALPHABET GAME

This is a great family game. Work through the alphabet starting with "A" and try to find objects outside or inside the car that begin with each letter. For example, if you see an *anteater*, that counts for "A." *Automobile* and *airplane* would also count. Sounds too easy? It's actually not as easy as it looks. Wait until you get to "V" and "Z." Sometimes "J" can be hard, too. Another way to play is to look for the actual letters on signs.

COUNTING COWS

Count all the cows you see on your side of the car. The person who counts the most wins! But there's a twist. If you pass a cemetery on your side of the car, and someone in the car yells "Your cows are buried!" you lose all your cows.

Keep in mind, this game doesn't have to be all about cows. Try counting burger restaurants, gas stations, or billboards.

Geography

What planet had a continent called Pangaea? ➤ page 87

Sizing up the Earth

The word "geography" comes from the Greek word *geographia*, meaning "writing about the Earth." It was first used by the Greek scholar Eratosthenes, who was head of the great library of Alexandria in Egypt. Around 230 B.C., when many people believed the world was flat, he did a remarkable thing. He calculated the circumference of the Earth. His figure of about 25,000 miles was close to the modern measurement at 24,901 miles!

Actually, the Earth is not perfectly round. It's flatter at the poles and bulges out a little at the middle. This bulge around the equator is due to centrifugal force from the Earth's rotation. ("Centrifugal" means "moving away from the center." Think of how a merry-go-round pushes you to the outside as it spins.) The Earth's diameter is 7,926 miles at the equator, but only 7,900 miles from North Pole to South Pole. The total surface area of the Earth is 196,940,000 square miles.

Geography 1-2-3

Longest Rivers	**1.** Nile (Egypt and Sudan)—4,160 miles **2.** Amazon (Brazil and Peru)—4,000 miles **3.** Chang (China)—3,940 miles (formerly called the Yangtze)
Tallest Mountains	**1.** Mount Everest (Tibet and Nepal)—29,035 feet **2.** K2 (Kashmir)—28,250 feet **3.** Kanchenjunga (India and Nepal)—28,208 feet
Biggest Islands	**1.** Greenland (Atlantic Ocean)—840,000 square miles **2.** New Guinea (Pacific Ocean)—306,000 square miles **3.** Borneo (Pacific Ocean)—280,100 square miles
Biggest Desert Regions	**1.** Sahara Desert (North Africa)—3.5 million square miles **2.** Australian Deserts—1.3 million square miles **3.** Arabian Peninsula—1 million square miles
Biggest Lakes	**1.** Caspian Sea (Europe and Asia)—143,244 square miles **2.** Superior (U.S. and Canada)—31,700 square miles **3.** Victoria (Kenya, Tanzania, Uganda)—26,828 square miles
Highest Waterfalls	**1.** Angel Falls (Venezuela)—3,212 feet **2.** Tugela Falls (South Africa)—2,800 feet **3.** Monge Falls (Norway)—2,540 feet

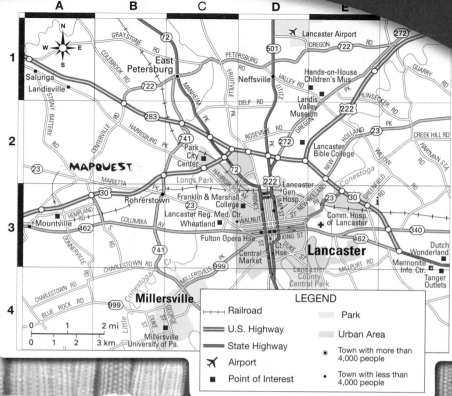

Reading a Map

DIRECTION Maps usually have a compass rose that shows you which way is north. On most maps, like this one, it's straight up. The compass rose on this map is in the upper left corner.

DISTANCE Of course the distances on a map are much shorter than the distances in the real world. The scale shows you how to estimate the real distance. This map's scale is in the lower left corner.

PICTURES Maps usually have little pictures or symbols to represent real things like roads, towns, airports, or other points of interest. The map legend (or key) tells what they mean.

FINDING PLACES Rather than use latitude and longitude to locate features, many maps, like this one, use a grid system with numbers on one side and letters on another. An index, listing place names in alphabetical order, gives a letter and a number for each. The letter and number tell you in which square to look for a place on the map's grid. For example, Landisville can be found at A-1 on this map.

USING THE MAP People use maps to help them travel from one place to another. What if you lived in Salunga and wanted to go to the Mapquest office? First, locate the two places on the map. Salunga is in A-1, and the Mapquest office is in A-3. Next, look at the roads that connect them and decide on the best route. (There could be several different ways to go.) The fastest way to go is to take Stony Battery Road to Donnerville Road, take a left on Donnerville, and then a right on Hempland Road.

81

EARLY EXPLORATION

AROUND 1000 — **Leif Ericson**, from Iceland, explored "Vinland," which may have been the coasts of northeast Canada and New England.

1271-95 — **Marco Polo** (Italian) traveled through Central Asia, India, China, and Indonesia.

1488 — **Bartolomeu Dias** (Portuguese) explored the Cape of Good Hope in southern Africa.

1492-1504 — **Christopher Columbus** (Italian) sailed four times from Spain to America and started colonies there.

1497-98 — **Vasco da Gama** (Portuguese) sailed farther than Dias, around the Cape of Good Hope to East Africa and India.

1513 — **Juan Ponce de León** (Spanish) explored and named Florida.

1513 — **Vasco Núñez de Balboa** (Spanish) explored Panama and reached the Pacific Ocean.

1519-21 — **Ferdinand Magellan** (Portuguese) sailed from Spain around the tip of South America and across the Pacific Ocean to the Philippines, where he died. His expedition continued around the world.

1519-36 — **Hernando Cortés** (Spanish) conquered Mexico, traveling as far west as Baja California.

1527-42 — **Alvar Núñez Cabeza de Vaca** (Spanish) explored the southwestern United States, Brazil, and Paraguay.

1532-35 — **Francisco Pizarro** (Spanish) explored the west coast of South America and conquered Peru.

1534-36 — **Jacques Cartier** (French) sailed up the St. Lawrence River to the site of present-day Montreal.

1539-42 — **Hernando de Soto** (Spanish) explored the southeastern United States and the lower Mississippi Valley.

1603-13 — **Samuel de Champlain** (French) traced the course of the St. Lawrence River and explored the northeastern United States.

1609-10 — **Henry Hudson** (English), sailing from Holland, explored the Hudson River, Hudson Bay, and Hudson Strait.

1682 — **Robert Cavelier**, sieur de La Salle (French), traced the Mississippi River to its mouth in the Gulf of Mexico.

1768-78 — **James Cook** (English) charted the world's major bodies of water and explored Hawaii and Antarctica.

1804-06 — **Meriwether Lewis and William Clark** (American) traveled from St. Louis along the Missouri and Columbia rivers to the Pacific Ocean and back.

1849-59 — **David Livingstone** (Scottish) explored Southern Africa, including the Zambezi River and Victoria Falls.

SOME FAMOUS EXPLORERS

These explorers, and many others, risked their lives on trips to explore faraway and often unknown places. Some sought fame. Some sought fortune. Some just sought challenge. All of them increased people's knowledge of the world.

MARCO POLO

(1254?-1324). You may have played "Marco Polo" in the swimming pool, but the original Marco Polo was an Italian traveler who journeyed by land all the way to China and back. He worked for the Chinese emperor Kublai Khan and even governed a Chinese city. For a long time his writings were the only knowledge people in Europe had about the Far East.

CHRISTOPHER COLUMBUS (1451-

1506), Italian navigator who sailed for Spain. He had hoped to find a fast route to Asia by going west from Europe. Instead he became the first European (other than the Vikings) to reach America, landing in the Bahamas in October 1492.

MERIWETHER

LEWIS (1774-1809) and WILLIAM CLARK (1770-1838), American soldiers and explorers. In 1804-06 they led an expedition 8,000 miles across the wilderness of the American West and back, gaining detailed knowledge of the huge Louisiana Territory that the United States had bought from France.

CAPTAIN JAMES

COOK (1728-1779), British explorer and navigator. He made three long voyages in the South Pacific Ocean and along the north coast of North America. Cook mapped many areas, including the coast of New Zealand and east coast of Australia, and was the first European to reach Hawaii. On a return trip there he was killed by islanders in a skirmish over a stolen boat.

MARY HENRIETTA

KINGSLEY (1862-1900), British explorer. At a time when women were discouraged from traveling into remote regions, she made two trips to West Africa, visiting areas never seen by Europeans. She studied and wrote about the customs and natural environment.

MATTHEW HENSON

(1866-1955), the first famous African American explorer. Hired as an assistant to explorer Robert Peary (1856-1920), he traveled on seven expeditions to Greenland and the Arctic region. In April 1909, Peary and Henson became the first to reach, or nearly reach, the North Pole. (Recent research suggests they may have fallen short by about 30 to 60 miles.)

JACQUES COUSTEAU

(1910-1997), French undersea explorer and environmentalist. He helped invent the Aqualung, allowing divers to stay deep underwater for hours, and made award-winning films of what he found there.

SIR EDMUND

HILLARY (1919-), New Zealand-born mountain climber and explorer. In 1953, he and his local guide Tenzing Norgay (1914-1986) became the first people ever to reach the top of Mount Everest, the world's highest mountain.

WEB SITE For a site about explorers with lots of useful links, try *www.kidinfo. com/American_History/ Explorers.html*

83

LOOKING at our WORLD

THINKING GLOBAL

Shaped like a ball or sphere, a globe is a model of our planet. Like Earth, it's not perfectly round. It is an oblate spheroid (called a "geoid") that bulges a little in the middle.

In 1569, Gerardus Mercator found a way to project the Earth's curved surface onto a flat map. One problem with a Mercator map is that land closer to the poles appears bigger than it is. Australia looks smaller than Greenland on this type of map, but in reality it's not.

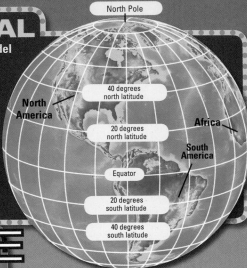

North Pole

North America

40 degrees north latitude

20 degrees north latitude

Africa

South America

Equator

20 degrees south latitude

40 degrees south latitude

South Pole

LATITUDE AND LONGITUDE

Imaginary lines that run east and west around Earth, parallel to the equator, are called **parallels**. They tell you the **latitude** of a place, or how far it is from the equator. The equator is at 0 degrees latitude. As you go farther north or south, the latitude increases. The North Pole is at 90 degrees **north latitude**. The South Pole is at 90 degrees **south latitude**.

Imaginary lines that run north and south around the globe, from one pole to the other, are called **meridians**. They tell you the degree of **longitude**, or how far east or west a place is from an imaginary line called the **Greenwich meridian** or **prime meridian** (0 degrees). That line runs through the city of Greenwich in England.

Which Hemispheres Do You Live In?

Draw an imaginary line around the middle of Earth. This is the **equator**. It splits Earth into two halves called **hemispheres**. The part north of the equator, including North America, is the **northern hemisphere**. The part south of the equator is the **southern hemisphere**.

You can also divide Earth into east and west. North and South America are in the **western hemisphere**. Africa, Asia, and most of Europe are in the **eastern hemisphere**.

THE TROPICS OF CANCER AND CAPRICORN

If you find the equator on a globe or map, you'll often see two dotted lines running parallel to it, one above and one below (see pages 143 and 152–153). The top one marks the Tropic of Cancer, an imaginary line marking the latitude (about 23°27' North) where the sun is directly overhead on June 21 or 22, the beginning of summer in the northern hemisphere.

Below the equator is the Tropic of Capricorn (about 23°27' South). This line marks the sun's path directly overhead at noon on December 21 or 22, the beginning of summer in the southern hemisphere. The area between these dotted lines is the tropics, where it is consistently hot because the sun's rays shine more directly than they do farther north or south.

THE SEVEN CONTINENTS AND FOUR OCEANS

ARCTIC OCEAN
5,105,700 square miles
3,407 feet avg. depth

ASIA
Area: 12,000,000 square miles
2005 population: 3,910,766,590
Highest pt.: Mt. Everest (Nepal/Tibet) 29,035 ft.
Lowest pt.: Dead Sea (Israel/Jordan) −1,348 ft.

OCEANIA (including Australia)
Area: 3,300,000 square miles
2005 population: 32,744,469
Highest pt.: Jaya, New Guinea 16,500
Lowest pt.: Lake Eyre, Australia −52 ft.

EUROPE
Area: 8,800,000 square miles
2005 population: 729,447,727
Highest pt.: Mt. Elbrus, Russia 18,510 ft.
Lowest pt.: Caspian Sea −92 ft.

INDIAN OCEAN
28,350,500 square miles
12,598 feet avg. depth

AFRICA
Area: 11,500,000 square miles
2005 population: 887,223,098
Highest pt.: Mt. Kilimanjaro (Tanzania) 19,340 ft.
Lowest pt.: Lake Assal (Djibouti) −512 ft.

ATLANTIC OCEAN
33,420,000 square miles
11,370 feet avg. depth

NORTH AMERICA
Area: 8,300,000 square miles
2005 population: 541,684,479
Highest pt.: Mt. McKinley (AK) 20,320 ft.
Lowest pt.: Death Valley (CA) −282 ft.

PACIFIC OCEAN
64,186,300 square miles
12,925 feet avg. depth

SOUTH AMERICA
Area: 6,800,000 square miles
2005 population: 371,271,037
Highest pt.: Mt. Aconcagua (Arg.) 22,834 ft.
Lowest pt.: Valdes Peninsula (Arg.) −131 ft.

ANTARCTICA
Area: 5,400,000 square miles
2005 population: no permanent residents
Highest pt.: Vinson Massif 16,864 ft.
Lowest pt.: Bently Subglacial Trench −8,327 ft.

N
E
S
W

WHAT'S INSIDE THE EARTH?

Starting at the Earth's surface and going down you find the lithosphere, the mantle, and then the core.

The lithosphere, the rocky crust of the Earth, extends for about 60 miles.

The dense, heavy inner part of the Earth is divided into a thick shell, the mantle, surrounding an innermost sphere, the core. The mantle extends from the base of the crust to a depth of about 1,800 miles and is mostly solid.

Then there is the Earth's core. It has two parts: an inner sphere of scorchingly hot, solid iron almost as large as the moon and an outer region of molten iron. The inner core is much hotter than the outer core. The intense pressure near the center of Earth squeezes the iron in the inner core into a solid ball nearly as hot as the surface of the Sun. Scientists believe the core formed billions of years ago during the planet's fiery birth. Iron and other heavy elements sank into the planet's hot interior while the planet was still molten. As this metallic soup cooled over millions of years, crystals of iron hardened at the center.

lithosphere

mantle about 1,800 miles

outer core about 1,300 miles

core about 1,500 miles

In 1996, after nearly 30 years of research, it was found that, like the Earth itself, the inner core spins on an axis from west to east, but at its own rate, outpacing the Earth by about one degree per year.

Homework Help

There are three types of rock:

1 IGNEOUS rocks form from underground magma (melted rock) that cools and becomes solid. Granite is an igneous rock made from quartz, feldspar, and mica.

2 SEDIMENTARY rocks form on low-lying land or the bottom of seas. Layers of small particles harden into rock such as limestone or shale over millions of years.

3 METAMORPHIC rocks are igneous or sedimentary rocks that have been changed by chemistry, heat, or pressure (or all three). Marble is a metamorphic rock formed from limestone.

CONTINENTAL DRIFT

The Earth didn't always look the way it does now. It was only in the early 20th century that a geologist named Alfred Lothar Wegener came up with the theory of continental drift. Wegener got the idea by looking at the matching rock formations on the west coast of Africa and the east coast of South America. He named the enormous first continent Pangaea. The continents are still moving, athough most move no faster than your fingernails grow.

Permian
225 million years ago

Triassic
200 million years ago

Jurassic
135 million years ago

Cretaceous
65 million years ago

Present Day

Health

What causes burps? ➤ page 93

Getting bigger isn't the only thing our bodies do as we get older. Our bodies go through many major changes throughout our lives.

When babies are first born, they are completely helpless. They cannot see too clearly or too far beyond a few feet, cannot feed themselves, and can't move around much. As they get older, they start to recognize faces and smile. They also learn how to use their little arms and legs. Before long, they start crawling and walking. And they gradually learn to talk and tell you what they want!

As kids get older, they get bigger and stronger. They have a lot of energy, but they also eat a lot and sleep a lot. Between ages 7 and 9, kids get much smarter and begin to think more independently. In addition, things start to get "hardwired" in their brains, meaning that a lot of interests and ideas that stick with people through life become ingrained on the brain. It's almost as if your brain is choosing what it will be good at later on in life.

Girls around the ages of 11 to 14 and boys around 13 to 16 go through a series of emotional and body changes. This is called puberty and is caused by hormones. The regions of the brain associated with reason, logic, and risk-taking are developing rapidly.

When people reach adulthood, their bodies are fully grown and their brains fully formed. As adults get older, more changes occur. Around age 40, many people become farsighted, meaning that they cannot see close things (like these words) clearly. Over half of all those over the age of 65 have some form of farsightedness.

Besides changes in vision, people's bodies begin to shrink a bit as they get older. This is because bones start to lose calcium. Also, even weirder, adult brains shrink. Human brains reach their full size around age 20. After that, they start shrinking. Men's brains tend to shrink faster than women's brains. But scientists don't think that it affects intelligence very much. However, some doctors think that because of changes in brain size, younger people are better at making quick decisions in pressure situations, whereas older brains are better at coming up with carefully thought-out decisions.

NEW FOOD PYRAMID

To stay healthy, it is important to eat the right foods and to exercise. In 2005, the U.S. government designed a new food pyramid to help people track what they should eat. The new pyramid shows that exercise is important to health and comes with rules recommending different amounts of food depending on your age, gender, and activity level. The different widths of each part of the pyramid help you remember about how much you should be eating of each group.

GRAINS
Eat whole grain bread, cereal, crackers, rice, and pasta.

VEGETABLES
Try more dark green and orange vegetables.

FRUITS
Choose from fresh, frozen, canned, or dried fruit.

OILS
Fish and nuts have oil. Vegetable oils are good, too. Butter and lard should be limited.

MILK
Low-fat or fat-free milk products are best.

MEAT & BEANS
Eat lean meats and poultry. Don't forget to try fish, beans, peas, and nuts.

MyPyramid.gov STEPS TO A HEALTHIER YOU

To figure out what you should be eating, based on your age, activity, and gender, use the calculator online: **WEB SITE** *www.mypyramid.gov*

For example, an active boy between ages 9 and 13 should eat about 2,600 calories daily, including:

Fruits	2 cups	Meat & Beans	6.5 ounces
Vegetables	3.5 cups	Milk	3 cups
Grains	9 ounces	Oils	8 teaspoons

YOUR BODY

Know What Goes Into It

NUTRITION FACTS: KNOWING HOW TO READ THE LABEL

Every food product approved by the Food and Drug Administration (FDA), whether it's a can of soup or a bag of potato chips, has a label that describes the nutrients derived from that product. For instance, the chips label on this page shows the total calories, fat, cholesterol, sodium, carbohydrate, protein, and vitamin content per serving.

A serving size is always defined (here, it is about 12 chips or 28 grams). This label shows that there are 9 servings per container. Don't be fooled by the calorie count of 140 –these are calories per serving and not per container. If you ate the entire chips bag, you would have eaten 1,260 calories!

Nutrition Facts

Serving Size 1 oz. (28g/About 12 chips)
Servings Per Container About 9

Amount Per Serving

Calories 140	Calories from Fat 60

	% Daily Value*
Total Fat 7g	11%
Saturated Fat 1g	5%
Trans Fat 0g	
Cholesterol 0mg	0%
Sodium 170mg	7%
Total Carbohydrate 18g	6%
Dietary Fiber 1g	4%
Sugars less than 1g	
Protein 2g	

Vitamin A 0%	•	Vitamin C 0%
Calcium 2%	•	Iron 2%
Vitamin E 4%	•	Thiamin 2%
Riboflavin 2%	•	Vitamin B6 4%
Phosphorus 6%	•	Magnesium 4%

* Percent Daily Values are based on a 2,000 calorie diet. Your daily values may be higher or lower depending on your calorie needs:

	Calories:	2,000	2,500
Total Fat	Less than	65g	80g
Sat Fat	Less than	20g	25g
Cholesterol	Less than	300mg	300mg
Sodium	Less than	2,400mg	2,400mg
Total Carbohydrate		300g	375g
Dietary Fiber		25g	30g

Calories per gram:
Fat 9 • Carbohydrate 4 • Protein 4

WHY YOU NEED TO EAT:

Fats are needed to keep people healthy and to help kids grow. Fats contain nine calories per gram—the highest calorie count of any type of food. So you should limit (but not avoid) intake of fatty foods.

Carbohydrates are a major source of energy for the body. Simple carbohydrates are found in regular white sugar, fruit, and milk. Complex carbohydrates, also called starches, are found in bread, pasta, and rice.

Cholesterol is a soft, fat-like substance mostly found in animal products such as meat, cheese, and eggs. Your body also produces some of it. Cholesterol is an important part of a healthy body because it helps with cell membrane and hormone production. There is good and bad cholesterol. Bad cholesterol, or LDL, gets stuck in blood vessels and can cause heart attack or stroke later on. Good cholesterol, or HDL, helps break down the bad cholesterol.

Proteins help your body grow and make your immune system stronger.

Vitamins and Minerals are good for all parts of your body. Examples: vitamin A, which is found in carrots, helps the eyes; calcium, which is found in milk, helps build bones; and vitamin C, which is found in fruits, helps cuts to heal.

SOME LOW-FAT FOODS

Crackers
Granola
Turkey Burger
Bagel
Almonds
Baked Potato

SOME FATTY FOODS

Chocolate-Chip Cookies
Bacon & Eggs
Hamburger
Donuts
M&Ms
French Fries

Have Fun Getting Fit

WHY WORK OUT?

Currently, one in three children in America has a weight problem, and over 9 million are obese or overweight. Overweight kids run the risk of developing serious health problems including diabetes, asthma, and high blood pressure.

Exercise is a great way to prevent obesity and improve health. The U.S. Surgeon General recommends that children get at least 60 minutes of some moderate exercise every day. Exercise can help reduce the risk of developing diseases like cancer or diabetes and also help build healthy bones, muscles, and joints.

HOW TO WORK OUT

▶ Begin with a five-minute warm-up! Warm-up exercises heat the body up, so that muscles become soft and limber and ready for more intense activity. Some warm-up exercises include jumping jacks, walking, and stretching.

▶ After your warm-up, do an exercise activity that you like, such as running or playing football with your friends; this increases your heart rate.

▶ After working out, cool down for 5 to 10 minutes and let your heart rate slow gradually. Cooling down is like a reverse warm-up. Walking is a good cooldown activity. Afterward, take the time to do some stretching. This helps your muscles remove waste, such as lactic acid, that your muscles make during exercise. Also remember to drink plenty of water during and after you exercise.

▶ Adding an element of strength training to your workout can be very beneficial. This doesn't mean you should lift the heaviest weights possible—far from it! Use light weights (1/2 lb or 1 lb) with controlled repetitions and rest between workouts.

did you know? Nearly 60% of all public and private middle schools and high schools sell soda for students to drink at lunch, according to the National Soft Drink Association. Kids who regularly consume soft drinks take in about 200 more calories each day than their classmates who don't.

ACTIVITY

Activity	CALORIES PER MINUTE
Jogging (6 miles per hour)	8
Jumping rope (easy pace)	7
Playing basketball	7
Playing soccer	6
Bicycling (9.4 miles per hour)	5
Skiing (downhill)	5
Raking the lawn	4
Rollerblading (easy pace)	4
Walking (4 miles per hour)	4
Bicycling (5.5 miles per hour)	3
Swimming (25 yards per minute)	3
Walking (3 miles per hour)	3

If you're interested in running, try **WEB SITE** www.kidsrunning.com
There you'll find advice, activities, stories, poems, and more—all about running.

Body Basics:

Your body is made up of many different parts that work together every minute of every day and night. It's more amazing than any machine or computer. Even though everyone's body looks different outside, people have the same parts inside. Each system of the body has its own job. Some of the systems also work together to keep you healthy and strong.

CIRCULATORY SYSTEM In the circulatory system, the **heart** pumps **blood**, which then travels through tubes, called **arteries**, to all parts of the body. The blood carries the oxygen and food that the body needs to stay alive. **Veins** carry the blood back to the heart.

DIGESTIVE SYSTEM The digestive system moves food through parts of the body called the **esophagus**, **stomach**, and **intestines**. As the food passes through, some of it is broken down into tiny particles called **nutrients**, which the body needs. Nutrients enter the bloodstream, which carries them to all parts of the body. The digestive system then changes the remaining food into waste that is eliminated from the body.

ENDOCRINE SYSTEM

The endocrine system includes **glands** that are needed for some body functions. There are two kinds of glands. **Exocrine** glands produce liquids such as sweat and saliva. **Endocrine** glands produce chemicals called **hormones**. Hormones control body functions, such as growth.

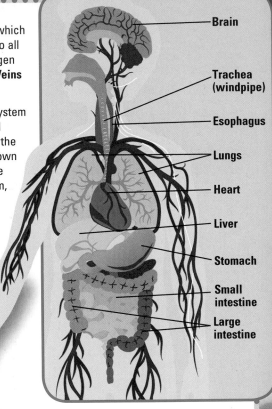

- Brain
- Trachea (windpipe)
- Esophagus
- Lungs
- Heart
- Liver
- Stomach
- Small intestine
- Large intestine

NERVOUS SYSTEM The nervous system enables us to think, feel, move, hear, and see. It includes the **brain**, the **spinal cord**, and **nerves** in all parts of the body. Nerves in the spinal cord carry signals back and forth between the brain and the rest of the body. The brain tells us what to do and how to respond. It has three major parts. The **cerebrum** controls thinking, speech, and vision. The **cerebellum** is responsible for physical coordination. The **brain stem** controls the respiratory, circulatory, and digestive systems.

RESPIRATORY SYSTEM The respiratory system allows us to breathe. Air comes into the body through the nose and mouth. It goes through the **windpipe** (or **trachea**) to two tubes (called **bronchi**), which carry air to the **lungs**. Oxygen from the air is taken in by tiny blood vessels in the lungs. The blood then carries oxygen to the cells of the body.

What the Body's Systems Do

MUSCULAR SYSTEM Muscles are made up of elastic fibers. There are three types of muscle: **skeletal, smooth,** and **cardiac.** The skeletal muscles help the body move—they are the large muscles we can see. Smooth muscles are found in our digestive system, blood vessels, and air passages. Cardiac muscle is found only in your heart. Smooth and cardiac muscles are **involuntary** muscles—they do their job without us having to think about them.

REPRODUCTIVE SYSTEM Through the reproductive system, adult human beings are able to create new human beings. Reproduction begins when a **sperm** cell from a man fertilizes an **egg** cell from a woman.

URINARY SYSTEM This system, which includes the **kidneys,** cleans waste from the blood and regulates the amount of water in the body.

IMMUNE SYSTEM The immune system protects your body from diseases by fighting against certain substances that come from outside, or **antigens.** This happens in different ways. For example, white blood cells called **B lymphocytes** learn to fight certain viruses and bacteria by producing **antibodies,** which spread around the body to attack them. Sometimes, as with **allergies,** the immune system makes a mistake and creates antibodies to fight a substance that's really harmless.

did you know?

Burps

are caused by gases flying out from the stomach. The gases come from the air we swallow when we swallow food. Fizzy drinks contain a lot of carbon dioxide gas that causes burps. Also, gases are released as our stomachs digest certain types of food.

A fart

is caused by gas escaping from your intestines. A fart is mostly made up of the gases released by bacteria that digest food in your intestines. Some of that gas was swallowed and wasn't burped out. But most of the gas is created as food is digested. The nasty smell comes from sulfur compounds in the food. Beans can cause you to have lots of farts, but overall they're not any more or less stinky. Eating lots of eggs, meat, or cauliflower can lead to really stinky farts.

THE FIVE SENSES

Your senses gather information about the world around you. The five senses are **hearing, sight, smell, taste,** and **touch.** You need senses to find food, resist heat or cold, and avoid situations that might be harmful. Your ears, eyes, nose, tongue, and skin sense changes in the environment. Then, nerve receptors send signals to the brain, where the information is processed.

HEARING

1

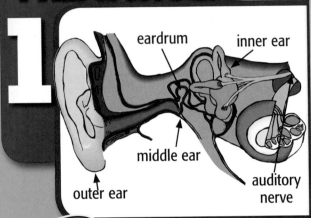

eardrum | inner ear
middle ear
outer ear
auditory nerve

did you know? *Some sounds are easier to hear than others. "AH," "AW," "EH," and "OO" are the easiest to hear.*

The human ear is divided into three parts—the outer, middle, and inner. The **outer ear** is mainly the flap we can see from the outside. Its shape funnels sound waves into the **middle ear**, where the **eardrum** is located. The eardrum vibrates when the sound waves hit it, causing three tiny bones behind it to vibrate as well. These vibrations are picked up in the **inner ear** by tiny filaments of the **auditory nerve**. This nerve changes the vibrations into nerve impulses and carries them to the brain.

SIGHT

2

The **lens** of the eye is the first stop for light waves, which tell you the shapes and colors of things around you. The lens focuses light waves onto the **retina**, located on the back wall of the eye. The retina has light-sensitive nerve cells. The cells translate the light waves into patterns of nerve impulses that travel along the **optic nerve** to your brain, where an image is produced. So in reality, all the eye does is collect light. It is the brain that actually forms the image.

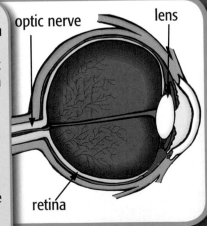

optic nerve | lens
retina

SMELL

3

In our noses we have nerve cells called **olfactory receptors**. Tiny mucus-covered hairs from these receptors detect chemicals in the air. These chemicals make what we call odor, or scent. Once detected, this information travels along the **olfactory nerves** to the brain. An interesting thing about smell is that it is linked closely to memory. The nerves from the olfactory receptors are linked directly to the **limbic system**, the part of the brain that deals with emotions. This is why we tend to like or dislike a smell right away. The smell can leave a strong impression on our memory, and very often a smell triggers a particular memory. Sometimes, smelling a perfume might make you think of a particular person.

TASTE

4

Taste buds are the primary receptors for taste. They are located on the surface and sides of the tongue, on the roof of the mouth, and at the back of the throat. These buds detect four qualities of a substance—**sweet** (like sugar), **sour** (like lemons), **salty** (like chips), and **bitter** (like tonic water). Scent and taste signals come together in the same part of your brain. That's why you need both taste and smell to get the full flavor of something. If you've ever had a stuffed up nose, you may have noticed that you can only taste the four things that a tongue can pick up, and nothing else.

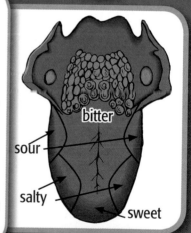

bitter

sour

salty

sweet

TOUCH

5

Your sense of touch allows you to feel heat, cold, pain, and pressure. These environmental factors are all sensed by nerve fibers located in the **epidermis** (outer layer of skin) and **dermis** (second layer of skin) in all parts of the body. Like with all the other senses, nerves send information to the brain through the nervous system.

STAYING ALIVE HOW TO DO IT

LEADING CAUSES OF DEATH IN THE U.S. (2003)

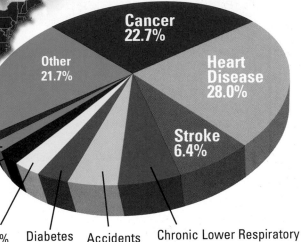

Cancer 22.7%

Heart Disease 28.0%

Other 21.7%

Stroke 6.4%

Blood poisoning 1.4%

Kidney disease 1.7%

Alzheimer's disease 2.6%

Influenza and Pneumonia 2.7%

Diabetes 3.0%

Accidents 4.5%

Chronic Lower Respiratory Disease 5.2%

DON'T SMOKE

The effects of smoking are responsible for one out of every five deaths in the U.S.—more than car accidents, homicides, or HIV/AIDS. Smoking can lead to cancer, respiratory disease, and cardiovascular (heart and circulatory system) disease. Smoking while underage can keep lungs from fully developing, and kids who smoke are more likely to become addicted. Despite the risks, in a recent survey 11.9% of kids between the ages of 12 and 17 had tried cigarettes in the month before the survey.

DON'T DRINK

Drinking alcoholic beverages can have a bad impact on the health of young people. It can also play a part in accidents and acts of violence and keep you from doing well in school. Some kids may feel pressured into taking a drink because "everyone else is doing it," but that's not actually true. Surveys show that only one in four 8th graders said that they used alcohol at all over a month-long period in 1994. By 2004 that number had decreased to only one in five.

STAY SAFE IN THE CAR

In 2004, 31,693 people in the U.S. were killed in motor vehicle accidents. Properly using seatbelts has been shown to reduce the risk of fatal injuries from accidents. In fact, research suggests that 5,839 people (about one in five deaths) could have been saved if they had been properly restrained. But not everyone uses safety belts, not even kids. That same year, 63% of all kids aged 13 to 15 who were killed in accidents were not using their seatbelts—the highest percentage for any age group.

Every year, 1 in 600,000 Americans are struck by lightning, but your actual odds of being struck vary widely, depending on your habits and where you live.

On the Job

Intensive Care Unit Nurse

Kareem Dally, RN

Scripps Mercy Hospital in San Diego, California

Q: What got you interested in nursing?

I grew up with my six siblings in a small village in Israel with no running water or electricity. Two of my older sisters became nurses. When my mom got sick, I decided that I wanted to go to school and be able to help her, so I became a nurse.

Q: What sort of special training did you need for your job?

I have a Bachelor of Science in Nursing, which is a four-year degree. ICU nurses need to take a specialized eight week training course. Also, nurses take continuing education classes to learn about any new treatments or procedures.

Q: What is it like on a typical day at work?

As an ICU nurse I work a 12-hour shift. The first thing I do when I start my shift is to get information from the outgoing nurse on the one or two patients I'll be caring for. I get information about why the patient is here, what their status is, and what the treatment plan will be. After that I listen to the patient's heart, lungs, and stomach, check his or her eyes, blood pressure, and heart rhythm, and make sure the patient is not in any pain. Patients in the ICU can be very sick and require a lot of care so I check on all of these things every four hours. If the patient needs medication, I give it to them, and I also answer the doctor's questions about how the patient is doing and offer advice.

I also am on the Code Blue Team, so if a patient stops breathing or their heart stops beating I do CPR or give them medications to help get them back to normal.

Q: What is the hardest thing about your job?

One of the hardest things I do is talking with a sick person's family. It's never easy to see someone you love in the hospital, especially in the ICU. Most of the time they are very scared, stressed-out, and worried.

Q: What do you like the most about your job?

The best part of my job is being able to make a difference in someone's life. It's so incredible to have someone who was once very sick walk back into the hospital to say thank you.

Q: Do you have any advice for kids who want to become nurses?

It would be good to volunteer at a local hospital and also to spend some time with a nurse to really see what they do. There are so many branches of nursing. Some of us are managers or teachers, some work in the emergency department or in the operating room. There's so much to choose from that I think it's good to explore a bit.

Holidays

When is Talk Like a Pirate Day? ➡ page 101

Fun Facts About Holidays

Some holidays "by the numbers."

1,070 pounds—the weight of the ball that drops at New York's Times Square to introduce the New Year.

152 million—the number of Mother's Day cards given every year, compared to only 95 million Father's Day cards.

150 million—the number of hot dogs Americans eat on the Fourth of July.

90—the percent of parents that admit sneaking Halloween candy from their kids' stashes. Keep an eye out!

24.5 million—the number of living U.S. military veterans honored on Veterans Day (November 11).

32 feet—the height of the world's largest menorah, built in New York City's Central Park, for Hanukkah in 1998. A cherry-picker crane from the electric company was needed to light it!

20.8 million—the number of Christmas trees cut down and decorated annually.

Do-It-Yourself Holidays

Some holidays came about because of popular demand. Here's a look at how people made it happen.

MOTHER'S DAY In 1907, Anna Jarvis of Philadelphia, Pennsylvania, began calling for a day to celebrate mothers. A successful letter-writing campaign, driven by Jarvis and other supporters, led President Woodrow Wilson to declare the second Sunday in May Mother's Day in 1914.

FATHER'S DAY Father's Day started in Spokane, Washington, in 1910. A city resident there called for a day to honor her father, a veteran and widower who had raised six children. The day was not formally recognized until 1972, when it was proclaimed by President Richard Nixon.

LABOR DAY This tradition started in the U.S. after the Knights of Labor union held a parade and picnic for about 10,000 workers on September 5, 1882, in New York City. The date was chosen because it was a halfway point between Independence Day and Thanksgiving. Congress formally recognized Labor Day a federal holiday in 1894.

MARTIN LUTHER KING JR. DAY Soon after Reverend Dr. Martin Luther King Jr. was assassinated in 1968, people began campaigning for a holiday in his honor. One campaign gathered 6 million petition signatures. President Ronald Reagan signed a bill making the third Monday in January a holiday in King's honor in 1983.

Holidays in the United States

There are no official holidays for the whole U.S. But there are federal holidays, when workers for the federal government get the day off. Many offices, and most banks and schools, in the 50 states are closed on these days.

There are also other holidays that may not be an occasion for a day off from school but are enthusiastically celebrated.

▶ **NEW YEAR'S DAY** The U.S. and most other countries celebrate the beginning of the new year on January 1.

▶ **MARTIN LUTHER KING JR. DAY** Observed on the third Monday in January, this holiday marks the birth (January 15, 1929) of the African American civil rights leader Rev. Dr. Martin Luther King Jr. In 2007, it will be celebrated on January 15.

VALENTINE'S DAY February 14 is a day for sending cards or gifts to people you love.

▶ **PRESIDENTS' DAY** On the third Monday in February (February 19, 2007), most states celebrate the births of both George Washington (born February 22, 1732) and Abraham Lincoln (born February 12, 1809).

MOTHER'S DAY Mothers are honored on the second Sunday in May (May 13, 2007).

▶ **MEMORIAL DAY OR DECORATION DAY** The last Monday in May (May 28, 2007) is set aside to remember those who died serving in the military.

FATHER'S DAY Fathers are honored on the third Sunday in June (June 17, 2007).

▶ **FOURTH OF JULY OR INDEPENDENCE DAY** July 4 is the anniversary of the day in 1776 when the American colonies signed the Declaration of Independence. People celebrate with parades, picnics, barbecues, and fireworks.

▶ **LABOR DAY** Labor Day, the first Monday in September, honors the workers of America. It falls on September 4 in 2006 and September 3 in 2007.

GRANDPARENTS' DAY This holiday to honor your grandparents comes every year on the first Sunday after Labor Day (September 10, 2006 and September 9, 2007).

▶ **COLUMBUS DAY** Celebrated on the second Monday in October, Columbus Day is the anniversary of October 12, 1492, the day Christopher Columbus was traditionally thought to have arrived in the Americas (on San Salvador Island). It falls on October 9 in 2006 and October 8 in 2007.

HALLOWEEN In ancient Britain, Druids wore grotesque costumes on October 31 to scare away evil spirits. Today while "trick-or-treating," children ask for candy and gather money for UNICEF, the United Nations Children's Fund.

ELECTION DAY The first Tuesday after the first Monday in November (November 7 in 2006 and November 13 in 2007), Election Day is a mandatory holiday in some states.

▶ **VETERANS DAY** Veterans Day, November 11, honors veterans of wars. First called Armistice Day, it marks the anniversary of the armistice (agreement) that ended World War I.

▶ **THANKSGIVING** Thanksgiving was first observed by the Pilgrims in 1621 as a harvest festival and a day for thanks and feasting. In 1863, Abraham Lincoln revived the tradition. It comes on the fourth Thursday in November—November 23 in 2006 and November 22 in 2007.

HANUKKAH (ALSO CHANUKAH) This eight-day Jewish festival of lights begins on the evening of December 15 in 2006 and December 4 in 2007.

▶ **CHRISTMAS** Christmas is both a religious holiday and a legal holiday. It is celebrated on December 25.

KWANZAA This seven-day African-American festival begins on December 26. It celebrates seven virtues, such as self-determination.

Holidays marked with a ▶ are federal holidays.

CALENDAR BASICS

Holidays and calendars go hand in hand. Using a calendar, you can see what day of the week it is and watch out for the next special day. Calendars divide time into days, weeks, months, and years. A year is the time it takes for one revolution of Earth around the Sun. Early calendars were lunar—based on the phases of the Moon. The ancient Egyptians were probably the first to develop a solar calendar, based on the movement of Earth around the Sun.

THE NAMES OF THE MONTHS

January	named for the Roman god Janus, guardian of gates (often shown with two faces, looking backward and forward)
February	named for Februalia, a Roman time of sacrifice
March	named for Mars, the Roman god of war (the end of winter meant fighting could begin again)
April	"aperire," Latin for "to open," as in flower buds
May	named for Maia, the goddess of plant growth
June	"Junius," the Latin word for the goddess Juno
July	named after the Roman ruler Julius Caesar
August	named for Augustus, the first Roman emperor
September	"septem," the Latin word for seven (the Roman year began in March)
October	"octo," the Latin word for eight
November	"novem," the Latin word for nine
December	"decem," the Latin word for ten

HOLIDAYS Around the World

CANADA DAY Canada's national holiday, July 1, commemorates the union of Canadian provinces in 1867.

CHINESE NEW YEAR China's biggest holiday starts the first month in the Chinese lunar calendar and falls on February 18 in 2007. Celebrations include parades, fireworks, and traditional meals.

CINCO DE MAYO Mexicans remember May 5, 1862, when their ancestors defeated the French army in the Battle of the Puebla.

DIWALI On October 21, 2006, Hindus across India and around the world decorate their homes with small oil lamps to celebrate this festival of lights.

Odd Holidays

You can chase away the "back-to-school blues" by observing **Hobbit Day** or **Elephant Appreciation Day** on September 22. Here are a few other odd "days" you've probably never heard of:

July 2006
- 10: International Town Criers Day
- 16: National Ice Cream Day (a.k.a. Sundae Sunday)
- 22: Rat-Catchers' Day
- 24: National Drive-Thru Day

August 2006
- 4: Work Like a Dog Day
- 6: National Fresh Breath Day
- 9: National Underwear Day
- 17: Sandcastle Day

September 2006
- 5: Be Late for Something Day
- 12: Video Games Day
- 13: Fortune Cookie Day
- 19: Talk Like a Pirate Day

October 2006
- 2: World Farm Animals Day
- 6: World Smile Day
- 15: National Grouch Day
- 31: National Knock-Knock Day

November 2006
- 4: National Chicken Lady Day
- 13: World Kindness Day
- 21: World Hello Day
- 24: Buy Nothing Day

December 2006
- 4: National Dice Day
- 15: Underdog Day
- 29: **No Interruptions** Day
- 31: Make Up Your Mind Day

January 2007
- 7: I'm Not Going to Take It Anymore Day
- 8: **Word Nerd Day**
- 21: Squirrel Appreciation Day
- 29: **Bubble Wrap Appreciation Day**

February 2007
- 1: **Bubble Gum Day**
- 2: **Wear Red Day**
- 14: Ferris Wheel Day
- 28: Inconvenience Yourself Day

March 2007
- 1: National Pig Day
- 18: Awkward Moments Day
- 22: International Goof-Off Day
- 25: Pecan Day

April 2007
- 10: National Siblings Day
- 11: Barbershop Quartet Day
- 10: **Blame Someone Else Day**
- 30: National Honesty Day

May 2007
- 1: Save the Rhino Day
- 5: Cartoonists Day
- 12: Limerick Day
- 16: International Sea Monkey Day

June 2007
- 2: National Bubba Day
- 8: Upsy Daisy Day
- 16: World Juggling Day
- 28: National Handshake Day

Homework Help

What type of paragraph expresses an opinion?
➡ **page 105**

If you need to study for an exam or write a research paper, there are helpful hints in this chapter.

In other chapters, you can find lots of information on topics you may write about or study in school. **Facts About Nations,** pages 154-179, and **Facts About U.S. States,** pages 260-307, are good places to look. For math tips and formulas, look up the chapter on **Numbers**. For good books to read, and write about, see the **Books** chapter. Plus, there are many other study and learning tips throughout the book. Look for the **"Homework Help" icon!**

Those Tricky Tests

Getting Ready

Being prepared for a test can relieve some of your jitters and can make test taking a lot easier! Here are some tips to help you get ready.

▶ Take good notes in class and keep up with assignments, so you don't have to learn material at the last minute! Just writing down the notes helps you remember the information.

▶ Make a study schedule and stick to it! Don't watch TV or listen to distracting music while studying.

▶ Start reviewing early if you can—don't wait until the night before the test.

▶ Go over the headings, summaries, and questions in each chapter to review key points. Read your notes and highlight the most important topics.

▶ Take study breaks so you can concentrate and stay alert.

▶ Get a good night's sleep and eat a good breakfast before the test.

The Big Event

Follow these suggestions for smooth sailing during test time:

▶ Take a deep breath and relax! That will help calm your nerves.

▶ If you are allowed, skim through the entire exam so you know what to expect and how long it may take.

▶ As you start each part of the exam, read directions carefully.

▶ Read each question carefully before answering. For a multiple choice question, check every possible answer before you decide on one. The best answer could be the last one.

▶ Don't spend too much time on any one question. Skip hard questions and go back to them at the end.

▶ Keep track of time so you can pace yourself. Use any time left at the end to go back and review your answers. Make sure you've written the answer you meant to select.

Grammar:
It's Easier than You Think

Here are a few rules to remember to help your writing.

Use a comma to show a pause—especially both before and after a group of words. This is called using **paired commas**. You should also use a comma after **introductory words and phrases** like "next" and "after a while."

▶ **RIGHT:** *My favorite aunt, Emily Jones, is an expert when it comes to using commas. The rules for good writing, I am afraid, are often hard to remember. After a while, I figured out the answer to the problem.*

Never let a sentence run on into another sentence without a period in between.

WRONG: *My teacher drives to school every day, she lives 12 miles away.*

▶ **RIGHT:** *My teacher drives to school every day. She lives 12 miles away.*

When a phrase at the beginning of a sentence has a verb form ending in -ing, make sure it does not refer to the wrong thing.

WRONG: *Walking into the cafeteria, my milk spilled onto the floor.*

▶ **RIGHT:** *Walking into the cafeteria, I spilled my milk onto the floor.* [Think about it… your milk wasn't walking into the cafeteria.]

Use the "subjective" form of personal pronouns (**I, we, he, she, they**) when something is the subject of a sentence. Use the "objective" [**me, us, him, her, them**] when it is the object of the sentence or of a preposition (like **with** or **by**).

WRONG: *Michael and me played basketball.* [You should use I, since it's the subject.]

WRONG: *Can you play with Ashley and I?* [You should use me since it's the object of the preposition with.]

Hint: Don't use myself in sentences like those two above. Never use myself when you could use me, or I, instead.

It's a Common Mistake.
Unlike nearly all other possessive words, its does not use an apostrophe to show possession.

WRONG: *Every game has it's rules.*

▶ **RIGHT:** *Every game has its rules.*

Use an apostrophe for it's only when you mean it is, as in the heading above. If you keep on the lookout you might find this mistake before long in something an adult has written.

IF NOTHING ELSE, REMEMBER THIS:

After you finish a writing assignment, look it over carefully. Be sure to read what is really on the paper and not what you think you wrote. Don't be surprised if you find some obvious mistakes—like a capital letter you forgot to use or a simple word that you misspelled. Even book editors have to check and re-check their work.

Different Types of Non-Fiction Writing

There are four main types of paragraphs or essays you might be asked to write in school: **expository**, **narrative**, **descriptive**, and **persuasive**.

EXPOSITORY

An expository paragraph "exposes" information about a subject. It is sometimes called an information paragraph because it gives information about a person, place, thing, or idea. Almost all of the writing in *The World Almanac for Kids* is expository. And most of the writing you do for school will be expository. Here are some expository writing suggestions:

- Summarize chapter 2 of your science textbook, "Animals in Their Habitats."
- Compare and contrast Rosa Parks and Martin Luther King Jr. What do they have in common? How are they different? How did they both contribute to civil rights?

transitional words help the paragraph hold together

The Koala

state the topic right away

details support the topic

Koala bears are not really bears—and that's only one surprising fact about them. To start with, they eat eucalyptus leaves, which other animals find poisonous. Also, they don't need to drink anything, because the eucalyptus leaves provide all the moisture they need. In addition, they are marsupials, which means that they carry their babies around in pouches on their bodies until the babies are ready to be on their own. Finally, they are only native to one place in the world, eastern Australia. In conclusion, this gentle animal is as unusual as it is adorable.

NARRATIVE

A narrative paragraph tells a story about an event. You can find narrative writing in a newspaper report on a local event. Here are some narrative writing suggestions:

- Write a report about a field trip to the science museum.
- Write an essay about what you did over your summer vacation.

use nouns, verbs, and adjectives to keep the action exciting

Roving Mars: My Favorite Field Trip

say what the event was right away

try to build suspense by telling the story with the most interesting details you can

Going to see my first IMAX movie, *Roving Mars*, was one of the most exciting movie experiences I've ever had. When my teacher took our class into the theater, I was immediately shocked by how enormous the screen was. When the lights went down, and the music started blasting out of the speakers, I was almost scared by how intense the experience was. As the cameras followed the adventures of the rovers *Spirit* and *Opportunity*, I felt like I was right there on Mars with them. After we got home from the theater, I scoured the Internet for more information about the Mars rover mission. If humans can ever go to Mars someday, I'd like to be one of them.

DESCRIPTIVE

A descriptive paragraph describes a person, place, thing, or idea. It uses sensory detail to give the reader a better idea of what the topic is really like. This is the kind of writing you will see in books about travel, food, art, and celebrities. Here are some descriptive writing suggestions:

- Who is your hero? Describe the qualities this person has that makes him or her special.
- What's your favorite part of your city? What's interesting about it?

use your five senses to help the reader imagine what the thing is like

Coney Island

In New York, there's an odd, dirty place that is still cool and a lot of fun—it's called Coney Island. It may not be the fanciest place you've ever been, but there are things that make it special. Families, the elderly, and teenagers all love to hang out on the hot beach. They sunbathe, swim, play beach sports, and listen to music along with the sound of the surf. In June, there is the annual Mermaid Parade, where you can see brightly-colored cars and costumes traveling down Boadway Avenue. If you're near Nathan's you can smell delicious hot dogs and fries that will make your mouth water. Best of all, there are rides for kids and adults. Just watch that you don't get whiplash going down the 80-year-old rollercoaster called The Cyclone!

name the thing you are describing right away

use many different details to paint a scene

PERSUASIVE

A persuasive paragraph tries to convince the reader of the writer's point of view. It uses facts, statistics, details, and logic to make an argument. Here are some persuasive writing suggestions:

- Why did the American colonists believe that they deserved independence from Great Britain?
- What improvement would you most like to see in your school?

connecting words help your ideas work together

Start Recycling: It's Easy!

Our school should start a paper-recycling program. The first thing to think about is that about 30% of the materials in landfills come from paper products, many of which could have been recycled. Another reason to start recycling is because it's educational. After asking my classmates, I found out that kids don't know how recycling works. Recycling would be an educational opportunity for our school. A final reason is because starting the program would be easy. Our city already has a recycling program. We just have to organize our own school to participate. In conclusion, starting a recycling program would be easy and also good for the environment and our community.

state your opinion in the topic sentence

provide specific reasons for your point of view

How to write a research paper

Doing Research

To start any research paper or project, the first thing to do is research.

Encyclopedias are a good place to start. They can give you a good overview of the subject.

▶ **The electronic catalog** of your school or town library will probably be your main source for finding books and articles about your subject. A librarian can help show you how this works.

▶ You can also use **the Internet** as a research tool (see opposite page).

▶ As you read each source, **write down the facts and ideas** that you may need. Include the title and author for each source and the page numbers for where you found the particular information. You might try using 3 x 5 index cards.

Writing It Down

The next step is to organize your facts. **Develop a rough outline** of your ideas in the order in which they'll appear. Then, write a draft of your paper. It should contain three main parts:

INTRODUCTION The introduction, or first paragraph, explains your topic and your point of view on it. It should draw readers into the paper and let them know what to expect.

BODY The body of the paper develops your ideas. Use specific facts, examples, and details to make your points clear and convincing. Use separate paragraphs for each new idea and use words and phrases that link one paragraph to the next so your ideas flow smoothly.

CONCLUSION Summarize your main points in the final paragraph, or conclusion.

Showing Your Sources

You may need to do a **bibliography** at the end of your paper. This is a list of all the sources you used to prepare the report.

FOR A BOOK: Author. *Title*. City Published: Publisher, Year.
> Kwek, Karen. *Welcome to Chile*. Milwaukee, Wisc.: Gareth Stevens, 2004.

FOR A MAGAZINE ARTICLE: Author. "Article Title." *Magazine Title*, Date of Issue, Pages.
> Silver, Michael. "Superbowl XXXIX: Three-Ring Circus." *Sports Illustrated*, February 14, 2005, 36-46.

FOR ONLINE (INTERNET): Author(s). Name of Page [online]. Date of Posting/ Revision. [cited year day month]. <URL>.
> The World Almanac for Kids. Animals. [cited 2006 March 4]. <http://www.worldalmanacforkids.com/explore/animals.html>.

Hint: You usually will not have a reason to use the same wording as your source. If you do, refer to your source and use quotation marks.

Research on the INTERNET

Using Library Resources

Your school or public library is a great place to start. It probably has a list (catalog) of its books and periodicals (newspapers and magazines) available from computers at the library, or even from home over the Internet through your library's web site. You can search using **keywords** (words that describe your subject) in three basic ways: by **author**, by **title**, or by **subject**.

For example, doing a subject search for "Benjamin Franklin" will give you a list of books and articles about him, along with their locations in the library.

Your library may also subscribe to online reference databases that companies like The World Almanac create especially for research. These are accessible over the Internet and could contain almanacs, encyclopedias, other reference books, or collections of articles. You can access these databases from the library, and maybe even from home from your library's web site.

When you write your report, don't copy directly from books, articles, or the Internet—that's **plagiarism**, a form of cheating. Keep track of all your **sources**—the books, articles, and web sites you use—and list them in a **bibliography**. (See page 106 for some examples.)

Why shouldn't I just search the Internet?

The library's list may look just like other information on the Internet. But these sources usually have been checked by experts. This is not true of all the information on the Internet. It could come from almost anybody, and may not be trustworthy.

When can I use the Internet?

The Internet is still a great way to look things up. You can find addresses or recipes, listen to music, or find things to do. You can look up information on hobbies or musical instruments, or read a magazine or newspaper online.

If you search the Internet on your own, make sure the web site you find is reliable. A U.S. government site or a site produced by a well-known organization or publication is usually your best bet.

Using a Search Engine

The best way to find web sites is to use a search engine. Here are some helpful ones:

Yahooligans (www.yahooligans.com)
Kidsclick (www.kidsclick.org)
Lycos Zone (lycoszone.lycos.com)
Ask Jeeves Kids (www.ajkids.com)

Start by typing one or two search terms—words that describe your topic. The search engine scans the Internet and gives you a list of sites that contain them. The results appear in a certain order, or **rank**. Search engines use different ways of measuring which web sites are likely to be the most helpful. One way is by counting how many times your search terms appear on each site. The site that's listed first may not have what you want. Explore as many of the sites as possible.

You might have to narrow your search by using more keywords. Or try using **directories** to help find what you need.

THE WORLD ALMANAC FOR KIDS

has its own website at:

www.worldalmanacforkids.com

Inventions

Which was invented first, the parachute or the sewing machine? ➡ page 109

Many important inventions and discoveries came before history was written. These include the wheel, pottery, many tools, and the ability to make fire. More recent inventions help us to travel faster, communicate better, and live longer.

Famous American Inventors

BENJAMIN FRANKLIN (1706-1790) American founding father whose famous kite experiment proved that lightning is a form of electricity. Besides being an accomplished statesman and philosopher, Franklin invented the lightning rod, a radiator stove, an odometer to record mileage traveled by his carriage, and bifocal glasses.

ALEXANDER GRAHAM BELL (1847-1922) Scottish American professor who invented the telephone. An expert in deaf education, Bell also founded the American Association to Promote the Teaching of Speech to the Deaf. In Boston in 1876, Bell spoke the first words transmitted over a distance. He said to his assistant, Thomas Watson, "Mr. Watson, come here; I want you."

THOMAS EDISON (1847-1931) American inventor who held more than 1,000 patents for such famous innovations as the electric light bulb, a motion picture viewer, and a phonograph. Founder of the world's first large central electric-power station in New York City, Edison is considered one of the most important inventors of the 20th century.

LEWIS LATIMER (1848-1928) American inventor and son of runaway slaves who patented a more durable version of Thomas Edison's light bulb by using a carbon filament instead of paper. He worked on the patent for the telephone and oversaw the installation of public lights throughout New York, Philadelphia, London, and Montreal. Another invention of his was the first railroad-car toilet.

WILBUR AND ORVILLE WRIGHT (1867-1912, 1871-1948) Ohio brothers who developed the world's first successful propeller airplane. In Kitty Hawk, NC, in 1903, Orville made history by flying their 605-pound machine for 12 seconds. The duo went on to engineer a plane that Orville flew for 62 minutes at an altitude of 130 feet, making the brothers world-famous.

BEULAH HENRY (1887-1973) Businesswoman and inventor known as "Lady Edison." Her first of 49 patents was for the vacuum ice cream freezer in 1912. Among her 100 or so inventions was a type of sewing machine, a typewriter that made four copies at once, and a doll whose eyes could change color.

Invention TIME LINE

YEAR	INVENTION	INVENTOR (COUNTRY)
105	paper	Ts'ai Lun (China)
1250	magnifying glass	Roger Bacon (England)
1447	moveable type	Johann Gutenberg (Germany)
1590	2-lens microscope	Zacharias Janssen (Netherlands)
1608	telescope	Hans Lippershey (Netherlands)
1714	mercury thermometer	Gabriel D. Fahrenheit (Germany)
1752	lightning rod	Benjamin Franklin (U.S.)
1785	parachute	Jean Pierre Blanchard (France)
1800	electric battery	Alessandro Volta (Italy)
1829	steam locomotive	George Stephenson (England)
1834	refrigeration	Jacob Perkins (England)
1837	telegraph	Samuel F. B. Morse (U.S.)
1842	anesthesia (ether)	Crawford W. Long (U.S.)
1846	sewing machine	Elias Howe (U.S.)
1852	elevator brake	Elisha G. Otis (U.S.)
1867	typewriter	Christopher Sholes, Carlos Glidden, & Samuel W. Soulé (U.S.)
1870s	*telephone	Antonio Meucci (Italy), Alexander G. Bell (U.S.) ▲
1879	practical light bulb	Thomas A. Edison (U.S.)
1886	automobile (gasoline)	Karl Benz (Germany)
1891	escalator	Jesse W. Reno (U.S.)
1891	submarine (modern)	John Holland (U.S.)
1893	moving picture viewer	Thomas A. Edison (U.S.)
1895	diesel engine	Rudolf Diesel (Germany)
1895	X-ray	Wilhelm Roentgen (Germany) ▶
1899	tape recorder	Valdemar Poulsen (Denmark)
1903	windshield wipers	Mary Anderson (U.S.)
1913	modern radio receiver	Reginald A. Fessenden (U.S.)
1922	insulin	Sir Frederick G. Banting (Canada)
1923	television**	Vladimir K. Zworykin** (U.S.)
1926	rocket engine	Robert H. Goddard (U.S.)
1929	penicillin	Alexander Fleming (Scotland)
1939	jet airplane	Hans van Ohain (Germany)
1942	electronic computer	John V. Atanasoff & Clifford Berry (U.S.)
1955	fiber optics	Narinder S. Kapany (England)
1958	laser	A. L. Schawlow & C. H. Townes (U.S.)
1965	word processor	IBM (U.S.)
1973	CAT scanner	Godfrey N. Hounsfield (England)
1977	space shuttle	NASA (U.S.)
1978	artificial heart	Robert K. Jarvik (U.S.)
1979	cellular telephone	Ericsson Company (Sweden)
1987	laptop computer	Sir Clive Sinclair (England) ▶
1994	digital camera	Apple Computer, Kodak (U.S.)
1995	DVD (digital video disk)	Matsushita (Japan)
2002	robot vacuum	iRobot Corp. (U.S.)

X ray of human hand

*Meucci developed a version of the telephone (early 1870s); Bell received a patent for another version. **Others who helped invent the television include Philo T. Farnsworth (1926) and John Baird (1928).

did you know

Swiss inventor George de Mestral was inspired to develop VELCRO® when one day in the early 1940s, he and his dog returned from a walk covered in cockleburs. Curious about the plant's natural sticking power, de Mestral examined it under a microscope. He then created a fastener that emulated the burs' hooks on one side and his pant-leg fabric's loops on the other. He patented the invention in 1948.

Language

What does "chew the fat" mean? ➡ page 112

TOP LANGUAGES

Mandarin, the principal language of China, has the most native speakers of any language. Spanish ranks second as the most common native, or first, language in the world.*

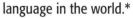

LANGUAGE	KEY PLACES WHERE SPOKEN	NATIVE SPEAKERS
Mandarin	China, Taiwan	873,014,298
Spanish	South America, Spain	322,299,171
English	U.S., Canada, Britain	309,352,280
Hindi	India	180,764,791
Portuguese	Portugal, Brazil	177,457,180
Bengali	India, Bangladesh	171,070,202
Russian	Russia	145,031,551
Japanese	Japan	122,433,899

*Estimates as of 2004.

Which LANGUAGES Are SPOKEN in the UNITED STATES?

Most Americans speak English at home. But since the beginning of American history, immigrants have come to the U.S. from all over the world. Many have brought other languages with them.

"¡Hola!" That's how more than 28 million Americans say "hi" at home.

The table at right lists the most frequently spoken languages in the U.S., as of the 2000 census.

	LANGUAGE USED AT HOME	SPEAKERS OVER 5 YEARS OLD
1	Speak only English	215,423,557
2	Spanish, Spanish Creole	28,101,052
3	Chinese	2,022,143
4	French	1,643,838
5	German	1,382,613
6	Tagalog (Philippines)	1,224,241
7	Vietnamese	1,009,627
8	Italian	1,008,370
9	Korean	894,063
10	Russian	706,242
11	Polish	667,414
12	Arabic	614,582
13	Portuguese	564,630
14	Japanese	477,997
15	French Creole	453,368
16	Greek	365,436
17	Hindi	317,057
18	Persian	312,085
19	Urdu	262,900
20	Gujarathi (from India & parts of Africa)	235,988

Language Express

 ¡Hola! (Spanish)

Hello! (English)

 Konnichi wa! (Japanese)

Surprise your friends and family with words from other languages.

English	Spanish	French	German	Chinese
January	enero	janvier	Januar	yi-yue
February	febrero	fevrier	Februar	er-yue
March	marzo	mars	Marz	san-yue
April	abril	avril	April	si-yue
May	mayo	mai	Mai	wu-yue
June	junio	juin	Juni	liu-yue
July	julio	juillet	Juli	qi-yue
August	agosto	aout	August	ba-yue
September	septiembre	septembre	September	jiu-yue
October	octubre	octobre	Oktober	shi-yue
November	noviembre	novembre	November	shi-yi-yue
December	diciembre	decembre	Dezember	shi er-yue
blue	azul	bleu	blau	lan
red	rojo	rouge	rot	hong
green	verde	vert	grün	lu
yellow	amarillo	jaune	gelb	huang
black	negro	noir	schwarz	hei
white	blanco	blanc	weiss	bai
happy birthday!	¡feliz cumpleanos!	joyeux anniversaire!	Glückwunsch zum Geburtstag!	sheng-ri kuai le!
hello!	¡hola!	bonjour!	hallo!	ni hao!
good-bye!	¡adios!	au revoir!	auf Wiedersehen!	zai-jian!
fish	pez	poisson	Fisch	yu
bird	pájaro	oiseau	Vogel	niao
horse	caballo	cheval	Pferd	ma
one	uno	un	eins	yi
two	dos	deux	zwei	er
three	tres	trois	drei	san
four	cuatro	quatre	vier	si
five	cinco	cinq	fünf	wu

 did you know?

- As of the end of 2005, the top five languages on the Internet, by the number of Internet users who speak that language, are 1. English, 2. Chinese, 3. Japanese, 4. Spanish, and 5. German.
- Because it is not related to any other language family, many people consider Basque to be the hardest language to master. It's spoken in the region around the Pyrenees Mountains, where France and Spain meet.

THE ENGLISH LANGUAGE

Facts About English

▶ According to the Oxford English Dictionary, the English language contains between 250,000 and 750,000 words. (The number depends on whether you count different meanings of the same word as separate words and on how many obscure technical terms you count.)

▶ The most frequently used letters of the alphabet are E, T, A, and O, in that order.

▶ Here are the 30 most common English words: the, of, and, a, to, in, is, that, it, was, he, for, as, on, with, his, be, at, you, I, are, this, by, from, had, have, they, not, or, one. Try to make a sentence with just these words. Here's an example: "I had to be with it for that is not the one they have."

New Words

English is always changing as new words are born and old ones die out. Many new words come from the field of electronics and computers, from the media, or from slang.

Lurk: to visit Internet communities or message boards often without contributing. ("That kid lurks through our web profiles but never leaves a comment.")

Ollie: no-handed skateboard jump where the board "sticks" to the rider's feet, from creator "Ollie" Gelfand. ("The skater ollied over the handrail and landed perfectly.")

Set-Jetter: a person who wants to visit a place featured in a book or movie they liked. ("Many set-jetters want to visit New Zealand because *Lord of the Rings* was filmed there.")

In Other Words: IDIOMS

Idioms are phrases that mean more than their words put together. Here are some to chew on:

bite off more than you can chew—"take on more than one can handle." Take a big bite out of a sandwich so that some of it is still sticking out past your lips. Now try chewing. Don't you wish you had bitten off less?

chew someone out—"to severely scold someone." The phrase supposedly came from the U.S. Army. It seems fitting that an angry, screaming general would make people feel as if they had just been chewed up and spit out.

chew the fat—"to have a long, friendly, and informal chat." Fat is tough to chew. The original phrasemakers probably had a fatty cut of meat and a whole lot of time to chew it. You'd probably want to chew the fat with your friends after school, but maybe not with your principal.

GETTING TO THE ROOT

Many English words and parts of words can be traced back to Latin or Greek. If you know the meaning of a word's parts, you can probably guess what it means.

A root (also called a stem) is the part of the word that gives its basic meaning, but can't be used by itself. Roots need other word parts to complete them: either a prefix at the beginning, or a suffix at the end, or sometimes both. The following tables give some examples of Greek and Latin roots, prefixes, and suffixes.

Latin

root	basic meaning	example
-alt-	high	altitude
-ject-	to throw	reject
-port-	to carry	transport
-scrib-/ -script-	to write	prescription
-vert-	turn	invert

prefix	basic meaning	example
de-	away, off	defrost
inter-	between, among	international
non-	not	nontoxic
pre-	before	prevent
re-	again, back	rewrite
trans-	across, through	trans-Atlantic

suffix	basic meaning	example
-ation	(makes verbs into nouns)	invitation
-fy/-ify	make or cause to become	horrify
-ly	like, to the extent of	highly
-ment	(makes verbs into nouns)	government
-ty/-ity	state of	purity

Greek

root	basic meaning	example
-anthrop-	human	anthropology
-biblio-	book	bible
-bio-	life	biology
-dem-	people	democracy
-phon-	sound	telephone
-psych-	soul	psychology

prefix	basic meaning	example
anti-/ant-	against	antisocial
auto-	self	autopilot
biblio-/ bibl-	book	bibliography
micro-	small	microscope
tele-	far off	television

suffix	basic meaning	example
-graph	write, draw, describe, record	photograph
-ism	act, state, theory of	realism
-ist	one who believes in, practices	capitalist
-logue/ -log	speech, to speak	dialogue
-scope	see	telescope

JOKES AND RIDDLES

1. Three men jump off the same diving board into a swimming pool. The first two men get their hair wet, and the third man doesn't. Why?

2. What has eighteen legs and catches flies?

3. A police officer was walking by a restaurant one afternoon when he heard a woman scream, "Please John, don't shoot!" Then the police officer heard a gun shot. He ran into the restaurant and found a milkman, a doctor, a lawyer, a cook, and a waitress. The police officer immediately arrested the milkman. Why?

4. Why did the computer go to the doctor?

5. How did the Vikings send secret messages?

6. I have five fingers but I'm not a hand. What am I?

7. When a teacher closes his eyes, why should it remind him of an empty classroom?

8. What do demons have on vacation?

9. What did the tie say to the hat?

10. What do you get if you cross a duck with a firecracker?

11. What is a parrot's favorite game?

12. What has a head and a foot but no arms?

13. Why did the robber take a bath before he stole from the bank?

14. What has 5 eyes, is blind, goes for miles, yet bumps into nothing?

15. What happens if you eat yeast and shoe polish?

16. What is the best day to cook in a wok?

17. What happens when you sit on a grape?

18. What was the pirate movie rated?

19. What do firemen put in their soup?

20. What did the duck say when she bought lipstick?

Knock-Knock
Who's there?
Butter.
Butter who?
Butter let me in.

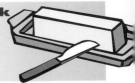

A sloth is out for a walk when he's mugged by four snails. After recovering his wits, he goes to make a police report. "Can you describe the snails?" asks the officer. "Not well; it all happened so fast," replies the sloth.

FATHER: How are your grades, son?
SON: Underwater, Dad.
FATHER: Underwater? What do you mean?
SON: They're below C level.

STUDENT: I don't think I deserve a zero on this exam.
TEACHER: Neither do I, but it's the lowest mark I can give you.

21. Why did the boy bring a ladder to school?

22. If April showers bring May flowers, then what do May flowers bring?

Girl: What did you get that little medal for?
Boy: For singing.
Girl: What did you get the big one for?
Boy: For stopping!

23. Why were the middle ages sometimes called the dark ages?

Knock-Knock
Who's there?
Little old lady.
Little old lady who?
Wow! I didn't know you could yodel.

24. Why did the baker stop making donuts?

25. What nails do carpenters hate to hit?

26. The person who makes it doesn't use it. The person who buys it does not want it. The person who is using it does not know it.

ANSWERS ON PAGES 334-337. FOR MORE PUZZLES GO TO WWW.WORLDALMANACFORKIDS.COM

27 Which weighs more, a pound of lead or a pound of feathers?

28 A father's child, a mother's child, yet no one's son. Who am I?

29 A 6-foot-tall magician held a water glass above his head and let it drop to the carpet without spilling a single drop of water. How could he manage to drop the glass from a height of 6 feet and not spill a drop of water?

Knock-Knock

Who's there?
Doris.
Doris who?
Doris locked, that's why I'm knocking.

30 Tall I am young,
Short I am old,
While with life I do glow,
Breath is my foe. What am I?

31 A doctor and a bus driver are both in love with an attractive girl named Sarah. The bus driver had to go on a long bus trip that would last a week. Before he left, he gave Sarah seven apples. Why?

A little girl goes to see the doctor. She's got a pea in one nostril, a grape in the other, and a string bean stuck in her ear. She says to the doctor, "I don't feel good." The doctor replies, "The problem is clear to me. You're not eating right!"

32 If two's company and three's a crowd, what are four and five?

33 What happens when you throw a green stone into the Red Sea?

34 What is a volcano?

35 Why is Alabama the smartest state in the USA?

WORD-CONNECT

Synonyms are words that have the same (or almost the same) meaning. For example, "large" and "big" are synonyms. The answers to this crossword puzzle are all synonyms of the clues given below. Can you fill in all the blanks?

ACROSS

2 Sketch
4 Wealthy
7 Drowsy
8 Difficult
9 Intelligent
11 Attempt
12 Presents
14 Dad
16 Shout
17 Chilly

DOWN

1 Small
3 Lumber
5 Pretty
6 Speedy
7 Noiseless
10 Mad
13 High
15 Headgear

ANSWERS ON PAGES 334-337. FOR MORE PUZZLES GO TO WWW.WORLDALMANACFORKIDS.COM

Magic

Who spent 60 hours in a block of ice? ➡ page 116

HARRY HOUDINI

(1874 – 1926)

Harry Houdini was born in Budapest, Hungary, and came to the U.S. at the age of four with the name Ehrich Weiss. As a young man, Houdini performed card tricks and other sleight-of-hand illusions, but moved on to more fantastic escapes that appeared to risk his life. By the time he was 25, Houdini was a celebrity in the U.S. and Europe.

Houdini's most famous escapes are still talked about today. He jumped into San Francisco Bay with a 75 pound ball and chain around his ankles while wearing handcuffs, and swam back to the surface unharmed. He escaped from a real prison cell. He even escaped from straitjackets while suspended from tall buildings upside-down.

DAVID BLAINE (1973 -)

David Blaine began performing card tricks at the age of four. He is a master of "street magic"—performing for small groups of people on city streets. In one trick, performed in his TV special *David Blaine: Street Magic*, Blaine appears to rise several inches off of the ground.

Blaine is also well-known for his feats of endurance. In 2000, he spent over sixty hours frozen in a block of ice in Times Square, in New York City. In 2002, Blaine spent thirty-five hours without food or water perched atop a 10-story-tall pillar in a New York park. And in 2003, Blaine spent forty-four days without food in a glass box suspended thirty feet in the air in London.

"CATCHING THE BURGLARS" Card Trick

❶ Get a regular deck of cards. Remove three Kings and all four Jacks. Place one of the four Jacks between two Kings, and place those three cards at the bottom of the deck. **PREPARE THE DECK BEFORE YOU DO THE TRICK; DO NOT LET YOUR AUDIENCE SEE YOU DO THIS.** You are now ready to perform the illusion.

❷ Gather your audience. Hold the remaining King and three Jacks in your left hand. Place the deck, face down, on the table. Tell your audience the following story: "Once upon a time, there was a house." Point to the face-down deck of cards. "The owners were out of town on vacation." Lay the three Jacks face up on the table.

Step 1

❸ Tell the audience, "These three burglars decided to steal everything from the house. The first one went through the back door." At this point, lift the face-down deck, put one of the Jacks face down on the table, and put the face-down deck on top of it.

❹ Tell the audience, "The second burglar went in through a window." Invite one of the audience members to slide the Jack (face down) anywhere in the middle of the deck.

❺ Tell the audience, "The last burglar just walked in the front door." Put the last Jack face down on top of the face-down deck.

Step 5

❻ Tell the audience, "The burglary was going according to plan until a detective saw what was happening. He raced into the house through the front door." Put the King (your final loose card) face down on top of the deck.

❼ Tell the audience, "As soon as the burglars heard the detective enter the house, they started to run. But the detective chased them around the house." Let an audience member cut the deck. You can allow other audience members to cut the deck as well, to build excitement.

❽ Tell the audience, "After that big chase, what do you suppose happened? There were three burglars and only one detective. How could one detective have captured three burglars?"

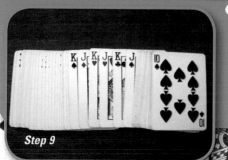

Step 9

❾ Turn the deck face up and fan out the cards in one long row. You will find the following series of cards: King – Jack, King – Jack, King – Jack. Point to the six cards and tell the audience, "As you can see, all of the burglars were caught by the detective—and his two magical assistants. You see, each burglar is being held by a detective!"

Military

What country maintains the largest military force? ➡ page 120

American Revolution

Why? The British king sought to control American trade and tax the 13 colonies without their consent. The colonies wanted independence.
Who? British and American loyalists vs. American revolutionaries with French support
When? 1775-1781
Result? The colonies gained independence.

George Washington

War of 1812

Why? Britain interfered with American commerce and forced American sailors to join the British navy.
Who? Britain vs. United States
When? 1812-1814
Result? There was no clear winner. The U.S. unsuccessfully invaded Canada, a British colony. The British burned Washington, D.C., and the White House but were defeated in other battles.

Francis Scott Key

The successful defense of Fort McHenry inspired Francis Scott Key to write "The Star-Spangled Banner."

Mexican War

Why? The U.S. annexed Texas. It also sought control of California, a Mexican province.
Who? Mexico vs. United States
When? 1846-1848
Result? Mexico ceded land in Texas, California, and New Mexico. The U.S. paid Mexico millions of dollars in return.

Mexican general Antonio López de Santa Anna, who fought in the Mexican War, defeated the American force inside the Alamo mission during the Texan war for independence.

Civil War

Why? The Southern states seceded from the U.S. The U.S. fought to keep them.
Who? Confederacy vs. Union
When? 1861-1865
Result? The United States remained a unified country. Slavery was abolished.

Battle of Antietam

Spanish-American War

Why? The Americans supported Cuban independence from Spain.
Who? United States vs. Spain
When? 1898
Result? Spain handed the Philippines, Guam, and Puerto Rico over to the U.S. Cuba became independent.

Sunken remains of the U.S.S. Maine

World War I

Why? Colonial and military competition between European powers.

Who? Allies (including the U.S., Britain, France, Russia, Italy, and Japan) vs. Central Powers (including Germany, Austria-Hungary, and Turkey)

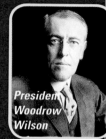
President Woodrow Wilson

When? 1914-1918

Result? The Allies defeated the Central Powers. An estimated 8 million soldiers and close to 10 million civilians were killed.

World War II

Why? The Axis sought world domination.

Who? Axis (including Germany, Italy, and Japan) vs. Allies (including the U.S., Britain, France, and the Soviet Union). The U.S. did not enter the war until Japan attacked Pearl Harbor in 1941.

When? 1939-1945 (U.S. dropped atomic bombs on Hiroshima and Nagasaki.)

Result? The Allies defeated the Axis. The Holocaust (the Nazi effort to wipe out the Jews and other minorities) was stopped. The U.S. helped rebuild Western Europe and Japan. The Soviet Union set up Communist governments in Eastern Europe.

D-Day

did you know

World War II was the deadliest conflict in history. More than 62 million people were killed.

Korean War

Why? North Korea invaded South Korea. In many ways, the conflict was part of the Cold War between the Communist and non-Communist nations.

Who? North Korea with support from China and the Soviet Union vs. South Korea backed by the United States and its allies

When? 1950-1953

Result? The war ended with a cease-fire agreement. North Korean forces retreated north of the 38th parallel. Korea remains divided.

Vietnam War

Why? Communists (Viet Cong) backed by North Vietnam attempted to overthrow South Vietnam's government.

Who? North Vietnam with support from the Soviet Union and China vs. South Vietnam with support from the U.S. and its allies

Burning Viet Cong base camp

When? 1959-1975

Result? The U.S. withdrew its troops in 1973. In 1975, South Vietnam surrendered. Vietnam became a unified Communist country.

did you know

Although the U.S. won every major military engagement, it still lost the war.

Persian Gulf War

Why? Iraq invaded and annexed Kuwait. It refused to withdraw despite United Nations demands.

Who? Iraq vs. U.S.-led coalition

When? 1991

Result? The coalition drove out Iraqi forces from Kuwait.

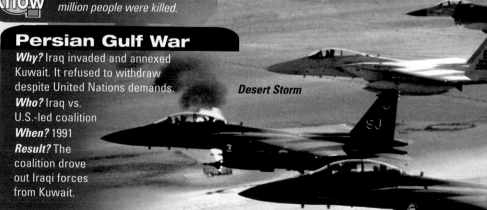
Desert Storm

Where Are We Now?

Afghanistan War

Why? The U.S. demanded that Afghanistan's Taliban regime turn over Osama bin Laden, the man who allegedly planned the 9/11 terrorist attacks. The Taliban claimed not to know bin Laden's whereabouts.

Who? Taliban regime vs. Afghani Northern Alliance fighters, supported by the United States and its allies

When? 2001-

Result? The Taliban regime was defeated, but U.S. troops are still fighting Taliban resisters and hunting for bin Laden.

The U.S. used unmanned aerial vehicles (robotic planes without pilots) to conduct round-the-clock surveillance.

Iraq War

Why? The U.S. accused Iraq of hiding weapons of mass destruction and supporting terrorism.

Who? Iraq vs. United States, Great Britain, and their allies

When? 2003-

Result? Saddam Hussein's government was toppled. Hussein was captured and put on trial. Attacks from different groups on U.S. troops and Iraqi civilians have been ongoing, however.

TOP 10 NATIONS WITH LARGEST ARMED FORCES

1. China	2,255,000	6. South Korea	688,000
2. United States	1,434,000	7. Pakistan	619,000
3. India	1,325,000	8. Iran	540,000
4. Russia	1,213,000	9. Turkey	515,000
5. North Korea	1,106,000	10. Myanmar	485,000

Source: International Institute for Strategic Studies

On the Job

U.S. COAST GUARD

BMC (CHIEF BOATSWAIN'S MATE)
LYNN FABBO, Cape May, New Jersey

What branch of the military do you work for?

I work for the Coast Guard. Our job is to save people's lives, stop drugs from coming into the country, and protect the marine environment.

What is a typical day like for you?

As a recruit company commander, I'm involved with training recruits, who come from all over the country and the world. (To join the military, you do not have to be a U.S. citizen.) The way a drill instructor is portrayed on TV, screaming at recruits, is not the way it really is. Our goal is to teach recruits everything they need to know, from military history to how to wear their uniforms properly. Recruit company commanders basically spend every waking minute with their recruits, from the time recruits wake up at 6 to the time we put them in the "rack" at 10.

What is your favorite part of your job?

Seeing the difference in recruits when they graduate. Some recruits don't have much self-esteem when they come to us. But at graduation, you see them standing up tall for the first time. One of my favorite recruits had a lot of problems early on in training. After talking to him, we found out he had come from an abusive home. He was never willing to give up, though. While he was in training, his mom checked into a home for abused women. She came to his graduation. She told me she had found strength and courage because of the strength her son had given her. And he had gotten this strength from his company commanders.

What is your least favorite part of your job?

When a young recruit really wants to do a good job but doesn't have the ability, we have to send him or her home. Even though we'd like to help everybody, sometimes it just doesn't work out that way. Maybe a recruit can't pass the physical fitness requirements or is stressed about being away from home for the first time.

What can kids do now to prepare for a career like yours?

They should keep themselves physically active and do their best while they're in school. I joined the U.S. Naval Sea Cadet Corps when I was in high school. Such programs can help kids decide if the military is for them.

Money

How long does a $1 bill last? ➡ page 123

▶ Where Does the U.S. Government Get Money?

Excise taxes (taxes on tobacco and alcohol, for example): **3%**

Estate and gift taxes: **1%**

Other sources: **3%**

Income taxes on businesses: **13%**

Income taxes on individuals: **43%**

Insurance, hospital, and retirement taxes: **37%**

▶ Where Does the U.S. Government Spend Money?

Social Security and income security (incl. public assistance and unemployment): **35%**

Education, training, employment, and social services: **4%**

Interest on the public debt: **7%**

Other, including agriculture, commerce, environment, international affairs, justice, space and technology, and transportation: **12%**

Health (including Medicare): **22%**

Defense (military): **20%**

How Much Money Is in Circulation?

As of September 2005, the total amount of money in circulation in the United States came to **$766,486,740,782**. About 35 billion dollars was in coins, the rest in paper money.

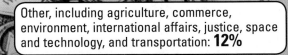

Paper Money

Coins

Making Money

What Is the U.S. Mint?

The U.S. Mint, founded in 1792, is part of the Treasury Department. The Mint makes all U.S. coins and safeguards the nation's $100 million in gold and silver bullion (uncoined bars of metal). Reserves of these precious metals are held at West Point, New York, and Fort Knox, Kentucky. The Mint turns out coins at four production facilities (Denver, Philadelphia, San Francisco, and West Point). For more information, visit the U.S. Mint's website at

WEB SITE **www.usmint. gov**

What Coins Does the Mint Make?

Branches of the U.S. Mint in Denver and Philadelphia currently make coins for circulation, or everyday use. In 2005, these two facilities made 15.2 billion coins, including 7.7 billion pennies, 1.7 billion nickels, 2.8 billion dimes, and 3.0 million quarters. A tiny "D" or "P" near the year, called a mint mark, tells you which one made the coin. A Lincoln cent or "penny" with no mint mark was probably made at the Philadelphia Mint, which has by tradition never marked pennies. The U.S. Mint also makes commemorative coins in honor of events, like the Olympics, or people, like Benjamin Franklin. The Franklin coin was released in January 2006.

Where is Paper Money Made?

The Bureau of Engraving and Printing (BEP), established in 1862, designs and prints all U.S. paper money. This agency, which is also part of the Treasury Department, prints postage stamps and other official certificates as well. The BEP's production facilities in Washington, D.C., and Ft. Worth, Texas, made almost 9 billion bills in 2005. About 95% of them are used to replace worn-out money. Even though bills are made of a special paper that is 75% cotton and 25% linen, they wear out pretty fast if they are used a lot. The $1 bill only lasts an average of 22 months, while the $50 bill lasts for about 5 years and the $100 bill lasts for about 8.5 years. For more information visit the BEP's website:

WEB SITE **www.money factory.com**

U.S. State Quarters

From 1999 to 2008, five new quarter designs are being minted each year. George Washington stays on the front, but a design honoring one of the 50 states appears on the back. The quarters for each state are coming out in the order in which the states joined the Union. In 2006, Nevada, Nebraska, Colorado, North Dakota, and South Dakota (pictured here) were put into circulation. Montana, Washington, Idaho, Wyoming, and Utah quarters are due in 2007.

Everybody knows that George Washington is on the U.S. one-dollar bill, but did you ever wonder what all that other stuff is?

Plate position
Shows where on the 32-note plate this bill was printed.

The Treasury Department seal: The balancing scales represent justice. The pointed stripe across the middle has 13 stars for the original 13 colonies. The key represents authority.

Plate serial number
Shows which printing plate was used for the face of the bill.

Serial number
Each bill has its own.

Federal Reserve District Number
Shows which district issued the bill.

Treasurer of the U.S. Signature

Series indicator (year note's design was first used)

Secretary of the Treasury signature

(Since 1949, every Treasurer of the U.S. has been a woman.)

Federal Reserve District Seal
The name of the Federal Reserve Bank that issued the bill is printed in the seal. The letter tells you quickly where the bill is from. Here are the letter codes for the 12 Federal Reserve Districts:

A: Boston **G:** Chicago
B: New York **H:** St. Louis
C: Philadelphia **I:** Minneapolis
D: Cleveland **J:** Kansas City
E: Richmond **K:** Dallas
F: Atlanta **L:** San Francisco

Front of the Great Seal of the United States: The bald eagle is the national bird. The shield has 13 stripes for the 13 original colonies. The eagle holds 13 arrows (symbol of war) and an olive branch (symbol of peace). Above the eagle is the motto "E Pluribus Unum," Latin for "out of many, one," and a constellation of 13 stars.

Plate serial number
Shows which plate was used for the back.

Reverse of the Great Seal of the United States:
The pyramid symbolizes something that lasts for ages. It is unfinished because the U.S. is always growing. The eye, known as the "Eye of Providence," probably comes from an ancient Egyptian symbol. The pyramid has 13 levels; at its base are the Roman numerals for 1776, the year of American independence. "Annuit Coeptis" is Latin for "God has favored our undertaking." "Novus Ordo Seclorum" is Latin for "a new order of the ages." Both phrases are from the works of the Roman poet Virgil.

THE WORLD'S RICHEST PEOPLE

These five people were the world's richest as of 2006, according to *Forbes* magazine. (The figure after each name is the person's net worth, or the cash value of everything the person owns minus any debts.)

1. William Gates III
$50.0 billion

1 William Gates III, $50.0 billion The world's richest man is also the biggest contributor to humanitarian causes. In 2000 the Microsoft chief and his wife started the Bill & Melinda Gates Foundation. It works to fight hepatitis B, AIDS, and malaria, help increase high school graduation rates, aid needy residents of the Pacific Northwest, and provide better Internet access at libraries.

2 Warren Buffett, $42.0 billion Buffett, an insurance and investment expert, has lived in the same gray stucco house on Farnam Street in Omaha, Nebraska for more than 40 years. He bought his first stock at age 11, and by 14, Buffett was renting out a farm he bought with his own money. He only invests in what he knows. Since his favorite dish is a burger and soda, his company owns Dairy Queen.

3 Carlos Slim Helu, $30.0 billion Helu, from Mexico, owns many industrial, shopping, and telecommunications companies. He puts in 14-hour work days. He has two charities for children and created the Foundation of the Historic Center of Mexico City to restore Mexico City's colonial buildings.

4 Ingvar Kamprad, $28.0 billion Kamprad, from Sweden, founded the discount furniture chain IKEA. He started the company at age 17 selling various items like pens and watches door-to-door. IKEA furniture is now sold in 44 countries.

5 Lakshmi Mittal, $23.5 billion Mittal oversees the world's largest steel company, Mittal Steel. He grew up penniless in India. He worked at his father's steel company before starting his own. He bought a mansion for a record $128 million in 2004.

MONEY CIRCUIT

Complete the circuit by filling in each blank to form a word from the list below. Each new word begins with the last letter of the word before it. We've given you the first and last letters, and two of the words. The words need to be spelled backwards on the bottom.

```
C o u n T_____L_____E_____G_____S
U                                                 ___
R                                                 ___
R                                                 ___
E                                                 ___
N                                                 ___
C                                                 ___
Y e n o M_____S_____L_____N_____Y
```

Security   Lire   Nickel   Count   Gilts   Money
    Yen   Earning   Total   Loans   Sum

Movies & TV

What famous children's book came out as a new movie in June 2006? ⟶ page 127

Movie & TV Facts

Walt Disney

Young Oscar
The youngest actor to ever receive an Oscar is Tatum O'Neal, who was only 10 years old when she received a Best Actress in a Supporting Role award for *Paper Moon* in 1973.

Oscar the Mouse!
Walt Disney won a record-breaking 26 Oscars over his career.

First on TV
The first public television broadcasts were made in England in 1927 and in the U.S. in 1930.

Grandma, Turn Off the TV!
Kids age 2-11 watch an average of over 21 hours of TV a week. Teens age 12-18 watch an average of over 20 hours a week. However, women over age 55 watch the most TV of all—an average of 44 hours a week!

Ready for Your Close-up?
Because of the limits of early cameras to capture realistic color and shading, newscasters and actors used to wear heavy orange "pancake makeup" to look "real" on-camera.

All-Time Top Movies*

1.	*Titanic* (1997)	$600.8
2.	*Star Wars: Episode IV - A New Hope* (1977)	460.9
3.	*Shrek 2* (2004)	436.5
4.	*E.T.: The Extra Terrestrial* (1982)	435.0
5.	*Star Wars: Episode I- The Phantom Menace* (1999)	431.1
6.	*Spider-Man* (2002)	403.7
7.	*Star Wars: Episode III-Revenge of the Sith* (2005)	380.3
8.	*The Lord of the Rings: The Return of the King* (2003)	377.0
9.	*Spider-Man 2* (2004)	373.4
10.	*The Passion of the Christ* (2004)	370.3

All-Time Top Animated Movies*

1.	*Shrek 2* (2004)	$436.5
2.	*Finding Nemo* (2003)	339.7
3.	*The Lion King* (1994)	328.4
4.	*Shrek* (2001)	267.7
5.	*The Incredibles* (2004)	261.4
6.	*Monsters, Inc.* (2001)	255.9
7.	*Toy Story 2* (1999)	245.8
8.	*Aladdin* (1992)	217.4
9.	*Madagascar* (2005)	193.1
10.	*Toy Story* (1995)	191.8

Source: Internet Movie Database
*Through March 30, 2006. Gross in millions of dollars based on box office sales in the U.S. and Canada.

Top TV Shows in 2005-2006

AGES 6-11

NETWORK

1. American Idol
2. Survivor: Panama-Exile Island
3. Extreme Makeover: Home Edition
4. Survivor: Guatemala
5. The Simpsons

CABLE

1. Drake & Josh
2. Zoey 101
3. Ned's Declassified School Survival Guide
4. SpongeBob SquarePants
5. All That

AGES 12-17

NETWORK

1. American Idol
2. Family Guy
3. Desperate Housewives
4. American Dad
5. The Simpsons

CABLE

1. WWE Entertainment
2. Family Guy
3. Zoey 101
4. Naruto
5. Drake & Josh

Ty Pennington
Extreme Makeover: Home Edition

Hitting Theaters in 2006...

Don't miss **Charlotte's Web**, based on the classic novel by E.B. White. You'll never feel the same way about spiders and pigs again (June).

The voice of Jennifer Love Hewitt brings **Garfield's A Tale of Two Kitties** to life (June).

Can the world live without Superman? Apparently not. **Superman Returns** for the first time in years to try to win back Lois Lane's heart and find a place for himself in society. Stars include Kate Bosworth and Brandon Routh (June).

Orlando Bloom, Johnny Depp, and Keira Knightly return in **Pirates of the Caribbean: Dead Man's Chest**, the second part to the at-sea thriller based on the popular Disneyland ride (July).

In **The Barnyard**, animals walk, sing, talk and party. But can Otis the cow stay in charge and keep his cool? Featuring the voices of Courteney Cox and Danny Glover (October).

Night at the Museum shows what happens when displays at a natural history museum come alive. Starring Ben Stiller, Robin Williams, and Ricky Gervais, this movie is guaranteed to be funny (December).

Shrek

...and in 2007

Spiderman 3 and **Shrek 3** will make May a blockbuster month for cartoon and comic-book fans everywhere.

Fantastic Four 2 and **Transformers** will set off fireworks in the theaters on the July 4th weekend.

In December, prepare to be wowed by book-to-movie spectacles **His Dark Materials: The Golden Compass** and **The Chronicles of Narnia: Prince Caspian**.

BIG HITS FOR THE SMALL SCREEN

Wonder what to rent next? These top movies for kids are available on video or DVD.

ANIMATION

▶ *The Incredibles* (2004) A family of superheroes lives a quiet life in Metroville until one day when they are forced to save the world.

▶ *The SpongeBob SquarePants Movie* (2004) SpongeBob's boss, Mr. Krab, is unfairly accused of stealing King Neptune's crown. Along with his best buddy, Patrick, SpongeBob sets out to Shell City to track down the crown and save Mr. Krab's life.

▶ *Toy Story* (1995) Woody, a toy cowboy, and Buzz Lightyear, a toy astronaut, don't like each other. But they call a truce and help each other get back to the toy room.

If you like animated movies, you might also want to check out *The Lion King, Finding Nemo,* and *Shrek.*

Toy Story

ADVENTURE

▶ *The Adventures of Shark Boy and Lava Girl* (2005) In order to escape ridicule from his classmates, Max makes up the dream world Planet Drool. He realizes his dream world is a powerful one when Shark Boy and Lava Girl, two made-up superheroes, show up on Earth and need his help.

▶ *Pee-wee's Big Adventure* (1985) After a fortune teller informs Pee-wee Herman that his stolen bicycle is in the basement of the Alamo, he sets off on a madcap road trip to recover it.

Looking for other wild adventures? Check out *The Goonies, The Neverending Story,* and *Spy Kids.*

The Adventures of Shark Boy and Lava Girl

MOVIE Match-Up

Match the character described in A with one in Column B then with their movie in Column C.

Character A	Character B	Movie C
A red headed girl	Evil green sorceress	*Annie*
Midwestern girl	Bald headed dad	*Whale Rider*
Large sea-dwelling mammal	Ice queen	*To Kill a Mockingbird*
Mysterious recluse	Two curious kids	*The Wizard of Oz*
A wild animal	Wannabe chief of the tribe	*The Chronicles of Narnia*

ANSWERS ON PAGES 334–337. FOR MORE PUZZLES GO TO WWW.WORLDALMANACFORKIDS.COM

DRAMA

▶ **Whale Rider** (2002) An 11-year-old girl believes she's destined to be the first woman chief of the Whangara people. But first she must overcome her grandfather and a thousand years of tradition to fulfill her destiny.

Love to curl up and watch dramatic flicks? Lose yourself in *It's A Wonderful Life* and *To Kill a Mockingbird*.

FANTASY

▶ **Charlie and the Chocolate Factory** (2005) A poor, young boy wins a tour of the most amazing chocolate factory in the world. The tour is led by Willy Wonka, the factory's unusual owner, and is full of many odd surprises.

▶ **The Chronicles of Narnia** (2005) Four kids find a secret passage through a wardrobe that leads to the mystical land of Narnia. With the guidance of a lion, they try to free Narnia from the evil witch who rules it.

▶ **The Wizard of Oz** (1939) A tornado sweeps Dorothy and her dog, Toto, to the strange land of Oz. In order to get back to Kansas, Dorothy embarks on a quest to see the wizard—the only person in Oz with the power to send her home.

Searching for other fantasy worlds worth getting lost in? Try *The Dark Crystal*, *Labyrinth*, and a Harry Potter film.

The Chronicles of Narnia

129

Museums

Where could you see a "Trash-o-saurus"? ➡ page 131

Museums collect things of great interest, such as works of art or everyday objects from different times in the past, and show them off to people who come there to visit.

The Louvre, in Paris, France, is one of the world's biggest and oldest museums. It began around the year 1200 as a fortress and palace built by the king of France, Philip Augustus. In 1546, Francis I started the royal collection of art. In 1793, the Louvre was opened up to the public as a museum. Its masterpieces include one of the most famous paintings ever made, the portrait known as the *Mona Lisa* by Leonardo DaVinci (see page 33).

The main entrance to the Louvre is through a big, glass pyramid, designed by I.M. Pei, that was added in 1989. Some people like it a lot; others hate it. **WEB SITE** *www.louvre.fr/louvrea.htm*

Exploratorium, in San Francisco, California, is a place to learn about everything from frogs to earthquakes to space weather. Grope through darkness in the Tactile Dome, where the sense of touch is your only guide. There are "hands-on" exhibits in all areas of science, with plenty of things to look at, pick up, and tinker with. **WEB SITE** *www.exploratorium.com*

The Smithsonian Institution, in Washington, D.C. is not just one museum, but 18 museums, most of them located along the Mall in Washington. It's the biggest museum complex in the world, holding about 142 million objects, from First Ladies' dresses to the first airplane flown by the Wright Brothers. **WEB SITE** *www.si.edu*

The American Museum of Natural History, in New York City, dates back to 1869, and is the biggest natural science museum in the world. It has everything from different kinds of rocks and famous jewels to huge dinosaur skeletons, lifelike scenes of animals in different environments, and exhibits that show humans as they lived tens of thousands of years ago. They also have fun programs. "Adventures in a Global Kitchen" invites kids to eat crickets! **WEB SITE** *www.amnh.org*

MUSEUMS
of all kinds

World's Largest Toy Museum in **Branson, Missouri.** Here you can see thousands of toys, from every generation, some dating back as far as the early 1800s. There are G.I. Joe figures, lots of Star Wars toys, and dolls of every kind from Raggedy Ann to Barbie, as well as planes, train sets, cap guns, cars, tops, robots, board games, and more.

WEB SITE *www.worldslargesttoymuseum.com*

Children's Garbage Museum in **Stratford, Connecticut.** Here you can watch cans and newspapers get recycled. At the door when you come in there's a 30-foot-long "Trash-o-saurus" made out of a ton of trash, the amount the average person throws away each year.

WEB SITE *www.crra.org/pages/education.htm*

The International UFO Museum and Research Center in **Roswell, New Mexico,** is dedicated to research into UFOs, or "unidentified flying objects" from outer space. Some say that a UFO crashed in the nearby desert back in 1947. **WEB SITE** *www.iufomrc.com*

National Museum of Health and Medicine in **Washington, D.C.** Founded during the Civil War as the Army Medical Museum, it holds specimens for research in military medicine and surgery. One of the most popular exhibits has artifacts from President Lincoln's assassination, including the bullet. There is an exhibit on battlefield surgery and the world's largest collection of microscopes. **WEB SITE** *nmhm.washingtondc.museum*

The Mütter Museum in Philadelphia, Pennsylvania is filled with strange medical wonders. The fascinating but gross items on display include buttons, safety pins, and children's toys removed from people's stomachs, as well as preserved brains, tumors, and various body parts.

WEB SITE *www.collphyphil.org/muttvisi.htm*

There are many other kinds of museums, ranging from the Fairbanks (Alaska) Ice Museum (with 40,000 pounds of ice carved into many different sculptures) to the World Kite Museum and Hall of Fame in Long Beach, Washington. Don't forget the Cockroach Museum and Hall of Fame in Plano, Texas, where you can see live hissing cockroaches, plus dead ones dressed up as famous people.

Music & Dance

When was the electric guitar invented? ➡ page 134

TOP ALBUMS of 2005

1. *The Massacre* .... 50 Cent*
2. *Encore* .... Eminem*
3. *American Idiot* .... Green Day
4. *The Emancipation of Mimi* .... Mariah Carey
5. *Breakaway* .... Kelly Clarkson
6. *Love. Angel. Music. Baby.* .... Gwen Stefani
7. *Destiny Fulfilled* .... Destiny's Child ▶
8. *How to Dismantle an Atomic Bomb* U2
9. *Greatest Hits* .... Shania Twain
10. *Feels Like Today* .... Rascal Flatts

These albums contain explicit lyrics. Edited versions suitable for kids are widely available.

All About AMERICAN IDOL

In June 2002, *American Idol*'s first season began on the FOX network. On September 4, 2002, Kelly Clarkson became the first American Idol as 22.8 million viewers watched. Auditions for the sixth season are expected to be held between August and October, 2006.

The goal of the show is to find undiscovered talented singers, and give them a shot at fame. So far, it has worked out. Kelly Clarkson won two Grammys in 2006. Other winners or contestants like Bo Bice, Carrie Underwood, Ruben Studdard, Clay Aiken, and Fantasia Barrino have also made popular albums.

One surprising effect of the show is that one of the least talented singers has become one of the most famous. William Hung didn't make it into the top 12 contestants when he auditioned to be in the Season 3 show, but his accidentally comical interpretation of Ricky Martin's "She Bangs" made him so popular with viewers that he landed a record deal of his own, several TV commercial roles, and one movie acting job.

Who's Hot NOW

USHER

Born: October 14, 1978, in Chattanooga, Tennessee

Albums: *Usher* (1994), *My Way* (1997), *Live* (1999), *8701* (2001), *Confessions* (2004)

Usher is a record-breaking music star at the top of his game. In 2004, he had the No. 1 bestselling album, *Confessions*, and during 2005, that same album ranked as the No. 11 bestselling album. Also in 2005, Usher starred in a new movie, *In the Mix*, and was in production on another film due out in 2006, *The Ballad of Walter Holmes*.

Usher started his career at age 12, when he was spotted at a talent show by a record producer. At age 15, he released his self-titled first album, and shortly after graduating from high school, he recorded his second album, *My Way*, for which he wrote several of his own songs. Since then, Usher has been touring the world as a singer-songwriter, as well as performing on TV and in movies.

GWEN STEFANI

Born: October 3, 1969, in Anaheim, California

Albums: *No Doubt* (1992), *The Beacon Street Collection* (1995), *Tragic Kingdom* (1995), *Return of Saturn* (2000), *Rock Steady* (2001), *Love. Angel. Music. Baby.* (2005)

Gwen Stefani might never have become a singer if her brother hadn't invited her to join his band when she was 17 years old. The band, No Doubt, had a rocky start with their self-titled debut that didn't sell well. After a modest success with their next album, No Doubt made it big on their third try, with *Tragic Kingdom*. Gwen had written the songs "Don't Speak," "Just a Girl," and "Spiderwebs," which sent the album to the No. 1 spot on the Billboard charts.

In 2002, Gwen became a crossover hit when she collaborated with rapper Eve on the song "Let Me Blow Ya Mind," which won a Grammy for best Rap/Sung Collaboration.

In 2004, Gwen decided to do a side project on her own. She put together an album inspired by some of her favorite artists like Prince and Madonna. Hits like "What You Waiting For?" and "Rich Girl" made Gwen famous as a soloist. "Hollaback Girl," her third hit single from the album, was the first single ever to reach digital download sales of over one million!

Gwen is reportedly working on a new solo album due out in late 2006.

Musical Instruments

There are many kinds of musical instruments. Instruments in an orchestra are divided into four groups, or sections: string, woodwind, brass, and percussion.

PERCUSSION INSTRUMENTS Percussion instruments make sounds when they are struck. They include drums, cymbals, triangles, gongs, bells, and xylophones. Keyboard instruments, like the piano, are sometimes included in percussion instruments.

BRASSES Brass instruments are hollow inside. They make sounds when air is blown into a mouthpiece. The trumpet, French horn, trombone, and tuba are brasses.

WOODWINDS Woodwinds are cylindrical and hollow inside. They make sounds when air is blown into them. The clarinet, flute, oboe, bassoon, and piccolo are woodwinds.

STRINGS Stringed instruments make sounds when the strings are either stroked with a bow or plucked with the fingers. The violin, viola, cello, bass, and harp are used in an orchestra. The guitar, banjo, and mandolin are other stringed instruments.

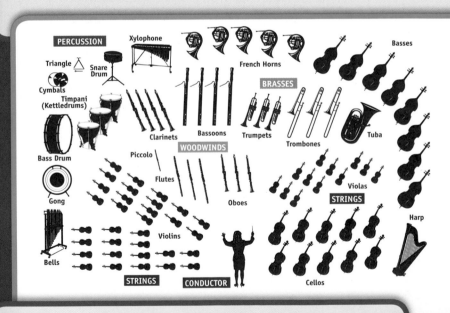

PERCUSSION — Xylophone — French Horns — Basses — Triangle — Snare Drum — Cymbals — Timpani (Kettledrums) — BRASSES — Bass Drum — Clarinets — Bassoons — Trumpets — Trombones — Tuba — Piccolo — WOODWINDS — Gong — Flutes — Oboes — Violas — STRINGS — Harp — Bells — Violins — STRINGS — CONDUCTOR — Cellos

OTHER MUSICAL INSTRUMENTS

There are more than 50 musical instruments native to Vietnam, including the Dan Nguyet, a two-stringed lute with a flat, circular body.

The Yoruba culture of Nigeria has a drum called a Iya'lu Dundun, which has bells and strings as well as a surface to strike with a stick.

The electric guitar was invented by George Beauchamp in the U.S. in 1931 and became popular by the 1950s.

How to **DANCE**

BALLET

Ballet has been performed for more than 500 years. Today, ballet is based on five basic positions. Try to do them yourself.

First Position   Second Position   Third Position   Fourth Position   Fifth Position

BREAKDANCING

Breakdancing can be done to any music with a strong beat. This dance form comes from the Bronx, New York, and became very popular during the 1980s. Try learning "The Worm."

1. Lie on your stomach in a push-up position, with your palms on the floor and legs together.

2. Lift up your legs high in the air, quickly, and as they come down, let your upper body and shoulders follow the motion, like a whip, rising, and then falling as well.

3. Repeat. When you get this right, you should look like an inchworm scooting along the ground.

HULA

The hula is the traditional dance of Hawaii. It was popular for centuries before it was banned by Captain James Cook, an English explorer who landed in Hawaii in 1778. However, the dance didn't die out, and is still popular today. The native Hawaiian language is still used to describe hula dancing. Here are a few steps:

Kaholo (also known as vamp): step to the right twice, bring your feet together, then step to the left twice, bring your feet together. Repeat.

Ami: rotate your hips counter-clockwise. Do not move your shoulders.

Ami Poe Poe: while doing the ami, keep your left foot in place, and rotate your whole body counter-clockwise by moving your right foot.

135

Mythology

What myth explains how the world was created by a god's vomit? ➡ page 139

MYTHS of the GREEKS

As the ancient Greeks went about their daily lives, they believed that a big family of gods and goddesses were watching over them from Mount Olympus. Farmers planting crops, sailors crossing the sea, and poets writing verses thought that these powerful beings could help or harm them. Stories of the gods and goddesses are called myths.

Some of the oldest myths came from the *Iliad* and *Odyssey*, long poems in Greek composed around 700 B.C.

After the Romans conquered Greece in 146 B.C., they adopted Greek myths but gave Roman names to the main gods and goddesses. Today, the other planets in our solar system are named after Roman gods.

GREEK & ROMAN GODS

The family of Greek and Roman gods and goddesses was large. Their family tree would have more than 50 figures on it. Here are some major gods. Those with * are children of Zeus (Jupiter).

Greek Name	Roman Name	Description
Aphrodite	Venus	Goddess of beauty and of love.
*Apollo	Phoebus	God of prophecy, music, and medicine.
*Ares	Mars	God of war; protector of the city.
*Artemis	Diana	Goddess of the Moon; a great huntress.
*Athena	Minerva	Goddess of wisdom and of war.
Cronus	Saturn	Father of Jupiter (Zeus), Neptune (Poseidon), Pluto (Hades), Juno (Hera), and Ceres (Demeter)
Demeter	Ceres	Goddess of crops and harvest, sister of Zeus (Jupiter).
*Dionysus	Bacchus	God of wine, dancing, and theater.
Hades	Pluto	Ruler of the underworld, brother of Zeus (Jupiter).
Hephaestus	Vulcan	God of fire.
Hera	Juno	Queen of the gods, wife of Zeus (Jupiter), goddess of marriage.
*Hermes	Mercury	Messenger god, had winged helmet and sandals.
Poseidon	Neptune	God of the sea and of earthquakes, brother of Zeus (Jupiter).
Zeus	Jupiter	Sky god, ruler of gods and mortals.

MAKING SENSE *of the* WORLD

Unlike folklore or fables, myths were once thought to be true. The Greeks and Romans explained many of the things in nature by referring to the gods. (So did other ancient peoples, such as the Egyptians and the Norse). To the Greeks a rough sea meant that POSEIDON was angry. Lightning was the work of ZEUS, ruler of the universe. The sun went across the sky because APOLLO was driving the chariot of the sun.

One of the most famous nature stories is about PERSEPHONE, or Proserpina, the daughter of Zeus and DEMETER. HADES, who fell in love with her, kidnapped her and carried her off to the Underworld (where people went after death). The gods asked Hades to bring her back, but while in the Underworld Persephone had eaten part of a pomegranate (the food of the dead), which meant she could not return. Eventually the gods worked out a deal. She could spend half of every year on Earth and half in the Underworld. When Persephone is on Earth, flowers bloom and crops grow, but when she is with Hades, plants wither and die. This is how the Greeks explained the seasons.

Statue of Poseidon

A famous place in ancient Greece was the TEMPLE OF APOLLO AT DELPHI. Inside it was a sacred stone that the Greeks believed to be the center of the world. The most important thing about Delphi, however, was its oracle. This was a priestess through whom, it was believed, Apollo spoke.

Greek & Roman HEROES

Besides the gods, Greek and Roman mythology has many stories about "heroes" who had superhuman qualities. They were somewhere between ordinary humans and full-blown gods. Often, a hero became famous for destroying some kind of monster:

- THESEUS went into the great maze known as the Labyrinth and killed the **Minotaur**, a man-eating creature with the head of a bull and the body of a man.

- PERSEUS cut off the head of **Medusa**, a terrifying woman who had snakes for hair and whose stare turned people to stone.

- BELLEROPHON, with the help of the famous winged horse **Pegasus**, killed the fire-breathing Chimaera.

Hercules

But the most popular hero was Herakles, or **Hercules**. ▶ The most famous of his deeds were his twelve labors. They included killing the **Hydra**, a many-headed monster, and capturing the horrible three-headed dog **Cerberus**, who guarded the gates of the Underworld. Hercules was so great a hero that the gods granted him immortality. When his body lay on his funeral pyre, Athena came and carried him off to Mount Olympus in her chariot.

137

NORSE MYTHOLOGY

You may never have heard of the gods and goddesses from Norse mythology, but you use their names all the time, in a way. Tuesday is named after the Norse god Tyr (later known as Tiw), Wednesday after Wodan (usually spelled Odin), Thursday after Thor, and Friday after Frigg and Freya. (Saturday is another story—you can look up the Roman god it was named after.)

Norse mythology was developed by peoples in far Northern Europe (Scandinavia). They sailed far from their homelands and carried their legends to Iceland, England, Germany, and the Netherlands.

The Norse myths tell us that the gods and goddesses live in the heavens in a place called **Asgard**, which is reached by a rainbow bridge. Other beings, such as giants, elves, and humans, have their own homes. The goddess Hel rules over **Niflheim**, the underworld or home of the dead. Humans live in **Midgard**, or Middle Earth. The end of the world, the myths say, will come in a great battle called **Ragnarök** (doomsday). In Asgard there is a great hall with a roof of shields, called **Valhalla**, where warriors killed in battle go. There they wait for the time when they will fight with Odin against the giants at the end of the world.

Major NORSE *Gods*

Name	Description
Odin	One-eyed king of the gods. God of war, death, poetry, wisdom, and magic.
Thor	Son of Odin. God of thunder, lightning, and rain.
Frigg	Wife of Odin. Goddess of marriage, motherhood, and the home.
Freya	Goddess of birth and of crops.
Tyr	Sky god and god of war and justice. His hand was bitten off by the wolf Fenrir.
Baldur	Son of Odin. God of light, purity, and beauty. Best loved of the gods.
Loki	Son of giants and father of Hel. Clever trickster who sometimes helped Thor and Odin and was sometimes their enemy.
Hel	Goddess of death. Daughter of Loki.
Heimdall	Son of nine giantesses. Watchman of the rainbow bridge. Known for his keen eyes and ears, he could hear grass growing.

MYTHOLOGY
Around the World

Every culture has myths, many of which explain how things came to be. These are called origin myths. Here are a few from around the world.

THE MYTH OF PAN GU

Where? *China and Southeast Asia*

How Old? *Three Kingdoms Period (220-265 A.D.)*

There was once a huge egg. Inside that egg was the first man, Pan Gu. After he broke out of the egg, Pan Gu was afraid that the two halves would join back together again and enclose him. So he separated the halves as far apart as he possibly could, and the upper half became heaven and the lower half became Earth. Pan Gu died 18,000 years later when he burst apart. At that moment, his left eye became the sun and his right eye became the moon. His hair changed into stars, his flesh into the ground, his bones into the mountains, and his blood into the oceans.

THE BUMBA MYTH

Where? *Boshongo Tribe in the Congo/Central Africa*

How Old? *Unknown*

In the beginning of time, the world was completely dark. The only thing that existed was water and the mighty god, Bumba. One day Bumba was plagued with a tremendous stomachache. Racked with pain, he vomited up the sun. The sun dried up some of the water, leaving vast areas of land. Still in pain, Bumba vomited again, spitting up the moon and the stars. Bumba kept vomiting, but this time it was living creatures—the leopard, the crocodile, the turtle, and so forth. The last living creature to come from his stomach was mankind.

THE RAVEN STEALS THE SUN

Where? *The Haida Tribe (Native American), in British Columbia*

How Old? *Unknown.*

Long ago, Gray Eagle was the guardian of the sun, moon, stars, fresh water, and fire. But he kept these things from the people and forced them to live in total darkness.

Gray Eagle had a beautiful daughter who the Raven—a handsome young male—fell in love with. One day the daughter invited the Raven to her father's house. Inside the house, the Raven saw what Gray Eagle had been hiding: the sun, moon, stars, fresh water, and fire and decided to steal these things and share them with the rest of the world. The Raven quickly flew into the dark sky and hung up the sun, the moon, and each of the stars. Then he flew over the earth and dropped all the water, creating the lakes, oceans, and the streams.

Nations

Which country is home to the Mosquito Coast? ➡ page 168

GOVERNMENTS & LEADERS

Among the world's 193 independent nations there are various kinds of governments.

Totalitarianism In totalitarian countries the rulers have strong power and the people have little freedom. Today, North Korea has a totalitarian government.

Monarchy A country with a king or queen can be called a **monarchy**. Monarchies are almost always hereditary, meaning the throne is passed down in one family.

Democracy The word **democracy** comes from the Greek words *demos* ("people") and *kratia* ("rule"). In a democracy, the **people** rule. Since there are too many people to agree on everyday decisions themselves, democracies nowadays are **representative** democracies; this means the people make decisions through the leaders they choose. In a democracy people can complain about the government and vote it out of office, which they often do. **Winston Churchill**, one of Britain's greatest prime ministers, probably had this in mind when he said, "Democracy is the worst form of government except for all those others that have been tried."

Female Firsts!

ELLEN JOHNSON-SIRLEAF, President of Liberia

In January 2006, Ellen Johnson-Sirleaf became the first female president of Liberia. She is also Africa's first elected woman leader. Earlier in her life, she was imprisoned and even forced to leave her country because of her political beliefs. However, she returned home in 1997, and Liberians hope that she will help rebuild their economy.

MICHELLE BACHELET, President of Chile

Michelle Bachelet was elected as Chile's first female president in January 2006. Her father was a general who opposed the dictator Augusto Pinochet in the 1970s. After her father died in prison, she and her mother were forced to leave the country. Bachelet became a medical doctor and returned to Chile in 1979. She has also held the positions of health minister and defense minister.

ANGELA MERKEL, Chancellor of Germany

Angela Merkel became Germany's first female chancellor (prime minister) in November 2005. She grew up in East Germany, and worked as a scientist. She joined the protests to end communist control of East Germany in 1989. After East Germany and West Germany reunified in 1990, she held many posts in government. She is the first person from the former East Germany to lead the reunified Germany.

A COMMUNITY of NATIONS

United Nations

The United Nations (UN) was started in 1945 after World War II. The first members were 50 nations that met in San Francisco, California. They signed an agreement known as the UN Charter. The UN now has 191 members—including Timor-Leste and Switzerland, both of which joined in 2002. Only two independent nations—Taiwan and Vatican City—are not members.

HOW THE UN IS ORGANIZED

▶ **GENERAL ASSEMBLY** **What It Does:** discusses world problems, admits new members, appoints the secretary-general, decides the UN budget. **Members:** all UN members belong to it; each country has one vote.

▶ **SECURITY COUNCIL** **What It Does:** handles questions of peace and security. **Members:** five permanent members (China, France, Great Britain, Russia, U.S.), each of whom can veto any proposed action; ten elected by the General Assembly for two-year terms. In early 2006 the ten were Argentina, Denmark, Greece, Japan, and Tanzania (terms ending Dec. 31, 2006) and Congo, Ghana, Peru, Qatar, and Slovakia (terms ending Dec. 31, 2007).

▶ **ECONOMIC AND SOCIAL COUNCIL** **What It Does:** deals with issues related to trade, economic development, industry, population, children, food, education, health, and human rights. **Members:** fifty-four member countries elected for three-year terms.

▶ **INTERNATIONAL COURT OF JUSTICE (WORLD COURT)** located at The Hague, Netherlands. **What It Does:** highest court for disputes between countries. **Members:** fifteen judges, each from a different country, elected to nine-year terms.

▶ **SECRETARIAT** **What It Does:** carries out day-to-day operations of the UN. **Members:** UN staff, headed by the secretary-general.

UN PEACEKEEPERS

The Security Council sets up UN peacekeeping missions to try to stop people from fighting while the countries or groups try to work out their differences. There were 15 peacekeeping missions operating around the globe in January 2006 such as one in southern Sudan and another in Kosovo. UN peacekeepers usually wear blue helmets or berets with white UN letters.

For more information about the UN, you can write to:
Public Inquiries Unit, United Nations, Room GA-57, New York, NY 10017
Website: www.un.org

Maps showing Nations of the World

AUSTRALIA · · · · · · · · · · · **142**
PACIFIC ISLANDS · · · · · **143**
NORTH AMERICA · · · · · **144**
SOUTH AMERICA · · · · · **146**
EUROPE · · · · · · · · · · · · · **148**
ASIA · · · · · · · · · · · · · · · · **150**
AFRICA · · · · · · · · · · · · · **152**

Maps showing the continents and nations of the world appear on pages 142-153. Flags of the nations appear on pages 154-177. A map of the United States appears on pages 286-287.

AUSTRALIA

- ✪ National Capital
- ★ State Capital
- • Other City

1:40,886,000

0   250   500 mi

0   250   500 km

Two-Point Equidistant Projection

©MAPQUEST.COM

PACIFIC ISLANDS

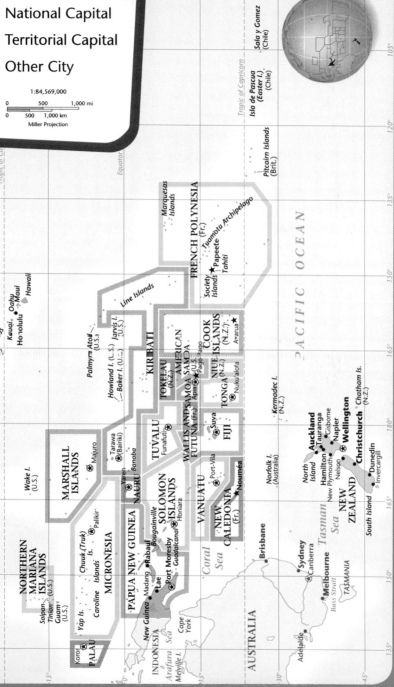

⊛ National Capital

★ Territorial Capital

● Other City

1:84,569,000

| 0 | 500 | 1,000 mi |
| 0 | 500 | 1,000 km |

Miller Projection

Sala y Gomez (Chile)

Isla de Pascua (Easter I.) (Chile)

Pitcairn Islands (Brit.)

Tropic of Capricorn

Marquesas Islands

FRENCH POLYNESIA (Fr.)

Tuamotu Archipelago

Society Islands ★ Papeete Tahiti

PACIFIC OCEAN

Line Islands

Kauai• Oahu Ho'olulu •Maui •Hawaii

Hawaiian Islands (U.S.)

Palmyra Atoll (U.S.)

Howland I. (U.S.) Baker I. (U.S.)

Jarvis I. (U.S.)

KIRIBATI

TOKELAU (N.Z.)

AMERICAN SAMOA (U.S.) Pago Pago

COOK ISLANDS (N.Z.)

★ Avarua

Wake I. (U.S.)

★ Tarawa (Bairiki)

WALLIS AND SAMOA FUTUNA (Fr.) ⊛ Apia

NIUE (N.Z.)

⊛ Nuku'alofa

Kermadec I. (N.Z.)

MARSHALL ISLANDS ⊛ Majuro

TUVALU Funafuti

Suva FIJI

Chuuk (Truk) Is. • Palikir

Yaren Banaba

Yap Is. Caroline Islands

NAURU

TONGA

Norfolk I. (Australia)

Chatham Is. (N.Z.)

NORTHERN MARIANA ISLANDS Saipan Tinian (U.S.) Guam (U.S.)

MICRONESIA

PAPUA NEW GUINEA Rabaul Bougainville

Madang Lae

New Guinea Port Moresby

SOLOMON ISLANDS Honiara Guadalcanal

VANUATU Port-Vila

NEW CALEDONIA (Fr.) Nouméa

North Island Auckland Hamilton Tauranga New Plymouth Nelson NEW ZEALAND South Island Dunedin Invercargill

Gisborne Napier ⊛ Wellington Christchurch

Koror PALAU

INDONESIA

Cape York

Brisbane

Sydney Canberra

Melbourne

TASMANIA

AUSTRALIA

Coral Sea

Tasman Sea

Arafura Sea Melville I.

Bass Strait

Adelaide

Equator

Tropic of Cap

NORTH AMERICA

⊛ National Capital

★ Territorial Capital

• Other City

1:39,978,000

0   350   700 mi

0   350   700 km

Azimuthal Equal Area Projection

ATLANTIC OCEAN

Bermuda (Brit.)

BARBADOS
GUADELOUPE (Fr.)
ANTIGUA & BARBUDA
DOMINICA
MARTINIQUE (Fr.)
ST. LUCIA
ST. VINCENT & THE GRENADINES
GRENADA
TRINIDAD & TOBAGO
Bonaire (Neth.)
Port-of-Spain

VENEZUELA

BRAZIL

COLOMBIA

ST. KITTS & NEVIS
VIRGIN IS. (U.S./Brit.)
PUERTO RICO (U.S.)
TURKS & CAICOS IS. (Brit.)
San Juan
Santo Domingo
HAITI
DOMINICAN REPUBLIC
Port-au-Prince
Curaçao (Neth.)
Aruba (Neth.)

Caribbean Sea

CUBA
Santiago de Cuba
Havana
CAYMAN IS. (Brit.)
JAMAICA
Kingston

Nassau
THE BAHAMAS

Panama City
PANAMA
COSTA RICA
San José
NICARAGUA
Managua
HONDURAS
Tegucigalpa
BELIZE
Belmopan
GUATEMALA
Guatemala City
San Salvador
EL SALVADOR

YUCATAN PENINSULA
Campeche
Mérida
Villahermosa
Tuxtla Gutiérrez
Oaxaca

Bay of Campeche

Gulf of Mexico

Straits of Florida

ATLANTIC OCEAN

MASS.
BOSTON
CONN.
R.I.
New York City
NEW JERSEY
DELAWARE
MARYLAND
Washington, D.C.
Baltimore
Philadelphia
PENN.
N.Y.
Richmond
VA.
W. VA.
N.C.
Raleigh
Charlotte
S.C.
Savannah
Jacksonville
GA.
FLA.
Tampa
St. Petersburg
Miami
Atlanta
Birmingham
ALA.
Mobile
New Orleans
Baton Rouge
LA.
Jackson
MISS.
Memphis
TENN.
Nashville
KY.
Louisville
Cincinnati
OHIO
Columbus
Cleveland
Pittsburgh
Buffalo
Rochester
Detroit
MICH.
Toronto
Ontario
Milwaukee
Minneapolis
WIS.
Lake Michigan
APPALACHIAN

UNITED STATES

Chicago
IND.
Indianapolis
ILL.
St. Louis
MO.
IOWA
Omaha
NEB.
Des Moines
KANS.
Wichita
Kansas City
OKLA.
Oklahoma City
ARK.
Little Rock
Shreveport
Dallas
TEXAS
Austin
San Antonio
Houston
Mississippi
Ohio
Platte
Arkansas
S. DAK.
Rapid City
Cheyenne
WYO.
Casper
Denver
COLORADO
Colorado Plateau
NEW MEXICO
Albuquerque
Santa Fe
El Paso
Ciudad Juárez
ARIZONA
Phoenix
Nogales
Mexicali
UTAH
Salt Lake City
Great Salt L.
NEVADA
Reno
Las Vegas
CALIF.
Sacramento
San Francisco
Fresno
Mt. Whitney 4,418 m. (14,494 ft.)
SIERRA NEVADA
Santa Barbara
Los Angeles
San Diego
Tijuana
Eureka
Boise
Snake
Pocatello
Great OREGON Plateau
COAST RANGES

PACIFIC OCEAN

Tropic of Cancer

Gulf of California

BAJA CALIFORNIA
La Paz
Mazatlán
Ciudad Obregón
Hermosillo
Chihuahua
Durango
Torreón
Monterrey
SIERRA MADRE ORIENTAL
SIERRA MADRE OCCIDENTAL
Culiacán

MEXICO

Mexico City
Guadalajara
León
San Luis Potosí
Puebla
Orizaba Pk. (18,405 ft.) 5,610 m.
Veracruz
Acapulco

Rio Grande

145

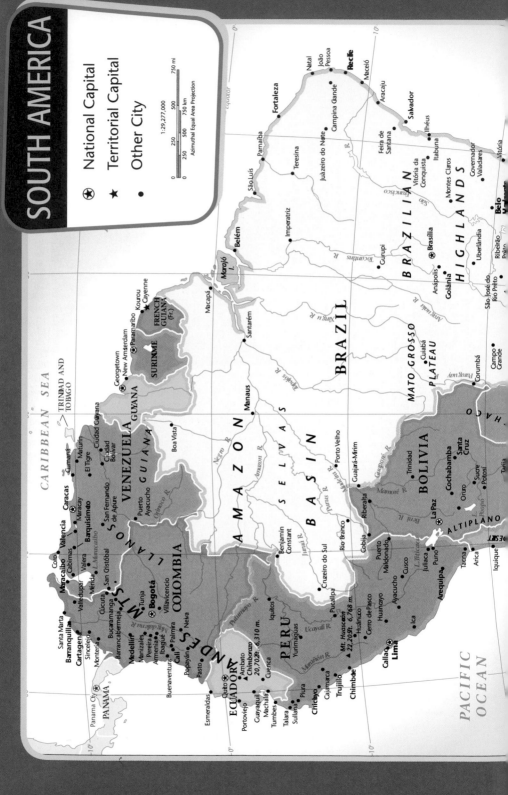

SOUTH AMERICA

⊛ National Capital
★ Territorial Capital
• Other City

1:29,277,000

0   250   500   750 km
0   250   500   750 mi

Azimuthal Equal Area Projection

CARIBBEAN SEA

PACIFIC OCEAN

Panama City ⊛ PANAMA

Santa Marta
Barranquilla
Cartagena
Sincelejo
Montería
Coro
Maracaibo
Cabimas
Valledupar
Valera
Mérida
Cúcuta
San Cristóbal
Bucaramanga
Barrancabermeja
Medellín
Manizales
Pereira
Armenia
Ibagué
Cali
Palmira
Popayán
Pasto

SANTA MARTA MTS.

COLOMBIA
⊛ Bogotá
Tunja
Villavicencio
Neiva

ANDES MTS.

Buenaventura

Esmeraldas
Quito ⊛ ECUADOR
Portoviejo
▲ Ambato
Chimborazo 20,702 ft. 6,310 m.
Guayaquil
Machala
Cuenca
Tumbes
Talara
Sullana
Piura

PERU

Loja
Chiclayo
Cajamarca
Trujillo
Chimbote ▲ Mt. Huascarán 22,205 ft. 6,768 m.
Huánuco
Callao ⊛ Lima
Cerro de Pasco
Huancayo
Ica
Ayacucho
Cusco
Juliaca
Puno
Arequipa
Tacna
Arica
Iquique

Valencia
Caracas ★
Maracay
Barquisimeto
San Fernando de Apure
Puerto Ayacucho

VENEZUELA

LLANOS

Maturín
El Tigre
Cumaná
Ciudad Guayana
Ciudad Bolívar

TRINIDAD AND TOBAGO

Georgetown ⊛
New Amsterdam

GUYANA

Paramaribo ⊛
SURINAME

Kourou
Cayenne
FRENCH GUIANA (Fr.)

GUIANA HIGHLANDS

Boa Vista

Orinoco R.

Negro R.

Amazon R.

AMAZON BASIN

SELVAS

Manaus

Santarém

Benjamín Constant

Cruzeiro do Sul

Rio Branco

Pucallpa

Iquitos

Yurimaguas

Puerto Maldonado

Guajará-Mirim

Riberalta

Cobija

Porto Velho

BOLIVIA

La Paz ⊛
ALTIPLANO
L. Titicaca
L. Poopó
Oruro
Cochabamba
Sucre ⊛
Potosí
Santa Cruz
Trinidad

CHACO

EAST

Marajó I.

Macapá

Belém

Imperatriz

São Luís

Parnaíba

Teresina

Fortaleza

Natal
João Pessoa
Recife
Maceió

Campina Grande

Juazeiro do Norte

Aracaju

Salvador

Ilhéus

Itabuna

Feira de Santana

BRAZIL

BRAZILIAN HIGHLANDS

Brasília ⊛

Gurupi

Anápolis

Goiânia

Uberlândia

São José do Rio Prêto

Ribeirão Prêto

Montes Claros

Governador Valadares

Vitória da Conquista

Vitória

Belo Horizonte

MATO GROSSO PLATEAU

Cuiabá

Campo Grande

Corumbá

equator

Ucayali R.

Marañón R.

Napo R.

Putumayo R.

Magdalena R.

L. Maracaibo

Xingu R.

Tapajós R.

Tocantins R.

São Francisco R.

Madeira R.

Purus R.

Juruá R.

Guaporé R.

Mamoré R.

Beni R.

Paraguay R.

Araguaia R.

146

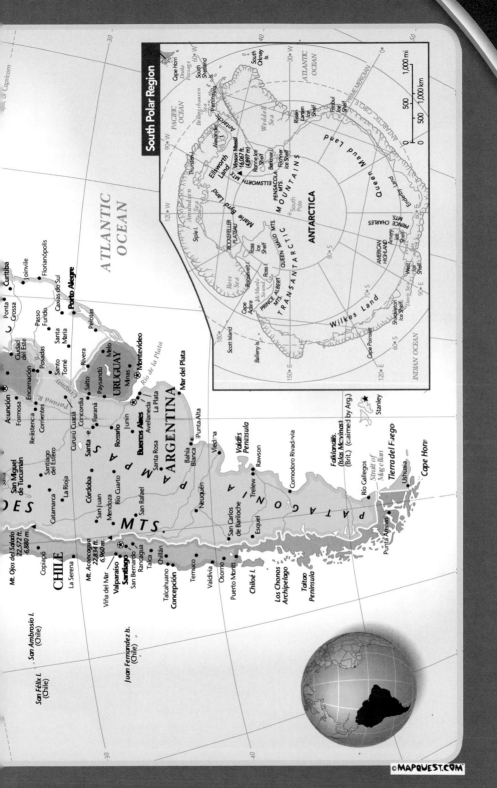

South Polar Region

©MAPQUEST.COM

ATLANTIC OCEAN

IRELAND

PORTUGAL

GREAT BRITAIN

SPAIN

MOROCCO

FRANCE

BEL. NETH. DEN.

GERMANY

NORWAY

SWEDEN

FINLAND

Murmansk

SWITZ.

E U R O P E

ESTONIA

Arkhangel'sk

St. Petersburg

ALGERIA

ITALY

AUS.

CZECH REP.

POLAND

LAT.

LITH.

Moscow

R U S S

TUNISIA

HUNG.

BELARUS

SERB. & MONT.

ROM.

MOL.

UKRAINE

URAL MOUNTAINS

Yekaterinburg

Chelyabinsk

Magnitogorsk

Omsk

Novosibir

ALB.

BUL.

Volgograd

Volga

Astrakhan'

LIBYA

GREECE

İstanbul

Black Sea

İzmir

Ankara ✪

TURKEY

Caspian Sea

Astana ✪

Pavlo

Mediterranean Sea

Tropic of Cancer

GEORGIA

Tbilisi ✪

ARMENIA

Yerevan ✪

KAZAKHSTAN

Karaganda

Semey (Semipalatinsk)

CYPRUS

Nicosia ✪

LEBANON

Beirut ✪

Tel Aviv

AZERBAIJAN

Baku ✪

Aral Sea

Lake Balkhash

CHAD

EGYPT

Jerusalem ✪

ISRAEL

SYRIA

Damascus ✪

Amman ✪

JORDAN

IRAQ

Tabriz

TURKMENISTAN

Ashgabat ✪

UZBEKISTAN

Bishkek ✪

Tashkent ✪

Almaty

KYRGYZSTAN

Kashi

Sinai

Baghdad ✪

Tehran ✪

Dushanbe ✪

Takla M Deser

SAUDI ARABIA

Al Basrah

Mashhad

TAJIKISTAN

A F R I C A

Red Sea

KUWAIT

Kuwait City ✪

Esfahan

IRAN

AFGHANISTAN

Kabul ✪

Islamabad ✪

Srinagar

XIZA (TIBI

Jeddah

Manama ✪

Shiraz

Kandahar

SUDAN

Mecca

Riyadh ✪

BAHRAIN

Kerman

Lahore

Amritsar

HIMALA

ERITREA

QATAR

Doha ✪

UNITED ARAB EMIRATES

Abu Dhabi ✪

PAKISTAN

Delhi ✪

NEPAL

Sukkur

New Delhi

Karachi

Muscat ✪

OMAN

Gulf of Oman

Hyderabad

Jaipur

Kanpur

Kathmande

Luckno

Gan

Sanaa ✪

Aden

YEMEN

ETHIOPIA

DJI.

Gulf of Aden

Ahmadabad

I N D I A

Nagpur

Socotra (Yemen)

Arabian Sea

Mumbai

Hyderabad

SOMALIA

Equator

Lakshadweep (India)

Bangalore

Chennai

Madurai

Kochi

SRI LANK

Colombo ✪

ishu

Male

MALDIVES

INDIAN

OCEA

ASIA

✪ National Capital

★ Territorial Capital

• Other City

1:51,084,000

0   500   1,000 mi

0   500   1,000 km

Two-Point Equidistant Projection

North Pole

CTIC
EAN

ARCTIC
OCEAN

*Chukchi
Sea*

*East
Siberian
Sea*

*Laptev
Sea*

B E R I A

Lena

ALASKA

*Bering
Sea*

Anadyr

KAMCHATKA
PENINSULA

Magadan

Petropavlovsk-
Kamchatskiy

*Sea of
Okhotsk*

Sakhalin

*Kuril
Islands
(Russia)*

Komsomolsk
na Amure

Khabarovsk

Blagoveshchensk

Sapporo

Bratsk

*Lake
Baikal*

Chita

Yakutsk

Irkutsk

Ulan-Ude

Harbin

Vladivostok

JAPAN

Sendai

Ulaanbaatar

Changchun

*Sea of
Japan
(East Sea)*

Tokyo

MONGOLIA

Shenyang

Pyongyang

N. KOREA

Yokohama

Kyoto

GOBI DESERT

Beijing

Hohhot

Dalian

Seoul

Kobe

Osaka

Tianjin

S. KOREA

Hiroshima

Jinan

Qingdao

Nagasaki

Taiyuan

*Yellow
Sea*

Lanzhou

Yellow (Huang)

Zhengzhou

Shanghai

HINA

CHINA

Xi'an

Nanjing

*East
China
Sea*

PACIFIC
OCEAN

Chengdu

Wuhan

Lhasa

Chongqing

Changsha

Wenzhou

Ryukyu Islands

Okinawa (Japan)

Yangtze (Chang)

Fuzhou

Kunming

Xiamen

Nanning

Taipei

TAIWAN

Guangzhou

Hong Kong

*Philippine
Sea*

Mandalay

Macao

Hanoi

*Gulf
of
Tonkin*

LUZON

MYANMAR
(BURMA)

LAOS

Mekong

Manila

PHILIPPINES

Yangon
(Rangoon)

Vientiane

Da Nang

THAILAND

VIETNAM

*South
China
Sea*

Cebu

MINDANAO

Bangkok

CAMBODIA

Davao

*Andaman
Sea*

Phnom
Penh

Ho Chi Minh City

*Sulu
Sea*

*Gulf of
Thailand*

Kota Kinabalu

Bandar Seri Begawan

*Celebes
Sea*

Manado

NEW GUINEA

Medan

BRUNEI

*Irian
Jaya*

Kuching

MALAYSIA

Kuala
Lumpur

BORNEO

SINGAPORE

*Banda
Sea*

*Arafura
Sea*

Singapore

SUMATRA

INDONESIA

Padang

Banjarmasin

*Java
Sea*

Makassar

*Timor
Sea*

Palembang

Jakarta

Surabaya

Dili

EAST
TIMOR

Bandung

JAVA

Kupang

AUSTRALIA

©MAPQUEST.COM

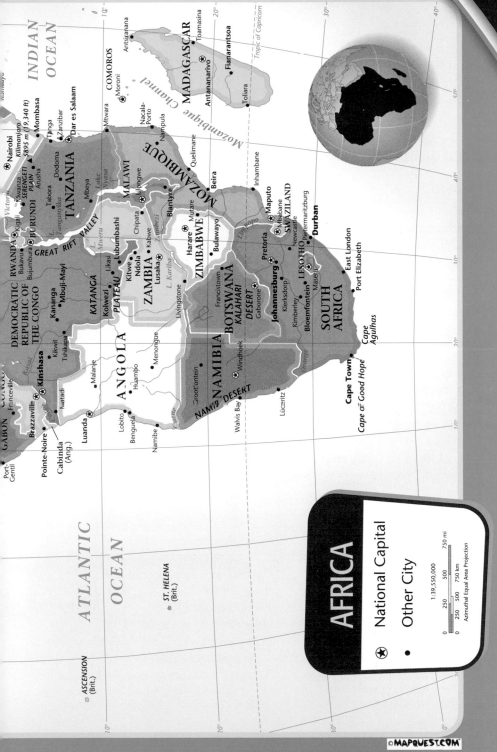

INDIAN OCEAN

COMOROS
Moroni

MADAGASCAR

Antsiranana
Toamasina

Antananarivo
Fianarantsoa

Toliara

Tropic of Capricorn

Mozambique Channel

Nairobi
Kilimanjaro
5895 m (9,340 ft)
Mombasa
Tanga
Zanzibar
Dar es Salaam

Mtwara
Nacala-Porto
Nampula

Kigali
Bukavu
Bujumbura
SERENGETI PLAIN
Mwanza
Arusha
Dodoma
Tabora
Mbeya

L. Victoria

RWANDA
BURUNDI

GREAT RIFT VALLEY

TANZANIA

MALAWI

Lilongwe

Quelimane

Beira

Inhambane

MOZAMBIQUE

L. Tanganyika
L. Mweru

Lubumbashi
Chipata
Blantyre

Lake Nyasa

Kananga
Mbuji-Mayi

Likasi
Kolwezi
Ndola
Kitwe
Lusaka
L. Kariba
Zambezi

KATANGA
PLATEAU

ZAMBIA

ZIMBABWE
Harare
Mutare
Bulawayo

Maputo
Mbabane
Newcastle
SWAZILAND
Pietermaritzburg
Durban

DEMOCRATIC
REPUBLIC OF
THE CONGO

Kilwit
Tshikapa

Francistown

Pretoria
Johannesburg
Klerksdorp
Kimberley
Bloemfontein
LESOTHO
Maseri

East London
Port Elizabeth

BOTSWANA
KALAHARI DESERT
Gaborone

SOUTH
AFRICA

Kinshasa
Matadi
Brazzaville

Menongue

ANGOLA

Malanje
Huambo

Grootfontein

NAMIBIA

Windhoek

Orange

Cape
Agulhas

GABON
Port-Gentil
Pointe-Noire
Cabinda
(Ang.)

Luanda
Lobito
Benguela

Namibe

Walvis Bay

NAMIB DESERT

Lüderitz

Cape Town
Cape of Good Hope

CONGO
Franceville

ATLANTIC
OCEAN

ST. HELENA
(Brit.)

ASCENSION
(Brit.)

AFRICA

⊛ National Capital

• Other City

1:39,550,000

0   250   500   750 mi
0   250   500   750 km
Azimuthal Equal Area Projection

153

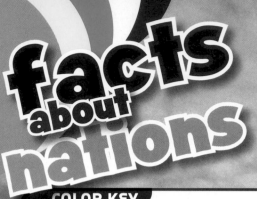

facts about nations

Here are basic facts about each of the 193 independent nations in the world. The color of the heading for each country tells you what continent it belongs in. The population is an estimate for mid-2006. The currency entry shows how much one U.S. dollar was worth in each country's currency as of early 2006. The language entry gives official languages and other common languages.

COLOR KEY

- Africa
- Asia
- Australia
- Europe
- North America
- Pacific Islands
- South America

Afghanistan

- **Capital:** Kabul
- **Population:** 31,056,997
- **Area:** 250,001 sq. mi. (647,500 sq. km.)
- **Currency:** $1 = 49.10 afghanis
- **Language:** Afghan Persian (Dari), Pashtu
- **Did You Know:** The national sport *buzkashi* is played on horseback and literally means "goat grabbing."

Albania

- **Capital:** Tirana
- **Population:** 3,581,655
- **Area:** 11,100 sq. mi. (28,748 sq. km.)
- **Currency:** $1 = 101.54 leke
- **Language:** Albanian, Greek
- **Did You Know:** In 2000, Tirana painted all the gray Communist-era buildings in the city in festive colors and patterns.

Algeria

- **Capital:** Algiers (El Djazair)
- **Population:** 32,930,091
- **Area:** 919,595 sq. mi. (2,381,740 sq. km.)
- **Currency:** $1 = 72.70 dinars
- **Language:** Arabic, French, Berber dialects
- **Did You Know:** Algeria's desert region contains large "sand seas" called *ergs* that have dunes up to 2,000 feet high.

Andorra

- **Capital:** Andorra la Vella
- **Population:** 71,201
- **Area:** 181 sq. mi. (468 sq. km.)
- **Currency:** $1 = .84 euros
- **Language:** Catalan, French, Castilian
- **Did You Know:** This tiny mountain nation's main sources of income are tourism and ski resorts.

Angola

- **Capital:** Luanda
- **Population:** 12,127,071
- **Area:** 481,354 sq. mi. (1,246,700 sq. km.)
- **Currency:** $1 = 80.18 kwanza
- **Language:** Portuguese, African languages
- **Did You Know:** Angola is the second largest oil-producer in sub-Saharan Africa after Nigeria.

Antigua & Barbuda

- **Capital:** St. John's
- **Population:** 69,108
- **Area:** 171 sq. mi. (443 sq. km.)
- **Currency:** $1 = 2.67 East Caribbean dollars
- **Language:** English
- **Did You Know:** Antigua and Barbuda were inhabited by the Carib Indians when Europeans arrived in the 17th century.

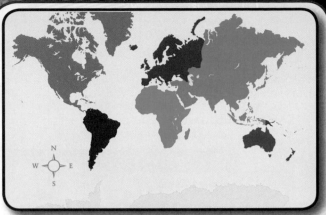

Argentina

- **Capital:** Buenos Aires
- **Population:** 39,921,833
- **Area:** 1,068,302 sq. mi. (2,766,890 sq. km.)
- **Currency:** $1 = 3.07 pesos
- **Language:** Spanish, English, Italian
- **Did You Know:** Argentina's central grasslands, called the "Pampas," are one of the world's largest cattle-producing areas.

Armenia

- **Capital:** Yerevan
- **Population:** 2,976,372
- **Area:** 11,506 sq. mi. (29,800 sq. km.)
- **Currency:** $1 = 439.50 drams
- **Language:** Armenian, Russian
- **Did You Know:** This nation has an average elevation of 5,900 feet, more than a mile above sea level.

Australia

- **Capital:** Canberra
- **Population:** 20,264,082
- **Area:** 2,967,909 sq. mi. (7,686,850 sq. km.)
- **Currency:** $1 = 1.35 Australian dollars
- **Language:** English, Aboriginal languages
- **Did You Know:** The Great Barrier Reef, running about 1,250 miles along Australia's coast, is the world's biggest coral reef.

Austria

- **Capital:** Vienna
- **Population:** 8,192,880
- **Area:** 32,382 sq. mi. (83,870 sq. km.)
- **Currency:** $1 = .84 euros
- **Language:** German, Serbian
- **Did You Know:** The composers Mozart, Strauss, Beethoven, Haydn, and Schubert all came to Vienna, which remains a center for classical music today.

Azerbaijan

- **Capital:** Baku
- **Population:** 7,961,619
- **Area:** 33,436 sq. mi. (86,600 sq. km.)
- **Currency:** $1 = 4,606 manats
- **Language:** Azeri, Russian, Armenian
- **Did You Know:** In ancient times, Azerbaijan was a major hub of the Great Silk Road between China and Italy.

The Bahamas

- **Capital:** Nassau
- **Population:** 303,770
- **Area:** 5,382 sq. mi. (13,940 sq. km.)
- **Currency:** $1 = .99 Bahamian dollars
- **Language:** English, Creole
- **Did You Know:** Christopher Columbus first landed in the New World on San Salvador, an island in the Bahamas.

facts about nations

Bahrain

- **Capital:** Manama
- **Population:** 698,585
- **Area:** 257 sq. mi. (665 sq. km.)
- **Currency:** $1 = .38 dinars
- **Language:** Arabic, English, Farsi, Urdu
- **Did You Know:** The four-lane King Fahd Causeway spans 16 miles, connecting the island of Bahrain to Saudi Arabia.

Bangladesh

- **Capital:** Dhaka
- **Population:** 147,365,352
- **Area:** 55,599 sq. mi. (144,000 sq. km.)
- **Currency:** $1 = 66.72 taka
- **Language:** Bangla, English
- **Did You Know:** From 1947 to 1971, Bangladesh was known as East Pakistan.

Barbados

- **Capital:** Bridgetown
- **Population:** 279,912
- **Area:** 166 sq. mi. (431 sq. km.)
- **Currency:** $1 = 1.99 Barbados dollars
- **Language:** English
- **Did You Know:** Barbados is named after the island's bearded fig trees (barbados means "bearded ones" in Spanish).

Belarus

- **Capital:** Minsk
- **Population:** 10,293,011
- **Area:** 80,155 sq. mi. (207,600 sq. km.)
- **Currency:** $1 = 2,154 rubli
- **Language:** Belarusian, Russian
- **Did You Know:** Belarus became independent when the Soviet Union broke up in late 1991.

Belgium

- **Capital:** Brussels
- **Population:** 10,379,067
- **Area:** 11,787 sq. mi. (30,528 sq. km.)
- **Currency:** $1 = .84 euros
- **Language:** Dutch, French, German
- **Did You Know:** Belgium's second largest city, Antwerp, has been a center for diamond-cutting since the 16th century.

Belize

- **Capital:** Belmopan
- **Population:** 287,730
- **Area:** 8,867 sq. mi. (22,966 sq. km.)
- **Currency:** $1 = 1.96 Belize dollars
- **Language:** English, Spanish, Mayan, Garifuna, Creole
- **Did You Know:** Belize's national motto is *Sub Umbra Florero*, which means "Under the shade, I flourish."

Benin

- **Capital:** Porto–Novo (constit.) Cotonou (admin.)
- **Population:** 7,862,944
- **Area:** 43,483 sq. mi. (112,620 sq. km.)
- **Currency:** $1 = 548 CFA francs
- **Language:** French, Fon, Yoruba
- **Did You Know:** The port city of Ouidah was a major center for the slave trade in the early 1700s.

Bhutan

- **Capital:** Thimphu
- **Population:** 2,279,723
- **Area:** 18,147 sq. mi. (47,000 sq. km.)
- **Currency:** $1 = 44.16 ngultrums
- **Language:** Dzongkha, Tibetan
- **Did You Know:** The government of Bhutan has stopped using Gross Domestic Product (a measure of economic output) as a measure of progress; it now measures "GNH" or Gross National Happiness instead.

COLOR KEY

- Europe
- Africa
- North America
- Asia
- Pacific Islands
- Australia
- South America

BRUSSELS, BELGIUM

Bolivia

- **Capital:** La Paz; Sucre (judiciary)
- **Population:** 8,989,046
- **Area:** 424,164 sq. mi. (1,098,580 sq. km.)
- **Currency:** $1 = 8.00 bolivianos
- **Language:** Spanish, Quechua, Aymara
- **Did You Know:** Bolivia and Paraguay are the only South American countries with no coastline.

Bosnia and Herzegovina

- **Capital:** Sarajevo
- **Population:** 4,498,976
- **Area:** 19,741 sq. mi. (51,129 sq. km.)
- **Currency:** $1 = 1.64 convertible marks
- **Language:** Bosnian, Croatian, Serbian
- **Did You Know:** There are three presidents of Bosnia and Herzegovina who rotate every eight months.

Botswana

- **Capital:** Gaborone
- **Population:** 1,639,833
- **Area:** 231,804 sq. mi. (600,370 sq. km.)
- **Currency:** $1 = 5.42 pulas
- **Language:** English, Setswana
- **Did You Know:** The Kalahari Desert, a land of bush and grasslands, covers 84% of this country.

Brazil

- **Capital:** Brasília
- **Population:** 188,078,227
- **Area:** 3,286,488 sq. mi. (8,511,965 sq. km.)
- **Currency:** $1 = 2.18 reais
- **Language:** Portuguese, Spanish, English
- **Did You Know:** Brazil is bigger than the 48 contiguous, or "touching," U.S. states.

Brunei

- **Capital:** Bandar Seri Begawan
- **Population:** 379,444
- **Area:** 2,228 sq. mi. (5,770 sq. km.)
- **Currency:** $1 = 1.62 Brunei dollars
- **Language:** Malay, English, Chinese
- **Did You Know:** This leading oil producer is located in the Pacific, not in the Middle East.

Bulgaria

- **Capital:** Sofia
- **Population:** 7,385,367
- **Area:** 42,823 sq. mi. (110,910 sq. km.)
- **Currency:** $1 = 1.63 leva
- **Language:** Bulgarian, Turkish
- **Did You Know:** Bulgaria has existed as a nation for more than 13 centuries.

Burkina Faso

- **Capital:** Ouagadougou
- **Population:** 13,902,972
- **Area:** 105,869 sq. mi. (274,200 sq. km.)
- **Currency:** $1 = 548 CFA francs
- **Language:** French, indigenous languages
- **Did You Know:** Since the government made them a protected species in the 1980s, the number of elephants in Burkina Faso has grown from 350 to as many as 5,000.

Burundi

- **Capital:** Bujumbura
- **Population:** 8,090,068
- **Area:** 10,745 sq. mi. (27,830 sq. km.)
- **Currency:** $1 = 971.50 francs
- **Language:** Kirundi, French, Swahili
- **Did You Know:** The Twa, a pygmy group (averaging about 5 feet tall), are thought to be the original inhabitants of Burundi.

facts about nations

Cambodia

- Capital: Phnom Penh
- Population: 13,881,427
- Area: 69,900 sq. mi. (181,040 sq. km.)
- Currency: $1 = 4,063 riels
- Language: Khmer, French
- Did You Know: A lake called the Tonle Sap expands from 1,200 to 3,000 square miles in area every year during the wet season.

Cameroon
- Capital: Yaoundé
- Population: 17,340,702
- Area: 183,568 sq. mi. (475,440 sq. km.)
- Currency: $1 = 547.98 CFA francs
- Language: English, French
- Did You Know: Cameroon has rain forests, sandy beaches, rolling savannas, volcanic mountain ranges, and over 200 ethnic groups in an area slightly larger than the state of California.

Canada
- Capital: Ottawa
- Population: 33,098,932
- Area: 3,855,103 sq. mi. (9,984,670 sq. km.)
- Currency: $1 = 1.15 Canada dollars
- Language: English, French
- Did You Know: The 2010 Olympic Winter Games will be held in Vancouver, British Columbia.

Cape Verde
- Capital: Praia
- Population: 420,979
- Area: 1,557 sq. mi. (4,033 sq. km.)
- Currency: $1 = 92.17 escudos
- Language: Portuguese, Crioulo
- Did You Know: These islands were uninhabited when the Portuguese arrived around 1460.

Central African Republic

- Capital: Bangui
- Population: 4,303,356
- Area: 240,535 sq. mi. (622,984 sq. km.)
- Currency: $1 = 547.98 CFA francs
- Language: French, Sangho
- Did You Know: Diamonds are the leading export of this developing nation.

Chad
- Capital: N'Djamena
- Population: 9,944,201
- Area: 495,755 sq. mi. (1,284,000 sq. km.)
- Currency: $1 = 547.98 CFA francs
- Language: French, Arabic, Sara
- Did You Know: Scientists believe Lake Chad once was roughly the same size as the Caspian Sea, the largest lake in the world at 144,000 sq. mi. but Lake Chad has shrunk down to 550 sq. mi.

Chile
- Capital: Santiago
- Population: 16,134,219
- Area: 292,260 sq. mi. (756,950 sq. km.)
- Currency: $1 = 526.70 pesos
- Language: Spanish, Indian languages
- Did You Know: Although separated by 2,300 miles of ocean, Easter Island, known for its giant Moai statues, has been a part of Chile since 1888.

China
- Capital: Beijing
- Population: 1,313,973,713
- Area: 3,705,407 sq. mi. (9,596,960 sq. km.)
- Currency: $1 = 8.06 yuan/renminbi
- Language: Mandarin, and many dialects
- Did You Know: At its peak in the 17th century, the Great Wall of China (actually a network of walls) extended some 3,700 miles.

Colombia

- **Capital:** Bogotá
- **Population:** 43,593,035
- **Area:** 439,736 sq. mi. (1,138,911 sq. km.)
- **Currency:** $1 = 2,258 pesos
- **Language:** Spanish
- **Did You Know:** This nation is the world's biggest source of emeralds.

Comoros

- **Capital:** Moroni
- **Population:** 690,948
- **Area:** 838 sq. mi. (2,170 sq. km.)
- **Currency:** $1 = 404.2 francs
- **Language:** Arabic, French, Shikomoro (a blend of Swahili and Arabic)
- **Did You Know:** Comoros is made up of mountainous islands of volcanic origin.

Congo, Democratic Republic of the

- **Capital:** Kinshasa
- **Population:** 62,660,551
- **Area:** 905,568 sq. mi. (2,345,410 sq. km.)
- **Currency:** $1 = 437 francs
- **Language:** French, Lingala, Kingwana, Kikongo, Tshiluba
- **Did You Know:** Rainwater drains into the Congo River from parts of seven different countries.

Congo, Republic of the

- **Capital:** Brazzaville
- **Population:** 3,702,314
- **Area:** 132,047 sq. mi. (342,000 sq. km.)
- **Currency:** $1 = 547.98 CFA francs
- **Language:** French, Lingala, Monokutuba, Kikongo
- **Did You Know:** Most people in the Republic of the Congo live in cities or towns; the rain forests there are largely uninhabited.

Costa Rica

- **Capital:** San José
- **Population:** 4,075,261
- **Area:** 19,730 sq. mi. (51,100 sq. km.)
- **Currency:** $1 = 499.40 colones
- **Language:** Spanish
- **Did You Know:** An early Spanish explorer gave Costa Rica its current name, which means "rich coast" in English.

Côte d'Ivoire (Ivory Coast)

- **Capital:** Yamoussoukro
- **Population:** 17,654,843
- **Area:** 124,503 sq. mi. (322,461 sq. km.)
- **Currency:** $1 = 548.05 CFA francs
- **Language:** French, Dioula
- **Did You Know:** This nation is the world's leading producer of cocoa beans.

Croatia

- **Capital:** Zagreb
- **Population:** 4,494,749
- **Area:** 21,831 sq. mi. (56,542 sq. km.)
- **Currency:** $1 = 6.15 kuna
- **Language:** Croatian, Serbian
- **Did You Know:** Croatia was part of Yugoslavia until declaring independence in 1991.

Cuba

- **Capital:** Havana
- **Population:** 11,382,820
- **Area:** 42,803 sq. mi. (110,860 sq. km.)
- **Currency:** $1 = 24.50 pesos
- **Language:** Spanish
- **Did You Know:** Cuban President Fidel Castro has ruled the country since 1959.

COLOR KEY

- Africa
- Asia
- Australia
- Europe
- North America
- Pacific Islands
- South America

facts about nations

Cyprus

- **Capital:** Nicosia
- **Population:** 784,301
- **Area:** 3,571 sq. mi. (9,250 sq. km.)
- **Currency:** $1 =.48 pounds
- **Language:** Greek, Turkish, English
- **Did You Know:** Cyprus is divided into Greek and Turkish areas.

Czech Republic

- **Capital:** Prague
- **Population:** 10,235,455
- **Area:** 30,450 sq. mi. (78,866 sq. km.)
- **Currency:** $1 = 23.84 koruny
- **Language:** Czech, German, Polish
- **Did You Know:** Except for adding more words, the Czech language has changed very little since the 16th century.

Denmark

- **Capital:** Copenhagen
- **Population:** 5,450,661
- **Area:** 16,639 sq. mi. (43,094 sq. km.)
- **Currency:** $1 = 6.25 kroner
- **Language:** Danish, Faroese
- **Did You Know:** Most of Denmark is located on a peninsula, but it also includes more than 400 islands.

Djibouti

- **Capital:** Djibouti
- **Population:** 486,530
- **Area:** 8,880 sq. mi. (23,000 sq. km.)
- **Currency:** $1 = 174.70 Djibouti francs
- **Language:** French, Arabic, Afar, Somali
- **Did You Know:** Two-thirds of the population of Djibouti live in the capital city.

Dominica

- **Capital:** Roseau
- **Population:** 68,910
- **Area:** 291 sq. mi. (754 sq. km.)
- **Currency:** 2.67 East Caribbean dollars
- **Language:** English, French patois
- **Did You Know:** Banana plantations are vital to Dominica's economy.

Dominican Republic

- **Capital:** Santo Domingo
- **Population:** 9,183,984
- **Area:** 18,815 sq. mi. (48,730 sq. km.)
- **Currency:** $1 = 34.55 Dominican pesos
- **Language:** Spanish
- **Did You Know:** The national music, Merengue, is a mix of African and Spanish styles.

Ecuador

- **Capital:** Quito
- **Population:** 13,547,510
- **Area:** 109,483 sq. mi. (283,560 sq. km.)
- **Currency:** $1 = 25,000 Ecuador sucre
- **Language:** Spanish, Quechua
- **Did You Know:** The equator passes through this small country whose name in English is "the Republic of the Equator."

Egypt

- **Capital:** Cairo
- **Population:** 78,887,007
- **Area:** 386,662 sq. mi. (1,001,450 sq. km.)
- **Currency:** $1 = 5.73 pounds
- **Language:** Arabic, English, French
- **Did You Know:** The 4,500-year-old Great Pyramid of Giza near Cairo is all that is left of the "Seven Wonders of the Ancient World."

COLOR KEY

- Africa
- Asia
- Australia
- Europe
- North America
- Pacific Islands
- South America

El Salvador

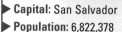

- **Capital:** San Salvador
- **Population:** 6,822,378
- **Area:** 8,124 sq. mi. (21,040 sq. km.)
- **Currency:** $1 = 8.75 colones
- **Language:** Spanish, Nahua
- **Did You Know:** This smallest of the Central American countries is the only one without a Caribbean coastline.

Equatorial Guinea

- **Capital:** Malabo
- **Population:** 540,109
- **Area:** 10,831 sq. mi. (28,051 sq. km.)
- **Currency:** $1 = 547.98 CFA francs
- **Language:** Spanish, French, Fang, Bubi
- **Did You Know:** Equatorial Guinea is the only country in Africa in which Spanish is an official languago.

Eritrea

- **Capital:** Asmara
- **Population:** 4,786,994
- **Area:** 46,842 sq. mi. (121,320 sq. km.)
- **Currency:** $1 = 15 nakfa
- **Language:** Tigrinya, Tigre, Kunama, Afar
- **Did You Know:** A mysterious language spoken by 3,000 Dahlak islanders was unknown to outsiders before 1996.

Estonia

- **Capital:** Tallinn
- **Population:** 1,324,333
- **Area:** 17,462 sq. mi. (45,226 sq. km.)
- **Currency:** $1 = 13.08 krooni
- **Language:** Estonian, Russian
- **Did You Know:** Estonia is about the size of Vermont and New Hampshire combined. In that small area, it contains over 1,400 lakes and 1,500 islands.

Ethiopia

- **Capital:** Addis Ababa
- **Population:** 74,777,981
- **Area:** 435,186 sq. mi. (1,127,127 sq. km.)
- **Currency:** $1 = 8.72 birr
- **Language:** Amharic, Tigrinya, Oromigna
- **Did You Know:** The 3.7-million-year-old skeleton of "Lucy," one of the earliest ancestors of modern humans, was found in Ethiopia.

Fiji

- **Capital:** Suva
- **Population:** 905,949
- **Area:** 7,054 sq. mi. (18,270 sq. km.)
- **Currency:** $1 = 1.73 Fiji dollars
- **Language:** English, Fijian, Hindustani
- **Did You Know:** Wearing a hat is a sign of disrespect in Fijian culture.

Finland

- **Capital:** Helsinki
- **Population:** 5,231,372
- **Area:** 130,559 sq. mi. (338,145 sq. km.)
- **Currency:** $1 = .84 euros
- **Language:** Finnish, Swedish, Russian, Sami
- **Did You Know:** Lapland in the north is home to the Saami (Lapps), traditionally a hunting, fishing, and reindeer-herding people.

France

- **Capital:** Paris
- **Population:** 60,876,136
- **Area:** 211,209 sq. mi. (547,030 sq. km.)
- **Currency:** $1 = .84 euros
- **Language:** French
- **Did You Know:** About one-fifth of the French people live in Paris or its suburbs.

facts about nations

Gabon

- **Capital:** Libreville
- **Population:** 1,424,906
- **Area:** 103,347 sq. mi. (267,667 sq. km.)
- **Currency:** $1 = 547.98 CFA francs
- **Language:** French, Bantu dialects
- **Did You Know:** Omar Bongo, who has been Gabon's president since 1967, is Africa's longest-serving head of state.

The Gambia

- **Capital:** Banjul
- **Population:** 1,641,564
- **Area:** 4,363 sq. mi. (11,300 sq. km.)
- **Currency:** $1 = 28.55 dalasi
- **Language:** English, Mandinka, Wolof
- **Did You Know:** One of the primary crops in the Gambia is peanuts, which are known as "groundnuts" there.

Georgia

- **Capital:** Tbilisi
- **Population:** 4,661,473
- **Area:** 26,911 sq. mi. (69,700 sq. km.)
- **Currency:** $1 = 1.81 laris
- **Language:** Georgian, Russian, Armenian, Azeri
- **Did You Know:** In 2004, the Georgian parliament adopted a new national flag.

Germany

- **Capital:** Berlin
- **Population:** 82,422,299
- **Area:** 137,847 sq. mi. (357,021 sq. km.)
- **Currency:** $1 = .84 euros
- **Language:** German
- **Did You Know:** Made up of many former principalities and kingdoms, Germany did not become a unified country until 1871.

Ghana

- **Capital:** Accra
- **Population:** 22,409,572
- **Area:** 92,456 sq. mi. (239,460 sq. km.)
- **Currency:** $1 = 9,068 cedis
- **Language:** English, Akan, Ewe, Moshi-Dagomba, Ga
- **Did You Know:** Before 1957, Ghana was part of the British Colony known as the Gold Coast.

Greece

- **Capital:** Athens
- **Population:** 10,688,058
- **Area:** 50,942 sq. mi. (131,940 sq. km.)
- **Currency:** $1 = .84 euros
- **Language:** Greek, English, French
- **Did You Know:** Ancient Greeks believed Mount Olympus (9,570 feet), the highest point in Greece, was the home of the gods.

Grenada

- **Capital:** Saint George's
- **Population:** 89,703
- **Area:** 133 sq. mi. (344 sq. km.)
- **Currency:** $1 = 2.67 East Caribbean dollars
- **Language:** English, French patois
- **Did You Know:** Grenada is the world's second-largest producer of nutmeg, after Indonesia.

Guatemala

- **Capital:** Guatemala City
- **Population:** 12,293,545
- **Area:** 42,043 sq. mi. (108,890 sq. km.)
- **Currency:** $1 = 7.59 quetzals
- **Language:** Spanish, Mayan languages
- **Did You Know:** There are 23 Amerindian dialects spoken in Guatemala.

COLOR KEY

- Africa
- Asia
- Australia
- Europe
- North America
- Pacific Islands
- South America

Guinea

- **Capital:** Conakry
- **Population:** 9,690,222
- **Area:** 94,926 sq. mi. (245,857 sq. km.)
- **Currency:** $1 = 4,280 francs
- **Language:** French, tribal languages
- **Did You Know:** Guinea has had only two presidents since 1958.

Guinea-Bissau

- **Capital:** Bissau
- **Population:** 1,442,029
- **Area:** 13,946 sq. mi. (36,120 sq. km.)
- **Currency:** $1 = 548 CFA francs
- **Language:** Portuguese, Crioulo, tribal languages
- **Did You Know:** At carnival time people here wear masks of sharks, hippos, and bulls.

Guyana

- **Capital:** Georgetown
- **Population:** 767,245
- **Area:** 83,000 sq. mi. (214,970 sq. km.)
- **Currency:** $1 = 189.50 Guyana dollars
- **Language:** English, Amerindian, Hindi
- **Did You Know:** Kaieteur Falls (740 feet) is one of the highest single-drop waterfalls in the world.

Haiti

- **Capital:** Port-au-Prince
- **Population:** 8,308,504
- **Area:** 10,714 sq. mi. (27,750 sq. km.)
- **Currency:** $1 = 43.60 gourdes
- **Language:** Haitian Creole, French
- **Did You Know:** Haiti gained independence from France in 1804 and, after the U.S., is the second oldest country in the Americas.

Honduras

- **Capital:** Tegucigalpa
- **Population:** 7,326,496
- **Area:** 43,278 sq. mi. (112,090 sq. km.)
- **Currency:** $1 = 18.84 lempiras
- **Language:** Spanish, Garifuna, Amerindian dialects
- **Did You Know:** Copán, once a center of the Mayan empire, is an important archaeological site in Honduras.

Hungary

- **Capital:** Budapest
- **Population:** 9,981,334
- **Area:** 35,919 sq. mi. (93,030 sq. km.)
- **Currency:** $1 = 209.43 forint
- **Language:** Hungarian (Magyar)
- **Did You Know:** Budapest was originally two separate cities, Buda and Pest. The two areas are separated by the Danube River.

Iceland

- **Capital:** Reykjavik
- **Population:** 299,388
- **Area:** 39,769 sq. mi. (103,000 sq. km.)
- **Currency:** $1 = 62.85 kronur
- **Language:** Icelandic (Islenska)
- **Did You Know:** The "Land of Fire and Ice" has more than 100 volcanoes and 120 glaciers.

India

- **Capital:** New Delhi
- **Population:** 1,095,351,995
- **Area:** 1,269,346 sq. mi. (3,287,590 sq. km.)
- **Currency:** $1 = 44.17 rupees
- **Language:** Hindi, English, Bengali, Urdu
- **Did You Know:** India has more people than the U.S., Indonesia, Brazil, Pakistan, and Bangladesh combined.

facts about nations

Indonesia

- **Capital:** Jakarta
- **Population:** 245,452,739
- **Area:** 741,100 sq. mi. (1,919,440 sq. km.)
- **Currency:** $1 = 9,185 rupiahs
- **Language:** Bahasa Indonesian, English, Dutch, Javanese
- **Did You Know:** This nation of 17,000 islands (6,000 inhabited) is home to the world's largest Muslim population.

Iran

- **Capital:** Tehran
- **Population:** 68,688,433
- **Area:** 636,296 sq. mi. (1,648,000 sq. km.)
- **Currency:** $1 = 9,112 rials
- **Language:** Farsi, Turkic, Kurdish
- **Did You Know:** Iran produces over a third of the world's pistachios—more than any other nation.

Iraq

- **Capital:** Baghdad
- **Population:** 26,783,383
- **Area:** 168,754 sq. mi. (437,072 sq. km.)
- **Currency:** $1 = 1,469 dinars
- **Language:** Arabic, Kurdish
- **Did You Know:** As of 2005, about 40% of the population of Iraq was age 14 or younger.

Ireland

- **Capital:** Dublin
- **Population:** 4,062,235
- **Area:** 27,135 sq. mi. (70,280 sq. km.)
- **Currency:** $1 = .84 euros
- **Language:** English, Gaelic
- **Did You Know:** The first known settlers at Dublin were Norsemen, or Vikings, who landed in the ninth century.

Israel

- **Capital:** Jerusalem
- **Population:** 6,352,117
- **Area:** 8,019 sq. mi. (20,770 sq. km.)
- **Currency:** $1 = 4.70 new shekels
- **Language:** Hebrew, Arabic, English
- **Did You Know:** Israel signed a peace treaty with Egypt in 1979, its first with an Arab nation.

Italy

- **Capital:** Rome
- **Population:** 58,133,509
- **Area:** 116,306 sq. mi. (301,230 sq. km.)
- **Currency:** $1 = .84 euros
- **Language:** Italian, German, French, Slovene
- **Did You Know:** The Renaissance, the 15th– and 16th–century revival of learning, began in Italy.

Jamaica

- **Capital:** Kingston
- **Population:** 2,758,124
- **Area:** 4,244 sq. mi. (10,991 sq. km.)
- **Currency:** $1 = 64.93 Jamaican dollars
- **Language:** English, Jamaican, Creole
- **Did You Know:** Jamaica's name comes from the Arawak Indian word Xaymaca, which means "isle of springs."

Japan

- **Capital:** Tokyo
- **Population:** 127,463,611
- **Area:** 145,883 sq. mi. (377,835 sq. km.)
- **Currency:** $1 = 117.96 yen
- **Language:** Japanese, Ainu, Korean
- **Did You Know:** The islands of Japan are very narrow. No part of Japan is more than 100 miles from the sea.

COLOR KEY

- Africa
- Asia
- Australia
- Europe
- North America
- Pacific Islands
- South America

Jordan

- **Capital:** Amman
- **Population:** 5,906,760
- **Area:** 35,637 sq. mi. (92,300 sq. km.)
- **Currency:** $1 = .71 dinars
- **Language:** Arabic, English
- **Did You Know:** The Dead Sea, on the Israel-Jordan border, is six times saltier than the ocean.

Kazakhstan

- **Capital:** Astana
- **Population:** 15,233,244
- **Area:** 1,049,155 sq. mi. (2,717,300 sq. km.)
- **Currency:** $1 = 132.05 tenge
- **Language:** Kazakh, Russian
- **Did You Know:** Baikonur Cosmodrome, the launching facility of the Russian Space Agency, is located in Kazakhstan.

Kenya

- **Capital:** Nairobi
- **Population:** 34,707,817
- **Area:** 224,962 sq. mi. (582,650 sq. km.)
- **Currency:** $1 = 70.95 shillings
- **Language:** Swahili, English
- **Did You Know:** Kenya's main port, Mombasa, was founded by Arab traders in the 11th century.

Kiribati

- **Capital:** Tarawa
- **Population:** 105,432
- **Area:** 313 sq. mi. (811 sq. km.)
- **Currency:** $1 = 1.35 Australian dollars
- **Language:** English, I-Kiribati
- **Did You Know:** Kiribati is a grouping of islands spread across an area of the Pacific Ocean about the same size as the continental U.S.

Korea, North

- **Capital:** Pyongyang
- **Population:** 23,113,019
- **Area:** 46,541 sq. mi. (120,540 sq. km.)
- **Currency:** $1 = 2.2 won
- **Language:** Korean
- **Did You Know:** North and South Korea have officially been at war for over 50 years. A ceasefire has maintained the peace since 1953.

Korea, South

- **Capital:** Seoul
- **Population:** 48,846,823
- **Area:** 38,023 sq. mi. (98,480 sq. km.)
- **Currency:** $1 = 966 won
- **Language:** Korean
- **Did You Know:** The martial arts form Taekwondo is Korea's national sport. It means "way of the foot and fist."

Kuwait

- **Capital:** Kuwait City
- **Population:** 2,418,393
- **Area:** 6,880 sq. mi. (17,820 sq. km.)
- **Currency:** $1 = .29 dinars
- **Language:** Arabic, English
- **Did You Know:** Women will be allowed to vote and run in parliamentary elections for the first time in 2007.

Kyrgyzstan

- **Capital:** Bishkek
- **Population:** 5,213,898
- **Area:** 76,641 sq. mi. (198,500 sq. km.)
- **Currency:** $1 = 41.4 soms
- **Language:** Kyrgyz, Russian, Uzbek
- **Did You Know:** The Manas, the Kyrgyz national epic, is thought to be the world's longest poem. The poem is more than half a million lines long.

SAVANNA IN KENYA

facts about nations

Laos

- Capital: Vientiane
- Population: 6,368,481
- Area: 91,429 sq. mi. (236,800 sq. km.)
- Currency: $1 = 10,157.55 kips
- Language: Lao, French, English
- Did You Know: Thousands of ancient stone jars can be found in Laos' Plain of Jars. Each jar is large enough to fit a person inside. Archaeologists are not sure who made them or why.

Latvia

- Capital: Riga
- Population: 2,274,735
- Area: 24,938 sq. mi. (64,589 sq. km.)
- Currency: $1 = .58 lat
- Language: Latvian, Russian, Lithuanian
- Did You Know: Festival sing-alongs are immensely popular in Latvia. Riga usually holds the largest annual gathering with over 30,000 dancers, singers, and musicians.

Lebanon

- Capital: Beirut
- Population: 3,874,050
- Area: 4,015 sq. mi. (10,400 sq. km.)
- Currency: $1 = 1,502 pounds
- Language: Arabic, French, English, Armenian
- Did You Know: Lebanon has been famous for cedar trees for over 4,000 years. The cedar even appears on the country's flag.

Lesotho

- Capital: Maseru
- Population: 2,022,331
- Area: 11,720 sq. mi. (30,355 sq. km.)
- Currency: $1 = 6.15 maloti
- Language: English, Sesotho, Zulu, Xhosa
- Did You Know: The Kingdom of Lesotho is completely surrounded by South Africa.

Liberia

- Capital: Monrovia
- Population: 3,042,004
- Area: 43,000 sq. mi. (111,370 sq. km.)
- Currency: $1 = 59 Liberian dollars
- Language: English, tribal languages
- Did You Know: Liberia was founded in 1822 by freed African American slaves from the United States. It became an independent republic in 1847.

Libya

- Capital: Tripoli
- Population: 5,900,754
- Area: 679,362 sq. mi. (1,759,540 sq. km.)
- Currency: $1 = 1.33 dinars
- Language: Arabic, Italian, English
- Did You Know: Libya was a colony of Italy from 1911 to 1943.

Liechtenstein

- Capital: Vaduz
- Population: 33,987
- Area: 62 sq. mi. (160 sq. km.)
- Currency: $1 = 1.30 Swiss francs
- Language: German, French
- Did You Know: Surrounded by Switzerland and Austria, which themselves also have no access to the sea, Liechtenstein is said to be "doubly landlocked."

Lithuania

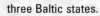

- Capital: Vilnius
- Population: 3,585,906
- Area: 25,174 sq. mi. (65,200 sq. km.)
- Currency: $1 = 2.89 litas
- Language: Lithuanian, Polish, Russian
- Did You Know: Lithuania is the largest of the three Baltic states.

Luxembourg

- **Capital:** Luxembourg
- **Population:** 474,413
- **Area:** 998 sq. mi. (2,586 sq. km.)
- **Currency:** $1 = .84 euros
- **Language:** French, German
- **Did You Know:** This country takes its name from a Roman castle on the Alzette River whose name, *Lucilinburhuc*, meant "Little Fortress."

Macedonia

- **Capital:** Skopje
- **Population:** 2,050,554
- **Area:** 9,781 sq. mi. (25,333 sq. km.)
- **Currency:** $1 = 51.55 denars
- **Language:** Macedonian, Albanian, Turkish
- **Did You Know:** Until 1913, Macedonia had been part of the Ottoman Empire for about 500 years.

Madagascar

- **Capital:** Antananarivo
- **Population:** 18,595,469
- **Area:** 226,657 sq. mi. (587,040 sq. km.)
- **Currency:** $1 = 2,160 ariary
- **Language:** Malagasy, French
- **Did You Know:** Madagascar, the world's fourth largest island, is home to about 90% of the known species of lemurs, and half the world's chameleons.

Malawi

- **Capital:** Lilongwe
- **Population:** 13,013,926
- **Area:** 45,745 sq. mi. (118,480 sq. km.)
- **Currency:** $1 = 128.22 kwacha
- **Language:** English, Chichewa
- **Did You Know:** Malawi means "flaming waters," and is named for the sun setting on Lake Malawi, the third largest lake in Africa.

Malaysia

- **Capital:** Kuala Lumpur
- **Population:** 24,385,858
- **Area:** 127,317 sq. mi. (329,750 sq. km.)
- **Currency:** $1 = 3.73 ringgits
- **Language:** Malay, English, Chinese dialects
- **Did You Know:** Malaysia's animal life includes elephants, tigers, and orangutans.

Maldives

- **Capital:** Male
- **Population:** 359,008
- **Area:** 116 sq. mi. (300 sq. km.)
- **Currency:** $1 = 12.58 rufiyaa
- **Language:** Maldivian, Divehi, English
- **Did You Know:** The capital island of this 1,190-coral-island nation is so overcrowded that a new artificial island is being created nearby to expand housing.

Mali

- **Capital:** Bamako
- **Population:** 11,716,829
- **Area:** 478,707 sq. mi. (1,240,000 sq. km.)
- **Currency:** $1 = 548.05 CFA francs
- **Language:** French, Bambara
- **Did You Know:** The city of Timbuktu was the center of the Mali empire in the 14th, 15th, and 16th centuries.

Malta

- **Capital:** Valletta
- **Population:** 400,214
- **Area:** 122 sq. mi. (316 sq. km.)
- **Currency:** $1 = .35 liri
- **Language:** Maltese, English
- **Did You Know:** Valletta is a 16th-century fortress-city built by the Knights of St. John.

COLOR KEY
- Africa
- Asia
- Australia
- Europe
- North America
- Pacific Islands
- South America

facts about nations

Marshall Islands

- **Capital:** Majuro
- **Population:** 60,422
- **Area:** 70 sq. mi. (181 sq. km.)
- **Currency:** U.S. dollar
- **Language:** English, Marshallese
- **Did You Know:** Bikini Atoll, where the first hydrogen bomb was tested, is located here.

Mauritania

- **Capital:** Nouakchott
- **Population:** 3,177,388
- **Area:** 397,956 sq. mi. (1,030,701 sq. km.)
- **Currency:** $1 = 266.60 ouguiyas
- **Language:** Hasaniya Arabic, Wolof, Pulaar
- **Did You Know:** About 40% of Mauritania's land area is covered by sand.

Mauritius

- **Capital:** Port Louis
- **Population:** 1,240,827
- **Area:** 788 sq. mi. (2,040 sq. km.)
- **Currency:** $1 = 30.10 Mauritian rupees
- **Language:** Creole, Bhojpuri, French
- **Did You Know:** The dodo became extinct here by 1681, 83 years after the Dutch arrived.

Mexico

- **Capital:** Mexico City
- **Population:** 107,449,525
- **Area:** 761,606 sq. mi. (1,972,550 sq. km.)
- **Currency:** $1 = 10.47 pesos
- **Language:** Spanish, Mayan dialects
- **Did You Know:** Before 1848, Mexico included the area now covered by Arizona, California, Nevada, New Mexico, western Colorado, Texas, and Utah.

Micronesia

- **Capital:** Palikir
- **Population:** 108,004
- **Area:** 271 sq. mi. (702 sq. km.)
- **Currency:** U.S. dollar
- **Language:** English, Trukese, Pohnpeian, Yapese
- **Did You Know:** Pohnpei is the largest of this nation's 600 islands. Its 133 square miles account for nearly half the total land area.

Moldova

- **Capital:** Chisinau
- **Population:** 4,466,706
- **Area:** 13,067 sq. mi. (33,843 sq. km.)
- **Currency:** $1 = 12.95 lei
- **Language:** Moldovan, Russian
- **Did You Know:** Grapes are a major crop in Moldova and winemaking is a major industry.

Monaco

- **Capital:** Monaco
- **Population:** 32,543
- **Area:** 1 sq. mi. (1.95 sq. km.)
- **Currency:** $1 = .84 euros
- **Language:** French, English, Italian
- **Did You Know:** Monaco is the most densely populated country in the world.

Mongolia

- **Capital:** Ulaanbaatar
- **Population:** 2,832,224
- **Area:** 603,909 sq. mi. (1,564,116 sq. km.)
- **Currency:** $1 = 1,224 tugriks
- **Language:** Khalkha Mongolian
- **Did You Know:** Mongolia is the most thinly populated country in the world.

Morocco

- **Capital:** Rabat
- **Population:** 33,241,259
- **Area:** 172,414 sq. mi. (446,550 sq. km.)
- **Currency:** $1 = 9.11 dirhams
- **Language:** Arabic, Berber dialects
- **Did You Know:** Casablanca is Morocco's largest city and main seaport.

Mozambique

- **Capital:** Maputo
- **Population:** 19,686,505
- **Area:** 309,496 sq. mi. (801,590 sq. km.)
- **Currency:** $1 = 25,020 meticals
- **Language:** Portuguese, native dialects
- **Did You Know:** The Chopi people who live here have orchestras of 30-50 different-sized *timbila*, which are xylophones.

Myanmar (Burma)

- **Capital:** Yangon (Rangoon)
- **Population:** 47,382,633
- **Area:** 261,970 sq. mi. (678,500 sq. km.)
- **Currency:** $1 = 6.42 kyats
- **Language:** Burmese
- **Did You Know:** More than 100 native languages are also spoken in Myanmar.

Namibia

- **Capital:** Windhoek
- **Population:** 2,044,147
- **Area:** 318,696 sq. mi. (825,418 sq. km.)
- **Currency:** $1 = 6.15 Namibian dollars
- **Language:** Afrikaans, English, German
- **Did You Know:** Until it gained independence from South Africa in 1990, Namibia was known as South West Africa.

Nauru

- **Capital:** Yaren district
- **Population:** 13,287
- **Area:** 8 sq. mi. (21 sq. km.)
- **Currency:** $1 = 1.35 Australian dollars
- **Language:** Nauruan, English
- **Did You Know:** Nauru is the smallest nation that holds regular elections (parliament).

Nepal

- **Capital:** Kathmandu
- **Population:** 28,287,147
- **Area:** 54,363 sq. mi. (140,800 sq. km.)
- **Currency:** $1 = 70.75 rupees
- **Language:** Nepali, many dialects
- **Did You Know:** Mt. Everest, the world's highest mountain, is partly in Nepal.

Netherlands

- **Capital:** Amsterdam
- **Population:** 16,491,461
- **Area:** 16,033 sq. mi. (41,526 sq. km.)
- **Currency:** $1 = .84 euros
- **Language:** Dutch
- **Did You Know:** Nowadays in the Netherlands, wooden shoes are worn mostly by farmers.

New Zealand

- **Capital:** Wellington
- **Population:** 4,076,140
- **Area:** 103,738 sq. mi. (268,680 sq. km.)
- **Currency:** $1 = 1.47 New Zealand dollars
- **Language:** English, Maori
- **Did You Know:** New Zealand was the first country to grant women full voting rights (in 1893).

Nicaragua

- **Capital:** Managua
- **Population:** 5,570,129
- **Area:** 49,998 sq. mi. (129,494 sq. km.)
- **Currency:** $1 = 17.23 gold córdobas
- **Language:** Spanish, Amerindian dialects
- **Did You Know:** The eastern shore is called Costa de Mosquitos (Mosquito Coast).

COLOR KEY
- Africa
- Asia
- Australia
- Europe
- North America
- Pacific Islands
- South America

THE TEMPLE OF THE INSCRIPTIONS, MAYAN RUINS OF PALENQUE, MEXICO

facts about nations

Niger

- **Capital:** Niamey
- **Population:** 12,525,094
- **Area:** 489,192 sq. mi. (1,267,001 sq. km.)
- **Currency:** $1 = 548.05 CFA francs
- **Language:** French, Hausa, Djerma, Fulani
- **Did You Know:** Temperatures can exceed 122° F in the hot season, which lasts from March to June.

Nigeria

- **Capital:** Abuja
- **Population:** 131,859,731
- **Area:** 356,669 sq. mi. (923,768 sq. km.)
- **Currency:** $1 = 128.50 nairas
- **Language:** English, Hausa, Yoruba, Ibo
- **Did You Know:** Nigeria is the biggest oil-producing country in Africa.

Norway

- **Capital:** Oslo
- **Population:** 4,610,820
- **Area:** 125,182 sq. mi. (324,220 sq. km.)
- **Currency:** $1 = 6.72 kroner
- **Language:** Norwegian, Sami, Finnish
- **Did You Know:** Norway is known for its many *fjords*—deep inlets with steep slopes that run up and down its coast.

Oman

- **Capital:** Muscat
- **Population:** 3,102,229
- **Area:** 82,031 sq. mi. (212,460 sq. km.)
- **Currency:** $1 = 0.39 rials
- **Language:** Arabic, English, Indian dialects
- **Did You Know:** The Arabian Oryx Sanctuary, which protects the endangered antelope, covers over a tenth of Oman's territory.

Pakistan

- **Capital:** Islamabad
- **Population:** 165,803,560
- **Area:** 310,403 sq. mi. (803,940 sq. km.)
- **Currency:** $1 = 59.82 rupees
- **Language:** Urdu, English, Punjabi, Sindhi
- **Did You Know:** Pakistan is mostly (97%) Muslim; its neighbor India is mostly Hindu (82%).

Palau

- **Capital:** Koror
- **Population:** 20,579
- **Area:** 177 sq. mi. (458 sq. km.)
- **Currency:** U.S. dollar
- **Language:** English, Palauan
- **Did You Know:** The islands of Palau are old coral reefs that have risen above the sea.

Panama

- **Capital:** Panama City
- **Population:** 3,191,319
- **Area:** 30,193 sq. mi. (78,200 sq. km.)
- **Currency:** $1 = 1 balboa
- **Language:** Spanish, English
- **Did You Know:** It takes 8 to 10 hours for a ship to travel through the 50-mile Panama Canal from the Caribbean Sea to the Pacific Ocean.

Papua New Guinea

- **Capital:** Port Moresby
- **Population:** 5,670,544
- **Area:** 178,704 sq. mi. (462,840 sq. km.)
- **Currency:** $1 = 3.01 kinas
- **Language:** English, Motu
- **Did You Know:** Papua New Guinea takes up the eastern half of New Guinea, the world's second largest island after Greenland.

COLOR KEY

- ● Africa
- ● Asia
- ● Australia
- ● Europe
- ● North America
- ● Pacific Islands
- ● South America

**CUPOLAS OF THE CHAPEL
OF CHRIST IN THE KREMLIN,
MOSCOW, RUSSIA**

Paraguay

- **Capital:** Asunción
- **Population:** 6,506,464
- **Area:** 157,047 sq. mi. (406,750 sq. km.)
- **Currency:** $1 = 6,130 guarani
- **Language:** Spanish, Guarani
- **Did You Know:** The capital of this landlocked South American nation is a port with access to the Atlantic Ocean through a system of rivers.

Peru

- **Capital:** Lima
- **Population:** 28,302,603
- **Area:** 496,226 sq. mi. (1,285,220 sq. km.)
- **Currency:** $1 = 3.29 nuevos soles
- **Language:** Spanish, Quechua, Aymara
- **Did You Know:** Scientists recently traced the origins of all the world's farmed potatoes to southern Peru.

Philippines

- **Capital:** Manila
- **Population:** 89,468,677
- **Area:** 115,831 sq. mi. (300,000 sq. km.)
- **Currency:** $1 = 51.61 pesos
- **Language:** Filipino, English
- **Did You Know:** The Philippines consist of about 7,100 islands, but most of the people live on one of the 11 largest islands.

Poland

- **Capital:** Warsaw
- **Population:** 38,536,869
- **Area:** 120,728 sq. mi. (312,685 sq. km.)
- **Currency:** $1 = 3.20 zlotych
- **Language:** Polish, Ukrainian, German
- **Did You Know:** In the 1500s, Poland was the largest country in Europe.

Portugal

- **Capital:** Lisbon
- **Population:** 10,605,870
- **Area:** 35,672 sq. mi. (92,391 sq. km.)
- **Currency:** $1 = .84 euros
- **Language:** Portuguese
- **Did You Know:** In 1497, a Portuguese captain, Vasco da Gama, became the first person to sail around the tip of Africa and into the Indian Ocean.

Qatar

- **Capital:** Doha
- **Population:** 885,359
- **Area:** 4,416 sq. mi. (11,437 sq. km.)
- **Currency:** $1 = 3.64 riyals
- **Language:** Arabic, English
- **Did You Know:** Workers from South Asia and other Arab states outnumber the citizens of Qatar by more than three to one.

Romania

- **Capital:** Bucharest
- **Population:** 22,303,552
- **Area:** 91,699 sq. mi. (237,500 sq. km.)
- **Currency:** $1 = 3.00 new lei
- **Language:** Romanian, Hungarian
- **Did You Know:** The coastal city of Varna, Romania's third largest, was founded by the Greeks in the sixth century.

Russia

- **Capital:** Moscow
- **Population:** 142,893,540
- **Area:** 6,592,772 sq. mi. (17,075,201 sq. km.)
- **Currency:** $1 = 28.28 rubles
- **Language:** Russian, many others
- **Did You Know:** The Trans-Siberian Railroad is the world's longest line, stretching over 5,000 miles from Moscow to Vladivostok.

facts about nations

Rwanda

- **Capital:** Kigali
- **Population:** 8,648,248
- **Area:** 10,169 sq. mi. (26,338 sq. km.)
- **Currency:** $1 = 540.66 francs
- **Language:** French, English, Kinyarwanda
- **Did You Know:** The source of the Nile River is located in Rwanda.

Saint Kitts and Nevis

- **Capital:** Basseterre
- **Population:** 39,129
- **Area:** 101 sq. mi. (261 sq. km.)
- **Currency:** $1 = 2.67 East Caribbean dollars
- **Language:** English
- **Did You Know:** St. Kitts was the first island in the West Indies settled by the British, in 1623.

Saint Lucia

- **Capital:** Castries
- **Population:** 168,458
- **Area:** 238 sq. mi. (616 sq. km.)
- **Currency:** $1 = 2.67 East Caribbean dollars
- **Language:** English, French patois
- **Did You Know:** The island has switched hands between the British and French 14 times.

Saint Vincent and the Grenadines

- **Capital:** Kingstown
- **Population:** 117,848
- **Area:** 150 sq. mi. (389 sq. km.)
- **Currency:** $1 = 2.67 East Caribbean dollars
- **Language:** English, French patois
- **Did You Know:** The deadly Soufriere volcano on St. Vincent last erupted in 1979.

COLOR KEY

- Africa
- Asia
- Australia
- Europe
- North America
- Pacific Islands
- South America

Samoa (formerly Western Samoa)

- **Capital:** Apia
- **Population:** 176,908
- **Area:** 1,137 sq. mi. (2,944 sq. km.)
- **Currency:** $1 = 2.75 tala
- **Language:** English, Samoan
- **Did You Know:** Most Samoans live in small seashore villages of 100 to 500 people.

San Marino

- **Capital:** San Marino
- **Population:** 29,251
- **Area:** 24 sq. mi. (61 sq. km.)
- **Currency:** $1 = .84 euros ▶**Language:** Italian
- **Did You Know:** San Marino claims to be Europe's oldest country, founded in AD 301.

São Tomé and Príncipe

- **Capital:** São Tomé
- **Population:** 193,413
- **Area:** 386 sq. mi. (1,001 sq. km.)
- **Currency:** $1 = 7,098 dobras
- **Language:** Portuguese, Creole, Fang
- **Did You Know:** Cocoa makes up about 95 percent of all the country's exports.

Saudi Arabia

- **Capital:** Riyadh
- **Population:** 27,019,731
- **Area:** 756,985 sq. mi. (1,960,582 sq. km.)
- **Currency:** $1 = 3.75 riyals ▶**Language:** Arabic
- **Did You Know:** Mecca, the birthplace of Muhammad, is the holiest city of Islam.

Senegal

- **Capital:** Dakar
- **Population:** 11,987,121
- **Area:** 75,749 sq. mi. (196,190 sq. km.)
- **Currency:** $1 = 548 CFA francs
- **Language:** French, Wolof, Pulaar
- **Did You Know:** The capital city, Dakar, is the westernmost point in Africa.

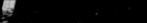

Serbia and Montenegro

- **Capital:** Belgrade
- **Population:** 10,832,545
- **Area:** 39,518 sq. mi. (102,350 sq. km.)
- **Currency:** $1 = 73.14 new dinars
- **Language:** Serbian, Albanian
- **Did You Know:** Ruins of the Roman town of Singidunum can still be seen in Belgrade.

Seychelles

- **Capital:** Victoria
- **Population:** 81,541
- **Area:** 176 sq. mi. (455 sq. km.)
- **Currency:** $1 = 5.19 rupees
- **Language:** English, French, Creole
- **Did You Know:** These islands were uninhabited when ships sailing for the British East India Company landed in 1609.

Sierra Leone
- **Capital:** Freetown
- **Population:** 6,005,250
- **Area:** 27,699 sq. mi. (71,740 sq. km.)
- **Currency:** $1 = 2,350 leones
- **Language:** English, Mende, Temne, Krio
- **Did You Know:** Portuguese explorer Pedro da Cintra called the area Serra Layoa, "Lion Mountains," in 1460.

Singapore
- **Capital:** Singapore
- **Population:** 4,492,150
- **Area:** 267 sq. mi. (693 sq. km.)
- **Currency:** $1 = 1.63 Singapore dollars
- **Language:** Chinese, Malay, Tamil, English
- **Did You Know:** Singapore is the world's second most densely populated country after Monaco.

Slovakia

- **Capital:** Bratislava
- **Population:** 5,439,448
- **Area:** 18,859 sq. mi. (48,845 sq. km.)
- **Currency:** $1 = 31.55 koruny
- **Language:** Slovak, Hungarian
- **Did You Know:** At many schools, students store their shoes in their school lockers and wear slippers to class.

Slovenia
- **Capital:** Ljubljana
- **Population:** 2,010,347
- **Area:** 7,827 sq. mi. (20,273 sq. km.)
- **Currency:** $1 = 200.10 tolars
- **Language:** Slovenian, Serbo-Croatian
- **Did You Know:** Slovenia has more than a thousand underground caves formed in rocky areas known as *karsts*.

Solomon Islands
- **Capital:** Honiara
- **Population:** 552,438
- **Area:** 10,985 sq. mi. (28,450 sq. km.)
- **Currency:** $1 = 7.33 Solomon Islands dollars
- **Language:** English, Melanesian
- **Did You Know:** Guadalcanal, one of the Solomon Islands, was the site of a key World War II battle.

Somalia
- **Capital:** Mogadishu
- **Population:** 8,863,338
- **Area:** 246,201 sq. mi. (637,657 sq. km.)
- **Currency:** $1 = 1,592 shillings
- **Language:** Somali, Arabic, Italian, English
- **Did You Know:** Iman, a supermodel from Somalia, speaks five languages and studied political science in college.

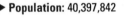

facts about nations

South Africa

- **Capital:** Pretoria (admin.)
  Cape Town (legisl.)
  Bloemfontein (judicial)
- **Population:** 44,187,637
- **Area:** 471,011 sq. mi. (1,219,912 sq. km.)
- **Currency:** $1 = 6.15 rand
- **Language:** Afrikaans, English, Ndebele, Sotho
- **Did You Know:** South Africa has 11 official languages; 9 of them are native.

Spain

- **Capital:** Madrid
- **Population:** 40,397,842
- **Area:** 194,897 sq. mi. (504,782 sq. km.)
- **Currency:** $1 = .84 euros
- **Language:** Castilian Spanish, Catalan, Galician
- **Did You Know:** Spain produces and exports the most olives and olive oil in the world.

Sri Lanka

- **Capital:** Colombo
- **Population:** 20,222,240
- **Area:** 25,332 sq. mi. (65,610 sq. km.)
- **Currency:** $1 = 102.03 rupees
- **Language:** Sinhala, Tamil, English
- **Did You Know:** In 1960, Sri Lanka chose the world's first elected female prime minister.

Sudan

- **Capital:** Khartoum
- **Population:** 41,236,378
- **Area:** 967,499 sq. mi. (2,505,810 sq. km.)
- **Currency:** $1 =250.07 dinars
- **Language:** Arabic, Nubian, Ta Bedawie
- **Did You Know:** Sudan is the largest country in Africa in total area, while Algeria is the largest in land area.

Suriname

- **Capital:** Paramaribo
- **Population:** 439,117
- **Area:** 63,039 sq. mi. (163,270 sq. km.)
- **Currency:** $1 = 2.74 Suriname dollars
- **Language:** Dutch, Sranang Tongo
- **Did You Know:** In 1677, Britain "traded" Suriname to the Dutch for New York City.

Swaziland

- **Capital:** Mbabane
- **Population:** 1,136,334
- **Area:** 6,704 sq. mi. (17,363 sq. km.)
- **Currency:** $1 = 6.08 lilangeni
- **Language:** English, siSwati
- **Did You Know:** Swaziland is the smallest country in Africa.

Sweden

- **Capital:** Stockholm
- **Population:** 9,016,596
- **Area:** 173,732 sq. mi. (449,964 sq. km.)
- **Currency:** $1 = 7.78 kronor
- **Language:** Swedish, Sami, Finnish
- **Did You Know:** In 1910, Sweden created Europe's first national park. In all, some 7,700 square miles of land are now preserved.

Switzerland

- **Capital:** Bern (admin.)
  Lausanne (judicial)
- **Population:** 7,523,934
- **Area:** 15,942 sq. mi. (41,290 sq. km.)
- **Currency:** $1 = 1.30 Swiss francs
- **Language:** German, French, Italian, Romansch
- **Did You Know:** Though it is home to the European headquarters of the United Nations, Switzerland did not join the UN until 2002.

Syria

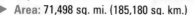

- Capital: Damascus
- Population: 18,881,361
- Area: 71,498 sq. mi. (185,180 sq. km.)
- Currency: $1 = 51.92 pounds
- Language: Arabic, Kurdish, Armenian
- Did You Know: Tablets found in Ugarit contain one of the world's oldest alphabets dating back to around 1400 BC.

Taiwan

- Capital: Taipei
- Population: 23,036,087
- Area: 13,892 sq. mi. (35,980 sq. km.)
- Currency: $1 = 32.18 Taiwan new dollars
- Language: Mandarin Chinese, Taiwanese
- Did You Know: Taipei 101, the world's tallest building, is 1,670 feet tall.

Tajikistan

- Capital: Dushanbe
- Population: 7,320,815
- Area: 55,251 sq. mi. (143,100 sq. km.)
- Currency: $1 = 2.79 somoni
- Language: Tajik, Russia
- Did You Know: Dust can take up to 10 days to settle after a strong dust storm here.

Tanzania

- Capital: Dar-es-Salaam
- Population: 37,445,392
- Area: 364,900 sq. mi. (945,087 sq. km.)
- Currency: $1 = 1,129 shillings
- Language: Swahili, English, Arabic
- Did You Know: Tanganyika and Zanzibar joined to form Tanzania in 1964.

Thailand

- Capital: Bangkok
- Population: 64,631,595
- Area: 198,457 sq. mi. (514,000 sq. km.)
- Currency: $1 = 39.51 baht
- Language: Thai, English
- Did You Know: Thailand is one of the world's largest tin producers and a major source of rubies and sapphires.

Timor-Leste (East Timor)

- Capital: Dili
- Population: 1,062,777
- Area: 5,794 sq. mi. (15,007 sq. km.)
- Currency: U.S. Dollar
- Language: Tetum, Portuguese, Indonesian, English
- Did You Know: Timor-Leste is the youngest nation in the world. It became independent on May 20, 2002.

Togo

- Capital: Lomé
- Population: 5,548,702
- Area: 21,925 sq. mi. (56,785 sq. km.)
- Currency: $1 = 548.05 CFA francs
- Language: French, Ewe, Kabye
- Did You Know: About 70% of Togolese people practice traditional African religions.

Tonga

- Capital: Nuku'alofa
- Population: 114,689
- Area: 289 sq. mi. (748 sq. km.)
- Currency: $1 = 2.07 pa'angas
- Language: Tongan, English
- Did You Know: The Polynesian people of Tonga trace heritage along their mothers' line, and newlyweds live near the bride's relatives.

Trinidad and Tobago

- Capital: Port-of-Spain
- Population: 1,065,842
- Area: 1,980 sq. mi. (5,128 sq. km.)
- Currency: $1 = 6.27 Trinidad and Tobago dollars
- Language: English, Hindi, French, Spanish
- Did You Know: Steel drums were first made in Trinidad in the 1940s.

COLOR KEY
- Africa
- Asia
- Australia
- Europe
- North America
- Pacific Islands
- South America

facts about nations

Tunisia

- **Capital:** Tunis
- **Population:** 10,175,014
- **Area:** 63,170 sq. mi. (163,610 sq. km.)
- **Currency:** $1 = 1.35 dinars
- **Language:** Arabic, French
- **Did You Know:** With more than 800 miles of coastline on the Mediterranean Sea, Tunisia is a popular vacation spot for European tourists.

Turkey

- **Capital:** Ankara
- **Population:** 70,413,958
- **Area:** 301,384 sq. mi. (780,580 sq. km.)
- **Currency:** $1 = 1.33 new lira
- **Language:** Turkish, Kurdish, Arabic
- **Did You Know:** Ruins at Hisarlik in northwest Turkey are believed to be those of the ancient city of Troy, site of the legendary Trojan War.

Turkmenistan

- **Capital:** Ashgabat
- **Population:** 5,042,920
- **Area:** 188,457 sq. mi. (488,100 sq. km.)
- **Currency:** $1 = 5,200 manats
- **Language:** Turkmen, Russian, Uzbek
- **Did You Know:** The Kara Kum desert covers about 90% of the country.

Tuvalu

- **Capital:** Funafuti
- **Population:** 11,810
- **Area:** 10 sq. mi. (26 sq. km.)
- **Currency:** $1 = 1.35 Tuvalu dollars
- **Language:** Tuvaluan, English
- **Did You Know:** These low-lying islands are threatened by rising sea levels.

Uganda

- **Capital:** Kampala
- **Population:** 28,195,754
- **Area:** 91,136 sq. mi. (236,040 sq. km.)
- **Currency:** $1 = 1,795 shillings
- **Language:** English, Luganda, Swahili
- **Did You Know:** Bwindi Impenetrable National Park is a home to endangered mountain gorillas.

Ukraine

- **Capital:** Kiev
- **Population:** 46,710,816
- **Area:** 233,090 sq. mi. (603,700 sq. km.)
- **Currency:** $1 = 5.06 hryvnia
- **Language:** Ukrainian, Russian
- **Did You Know:** In the 1840s, Russian rulers banned the Ukrainian language from schools here.

United Arab Emirates

- **Capital:** Abu Dhabi
- **Population:** 2,602,713
- **Area:** 32,000 sq. mi. (82,880 sq. km.)
- **Currency:** $1 = 3.67 dirhams
- **Language:** Arabic, Persian, English, Hindi, Urdu
- **Did You Know:** Man-made resort islands several miles wide are being constructed off the coast of Dubai. Three are shaped like date palm trees and another group of islands will look like a world map.

United Kingdom (Great Britain)

- **Capital:** London
- **Population:** 60,609,153
- **Area:** 94,526 sq. mi. (244,820 sq. km.)
- **Currency:** $1 = .57 pounds
- **Language:** English, Welsh, Scottish, Gaelic
- **Did You Know:** The prehistoric monument, Stonehenge, was built in England around 1500 BC.

COLOR KEY

- Europe
- Africa
- North America
- Asia
- Pacific Islands
- Australia
- South America

United States

- **Capital:** Washington, D.C.
- **Population:** 298,444,215
- **Area:** 3,718,712 sq. mi. (9,631,420 sq. km.)
- **Currency:** U.S. dollar
- **Language:** English, Spanish
- **Did You Know:** The southernmost point in the U.S. is Ka Lae (South Cape), Hawaii.

Uruguay

- **Capital:** Montevideo
- **Population:** 3,431,932
- **Area:** 68,039 sq. mi. (176,220 sq. km.)
- **Currency:** $1 = 24.15 pesos
- **Language:** Spanish, Portunol/Brazilero
- **Did You Know:** Uruguay hosted, and won, soccer's first World Cup in 1930.

Uzbekistan

- **Capital:** Tashkent
- **Population:** 27,307,134
- **Area:** 172,742 sq. mi. (447,400 sq. km.)
- **Currency:** $1 = 1,161 sumy
- **Language:** Uzbek, Russian, Tajik
- **Did You Know:** The Muruntau gold mine is the world's largest open pit gold mine.

Vanuatu

- **Capital:** Port-Vila
- **Population:** 208,869
- **Area:** 4,710 sq. mi. (12,200 sq. km.)
- **Currency:** $1 = 112 vatus
- **Language:** French, English, Bislama
- **Did You Know:** Before independence in 1980, Britain and France jointly ruled these islands.

Vatican City

- **Population:** 921
- **Area:** .17 sq. mi. (.44 sq. km.)
- **Currency:** $1 = .84 euros
- **Language:** Italian, Latin
- **Did You Know:** The world's smallest country is less than 0.2 square miles in area and is surrounded by the city of Rome.

Venezuela

- **Capital:** Caracas
- **Population:** 25,730,435
- **Area:** 352,145 sq. mi. (912,050 sq. km.)
- **Currency:** $1 = 1,915 boliviares
- **Language:** Spanish, Amerindian languages
- **Did You Know:** Venezuela's Lake Maracaibo is the largest in South America at 5,217 sq. miles.

Vietnam

- **Capital:** Hanoi
- **Population:** 84,402,966
- **Area:** 127,244 sq. mi. (329,560 sq. km.)
- **Currency:** $1 = 15,877 dong
- **Language:** Vietnamese, French, Chinese
- **Did You Know:** Vietnam grows a third of the world's cashew nuts, the most of any nation.

Yemen

- **Capital:** Sana'a
- **Population:** 21,456,188
- **Area:** 203,850 sq. mi. (527,970 sq. km.)
- **Currency:** $1 = 196.07 rials
- **Language:** Arabic
- **Did You Know:** "Mocha" coffee takes its name from a Yemeni seaport.

Zambia

- **Capital:** Lusaka
- **Population:** 11,502,010
- **Area:** 290,586 sq. mi. (752,614 sq. km.)
- **Currency:** $1 = 3,185 kwacha
- **Language:** English, native languages
- **Did You Know:** Fossils show that humans inhabited Zambia 100,000 years ago.

Zimbabwe

- **Capital:** Harare
- **Population:** 12,236,805
- **Area:** 150,804 sq. mi. (390,580 sq. km.)
- **Currency:** $1 = 99,202 Zimbabwe dollars
- **Language:** English, Shona, Sindebele
- **Did You Know:** Ruins called Great Zimbabwe were the center of a trading empire from the 12th to the 15th centuries.

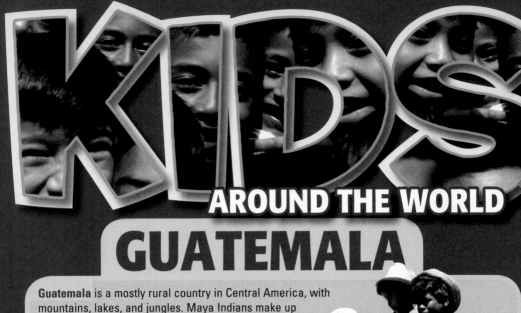

KIDS
AROUND THE WORLD

GUATEMALA

Guatemala is a mostly rural country in Central America, with mountains, lakes, and jungles. Maya Indians make up nearly half of the population; the rest are mainly people of mixed Indian and Spanish descent called mestizos. Most are Catholic. Spanish is the official language, but 20 Mayan languages are also widely spoken. The customs and traditions of the Mayans are still a big part of the culture. Their hand-woven clothing is very bright and colorful, like the clothes these boys are wearing. The patterns on the clothing can show a lot about people's lives, such as which village they are from and whether or not they are married.

JORDAN

 is a kingdom located in the Middle East, and is bordered by Iraq, Israel, Saudi Arabia, and Syria. Its history goes back thousands of years, and it has had many different rulers. Most of the people are Arabs, who practice Islam. Roughly 90% of the people live in the cities, although some Bedouin nomads still live in tents in the desert. About half of the population is Palestinian. Since much of the country is too dry for farming and lacks natural resources, Jordan depends a lot on foreign aid and tourism. Family life is very important in Jordan, and children live with their extended families. Almost half of the population is under the age of 20. Each year, thousands of tourists flock to the ruins of Petra, an ancient city over 2,000 years old, carved from red sandstone cliffs.

ENGLAND

England, Scotland, and Wales make up Great Britain, which along with Northern Ireland is the nation officially known as the United Kingdom of Great Britain and Northern Ireland. (It's often called Great Britain for short.) During its long history, many people from northern and western Europe settled in England. More recently, immigrants from former British colonies in Asia and Africa have also come. The United Kingdom has a queen and royal family, but it is also one of the world's oldest democracies. Children in England lead similar lives to kids in the U.S. and love soccer and rugby (a sport similar to American football). They must take a big test when they are 16, to see whether they can go on to college or not. It's usually cool in England, especially at the beach. But in the summer of 2003, there was a record heat wave. The temperature in London reached 100° F for the first time!

ROMANIA

One of the most famous kids from Romania was Nadia Comaneci, who won five medals (three were gold) as an Olympic gymnast in 1976 when she was only 14. Romania is also famous for its medieval castles and the legendary Count Dracula, based on the real-life noble Vlad Dracula, nicknamed "Vlad the Impaler."

Besides ethnic Romanians, about 500,000 Roma people (Gypsies) live in Romania. The Roma came from northorn India in the 12th century. They are the largest minority group in Europe with 7 to 9 million across the continent. Roma-rights groups are working for equal treatment in Romania, much like African-Americans did in the U.S. during the 1950s and 1960s.

Most Roma families live in very poor conditions, and schools are often in buildings without central heat or plumbing. Despite that, children still learn, play with siblings and friends, and enjoy life.

SOUTH KOREA

Korea is located on a peninsula in Asia between China and Japan. It was once called the Hermit Kingdom by European traders who first visited in the 1800s. Buddhism is the main religion, and there are many temples where people can go to worship their ancestors. A set of more than 80,000 wood blocks used to print Buddhist scriptures, the Tripitaka Koreana, was made in the 13th century and is kept at the Haeinsa Temple. Kids in Korea are high-tech, and almost everybody has a cell phone and a high-speed Internet connection. The national Korean dish, *kimchee*, is made with cabbage and is very spicy.

Native Americans

What Native American became an Olympic superstar? ➡ page 183

Native Americans are thought to have arrived in the Americas 18,000 years ago, most likely from northeast Asia. Although their population decreased significantly through the 17th, 18th, and 19th centuries from disease and war, there are still hundreds of tribes or nations, each with its own unique language and traditions. From the names of states and towns to foods like corn and squash, the influence of Native American cultures can be found everywhere in America.

Totem pole from the Pacific Northwest

TIMELINE NORTH AMERICAN INDIANS

1492	Christopher Columbus made contact with Taino tribes on the island he named Hispaniola.
c.1600	Five tribes—Mohawk, Oneida, Onondaga, Cayuga, and Seneca—formed the Iroquois Confederacy in the Northeast.
1754-63	Many Native Americans fought with both French and British troops in the "French and Indian War."
1821	Sequoyah completed an alphabet for the Cherokee language.
1827	Cherokee tribes in what is now Georgia formed the Cherokee Nation with a constitution and elected government positions.
1830	Congress passed the Indian Removal Act, the first law that forced tribes to move so that U.S. citizens could settle certain areas of land.
1834	Congress created the Indian Territory for tribes removed from their lands. It covered the present-day states of Oklahoma, Kansas, and Nebraska.
1890	During the Wounded Knee Massacre, about 200 Sioux men, women, and children were killed in a battle with U.S. soldiers on a South Dakota reservation. It was the last major battle between Native Americans and U.S. forces.
1924	Congress granted all Native Americans U.S. citizenship.
1929	Charles Curtis, a Kaw, became the first American of Indian ancestry elected vice president.
1985	Wilma Mankiller became the first female chief of the Cherokee Nation.

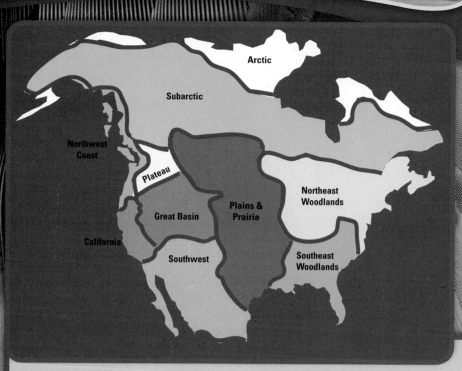

MAJOR CULTURAL AREAS of
Native North Americans

Climate and geography influenced the culture of the people who lived in these regions. On the plains, for example, people depended on the great herds of buffalo for food. For Aleuts and Eskimos in the far north, seals and whales were an important food source. There are more than 560 tribes officially recognized by the U.S. government today and more than 56 million acres of tribal lands. Below are just a few well-known tribal groups that have lived in these areas.

NORTHEAST WOODLANDS The Illinois, Iroquois (Mohawk, Onondaga, Cayuga, Oneida, Seneca, and Tuscarora), Lenape, Menominee, Micmac, Narragansett, Potawatomi, Shawnee.

SOUTHEAST WOODLANDS The Cherokee, Chickasaw, Choctaw, Creek, Seminole.

PLAINS & PRAIRIE The Arapaho, Blackfoot, Cheyenne, Comanche, Hidatsa, Kaw, Mandan, Sioux.

SOUTHWEST The Navajo, Apache, Havasupai, Mojave, Pima, Pueblo (Hopi, Isleta, Laguna, Zuñi).

GREAT BASIN The Paiute, Shoshoni, Ute.

CALIFORNIA The Klamath, Maidu, Miwok, Modoc, Patwin, Pomo, Wintun, Yurok.

PLATEAU The Cayuse, Nez Percé, Okanagon, Salish, Spokan, Umatilla, Walla Walla, Yakima.

NORTHWEST COAST The Chinook, Haida, Kwakiutl, Makah, Nootka, Salish, Tlinigit, Tsimshian, Tillamook.

SUBARCTIC The Beaver, Cree, Chipewyan, Chippewa, Ingalik, Kaska, Kutchin, Montagnais, Naskapi, Tanana.

ARCTIC The Eskimo (Inuit and Yipuk), Aleut.

Inuit girls with sled dogs

Largest U.S. Tribal Groupings*

1. Cherokee, 281,069
2. Navajo, 269,202
3. Sioux, 108,272
4. Chippewa, 105,907
5. Latin American Indian, 104,354

6. Choctaw, 87,349
7. Pueblo, 59,533
8. Apache, 57,060
9. Eskimo, 45,919
10. Iroquois, 45,212

*According to the U.S. Census 2000. Figures are for people reporting only one tribal grouping.

NATIVE AMERICAN
POPULATIONS BY STATE*

State	Population	State	Population
Alabama	23,095	Nebraska	16,562
Alaska	103,617	Nevada	33,045
Arizona	288,918	New Hampshire	3,214
Arkansas	19,555	New Jersey	26,625
California	416,646	New Mexico	192,135
Colorado	52,334	New York	103,443
Connecticut	11,812	North Carolina	110,198
Delaware	3,263	North Dakota	33,032
Florida	73,606	Ohio	26,025
Georgia	27,457	Oklahoma	283,844
Hawaii	4,299	Oregon	49,138
Idaho	19,891	Pennsylvania	21,900
Illinois	38,997	Rhode Island	6,366
Indiana	17,532	South Carolina	15,677
Iowa	10,338	South Dakota	66,535
Kansas	26,193	Tennessee	17,005
Kentucky	9,220	Texas	153,353
Louisiana	27,331	Utah	32,191
Maine	7,454	Vermont	2,326
Maryland	17,860	Virginia	24,314
Massachusetts	18,404	Washington	101,384
Michigan	60,462	West Virginia	3,729
Minnesota	59,411	Wisconsin	51,463
Mississippi	13,448	Wyoming	12,224
Missouri	26,493	Wash., D.C.	1,873
Montana	59,514	U.S. total	2,824,751

*2004 U.S. Census estimates. Figures do not include people who reported belonging to other ethnic groups in addition to Native American.

TOTEM POLES

Northwest Coast Indians carve totem poles with painted images of animals and human faces. The carvings represent animals and spirits and may also tell stories about specific people or events. The poles are carved from tree trunks or smaller pieces of wood and may be used as memorials, gravemarkers, and as welcome signs in front of homes. The tallest totem pole, erected in 1994, is located in Victoria, British Columbia, Canada. It was 180 feet, 3 inches tall.

FAMOUS NATIVE AMERICANS

Here are a few famous Native Americans who are admired for their bravery, leadership, and contributions to American history.

SACAGAWEA (1787?-1812), of the Shoshone tribe, served as an interpreter and guide for Meriwether Lewis and William Clark, who explored the American Northwest from 1804 to 1806. It's doubtful that the expedition could have succeeded without her. She showed the explorers what plants to use for food and medicine, guided them along trails, saved their supplies from a capsized boat, and persuaded the Native Americans they met that their intentions were peaceful.

Golden Dollar Obverse © 1999
U.S. Mint All Rights Reserved

CHIEF JOSEPH (1840-1904) was a leader of the Nez Percé tribe in present-day Idaho and Oregon. In 1868 he refused to sign a treaty with the U.S. to give away tribal land. After fighting broke out, he led nearly 800 men, women, and children from his tribe on a trek for more than 1,000 miles from Oregon to Montana toward escape in Canada. Cornered only 40 miles from the border, Chief Joseph sought peace rather than more fighting, saying "I will fight no more forever." Late in life he became a prominent critic of injustice to Indians.

CRAZY HORSE (1842?-1877) was an Oglala Sioux chief who refused to move his tribe to a reservation and led several battles against the U.S. Army. In 1876 he fought a victorious battle against General Custer's forces at the Battle of Little Bighorn ("Custer's Last Stand") in present-day Montana. He was captured at the end of 1876 and died in prison in 1877. Many Native Americans consider him a great hero. The Crazy Horse Memorial, carved from a mountain in South Dakota 17 miles from Mt. Rushmore, was started in 1948.

JIM THORPE (1888-1953). Born in Oklahoma of Sauk and Fox Indian ancestry, Jim Thorpe was one of America's greatest athletes of all time. He was an All-American in football and excelled in track and field, baseball, lacrosse, basketball, hockey, swimming, boxing, tennis, and archery. In the 1912 Olympic Games, he won the decathlon (10 events) and pentathlon (5 events). From 1913 to 1919, he played major league baseball with teams in New York, Cincinnati, and Boston. He also played professional football in Ohio, New York, and Chicago from 1919 to 1926.

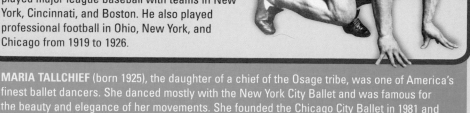

MARIA TALLCHIEF (born 1925), the daughter of a chief of the Osage tribe, was one of America's finest ballet dancers. She danced mostly with the New York City Ballet and was famous for the beauty and elegance of her movements. She founded the Chicago City Ballet in 1981 and entered the National Women's Hall of Fame in 1996.

Numbers

How many sides does a heptagon have? ⟹ page 187

Math News

ANIMAL MATH

Have you ever used math to try to find the fastest way of getting from one place to another? Professor Tim Pennings from Hope College in Michigan discovered that his dog, Elvis, also uses math, whether Elvis knows it or not. When Professor Pennings throws a ball into Lake Michigan, Elvis runs along the shore for a while, then swims for the ball (which is slower than running) at a more direct angle. After making careful measurements over 35 throws, the professor discovered that Elvis succeeded in calculating the exact point at which to jump in to get to the ball the fastest.

Prime Time!

A prime number is a number that can only be divided by itself and the number 1. So, prime numbers include: 2, 3, 5, 7, 11, 13, 17, and so on. All other positive numbers (other than 1) are called composite numbers, because they have at least two factors (numbers they can be divided by) other than 1. For example, 6 is a composite number: its factors are 1, 2, 3, and 6.

Mathematicians around the world participate in the Great Internet Mersenne Prime Search (GIMPS) project. These mathematicians use powerful computers to search for the biggest prime number.

In December 2005, two Missouri professors—Steven Boone and Curtis Cooper—found the biggest prime number yet discovered. It's expressed as a power. "Powers" work by multiplying the main number by as many times as the little number shows. So, $2^3 = 2 \times 2 \times 2 = 8$.

The prime number they found is $2^{30,402,457}$, minus 1. The number has 9,152,052 digits, enough to fill at least 10 World Almanacs for Kids.

Math can be very dangerous

According to legend, the ancient Greek Hippasus, from the fifth century B.C., discovered the existence of numbers which can't be represented by a fraction, called irrational numbers. Pi (π) (see page 186) is an example of an irrational number. Unfortunately, Hippasus was part of the Pythagoreans, a cult that believed that math had mystical powers. His fellow mathematicians found his idea so upsetting that they threw him overboard while they were at sea and he drowned, or so the story goes.

184

Homework Help

Have you ever wanted to be a human calculator?
Here are some tricks to help you on your way.

→ Multiplying by 10, 100, or any other number that starts with a 1 and is followed by zeros is really easy. Just add the number of zeros to the number you are multiplying by. So, 6 x 1,000,000 = 6,000,000.

→ Multiplying by 5 can be easy. To multiply 5 by 6, count by fives six times until you get to 30. All multiplication is really a series of additions: 3 x 5 is the same as 5 + 5 + 5 = 15.

→ To multiply any single digit by 9, it's easiest to use your hands. Spread all ten fingers in front of you. For 9 x 3, put down your third finger from the left, your left middle finger. Then, count how many fingers are to the left of that finger (2) and how many fingers are to the right (7). So, 9 x 3 = 27. Try this trick with other factors.

→ Multiplying by 4 is a little harder. But think about this and it will make it easy: To multiply something by 4, just double the number twice. So, instead of thinking about 8 x 4, think of the operation as 8 + 8 = 16; 16 + 16 = 32. So, 8 x 4 = 32.

→ To multiply any two-digit number by 11 is a little harder, but there is a trick.
   ▶ For this example we will use 36.
   ▶ Separate the two digits (3__6). (Notice the space between them.)
   ▶ Add the 3 and the 6 together (3 + 6 = 9).
   ▶ Put the resulting 9 in the hole 396. That's it! 11 x 36 = 396.

The only thing tricky to remember is that if the result of the addition is greater than 9, you only put the "ones" digit in the hole and carry the "tens" digit from the addition. For example 11 x 57 ... 5__7 ... 5 + 7 = 12 ... put the 2 in the hole and add the 1 from the 12 to the 5 in to get 6 for a result of 627 ... 11 x 57 = 627.

TRY IT!

Now—for a really tricky problem. If you practice this on your own, you can soon impress your friends and family. This is how you can add a range of even numbers quickly, starting with 2, and ending at any two-digit even number.

1. **Divide the two-digit number by 2.**
2. **Multiply that result by the next largest whole number.**

Example: What is the sum of all the even numbers between 2 and 22?
1. **22 ÷ 2 = 11**
2. **11 x 12 = 132**

Double check with a calculator to see if it works. Then try some other numbers before showing off your new trick.

Homework Help

Finding an area can be easy, if you know the not-so-secret formula.

AREA OF A SQUARE:

A plane figure with four sides is called a **quadrilateral**. A square is a quadrilateral with four right angles and four equal sides, like the figure you see here. To find the area for a square, use this formula: **SIDE X SIDE** (**SIDE X SIDE** can also be written as s^2, pronounced "side squared").

3 cm

3 cm

The sides of this square are each 3 centimeters long. So the area is 3 x 3, or 9. These are no longer centimeters but **square centimeters**.

AREA OF A RECTANGLE:

Rectangles are another type of quadrilateral. They have four right angles, but unlike a square, the sides are not all equal. To find the area of a rectangle, multiply **BASE x HEIGHT** (length x width).

4 cm

2 cm

This rectangle has a base of 2 centimeters and a height of 4 centimeters. Its area is 8 square centimeters.

AREA OF A PARALLELOGRAM:

Parallelograms are quadrilaterals that have parallel opposite sides but no right angles. The formula for the area of a parallelogram is the same as for a rectangle—**BASE x HEIGHT**.

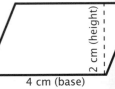

2 cm (height)

4 cm (base)

AREA OF A TRIANGLE:

A triangle is a three-sided plane figure. The prefix "tri" means three, which refers to the three points where the sides of a triangle meet.

To find the area for a triangle use **1/2 x (BASE x HEIGHT)** (first multiply the base by the height, then multiply that number by ½).

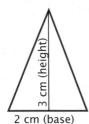

3 cm (height)

2 cm (base)

This triangle has a base of 2 centimeters and a height of 3 centimeters. So the area will be 3 square centimeters.

AREA OF A CIRCLE:

The distance around a circle is called its **circumference**. All the points on the circumference are an equal distance from the center. That distance is called the **radius**. A **diameter** is any straight line that has both ends on the circle and passes through its center. The diameter is twice the radius. To find a circle's area you need to use a number called **pi** (π) that equals about 3.14. The formula for a circle's area is **π x RADIUS x RADIUS** (or **π x RADIUS SQUARED**).

For instance, this circle has a radius of 3 centimeters, so its area = π x 3 x 3, or π x 3^2; that is, about 3.14 x 9. This comes to 28.26 square centimeters.

3 cm (radius

What Is Pi? *The Greek letter pi (π) stands for the number you get when you divide the circumference of a circle by its diameter. This number is always the same, no matter how big the circle is! The Babylonians discovered this in 2000 B.C. Actually, no one can say exactly what the value of π is. When you divide the circumference by the diameter it does not come out even, and you can keep going as many places as you want: 3.14159265 . . . it goes on forever.*

How Many SIDES and FACES Do They Have?

When a figure is flat (two-dimensional), it is a **plane** figure. When a figure takes up space (three-dimensional), it is a **solid** figure. The flat surface of a solid figure is called a **face**. Plane and solid figures come in many different shapes.

TWO-DIMENSIONAL

square

circle

triangle

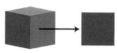
The flat surface of a cube is a square.

THREE-DIMENSIONAL

cube

sphere

tetrahedron

What Are POLYGONS?

A **polygon** is a two-dimensional figure with three or more straight sides (called line **segments**). A square is a polygon. Polygons have different numbers of sides—and each polygon has a different name. If the sides are all the same length and all the angles between the sides are equal, the polygon is called regular. If the sides are of different lengths or the angles are not equal, the polygon is called irregular. At right are some regular and irregular polygons.

NAME & NUMBER OF SIDES	REGULAR	IRREGULAR
triangle – 3		
quadrilateral or tetragon – 4		
pentagon – 5		
hexagon – 6		
heptagon – 7		
octagon – 8		
nonagon – 9		
decagon – 10		

What Are **Polyhedrons?**

A polyhedron is a three-dimensional figure with four or more faces. Each face on a polyhedron is a polygon. Below are some polyhedrons with many faces.

tetrahedron	hexahedron	octahedron	dodecahedron	icosahedron
4 faces	6 faces	8 faces	12 faces	20 faces

◀ Great Pyramid of Khefren (a half-octahedron)

187

Pascal's Triangle

Mathematicians spend a lot of time looking for patterns. Sometimes, they find a pattern of numbers that can be useful for all sorts of things. Pascal's Triangle is just that kind of pattern.

WHO WAS PASCAL?

Blaise Pascal was a mathematician from the seventeenth century. He wrote his first book on mathematics when he was only 16 years old, in 1639. He spent his life trying to solve problems in math and science.

HOW IS THE TRIANGLE PUT TOGETHER?

Notice that all of the numbers on the sides of the triangle are the number 1. The top row is called row 0, the second, row 1, the third, row 2. Look at row 2. The number 2 in the middle of the row comes from adding the two numbers directly above it (1 + 1). This is the way the triangle works—as you go down the rows, each number is the sum of the two numbers directly above it. Look for yourself and check to see if that's true. Can you figure out what the numbers in row 8 will be?

WHAT CAN THIS TRIANGLE DO?

This triangle can help you with probability and combinations. All of the numbers in the triangle have a place. To name the place, count in from the left, starting at 0. So, the first "2", closest to the top, would be in row 2 (remember, rows start at 0, too), place 1.

▶ HERE'S A QUESTION THIS TRIANGLE CAN HELP YOU SOLVE:

You are taking a special trip for your birthday and you can only invite two friends. But you have five friends you would enjoy taking along with you. How many choices do you have for the combination of friends on your birthday trip? Or, simply—how many different ways can you pick two things from a set of five things?

The answer is the number in row 5, place 2. There are ten different combinations of friends you could bring.

That's just the start. You can use this triangle for many other mathematical problems.
Look up Pascal's Triangle at
WEB SITE *mathforum.org*

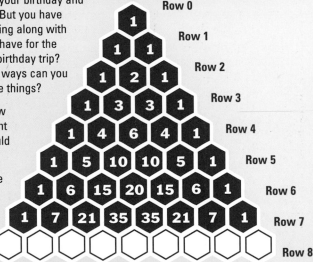

One very famous mathematical idea is Fermat's Last Theorem. Fermat wrote down a theorem, or a mathematical idea, in the margin of a book in the seventeenth century. He also wrote, "I have a truly marvelous demonstration of this proposition which this margin is too narrow to contain." No one was able to figure out what the demonstration was for more than 300 years. Finally, in 1993, mathematician Andrew Wiles announced that he had found a demonstration that worked. Wiles was convinced that Fermat never had a demonstration, because he had to use modern methods that Fermat wouldn't have known about to solve the problem.

Fun with Numbers

1 Derek and Aisha, 10-year-old twins, each got to negotiate their own allowances. Derek asked for $10 a week until he turned 18 years old. Aisha asked for a starting allowance of 1 cent, which would then double every day, but only for 30 days. Then, she would never ask for an allowance again. Their silly parents agreed to this request. Who made the smarter decision, Derek or Aisha?

2 June and November have 30 days. Some others months, like July and August have 31. How many months have 28 days?

3 You wake up in a dark bedroom. You want a matching pair of socks, but you don't want to turn the light on. You only have black socks and white socks in your drawer. How many socks do you need to pull out to get a matching pair?

4 Theresa is waiting in line for ice cream. She wants to order a double-scoop cone. The vendor says, "You have three options: chocolate, strawberry, or vanilla." Theresa says, "Actually, I have six options." How is she correct?

Sudoku

A Sudoku puzzle follows a few simple rules. Each square needs one number in it between 1 and 9. Each row must contain all numbers 1-9, each column must contain all numbers 1-9, and each of the nine-square units must have all numbers 1-9.

2	6			1				
7	8	4	2	5				
3	9	1	4	7	6	2	8	5
		3	7				1	
			3	8	5		2	4
	7		6		4	9		
1	4	8	5	3				
			8	6		4	7	1
	2		9				3	8

ANSWERS ON PAGES 334-337.
FOR MORE PUZZLES GO TO
WWW.WORLDALMANACFORKIDS.COM

Population

Which state is most popular among immigrants? ➡ page 195

WHERE DO PEOPLE LIVE?

In 1959, there were three billion people in the world. In 1999, the number hit six billion. According to the latest estimates by the United Nations, the world population will have reached 6.5 billion by mid-2006, and will grow to 9.2 billion by 2050. This is a lot of people, but not as many as predicted a few years ago. The United Nations lowered its estimates of how many people will be born and increased its estimates of deaths from the deadly AIDS epidemic.

It's a big world out there! Our planet has about 196,940,000 square miles of surface area. However, about 70 percent of that area is water. The total land area, 57,506,000 square miles, is about 16 times the area of the United States.

So, which nation is the largest in area? Russia is on top with over 6.5 million square miles of land area. China comes in a distant second with 3.6 million square miles, while the U.S. and Canada are close behind.

The smallest countries are Vatican City, Monaco, and Nauru. These countries are also among the most crowded (densely populated).

POPULATIONS

Smallest (2006)

	COUNTRY	POPULATION
1.	Vatican City	921
2.	Tuvalu	11,636
3.	Nauru	13,048
4.	Palau	20,303
5.	San Marino	28,880

Source: U.S. Census Bureau, CIA World Factbook

Largest (2006)

	COUNTRY	POPULATION
1.	China*	1,313,973,713
2.	India	1,095,351,995
3.	United States	298,444,215
4.	Indonesia	245,452,739
5.	Brazil	188,078,227

* Excluding Taiwan, pop. 23,036,087; Hong Kong, pop. 6,940,432; and Macau, pop. 453,125.

To get the population density, divide the population by the area. Density is calculated here according to land area, based on 2006 population.

MOST DENSELY POPULATED

	COUNTRY	PERSONS PER SQ MI*
1.	Monaco	43,218
2.	Singapore	17,016
3.	Vatican City	5,418
4.	Malta	3,280
5.	Maldives	3,095

* For comparison, New Jersey is the most densely populated state, with 1,176 people per square mile.

MOST SPARSELY POPULATED

	COUNTRY	PERSONS PER SQ MI
1.	Mongolia	4.7
2.	Namibia	6.4
3.	Australia	6.9
4.	Suriname	7.0
5.	Botswana	7.3

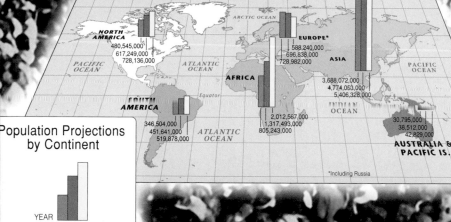

NORTH AMERICA
480,545,000
617,249,000
728,136,000

EUROPE*
588,240,000
696,838,000
728,982,000

ASIA
3,688,072,000
4,774,050,000
5,406,328,000

AFRICA
2,012,567,000
1,317,493,000
805,243,000

SOUTH AMERICA
346,504,000
451,641,000
519,878,000

AUSTRALIA & PACIFIC IS.
30,795,000
38,512,000
42,829,000

*Including Russia

Population Projections by Continent

YEAR
2000 2025 2050

Source: U.S. Bureau of the Census, International Data Division

FIVE LARGEST CITIES IN THE WORLD

Here are the five cities that had the most people, according to UN estimates for 2005. Numbers include people from the built-up area around each city (metropolitan area), not just the city. (See page 192 for the ten biggest U.S. cities.)

	CITY, COUNTRY	POPULATION
1.	Tokyo, Japan	35,327,000
2.	Mexico City, Mexico	19,013,000
3.	New York, U.S.	18,498,000
4.	Mumbai (Bombay), India	18,336,000
5.	São Paulo, Brazil	18,333,000

POPULATION OF THE UNITED STATES, 2005

Estimated U.S. Population on July 1, 2005: 296,410,404.
The population was projected to go past 300 million in October 2006.

RANK & STATE NAME	POPULATION	RANK & STATE NAME	POPULATION
1. California (CA)	36,132,147	27. Oregon (OR)	3,641,056
2. Texas (TX)	22,859,968	28. Oklahoma (OK)	3,547,884
3. New York (NY)	19,254,630	29. Connecticut (CT)	3,510,297
4. Florida (FL)	17,789,864	30. Iowa (IA)	2,966,334
5. Illinois (IL)	12,763,371	31. Mississippi (MS)	2,921,088
6. Pennsylvania (PA)	12,429,616	32. Arkansas (AR)	2,779,154
7. Ohio (OH)	11,464,042	33. Kansas (KS)	2,744,687
8. Michigan (MI)	10,120,860	34. Utah (UT)	2,469,585
9. Georgia (GA)	9,072,576	35. Nevada (NV)	2,414,807
10. New Jersey (NJ)	8,717,925	36. New Mexico (NM)	1,928,384
11. North Carolina (NC)	8,683,242	37. West Virginia (WV)	1,816,856
12. Virginia (VA)	7,567,465	38. Nebraska (NE)	1,758,857
13. Massachusetts (MA)	6,398,743	39. Idaho (ID)	1,429,096
14. Washington (WA)	6,287,759	40. Maine (ME)	1,321,505
15. Indiana (IN)	6,271,973	41. New Hampshire (NH)	1,309,940
16. Tennessee (TN)	5,962,959	42. Hawaii (HI)	1,275,194
17. Arizona (AZ)	5,939,292	43. Rhode Island (RI)	1,076,189
18. Missouri (MO)	5,800,310	44. Montana (MT)	935,670
19. Maryland (MD)	5,600,388	45. Delaware (DE)	843,524
20. Wisconsin (WI)	5,536,201	46. South Dakota (SD)	775,933
21. Minnesota (MN)	5,132,799	47. Alaska (AK)	663,661
22. Colorado (CO)	4,665,177	48. North Dakota (ND)	636,677
23. Alabama (AL)	4,557,808	49. Vermont (VT)	623,050
24. Louisiana (LO)	4,523,628	50. District of Columbia (DC)	550,521
25. South Carolina (SC)	4,255,083	51. Wyoming (WY)	509,294
26. Kentucky (KY)	4,173,405		

Largest Cities in the United States

Cities grow and shrink in population. Below is a list of
the largest cities in the United States in 2004 compared
with their populations in 1950. Populations are for people
living within the city limits only.

RANK & CITY	2004	1950
1. New York, NY	8,104,079	7,891,957
2. Los Angeles, CA	3,845,541	1,970,358
3. Chicago, IL	2,862,244	3,620,962
4. Houston, TX	2,012,626	596,163
5. Philadelphia, PA	1,470,151	2,071,605
6. Phoenix, AZ	1,418,041	106,818
7. San Diego, CA	1,263,756	334,387
8. San Antonio, TX	1,236,249	408,442
9. Dallas, TX	1,210,393	434,462
10. San Jose, CA	904,522	95,280

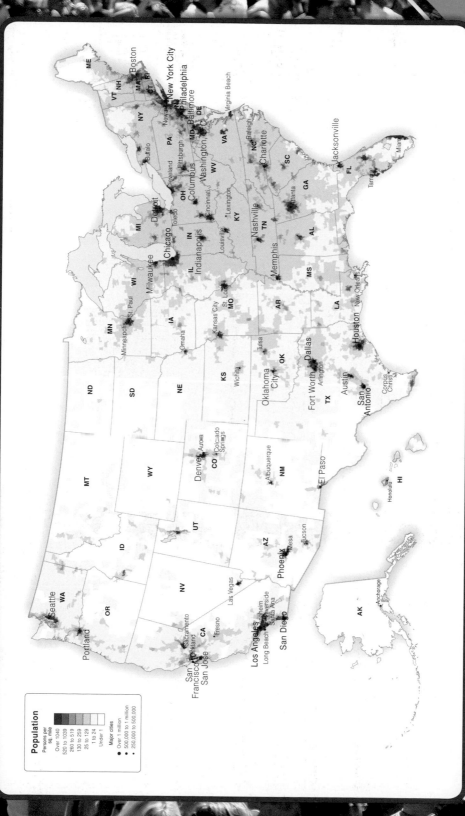

Population

Persons per sq. mile

Over 1040
520 to 1039
260 to 519
130 to 259
25 to 129
1 to 24
Under 1

Major cities
• Over 1 million
•• 500,000 to 1 million
•• 250,000 to 500,000

The Growing U.S. Population

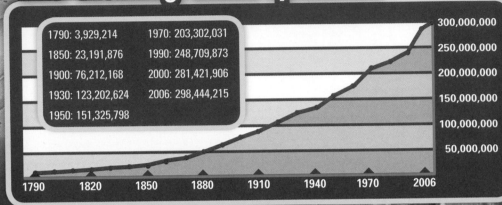

1790: 3,929,214	1970: 203,302,031
1850: 23,191,876	1990: 248,709,873
1900: 76,212,168	2000: 281,421,906
1930: 123,202,624	2006: 298,444,215
1950: 151,325,798	

U.S. Population, by Age

Source: Bureau of the Census, U.S. Dept. of Commerce;
2004 mid-year estimate

	Number	%
Total population	293,655,404	100
AGE		
Under 5 years	20,071,268	6.8
5 to 13 years	36,375,652	12.4
14 to 17 years	16,831,078	5.7
18 to 24 years	29,245,102	10.0
25 to 44 years	84,140,590	28.7
45 to 64 years	70,697,729	24.1
65 to 84 years	31,434,354	10.7
85 years and over	4,859,631	1.7

In 2004, the number of legal immigrants entering the U.S. was 946,142, up significantly from 705,827 in 2003.

The Many Faces of America:
IMMIGRATION

▼ Immigrants entering the U.S. at Ellis Island, early 1900s

The number of people in the U.S. who were born in another country (foreign-born) reached 34.2 million in 2004, or 11.7% of the population. This percentage has been rising since 1970, when it was down to 4.7%, and is at its highest since 1930. In the early 1900s, most immigrants came from Europe; in 2004, 54% of the foreign-born population were born in Latin America, and 25% were born in Asia.

Immigrants come for various reasons, such as to live in freedom, to escape poverty or oppression, and to make better lives for themselves and their children. The figures below, from U.S. Citizenship and Immigration Services, part of the Department of Homeland Security, cover legal immigrants only. In addition, the U.S. government estimates that in the 1990s about 350,000 people each year came across the border illegally or overstayed their temporary visa. There were an estimated 11 million unauthorized immigrants in the U.S. in 2006; more than half of these were from Mexico.

What Countries Do Immigrants Come From?

Below are some of the countries by birth of immigrants to the U.S. in 2004.
Legal immigration from all countries to the U.S. totaled 946,142 in 2004.

	Number	Percent of total
Mexico	175,364	18.5
India	70,116	7.4
Philippines	57,827	6.1
China	51,156	5.4
Vietnam	31,514	3.3
Dominican Republic	30,492	3.2
El Salvador	29,795	3.1
Cuba	20,488	2.2
Korea	19,766	2.1
Colombia	18,678	2.0
Guatemala	17,999	1.9
Canada	15,567	1.6
United Kingdom	14,915	1.6
Jamaica	14,414	1.5
Poland	14,250	1.5

Where Do Immigrants Settle?

In 2004, about 65% of all immigrants to the U.S. moved to the states below. California received roughly 45% of those immigrants born in Vietnam, Mexico, and the Philippines and one-third of immigrants from China and Korea. Florida received 73% of immigrants born in Cuba, nearly half of those from Haiti, and about one-third of those from Colombia. Nearly half of those born in the Dominican Republic chose to settle in New York.

California
252,920

New York
102,390

Texas
91,799

Florida
75,644

New Jersey
50,303

Illinois
46,314

This bar chart shows the states that received the highest number of immigrants in 2004.

Prizes & Contests

What is a "cow chip"? ➡ page 201

NOBEL PRIZES

The Nobel Prizes are named after Alfred B. Nobel (1833–1896), a Swedish scientist who invented dynamite, and left money for these prizes. They are given every year for promoting peace, as well as for physics, chemistry, medicine, physiology, literature, and economics.

▲ In 2005, the International Atomic Energy Agency and its director, Mohamed ElBaradei, were awarded the Nobel Peace Prize "for their efforts to prevent nuclear energy from being used for military purposes and to ensure that nuclear energy for peaceful purposes is used in the safest possible way."

PAST WINNERS OF THE NOBEL PEACE PRIZE INCLUDE:

2003 Shirin Ebadi, Iranian activist for democracy and human rights

2002 Jimmy Carter, former U.S. president and peace negotiator

1999 Médecins Sans Frontières (Doctors Without Borders), an organization that gives medical help to underserved populations

1997 Jody Williams and the **International Campaign to Ban Landmines**

1994 Yasir Arafat, Palestinian leader; **Shimon Peres,** foreign minister of Israel; **Yitzhak Rabin,** prime minister of Israel

1993 Nelson Mandela, leader of South African blacks; **F.W. de Klerk** president of South Africa

1989 The Dalai Lama, Tibetan Buddhist leader, forced into exile in 1959

1987 Oscar Arias Sánchez, president of Costa Rica, initiator of peace negotiations in Central America

◄ **1986 Elie Wiesel,** Holocaust survivor and author

1979 Mother Teresa, leader of the order of the Missionaries of Charity, who care for the sick and dying in India

1964 Martin Luther King Jr., civil rights leader

1906 Theodore Roosevelt, U.S. president who helped settle the Russo-Japanese War

ENTERTAINMENT Awards

2006 KIDS' CHOICE AWARDS

The 2006 Kids' Choice Awards were held Saturday, April 1, 2006, and hosted by ◄Jack Black. For more information, go to:

WEB SITE www.nick.com

KIDS' CHOICE AWARDS

25 million kids voted in the 2006 Nickelodeon's Kids' Choice Awards. Winners included:

Music Group: . . . . Green Day
Movie: . . . . *Harry Potter and the Goblet of Fire*
Book: . . . . Harry Potter series
Video Game: . . . . *Madagascar, Operation Penguin*
Favorite TV Show: . . . . . . *Drake and Josh*
Cartoon: . . . . *SpongeBob SquarePants*
TV Actor: . . . . Drake Bell
TV Actress: . . . . Jamie Lynn Spears
Movie Actor: . . . . Will Smith
Movie Actress: . . . . Lindsay Lohan ▶
Favorite Voice from
an Animated Movie: . . . . Chris Rock
Male Singer: . . . . Jesse McCartney
Female Singer: . . . . Kelly Clarkson
Song: . . . . "Wake Me Up When September Ends" (Green Day)
Athlete: . . . . Lance Armstrong
Wannabe Award: . . . . . . Chris Rock

Contests for Kids

SCIENCE AND TECHNOLOGY

Sponsored by Toshiba and the NSTA (National Science Teachers Association), the **ExploraVision Awards** reward kids who research a technology and imagine how that technology might change the future. Each team also builds web pages describing their project. Some of the 2005 winners were:

Grades 4-6 First Place Winner

VEWS: Volcano Early Warning System, by Home Connection-Oak Harbor School District, Oak Harbor, WA

People living in areas prone to volcanoes or mudslides will get to safer ground thanks to this system, which uses holographic GPS maps and relays an emergency signal that informs people of the best safety route.

WEB SITE *http://dev.nsta.org/ evwebs/2947/*

Grades 7-9 First Place Winner

Visible-Light Photocatalysis by Hawken Middle School, Lyndhurst, OH ▲

This invention uses nanotechnology to detoxify and clean polluted water and air. It can also clean facilities such as hospitals to prevent the spread of disease.

WEB SITE *http://dev.nsta.org/evwebs/1952/*

ART AND WRITING

The Scholastic Art and Writing Awards have celebrated the best in student work since 1923. In the past, award winners have included writers and artists who went on to become famous as adults, like author Joyce Carol Oates, artist Andy Warhol, and poet Sylvia Plath. The contest is open to middle and high school students. **WEB SITE** *www.artandwriting.org*

Andy Warhol's "Campbell's Soup Cans, 1962" on display at the Museum of Modern Art

BEE INVOLVED

If you have a knack for spelling or an interest in world geography, then these two national contests may be for you.

NATIONAL SPELLING BEE

The **National Spelling Bee** was started in Louisville, Kentucky, by the *Courier-Journal* in 1925. Newspapers across the U.S. run spelling bees for kids 15 and under. Winners may qualify for the Scripps National Spelling Bee held in Washington, D.C., in late May or early June. If interested, ask your school principal to contact your local newspaper. (For a behind-the-scenes look at the National Spelling Bee, try the 2002 film *Spellbound*.)

Anurag Kashyap, 13, from Poway, CA, won the 78th Annual Scripps National Spelling Bee contest on June 2, 2005. After 19 rounds, he won the bee by correctly spelling the word "appoggiatura," which is defined as "an accessory embellishing note or tone preceding an essential melodic note or tone." This is the second time Anurag has competed in the National Spelling Bee. He placed 47th in 2004.

WEB SITE *www.spellingbee.com*

Here are the words Anurag spelled on his way to the top. Some of them are just a little bit difficult!

cabochon	schefflera
priscilla	ornithorhynchous
oligopsony	agio
sphygmomanometer	agnolotti
prosciutto	peccavi
rideau	ceraunograph
pompier	exsiccosis
terete	hodiernal
tristachyous	appoggiatura

National Geographic Bee

After 10+ rounds, the winner is . . .

Nathan Cornelius, a 13-year-old from Cottonwood, Minnesota. After 10 rounds of regular questions and a lightning elimination set, Nathan advanced to the championship round. He won with the question: Lake Gatún, an artificial lake that constitutes part of the Panama Canal system, was created by damming which river?
(The answer: Chagres River)

Nathan won a $25,000 scholarship for college. He also won lifetime membership in the National Geographic Society. Nathan had already won the Minnesota state-level bee in 2003, 2004, and 2005. "I spend a couple of hours a day studying geography by looking at atlases and geography books," he said.

Nathan also got help from last year's champ. He read *Afghanistan to Zimbabwe: Country Facts That Helped Me Win the National Geographic Bee*, a book written by last year's Bee champion, Andrew Wojtanik of Kansas.

This contest draws five million contestants from nearly 15,000 schools across the United States. To enter, you must be in grade 4-8. School-level bees are followed by state-level bees and then the nationals. For more information: **WEB SITE** *www.nationalgeographic.com/geobee*

CONTESTS, CONTESTS EVERYWHERE!

It just seems to be part of human nature to find out who is the best at something, no matter what it is! There are state, national, and international competitions in a wild variety of events. Here are some contests that are a strain on your brain, some that are just fun—and some that are both. Contests like these may take place near you.

ROTTEN SNEAKER CONTEST Held annually in Montpelier, Vermont, the Odor-Eaters Rotten Sneaker Contest was won in March 2006 by seven-year-old McKenna Dinkel of Wasilla, Alaska. McKenna's sneakers were judged smelliest by a panel that included NASA's "Master Sniffer." Her secret to super smelly sneaks was to wear them around her family's farm with no socks. McKenna was awarded a $500 savings bond, $100 (to spend on new sneakers), and a lifetime supply of Odor-Eaters. Her sneakers will be enshrined with other winners' in the Odor-Eaters Hall of Fumes. For more information, visit the Odor-Eaters **WEB SITE** *www.odoreaters.com*

GO FLY A KITE! Children of all ages are invited to enter their own handmade kites into the Smithsonian Kite Festival, which is held every year in Washington, D.C., at cherry blossom time (late March to early April) on the National Mall. There are first, second, and third place prizes offered in categories for kids 11-and-under and 12-15.

The event was founded by aviation pioneer Paul E. Garber and is sponsored by the Smithsonian Associates and the National Air and Space Museum. Kite fliers from across the U.S. and all over the world participate. The sky is filled with all types of kites, from bowed to box/cellular to fighter and delta kites. There are also exhibitions by kite-flying masters and kite-making activities.

For more information, visit the festival's **WEB SITE** *www.kitefestival.org*

NATIONAL SCHOOL SCRABBLE TOURNAMENT Held in Boston every April, this contest is open to kids in grades 5 through 8. Regional tournaments, with 44-minute rounds, can be held within clubs, classrooms, schools, districts, regions, or states. **WEB SITE** *school.scrabble-assoc.com*

U.S. NATIONAL SNOW SCULPTING COMPETITION

Usually held in February, this contest gives each team a 7-foot-by-9-foot block of snow to carve. People carve enormous fish, realistic people, trees, and even scenes from fairy tales. There are special events for kids. The 2006 contest was held in Lake Geneva, Wisconsin.

WEB SITE www.usnationals.org

INTERNATIONAL CHERRY PIT SPITTING CHAMPIONSHIP

Open to spitters of all ages, this competition is held every year in Eau Claire, Michigan, in July. The world record is over 90 feet! (Watermelon seeds are often used in other spitting contests. And every April at Purdue University's "Bug Bowl" there is a cricket spitting contest!)

WEB SITE *www.treemendus-fruit.com*

WORLD COW CHIP THROWING CONTEST Held every

April in Beaver, Oklahoma. The object is to throw a hunk of dried cow dung (a "cow chip") as far as you can. The record is over 185 feet. This is one of many throwing contests. Eggs, fish, squid, pumpkins, and fruitcake are just a few of the other things people may throw.

Another Way of Saying It

The names on the left are another way of saying the famous names of prizewinners from the Kids' Choice Awards on page 197. See if you can guess who the name or what the thing is, and then draw a line to the award each won.

1. 24 Hours Filled With Grassy Colors — Cartoon
2. Set the Alarm for October 1 — Athlete
3. Duck and Joke — Music Group
4. Sharp Stick, Powerful Limb — TV Show
5. Dishwasher with Quadrilateral Slacks — Song

**ANSWERS ON PAGES 334-337.
FOR MORE PUZZLES GO TO
WWW.WORLDALMANACFORKIDS.COM**

201

Religion

What religion do the "Old Order" Amish belong to? ➡ page 205

How did the universe begin? Why are we here on Earth? What happens to us after we die? For most people, religion provides answers to questions like these. Believing in a God or gods, or in a higher power, is one way people make sense of the world around them. Religion can also help guide people's lives. An estimated six billion people all over the world believe in a religion.

Different religions have different beliefs. For example, Christians, Jews, and Muslims are monotheists, meaning they believe in only one God. Hindus, meanwhile, are polytheists, meaning they believe in many gods. On this page and the next are some facts about the world's major religions.

Christianity

WHO STARTED CHRISTIANITY? Christianity is based on the teachings of Jesus Christ. He was born in Bethlehem between 8 B.C. and 4 B.C. and died about A.D. 29.

WHAT WRITINGS ARE THERE? The **Bible**, consisting of the Old Testament and New Testament, is the main spiritual text in Christianity.

WHAT DO CHRISTIANS BELIEVE? There is only one God. God sent his Son, Jesus Christ, to Earth. Jesus died to save humankind but later rose from the dead.

HOW MANY ARE THERE? Christianity is the world's biggest religion. In mid-2004, there were more than 2.1 billion Christians worldwide.

WHAT KINDS ARE THERE? More than one billion Christians are **Roman Catholics**, who follow the Pope's leadership. **Orthodox Christians** accept similar teachings but follow different leadership. **Protestants** disagree with many Catholic teachings. They believe in the Bible's authority.

Buddhism

WHO STARTED BUDDHISM? Siddhartha Gautama (the Buddha), around 525 B.C.

WHAT WRITINGS ARE THERE? The **Tripitaka**, or "Three Baskets," contains three collections of teachings, rules, and commentaries. There are also other texts, many of which are called **sutras**.

WHAT DO BUDDHISTS BELIEVE? Buddha taught that life is filled with suffering. Through meditation and deeds, one can end the cycle of endless birth and rebirth and achieve a state of perfect peace known as **nirvana**.

HOW MANY ARE THERE? In mid-2004, there were about 375 million Buddhists in the world, 98% of them in Asia.

WHAT KINDS ARE THERE? There are two main kinds: **Theravada** ("Way of the Elders") Buddhism, the older kind, is more common in countries such as Sri Lanka, Myanmar, and Thailand. **Mahayana** ("Great Vehicle") Buddhism is more common in China, Korea, Japan, and Tibet.

Hinduism

WHO STARTED HINDUISM? The beliefs of Aryans, who migrated to India around 1500 B.C., intermixed with the beliefs of the people who already lived there.

WHAT WRITINGS ARE THERE? The **Vedas** ("Knowledge") collect the most important writings in Hinduism, including the ancient hymns in the **Samhita** and the teachings in the **Upanishads**. Also important are the stories the **Bhagavad-Gita** and the **Ramayana**.

WHAT DO HINDUS BELIEVE? There is one divine principle, known as **brahman**; the various gods are only aspects of it. Life is an aspect of, yet separate from the divine. To escape a meaningless cycle of birth and rebirth (**samsara**), one must improve one's **karma** (the purity or impurity of one's past deeds).

HOW MANY ARE THERE? In mid-2004, there were about 851 million Hindus, mainly in India and places where people from India have immigrated to.

WHAT KINDS ARE THERE? Most Hindus are primarily devoted to a single deity, the most popular being the gods **Vishnu** and **Shiva** and the goddess **Shakti**.

Islam

WHO STARTED ISLAM? Muhammad, the Prophet, about A.D. 622.

WHAT WRITINGS ARE THERE? The **Koran** (*al-Qur'an* in Arabic), regarded as the word of God. The **Sunna**, or example of the Prophet, is recorded in the **Hadith**.

WHAT DO MUSLIMS BELIEVE? People who practice Islam are known as Muslims. There is only one God. God revealed the Koran to Muhammad so he could teach humankind truth and justice. Those who "submit" (literal meaning of "Islam") to God will attain salvation. The wicked will go to hell.

HOW MANY ARE THERE? In mid-2004, there were approximately 1.3 billion Muslims, mostly in parts of Africa and Asia.

WHAT KINDS ARE THERE? There are two major groups: the **Sunni**, who in mid-2004 made up about 83% of all Muslims, and the **Shiite**, who broke away in a dispute over leadership after Muhammad died in 632.

Judaism

WHO STARTED JUDAISM? Abraham is thought to be the founder of Judaism, one of the first monotheistic religions. He probably lived between 2000 B.C. and 1500 B.C.

WHAT WRITINGS ARE THERE? The most important is the **Torah** ("Law"), comprising the five books of Moses. The **Nevi'im** ("Prophets") and **Ketuvim** ("Writings") are also part of the Hebrew Bible.

WHAT DO JEWS BELIEVE? There is one God who created and rules the universe. One should be faithful to God and observe God's laws.

HOW MANY ARE THERE? In mid-2004, there were close to 15 million Jews around the world. Many live in Israel and the United States.

WHAT KINDS ARE THERE? In the U.S. there are three main forms: **Orthodox**, **Conservative**, and **Reform**. Orthodox Jews are the most traditional, following strict laws about dress and diet. Reform Jews are the least traditional. Conservative Jews are somewhere in-between.

Major Holy Days for
CHRISTIANS, JEWS, MUSLIMS, BUDDHISTS, AND HINDUS

CHRISTIAN HOLY DAYS

	2006	2007	2008
Ash Wednesday	March 1	February 21	February 6
Good Friday	April 14	April 6	March 21
Easter Sunday	April 16	April 8	March 23
Easter for Orthodox Churches	April 23	April 8	April 27
Christmas	December 25	December 25	December 25

*Russian and some other Orthodox churches celebrate Christmas in January.

JEWISH HOLY DAYS

The Jewish holy days begin at sundown the night before the first full day of the observance. The dates of first full days are listed below.

	2006-07 (5767)	2007-08 (5768)	2008-09 (5769)
Rosh Hashanah (New Year)	September 23, 2006	September 13, 2007	September 30, 2008
Yom Kippur (Day of Atonement)	October 2, 2006	September 22, 2007	October 9, 2008
Hanukkah (Festival of Lights)	December 16, 2006	December 5, 2007	December 22, 2008
Passover	April 3, 2007	April 20, 2008	April 9, 2009

ISLAMIC (MUSLIM) HOLY DAYS

The Islamic holy days begin at sundown the night before the first full day of the observance. The dates of first full days are listed below.

	2006 (1427)	2007 (1428)	2008 (1429)
Muharram 1 (New Year)	January 30	January 20	January 9
Mawlid (Birthday of Muhammad)	April 10	March 31	March 20
Ramadan (Month of Fasting)	September 23	September 12	September 1
Eid al-Fitr (End of Ramadan)	October 23	October 12	September 30
Eid al-Adha	December 30	December 20	December 8

BUDDHIST HOLY DAYS

Not all Buddhists use the same calendar to determine holidays and festivals. A few well-known Buddhist observances and the months in which they may fall are listed below.

The Dalai Lama

Nirvana Day, February: Marks the death of Siddhartha Gautama (the Buddha).

Vesak or Visakah Puja (Buddha Day), April/May: The most important holiday. Celebrates the birth, enlightenment, and death of the Buddha.

Asalha Puja (Dharma Day), July: Commemorates the Buddha's first teaching.

Magha Puja or Sangha Day, February: Commemorates the day when 1,250 of Buddha's followers (**sangha**) visited him without his calling them.

Vassa (Rains Retreat), July-October: A three-month period during Asia's rainy season when monks travel little and spend more time on meditation and study. Sometimes called Buddhist Lent.

HINDU HOLY DAYS

Different Hindu groups use different calendars. A few of the many Hindu festivals and the months in which they may fall are listed below.

Maha Shivaratri, February/March: Festival dedicated to Shiva, creator and destroyer.

Holi, February/March: Festival of spring.

Ramanavami, March/April: Celebrates the birth of Rama, the seventh incarnation of Vishnu.

Diwali, October/November: Hindu New Year, the Festival of Lights.

All About THE AMISH

In the major religions there are different groups, or denominations, each with some unique customs and beliefs of its own. For example, many Christians are Protestants, and among Protestants there are Southern Baptists (the biggest Protestant group in the U.S.), Methodists, and Lutherans.

The Old Order Amish stand out because of their customs. They believe in a simple lifestyle, wear very plain, old-fashioned clothes, and shun the use of electricity. Instead of cars, they drive horse-drawn buggies. Their communities are mainly in Ohio and Pennsylvania.

Many of these Amish are farmers. They live in communities where they can all be together and have their own schools. The children are expected to marry other Amish and continue the same way of life when they grow up. The Amish are pacifists; that is, they believe war is wrong and do not fight in wars.

Science

What are the six simple machines? ➡ page 211

THE WORLD OF Science

The Latin root of the word "science" is *scire* meaning "to know." There are many kinds of knowledge, but when people use the word *science* they usually mean a kind of knowledge that can be discovered and backed up by observation or experiments.

The branches of scientific study can be loosely grouped into the four main areas shown below. Each branch of science has more specific areas of study within it than can be listed here. For example zoology includes entomology (study of insects), which in turn includes lepidopterology, the study of butterflies and moths!

In answering questions about our lives, our world, and our universe, scientists must often draw from more than one discipline. Biochemists, for example, deal with the chemistry that happens inside living things. Paleontologists study fossil remains of ancient plants and animals. Astrophysicists study matter and energy in outer space. And mathematics, considered by many to be an art and a science by itself, is used by all scientists.

Physical Science

ASTRONOMY—stars, planets, outer space

CHEMISTRY—properties and behavior of substances

PHYSICS—matter and energy

Life Science (Biology)

ANATOMY—structure of the human body

BOTANY—plants

ECOLOGY—living things in relation to their environment

GENETICS—heredity

PATHOLOGY—diseases and their effects on the human body

PHYSIOLOGY—the body's biological processes

ZOOLOGY—animals

Earth Science

GEOGRAPHY—Earth's surface and its relationship to humans

GEOLOGY—Earth's structure

MINERALOGY—minerals

PETROLOGY—rocks

SEISMOLOGY—earthquakes

VOLCANOLOGY—volcanoes

HYDROLOGY—water

METEOROLOGY—Earth's atmosphere and weather

OCEANOGRAPHY—the sea, including currents and tides

Social Science

ANTHROPOLOGY—human cultures and physical characteristics

ECONOMICS—production and distribution of goods and services

POLITICAL SCIENCE—governments

PSYCHOLOGY—mental processes and behavior

SOCIOLOGY—human society and community life

HOW DO SCIENTISTS
MAKE DISCOVERIES? THE SCIENTIFIC METHOD

The scientific method was developed over many centuries:
You can think of it as having five steps:

1. Ask a question.
2. Gather information through observation.
3. Based on that information, make an educated guess—or hypothesis—about the answer to your question.
4. Design an experiment to test that hypothesis.
5. Evaluate the results.

If the experiment shows that your hypothesis is wrong, make up a new hypothesis. If the experiment supports your hypothesis, then your hypothesis may be correct! However, it is usually necessary to test a hypothesis with many different experiments before it can be accepted as a scientific law—something that is generally accepted as true.

You can apply the scientific method to problems in everyday life. For example, suppose you plant some seeds and they fail to sprout. You would probably ask yourself, "Why didn't they sprout?"—and that would be step one of the scientific method. The next step would be to make observations; for example, you might take note of how deep the seeds were planted, how often they

were watered, and what kind of soil was used. Then, you would make an educated guess about what went wrong—for example, you might hypothesize that the seeds didn't sprout because you didn't water them enough. After that, you would test your hypothesis—perhaps by trying to grow the seeds again, under the exact same conditions as before, except that this time you would water them more frequently.

Finally, you would wait and evaluate the results of your experiment. If the seeds sprouted, then you could conclude that your hypothesis may be correct. If they don't sprout, you'd continue to use the method to find a scientific answer to your original question.

Who Discovered What?

These famous scientists made groundbreaking discoveries. Unscramble the mixed up words to find out what!

1. Using an early microscope, Anton van Leeuwenhoek discovered **OIOIRCRNSGMMAS** in the 1670s and 1680s.

2. Isaac Newton developed the laws of **RIGTAYV** in 1687.

3. Joseph Priestley discovered **EXGNYO** in 1774, and later created carbonated water, our modern-day soda!

4. Alessandro Volta experimented with the flow of **ECYICLTERIT** and created the battery in 1800.

5. Wilhelm Roentgen discovered **YASXR** by accident in 1895.

ANSWERS ON PAGES 334-337.
FOR MORE PUZZLES GO TO
WWW.WORLDALMANACFORKIDS.COM

WHAT EVERYTHING *IS* MADE OF

Everything we see and use is made up of basic ingredients called elements. There are more than 100 elements. Most have been found in nature. Some are created by scientists in labs.

Elements in Earth's Crust
(percent by weight)

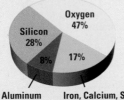

Oxygen 47%
Silicon 28%
8%
17%
Aluminum
Iron, Calcium, Sodium, Potassium, Others

Elements in the Atmosphere
(percent by volume)

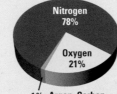

Nitrogen 78%
Oxygen 21%
1% Argon, Carbon Dioxide, Others

How Elements Are Named

How many of these elements have you heard of?

Elements are named after places, scientists, figures in mythology, or properties of the element. But no element gets a name until the International Union of Pure and Applied Chemistry (IUPAC) accepts it. In November 2004, the 111th element was approved and named. Roentgenium, with symbol Rg, was discovered by German scientists in 1995.

NAME	SYMBOL	WHAT IT IS	WHEN FOUND	NAMED FOR
Aluminum	Al	metal	1825	*alumen*, Latin word for "alum"
Californium	Cf	radioactive metal	1950	state of California, and the University of California
Helium	He	gas	1868	the Greek work *helios*, meaning sun
Iodine	I	nonmetallic solid	1811	the Greek word *iodes*, meaning violet
Iridium	Ir	transitional metal	1804	the Latin word *iridis*, meaning rainbow
Krypton	Kr	gas	1898	the Greek word *kryptos*, meaning hidden
Mercury	Hg	transitional metal	1500 B.C.	the Roman god Mercury
Neon	Ne	gas	1898	the Greek word *neon*, meaning new
Polonium	Po	metal	1898	Poland, native land of chemist Marie Curie; she and her husband discovered it.
Uranium	U	radioactive metal	1789	the planet Uranus

All About...
Compounds

Carbon, hydrogen, nitrogen, and oxygen are the most common chemical elements in the human body. Many other elements may be found in small amounts. These include calcium, iron, phosphorus, potassium, and sodium.

When elements join together, they form compounds. Water is a compound made up of hydrogen and oxygen. Salt is a compound made up of sodium and chlorine.

Common Name	Contains the Compound	Contains the Elements
Baking soda	sodium bicarbonate	sodium, hydrogen, carbon, oxygen
Chalk	calcium carbonate	calcium, carbon, oxygen
Soda bubbles	carbon dioxide	carbon, oxygen
Rust	iron oxide	iron, oxygen
Sugar	sucrose	carbon, hydrogen, oxygen
Toothpaste	sodium fluoride	sodium, fluorine
Vinegar	acetic acid	carbon, hydrogen, oxygen

CHEMICAL SYMBOLS ARE SCIENTIFIC SHORTHAND

When scientists write the names of elements, they often use a symbol instead of spelling out the full name. The symbol for each element is one or two letters. Scientists write O for oxygen and He for helium. The symbols usually come from the English name for the element (C for carbon). The symbols for some of the elements come from the element's Latin name. For example, the symbol for gold is Au, which is short for aurum, the Latin word for gold.

Mini Experiment: MAKE PLASTIC

One of the most common compounds is plastic. Plastics are made of polymers, which are really long molecules chained together. Most plastics we use are made from oil, but not all. Try making some. CAUTION: this may smell funny.

You'll need:
- 1 cup of whole milk (or heavy cream—the fattier, the better)
- Vinegar (or lemon juice)
- Saucepan
- Strainer

In the saucepan, heat the milk and bring it to a simmer. Do not let it boil. Adding a few tablespoons at a time, stir in the vinegar with a spoon until the milk starts to separate into solids and liquids. Remove from heat. Strain the mixture when it's cool enough to handle. The rubbery and soft stuff in the strainer is plastic. By heating the milk and adding the vinegar, you started a chemical reaction that brought out the natural polymers in the milk, and made a natural plastic. See how your plastic stuff reacts when pinched, stretched, or dropped. If you let it sit for a while, or put it in the freezer, it will get hard.

Physical Science
SOUND and LIGHT

Sound

Sound is a form of energy that is made up of waves traveling through mass. When you "hear" a sound, it is actually your ear detecting the vibrations of molecules as the sound wave passes through. To understand sound, you first have to understand waves. Take a bowl full of water and drop a penny into the middle of it. You'll see little circular waves move away from the area where the penny hit, spread out to the bowl's edges, and bounce back. Sound moves in the same way. The waves must travel through a gas, liquid, or a solid. In the vacuum of space, there is no sound because there are no molecules to vibrate. When you talk, your vocal chords vibrate to produce sound waves.

Light

Light is a little more tricky. It is a form of energy known as electromagnetic radiation that is emitted from a source. It travels as waves in straight lines and spreads out over a larger area the farther it goes. Scientists also think it goes along as particles known as photons. Light is produced in many ways, but mostly it comes from electrons that vibrate at high frequencies when heated to a high enough temperature.

Regular white light is made up of all the colors of the spectrum from red to violet. Each color has its own frequency. When you see a color on something, such as a red apple, that means that the apple absorbed all other colors of the spectrum and only reflected the red light. Things that are white reflect almost all the light that hits them. Things that are black, on the other hand, absorb all the light that hits them.

Moving Fast

Sound travels fast but light travels unbelievably faster. You've probably noticed that when you see lightning, you don't hear the thunder until several seconds after. That's because the light reaches you before the sound. The speed of sound varies depending on temperature and air pressure (it also travels faster through liquids and solids). A jet traveling at about 761 miles per hour is considered to be flying at the "speed of sound." But this is nothing compared to light. It goes 186,000 miles per second! It goes the same speed no matter what. Scientists don't think anything in the universe can travel faster.

Physical Science

How Simple Machines Work

Simple machines are devices that make our lives easier. Cars could not run, skyscrapers couldn't be built, and elevators couldn't carry people up if it were not for simple machines.

Inclined Plane When trying to get a refrigerator onto the back of a truck, a worker will use a ramp, or inclined plane. Instead of lifting something heavy a short distance, we can more easily push it over a longer distance, but to the same height.
Some Other Examples: escalators, staircases, slides.

Lever Any kind of arm, bar, or plank that can pivot on something (known as a fulcrum), is a lever. Depending on where the fulcrum is located on the lever, it can be used for different things.
Some Other Examples: shovel, bottle opener, back part of a hammer used for prying out nails, seesaw.

Wedge These machines are two inclined planes fastened onto each other to make a point. Wedges are used to pull things apart and even cut.
Some Other Examples: axes, knives.

Wheel and Axle This is another kind of lever, but instead of going up and down, it goes around. The wheel is the lever and the axle on which it turns is the fulcrum.
Some Other Examples: cars, bicycles, wagons.

Pulley A pulley is similar to a wheel and axle, except that there's no axle. It can be used to change both the direction and level force needed to move an object. The best example is a crane. An object is tied to a cable, which goes up and around the pulley, and down to the crane engine which is pulling it.
Some Other Examples: a block and tackle, a flag pole, tow trucks.

Screw A screw is an inclined plane wrapped around a cylinder. In the case of a wood screw, as it is turned it embeds itself farther into the piece of wood. Another use of a screw is to hold things in place such as the lid on a jar.
Some Other Examples: drills, corkscrews.

All About... Cells

Cells are sometimes called the "building blocks" of all living things. Complex life forms have many cells. There are trillions of them in the human body.

There are two main kinds of cells: **eukaryotic** and **prokaryotic**. All the cells in your body—along with the cells of other animals, plants, and fungi—are eukaryotic. These contain several different structures, called **organelles**. Like tools in a toolbox, each kind of organelle has its own function. The **nucleus**, for example, contains most of the cell's DNA, while the **mitochondria** provide energy for the body. The **ribosomes** are involved in making proteins.

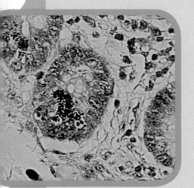

▲ Plant cell

Though both plant and animal cells are eukaryotic, they are different in a few ways. Animal cells rely only on mitochondria for energy, but plant cells also make use of another kind of organelle called a **chloroplast**. Chloroplasts contain chlorophyll, a green chemical plants use to make oxygen and energy from sunlight and water. This process is called **photosynthesis**. And unlike animal cells, plant cells are surrounded by a nonliving, rigid cell wall made of **cellulose**.

Prokaryotes (organisms with prokaryotic instead of eukaryotic cells) are all around you—and even inside of you. Most prokaryotes, such as bacteria, are single-celled. They don't have the variety of organelles that eukaryotic cells do.

WHAT IS DNA?

Every cell in every living thing (or organism) has **DNA**, a molecule that holds all the information about that organism. The structure of DNA was discovered in 1953 by the British scientist Francis Crick and the American scientist James Watson. James Watson was a World Almanac reader as a kid.

Lengths of connected DNA molecules, called **genes**, are tiny pieces of code. They determine what each organism is like. Almost all the DNA and genes come packaged in thread-like structures called **chromosomes**—humans have 46. There are 22 almost identical pairs, plus the X and Y chromosomes, which determine whether a human is male (one X chromosome and one Y chromosome) or female (two X chromosomes).

Genes are passed on from parents to children, and no two organisms (except clones or identical twins) have the same DNA.

Many things—the color of our eyes or hair, whether we're tall or short, our chances of getting certain diseases—depend on our genes.

The Human Genome

In 2000, the U.S. Human Genome Project and the company Celera Genomics identified the 3.1 billion separate codes in human DNA. In 2003, researchers succeeded in mapping out all the human chromosomes.

The human genome contains 20,000 to 25,000 genes. That's fewer than the 50,000-plus genes of a rice plant! But unlike many other genes, human genes can produce more than one kind of protein. Proteins perform most life functions and make up a large part of cellular structures.

By studying human genes, scientists can learn more about hereditary diseases and get a better idea of how humans evolved.

Tiny Creatures

Microbes Anton van Leeuwenhoek (pronounced Lay-wen-ook) made the first practical microscope in 1674. When he looked through it, he saw tiny bacteria, plant cells, and fungi, among other things. When he wrote about his findings, Leeuwenhoek called the creatures "wee beasties." We call them **microorganisms** ("micro" means *little*), or microbes. Before the microscope, people had no idea that there were millions of tiny living things crawling all over them.

Amoebas Amoebas are eukaryotic jelly-like blobs of protoplasm that ooze through their microscopic world. They eat by engulfing their food and slowly digesting it. To move around, the cell extends a part of its goo to create something called a **pseudopod** (soo-doh-pod), which means "false foot." The amoeba uses this to pull the rest of its "body" along. Amoebas normally live in water or on moist surfaces. In humans, most kinds of amoebas are harmless, but some cause diseases.

Diatoms Diatoms are one-celled algae that make glass shells to protect themselves. When they die, their shells collect at the bottom of the ocean in great numbers and form something called **diatomaceous earth**. It's gritty like sandpaper. Diatomaceous earth was once used in toothpaste to help scrape plaque off teeth. Nowadays, among other things, it is used as a pesticide—when sprayed in the air, it gets caught in the lungs of insects and slowly suffocates them.

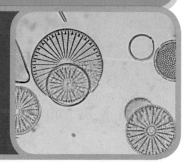

Mini Experiment: GROW SOME FUNGI

You can't see individual microbes without a microscope, but you can see groups of them. The easiest to see and grow are fungi—plant-like organisms that unlike regular plants, cannot make their own food but instead feed off other organisms. Sometimes fungi can grow in places where they aren't wanted, like bread. You can try growing some bread mold at home.

You'll need:
- 2 slices of white bread
- 2 tablespoons of water mixed with about 1 teaspoon of sugar
- 2 clear-plastic resealable bags (or glass jars with lids if you have them)

Take both pieces of white bread, and sprinkle them with the sugar water. Seal them each in their own resealable bag. Put all the bags in a warm dark place such as a cupboard or a drawer in your house. Check your bags each day for about 2 weeks. If all goes well, you should be seeing some fuzzy stuff growing on your bread. These are groups of fungi. Look closely at the different colors of the mold as it eats away at the bread. Try the experiment again using other liquids and other types of bread.

Whatever you do, wash your hands each time after you've finished.

SCIENCE q&a

WHY DO PLANTS NEED SUNLIGHT? Sunlight—along with water and carbon dioxide, a gas found in the air—is necessary for photosynthesis. That's the process by which plants make their food. In fact, the word *photosynthesis* means *putting together* (synthesis) with *light* (photo). Leaves are the food factories in plants, where photosynthesis takes place. Chlorophyll, a chemical that gives leaves their green color, plays a key role in the process. Photosynthesis also releases oxygen into the atmosphere—a good thing, since that's what people breathe! In winter when there is less sunlight, photosynthesis slows down and then stops, and plants live off the food they have stored. When the green chlorophyll goes out of the leaves, they take on the color of other chemicals in them—that's how trees get their beautiful autumn leaves.

CAN YOU HEAR THE OCEAN IN A CONCH SHELL? No. What you really hear are sounds from the air around you. The shell acts as a mini-echo chamber, increasing and distorting the sounds so that they resemble the roar of ocean waves.

IS QUICKSAND FOR REAL? Yes, but it's not as deadly as it is in the movies. Quicksand forms when sand gets mixed with too much water and becomes loosened and soupy. It may look like normal sand, but if you were to step on it, the pressure from your foot would cause the sand to act more like a liquid, and you'd sink right in. In quicksand, the more you struggle, the more you'll sink. But if you remain still, you'll start to float. So if you ever do fall into quicksand, remember to stay calm, and don't move until you've stopped sinking. Then very slowly try to get flat on your stomach and crawl out. Quicksand isn't very common, but if you were to step in some, you're not likely to sink deeper than up to your waist.

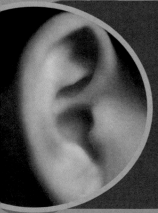

WHY DO MY EARS POP WHEN I GO UP IN A PLANE? Ear popping is the sound made when the air pressure in your ears needs to even out with the air outside. In the middle part of each ear, there is a sac of air behind the eardrum. The air there usually has the same air pressure as the air outside. When you take off in an airplane, the air pressure outside the ear goes down, but the pressure inside the ear is still at the same as it was on the ground. The inside air starts to push against the eardrum, causing pain. From the sac of air in each ear leads a tube called the Eustachian tube, which connects to the nasal passages and outside into the environment. When we swallow or yawn, the tubes open up allowing the pressure in the ear to become more like the pressure outside the ear. This causes the popping sound. The same thing happens when your plane goes to land.

WHY CAN'T SCUBA DIVERS GO TO THE BOTTOM OF THE OCEAN? Pressure, that's why. On dry land at sea level, there is about 14.7 pounds per square inch (psi) of atmospheric pressure pressing down on you. That's like having a 14.7 pound weight placed on top of you. We don't feel it because we've adapted to it. In water, the pressure increases the deeper you go. For every 33 feet a person dives, it goes up by 14.7 psi. The pressure can get to be so great that it literally crushes people. Scuba divers don't normally go deeper than 100 feet without specialized equipment. Even then, it's hard to go lower than 300 feet because of the effects of pressure on the human body. Instead, people use specially-built submarines to reach the deepest parts of the oceans.

HOW STRONG IS GRAVITY? Compared to other forces, gravity is weak. It may feel powerful on Earth, where it takes lots of energy for airplanes and rockets to leave the ground. But this is only because the planet is so massive that it pulls everything toward its center. Magnets use a force stronger than gravity when they stick on metal. And static electricity defies gravity when it makes your hair stand on end.

WHAT IS AN ECHO? An echo is a reflection of a sound. Sound travels in waves, which can bounce off another surface. The speed of sound is slow enough so that you can hear a repeat of the sound after a slight delay when the sound waves bounce back to you. When sound waves bounce off many surfaces, such as in a cave or a canyon, you might hear several echoes.

CAN A BASEBALL PITCHER REALLY MAKE A BALL CURVE? Pitchers can make a ball curve as much as 17 1/2 inches from its path. A snap of the wrist puts extra spin on the ball. As it spins, the stitches on one side move with the airflow around it. The stitches on the other side move against the airflow. When stitches and air move together, the flow is faster. The increased speed reduces the air pressure on that side. On the opposite side, the air pressure is increased. The ball moves—curves—toward the side of the ball with the lower pressure.

WHAT CAUSES RAINBOWS? The light we usually see (visible light) is made up of different frequencies, or colors, in a certain range, called the spectrum. The colors of the visible spectrum are red, orange, yellow, green, blue, indigo, and violet. White light is a mixture of all these colors. A prism can separate the frequencies mixed in a beam of white light. When you see a rainbow, the tiny water droplets in the air act as many tiny prisms, separating the Sun's white light into the colors of the spectrum.

Homework Help

Here's a useful way to remember the order of the colors of the spectrum. Remember the name ROY G. BIV
R = red, O = orange, Y = yellow, G = green, B = blue, I = indigo, V = violet

Some FAMOUS Scientists

NICOLAUS COPERNICUS (1473–1543), Polish scientist who is known as the founder of modern astronomy. He came up with the theory that Earth and other planets revolve around the Sun. But most thinkers continued to believe that Earth was the center of the universe.

JOHANNES KEPLER (1571–1630), German astronomer who developed three laws of planetary motion. He was the first to propose a force (later named gravity) that governs planets' orbits around the Sun.

SIR ISAAC NEWTON (1642–1727), British scientist who worked out the basic laws of motion and gravity. He also showed that sunlight is made up of all the colors of the rainbow. He invented the branch of mathematics called calculus about the same time as the German scientist Gottfried von Leibniz (1646–1716), who was the first to make it widely known.

CHARLES DARWIN (1809–1882), British scientist who is best known for his theory of evolution by natural selection. According to this theory, living creatures, by gradually changing so as to have the best chances of survival, slowly developed over millions of years into the forms they have today.

GEORGE WASHINGTON CARVER (1864–1943), born in Missouri of slave parents, became world-famous for his agricultural research. He found many nutritious uses for peanuts and sweet potatoes, and taught farmers in the South to rotate their crops to increase their yield.

MARIE CURIE (1867–1934), a Polish-French physical chemist known for discovering radium, which is used to treat some diseases. She won the Nobel Prize for chemistry in 1911. She and her husband, Pierre Curie, also won the Nobel Prize for physics in 1903 for their work in radiation.

ALBERT EINSTEIN (1879–1955), German-American physicist who developed revolutionary theories about the relationships between time, space, matter, and energy. Probably the most famous and influential scientist of the 20th century, he won a Nobel Prize in 1921.

JANE GOODALL (1934-), British scientist who is a leading authority on chimpanzee behavior. Goodall discovered that chimpanzees use tools, such as twigs to "fish" for ants. She also found that chimpanzees have complex family structures and personalities. She has written widely and is an advocate for the preservation of wild habitats.

STEPHEN HAWKING (1942-), British physicist and leading authority on black holes—dense objects in space whose gravity is so strong that not even light can escape them. Hawking has also written best-selling books, including *A Brief History of Time* (1988) and *The Universe in a Nutshell* (2001).

PAUL SERENO (1957-), American paleontologist who has traveled over much of the world to discover and study early dinosaur fossils. His research has helped explain dinosaur evolution and behavior.

Science Word Search

```
T S A L P O R O L H C T T T F C D M S F
C D I S K F P Y P R S G S F Y E N O I V
H G P B E R N X X I M I H S G L U T M T
M Y U H O M H O M B C B J I O L O A P T
S M P T O R O E X I M O T A L U P I L V
I E O O A T H S S Y V H L L O L M D E I
U N M D T C O Y O Y G J A H R O O Y M Z
S L Z O O H H S O M H E M B O S C Z A Z
X J M I S P E J Y D O I N W E E U H C Z
N M B O O O N S F N T R S D T O A H H H
I Z D R V U B R I O T A H I E B M T I E
X J T B D W I I C S U H F C M Y K A N Z
N S S G A V P H R K Q C E P F A X E E S
A Y G O L O O Z U D C I R S D J U B N C
P A L E O N T O L O G I S T I K C O I A
R R R C D N A S K C I U Q E A S R C H R
F I E R E I N S T E I N M R L T C N C B
I W I S B P U L L E Y O Y E U K B Y L O
E A O F S J O L S T N O V C Y I P M A N
R D A I N U S D O E T E N Y B N L U J Y
P H Y Z I S R I G E R I F Q W E W E B A
L U R Y N F R E L V C R A X W T V J R H
L Y V G O O R G A N E L L E S I Y A P Z
G J R L C M Q A M J F W E U Y C G U W C
Q G Z N E J T G L T I K I Z C U I Z M A
```

CAN YOU FIND THESE WORDS?

They go across, up , down, backward, and diagonally. Some letters are used for more than one word, and some are not used at all.

AMOEBA
ASTROPHYSICIST
ATOM
BIOCHEMIST
CARBON
CELLULOSE
CHLOROPLAST
CHROMOSOMES
COMPOUND
DIATOM
EINSTEIN
EUKARYOTE
GENOME
HYPOTHESIS
KINETIC
LEVER
METEOROLOGY
MITOCHONDRIA
NEUTRONS
ORGANELLES
OXYGEN
PALEONTOLOGIST
PHOTOSYNTHESIS
PRESSURE
PROTONS
PULLEY
QUICKSAND
RIBOSOMES
SIMPLEMACHINE
ZOOLOGY

ANSWERS ON PAGES 334-337.
FOR MORE PUZZLES GO TO
WWW.WORLDALMANACFORKIDS.COM

Space

What is the hottest planet? ➡ page 223

The SOLAR SYSTEM

Earth and the planets travel around the Sun. Together with the Sun, they are part of the solar system.

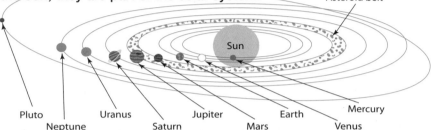

Asteroid belt

Sun

Pluto

Neptune

Uranus

Saturn

Jupiter

Mars

Earth

Venus

Mercury

The SUN is a STAR

Did you know that the Sun is a star, like the other stars you see at night? It is a typical, medium-size star. But because the Sun is much closer to our planet than any other star, we can study it in great detail. The diameter of the Sun is 865,000 miles—more than 100 times Earth's diameter. The gravity of the Sun is nearly 28 times the gravity of Earth.

How Hot Is the Sun? The surface temperature of the sun is close to 10,000° F, and it is believed that the Sun's inner core may reach temperatures around 30 million degrees! The Sun provides enough light and heat energy to support all forms of life on our planet.

The Planets Are in Motion

The planets move around the Sun along elliptical paths called **orbits**. One complete path around the Sun is called a **revolution**. Earth takes one year, or 365¼ days, to make one revolution around the Sun. Planets that are farther away from the Sun take longer. Most planets have one or more moons. A moon orbits a planet in much the same way that the planets orbit the Sun. Each planet also spins or rotates on its axis. An axis is an imaginary line running through the center of a planet. The time it takes Earth to rotate on its axis equals one day.

Homework Help

Here's a useful way to remember the names of planets in order of their usual distance from the Sun. Think of this sentence: My Very Excellent Mother Just Sent Us Nine Pizzas.

M = Mercury, **V** = Venus, **E** = Earth, **M** = Mars, **J** = Jupiter, **S** = Saturn, **U** = Uranus, **N** = Neptune, **P** = Pluto

The MOON

The Moon is about 238,900 miles from Earth. It is 2,160 miles in diameter and has no atmosphere. The dusty surface is covered with deep craters. It takes the same time for the Moon to rotate on its axis as it does to orbit Earth (27 days, 7 hours, 43 minutes). This is why one side of the Moon is always facing Earth. The Moon has no light of its own but reflects light from the Sun. The lighted part of the Moon that we see changes in a regular cycle, waxing (growing) and waning (shrinking). It takes the Moon about 29½ days to go through all the "phases" in this cycle. This is called a lunar month.

PHASES of the MOON

| New Moon | Waxing Crescent | First Quarter | Waxing Gibbous | Full Moon | Waning Gibbous | Last Quarter | Waning Crescent | New Moon |

What is an ECLIPSE?

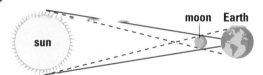

moon   Earth

sun

During a solar eclipse, the Moon casts a shadow on Earth. A total solar eclipse is when the Sun is completely blocked out. When this happens, the halo of gas around the Sun, called the **corona**, can be seen.

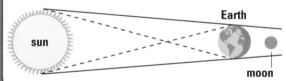

Earth

sun

moon

Sometimes Earth casts a shadow on the Moon. During a total lunar eclipse, the Moon remains visible, but it looks dark, often with a reddish tinge (from sunlight bent through Earth's atmosphere).

Upcoming Total Solar Eclipses

Total Solar Eclipses
August 1, 2008
Will be seen in northern Canada, Greenland, and Asia.
July 22, 2009
Will be seen in eastern Asia and the central Pacific Ocean.
July 11, 2010
Will be seen in the south Pacific Ocean and South America.

Upcoming Total Lunar Eclipses

Total Lunar Eclipses
March 3-4, 2007
Will be seen in Africa, Europe, and most of Asia.
August 28, 2007
Will be seen in eastern Asia, Australia, the Pacific Ocean, and the Americas.
Feb. 21, 2008
Will be seen in the Americas, Europe, Africa, and the Pacific.

PLANET EARTH
SEASONS

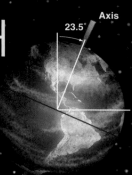

Axis

23.5°

The Earth spins on its axis of rotation. That's how we get day and night. But the Earth's axis isn't straight up and down. It is tilted about 23½ degrees. Because of this tilt, different parts of the globe get different amounts of sunlight during the year as the Earth orbits the Sun. This is how we have seasons.

SPRING At the vernal equinox (around March 21), daylight is 12 hours long throughout the world because the Earth is not tilted toward or away from the Sun. Days continue to get longer and the sunlight gets more direct in the Northern Hemisphere during spring.

WINTER Winter begins at the winter solstice (around December 21) in the Northern Hemisphere (north of the equator, where we live). Our hemisphere is tilted away from the Sun, so the Sun's rays reach us less directly. While days get longer during winter, they are still shorter than in spring and summer, so it's cold. Everything is reversed in the Southern Hemisphere, where it's summer!

Vernal Equinox

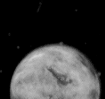

Summer Solstice

Winter Solstice

SUMMER The summer solstice (around June 21) marks the longest day of year in the Northern Hemisphere and the beginning of summer. The build-up of heat caused by more-direct sunlight during the long late spring and early summer days in the Northern Hemisphere makes summer our warmest season.

FALL After the autumnal equinox (around September 21) the Northern Hemisphere tilts away from the sun; sunlight is less direct and lasts less than 12 hours. The hemisphere cools off approaching winter.

Autumnal Equinox

NGC 4414 Galaxy, as seen by Hubble Space Telescope

What's Out There?

What else is in space besides planets?

A GALAXY is a group of billions of stars held close together by gravity. The universe may have as many as 100 billion galaxies! The one we live in is called the Milky Way. Our Sun and planets are only a small part of it. Scientists think there are as many as 200 billion stars in the Milky Way!

NEBULA is the name astronomers give to any fuzzy patch in the sky, even galaxies and star clusters. Planetary nebulas come from the late stages of some stars, while star clusters and galaxies are groups of stars. Emission nebulas, reflection nebulas, and dark dust clouds are regions of gas and dust that may be hundreds of light-years wide and are often birthplaces of stars. Emission nebulas often give off a reddish glow, caused when their hydrogen gas is heated by hot, newly formed stars nearby. Dust particles in some areas reflect hot blue starlight and appear as reflection nebulas. Dark dust clouds, though still mainly gas, contain enough dust to absorb starlight and appear as dark nebulas.

BLACK HOLE is the name given to a region in space with gravity so strong that nothing can get out—not even light. Many black holes are probably formed when giant stars at least 20 times as massive as our Sun burn up their fuel and collapse, creating very dense cores. Scientists think bigger, "supermassive" black holes may form from the collapse of many stars in the centers of galaxies. Astronomers can't see black holes, because they do not give off light. They watch for signs, such as effects on the orbits of nearby stars, or X-ray bursts from matter being sucked into the black hole.

SATELLITES are objects that move in an orbit around a planet. Moons are natural satellites. Artificial satellites, launched into orbit by humans, are used as space stations and observatories. They are also used to take pictures of Earth's surface and to transmit communications signals.

ASTEROIDS (or minor planets) are solid chunks of rock or metal that range in size from small boulders to hundreds of miles across. Ceres, the largest, is about 600 miles in diameter. Hundreds of thousands of asteroids orbit the Sun between Mars and Jupiter in the asteroid belt.

COMETS are moving chunks of ice, dust, and rock that form huge gaseous heads and tails as they move nearer to the Sun. One of the most well-known is Halley's Comet. It can be seen about every 76 years and will appear again in the year 2061.

Comet Hale-Bopp, discovered in 1995

METEOROIDS are small pieces of stone or metal traveling in space. Most meteoroids are fragments from comets or asteroids that broke off from crashes in space with other objects. A few are actually chunks that blew off from the Moon or Mars after an asteroid hit. When a meteoroid enters the Earth's atmosphere, it usually burns up completely. This streak of light is called a meteor, or **shooting star**. If a piece of a meteoroid survives its trip through our atmosphere and lands on Earth, it is called a **meteorite**.

221

THE PLANETS

1 MERCURY

Average distance from
the Sun: 36 million miles

Diameter: 3,032 miles

Average temp.: 333° F

Surface: silicate rock

Time to revolve around the Sun: 88 days

Day (synodic—midday to midday): 175.94
days

Number of moons: 0

 *Mercury is the closest planet to
the Sun, but it gets very cold there.
Since Mercury has almost no
atmosphere, most of its heat escapes at night,
and temperatures can fall to −300°.*

3 EARTH

Average distance from
the Sun: 93 million miles

Diameter: 7,926 miles

Average temp.: 59° F

Surface: water, basalt, and
granite rock

Time to revolve around the Sun: 365¼ days

Day (synodic—midday to midday): 24 hours

Number of moons: 1

 *The Earth travels around the Sun
at a speed of more than 66,000
miles per hour.*

5 JUPITER

Average distance from the
Sun: 484 million miles

Diameter: 88,732 miles

Average temp.: −162° F

Surface: liquid hydrogen

Time to revolve around the Sun: 11.9 years

Day (synodic—midday to midday): 9h 55m 30s

Number of moons: 63

 *The 4 largest moons were
discovered by Galileo in 1610; 21
others were not found until 2003.*

2 VENUS

Average distance from
the Sun: 67 million miles

Diameter: 7,521 miles

Average temp.: 867° F

Surface: silicate rock

Time to revolve around the Sun: 224.7 days

Day (synodic—midday to midday): 116.75 days

Number of moons: 0

 *Venus rotates in the opposite
direction from all the other planets.
Unlike on Earth, on Venus the Sun
rises in the west and sets in the east.*

4 MARS

Average distance from
the Sun: 142 million miles

Diameter: 4,213 miles

Average temp.: −81° F

Surface: iron-rich basaltic rock

Time to revolve around the Sun: 687 days

Day (synodic—midday to midday):
24h 39m 35s

Number of moons: 2

 *In 1877, astronomer Giovanni
Schiaparelli thought he saw lines
on Mars, which he called
"channels," or canali in Italian. This was
mistranslated into English as "canals,"
making people think there were canal-
building Martians.*

6 SATURN

Average distance from
the Sun: 887 million miles

Diameter: 74,975 miles

Average temp.: −218° F

Surface: liquid hydrogen

Time to revolve around the Sun: 29.5 years

Day (synodic—midday to midday): 10h 39m 23s

Number of moons: 47

 *Using a simple early telescope,
Galileo discovered what turned
out to be rings around Saturn.*

7 URANUS

Average distance from the Sun: 1.8 billion miles

Diameter: 31,763 miles

Average temp.: −323° F

Surface: liquid hydrogen and helium

Time to revolve around the Sun: 84 years

Day (synodic—midday to midday): 17h 14m 23s

Number of moons: 27

 Because Uranus is tipped 98 degrees on its axis, its north pole is dark for 42 years at a time.

8 NEPTUNE

Average distance from the Sun: 2.8 billion miles

Diameter: 30,603 miles

Average temp.: −330° F

Surface: liquid hydrogen and helium

Time to revolve around the Sun: 164.8 years

Day (synodic—midday to midday): 16d 6h 37m

Number of moons: 13

 Neptune was discovered in 1846, after British astronomer John Adams and French mathematician Urbain Le Verrier independently predicted where it would be, based on its effect on Uranus's orbit.

9 PLUTO

Average distance from the Sun: 3.6 billion miles

Diameter: 1,485 miles

Average temp.: −369° F

Surface: rock and frozen gases

Time to revolve around the Sun: 247.7 years

Day (synodic—midday to midday): 6d 9h 17m

Number of moons: 3

 Two new moons were discovered in 2005. They are called S/2005 P1 and S/2005 P2. Some scientists do not consider Pluto to be a planet.

THE 10TH PLANET?

In February 2006, astronomers found that an object, discovered in 2003 and located 97 AUs (about 9 billion miles) from the Sun, is bigger than Pluto. Called Xena (astronomers call it 2003 UB313), it is about 1,490 miles across. It may one day be considered the 10th planet.

More Planet Facts

Largest planet:
Jupiter (88,732 miles diameter)

Smallest planet:
Pluto (1,485 miles diameter)

Fastest orbiting planet:
Mercury (88 days)

Slowest orbiting planet:
Pluto (247.7 years)

Tallest mountain:
Mars (Olympus Mons, 15 miles high)

Hottest planet:
Venus (867° F)

Coldest planet:
Pluto (−369° F)

Shortest day:
Jupiter (9 hours, 55 minutes, 30 seconds)

Longest day:
Mercury (175.94 days)

No moons:
Mercury, Venus

Most moons:
Jupiter (63 known satellites)

EXPLORING SPACE

SOME UNMANNED MISSIONS
in the Solar System

LAUNCH DATE

1962 — **Mariner 2** First successful flyby of Venus.

1964 — **Mariner 4** First probe to reach Mars, 1965.

1972 — **Pioneer 10** First probe to reach Jupiter, 1973.

1973 — **Mariner 10** Only U.S. probe to reach Mercury, 1974.

1975 — **Viking 1 and 2** Landed on Mars in 1976.

1977 — **Voyager 1** Reached Jupiter in 1979 and Saturn in 1980.

1977 — **Voyager 2** Reached Jupiter in 1979, Saturn in 1981, Uranus in 1986, Neptune in 1989.

1989 — **Magellan** Orbited Venus and mapped its surface.

1989 — **Galileo** Reached Jupiter, 1995.

1996 — **Mars Global Surveyor** Began mapping surface in 1999.

1996 — **Mars Pathfinder** Landed on Mars. Carried a roving vehicle (Sojourner).

1997 — **Cassini** Reached Saturn in June 2004.

2001 — **Mars Odyssey** Began mapping and studying Mars in early 2002.

2003 — **Mars rovers Spirit and Opportunity** Landed on Mars in early 2004.

2005 — **Deep Impact** Reached comet Tempel 1 July 4, 2005. See page 226.

2006 — **New Horizons** Launched January 19. Due to reach Pluto in 2015. See page 226.

Mariner 2

Mars Odyssey

Milestones in Human Spaceflight

The U.S. formed NASA in 1958. It was in response to the Soviet Union's launching of the first artificial satellite *Sputnik I* on October 4, 1957. Since then, more than 400 astronauts have made trips into space to conduct research, visit orbiting space stations, and explore the Moon. Below are some of the biggest moments in human space flight.

1961	On April 12, Soviet cosmonaut Yuri Gagarin, in *Vostok 1*, became the first person to orbit Earth. On May 5, U.S. astronaut Alan B. Shepard Jr. during the *Mercury 3* mission became the first American in space.
1962	On February 20, U.S. astronaut John H. Glenn Jr. during the *Mercury 6* mission became the first American to orbit Earth.
1963	From June 16 to 19, the Soviet spacecraft *Vostok 6* carried the first woman in space, Valentina V. Tereshkova.
1965	On March 18, Soviet cosmonaut Aleksei A. Leonov became the first person to "walk" in space.
1966	On March 16, U.S. *Gemini 8* became the first craft to dock with (become attached to) another vehicle (an unmanned Agena rocket).
1969	On July 20, U.S. *Apollo 11's* lunar module *Eagle* landed on the Moon's surface in the area known as the Sea of Tranquility. Neil Armstrong was the first person ever to walk on the Moon.
1070	In April, *Apollo 13* astronauts returned safely to Earth after an explosion damaged their spacecraft and prevented them from landing on the Moon.
1973	On May 14, the U.S. put its first space station, *Skylab*, into orbit. The last *Skylab* crew left in January 1974.
1975	On July 15, the U.S. launched an *Apollo* spacecraft and the Soviet Union launched a *Soyuz* spacecraft. Two days later, the American and Soviet crafts docked, and for several days their crews worked and spent time together in space.
1981	*Columbia* was launched and became the first space shuttle to reach space.
1986	On January 28, space shuttle *Challenger* exploded 73 seconds after takeoff. All seven astronauts, including teacher Christa McAuliffe, died. In February, the Soviet space station *Mir* was launched into orbit.
1995	In June, Atlantis docked with *Mir* for the first time.
1998	In December, *Endeavour* was launched with *Unity*, a U.S.-built part of the International Space Station (ISS). The crew attached it to the Russian-built *Zarya* control module.
2000	The first crew arrived at the ISS in November.
2001	The 15-year Russian *Mir* program ended. Parts of it splashed down in the Pacific in March.
2003	On February 1, space shuttle *Columbia* disintegrated during its reentry into the Earth's atmosphere, killing the seven-member crew.
2005	Space shuttle *Discovery* was launched July 26. Its 13-day mission was to test new safety upgrades to the shuttle. Though successful, NASA decided to ground all other shuttles until they could be absolutely sure they were safe to fly.

SPACE NEWS

Deep Impact Slams Into Comet

Scientists wanted to see what was inside a comet. Since they couldn't fly onto one and start digging, they did the next best thing—they blew a hole in one using a small craft. The *Deep Impact* space probe was launched January 12, 2005. It carried with it an 820-pound, coffee table-sized impact probe. On July 4, 2005, it detached its probe near comet Tempel 1. *Deep Impact* itself stayed back to take pictures. The impact probe cruised along and slammed into the comet at a speed of about 23,000 mph (about 30 times the speed of sound on Earth). It blew a hole about the size of a football field and kicked up tons of dust and debris. One of the reasons scientists are so interested in comets is that understanding what's inside comets can help us to understand how the solar system was formed. Scientists are still analyzing the data from the impact.

Deep Impact

New Horizons Takes Off for Pluto

The *New Horizons* spacecraft blasted off from Cape Canaveral, Florida, on January 19, 2006. It will be the first probe to explore Pluto and its moon Charon. From Earth, only the most powerful telescopes can see Pluto, so it has been difficult for scientists to study it.

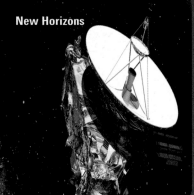

New Horizons

New Horizons will fly by Jupiter in February 2007. There scientists will test the probe's instruments to make sure everything is working okay. Afterward, the craft will use Jupiter's gravity to sling itself towards Pluto. It's due to reach that icy world in July 2015. There it will take pictures of the planet and take readings of its atmosphere and terrain.

Finally, the craft will continue on toward an area of the solar system known as the Kuiper Belt. Scientists think that comets come from the Kuiper Belt. Some think that even Pluto came from the Kuiper Belt. *New Horizons* is due to reach that area sometime between 2016 and 2020.

Massive Lightning Storm on Saturn

The *Cassini* space probe detected a huge lightning storm on Saturn in February 2006. It turned out to be the biggest lightning storm ever seen. According to NASA scientists, the storm covered an area about 2,175 miles long. A storm that size on Earth would cover almost all of the continental U.S.! In addition, the lightning activity was 1,000 times stronger than the lightning on Earth. Lightning has been seen in our solar system only on Earth, Jupiter, and Saturn.

Lightning storm on Saturn

Same Stars,
Different Pictures

When we look up in the sky, we see constellations such as the Big Dipper and the Pleiades. But throughout human history, people from different cultures have seen different things.

THE PLEIADES

The Pleiades star cluster is also known as the "seven sisters." It was named by the ancient Greeks after the seven daughters of Atlas and Pleione, who were titans according to myth. The Aztecs, on the other hand, called them *Tianquiztli*, which means "marketplace."

Aztec priests followed the movements of Tianquiztli over 52-year cycles. At the end of each cycle, they held an event known as the New Fire Ceremony. During this ceremony, if Tianquiztli reached its highest point in the sky that night, then the world would be well for another 52 years. If it didn't, the Aztecs believed that demons would come up from the ground and destroy the world.

The Hopi Indians of the American southwest called the cluster *Chuhukon*, which means "those who cling together." The Hopi thought that they were descendants of the Chuhukon.

THE BIG DIPPER

We call it "the big dipper" because to us it looks like a big dipping cup with a handle in the sky. The ancient Greeks saw the constellation as part of a larger grouping called *Ursa Major*. That means "big bear." In Greek myth, Zeus changed Callisto into a bear to hide her from his wife Hera. As the story goes, Callisto's son accidentally killed his mother, not knowing that she was the bear.

The ancient Chinese thought of this constellation of stars as a chariot for the emperor.

Arabians saw the cup part of the Big Dipper as a coffin. The stars making up the handle were mourners.

Ancient Germanic tribes thought it was a big wagon in the sky.

Before the American Civil War (1861-1865), slaves escaping plantations would travel toward northern U.S. states and Canada, where slavery was outlawed. They called the Big Dipper the "Drinking Gourd" and it was thought of as a sign in the sky pointing the way north to freedom.

Celaeno
Electra
Taygeta
Asterope   Maia
Merope
Alcyone

Pleione   Atlas

Big Dipper

Ursa Major

Sports

What NFL team won an "Ice Bowl" in 1967? ➡ page 239

Can you "bend it like Beckham"? Drive through the paint all the way to the hoop? Nail a 360°? Whether you play in a league or with friends in the neighborhood, prefer a solo bike trip or a hike through a nearby park, there are lots of awesome ways to stay fit, have fun, and get your game on.

FAVORITE SPORTS

Here are some favorite sports or activities, and the number of U.S. kids who enjoy each.

Boys (ages 6-17)		Girls (ages 6-17)	
1. Bicycling	11.3 million	1. Bicycling	10.1 million
2. Basketball	9.8 million	2. Walking/Hiking	9.0 million
3. Bowling	8.2 million	3. Bowling	8.9 million
4. Football	8.1 million	4. Volleyball	7.6 million
5. Soccer	6.8 million	5. Basketball	6.2 million
6. Skateboarding	6.6 million	6. Soccer	6.2 million
7. Walking/Hiking	5.3 million	7. In-Line Skating	5.5 million
8. In-Line Skating	4.9 million	8. Softball	5.0 million
9. Baseball	4.8 million	9. Scooter Riding	4.5 million
10. Scooter Riding	4.5 million	10. Ice Skating	4.3 million

LITTLE LEAGUE

Little League Baseball is the largest youth sports program in the world. It began in 1939 in Williamsport, Pennsylvania, with 45 boys playing on three teams. Now about 2.6 million boys and girls ages 5 to 18 play on over 200,000 Little League teams in more than 100 countries.

WEB SITE *www.littleleague.org*

STRANGE SPORTS

Most American kids are familiar with sports like soccer, basketball, baseball, and football, because they see them (and play them!) all the time. But some sports are seldom played on American fields, courts, or gridirons. Imagine yourself playing one of these somewhat unfamiliar sports.

CURLING

Curling dates back to the early 16th century in Scotland. It's like shuffleboard on ice. Matches take place on an ice rink or a natural ice field and are played by two teams of four. Each player slides a 42-pound "stone" across the ice toward the "button," a mark at the center of a circle. The other three players on the ice help the stone along, using long-handled brooms or brushes on the ice just ahead of the stone. Each team's goal is to get its stones closest to the button. Blocking and knocking out an opponent's stone are important parts of the game. A game is made up of 10 "ends." An end is over when each team has thrown 16 stones. Curling became an official Winter Olympics medal sport in 1998 in Nagano, Japan.

JOGGLING

Joggling is a combination of juggling and jogging. Contestants run races while juggling three, five, or seven balls at a time. The races range in length from short sprints to 5 kilometers (a little over 3 miles). Relay races, which involve exchanging juggled balls with team members, are also run. The Joggling World Championships are held every year as part of the International Jugglers' Association's summer festival. The first took place in 1980; the 2006 event will be held July 17-23 in Portland, Oregon.

UNDERWATER HOCKEY

Underwater hockey, also known as "octopush," was invented by four English scuba divers in 1954. The game is played at the bottom of a swimming pool between two teams of six. Players wear fins, a diving mask, and a snorkel to play. They use a short stick 10-12 inches long to slide a 3-pound puck into the opposing team's goal underwater. Everyone on a team has to work together to score, since no one can go too long without coming up for air! World championships are held every two years. The 2006 tournament was scheduled to take place August 13-26, 2006, in Sheffield, Great Britain.

I was born on September 3, 1986. I won my first amateur snowboarding competition at the age of 7, and turned pro when I was only 13. When I was 15, I just missed making the 2002 Winter Olympic snowboarding team. In 2006, I made it to the Winter Olympics in Turin, Italy, and won a gold medal in the Men's Halfpipe. I'm also a pro skateboarder. I was the first athlete ever to compete—and medal—in both the Summer and Winter X Games. If you don't remember my name, you may remember me better as the "Flying Tomato."

WHO AM I?

Answer: Shaun White

The **OLYMPIC GAMES**

The first Olympics were held in Greece more than 2,500 years ago. In 776 B.C. they featured just one event—a footrace. Boxing, wrestling, chariot racing, and the pentathlon (which consisted of five different events) came later. The Olympic Games were held every four years for more than 1,000 years, until A.D. 393, when the Roman emperor Theodosius stopped them. The first modern games were held in Athens in 1896. Winter Olympics were added in 1924.

2006 WINTER OLYMPICS: TURIN, ITALY

Turin, Italy, hosted 2,600 athletes and over 1 million spectators in 2006 at the 20th Winter Games, February 10-26.

The athletes in Turin represented 85 countries and competed for 84 gold medals in the sports listed below. Germany finished the games with the most medals (29), followed by the U.S. (25) and Canada (24). 2006 U.S. women's figure skating champion Sasha Cohen picked up the silver medal in Turin. The U.S. also won 3 out of the 6 snowboarding events.

Originally, the winter and summer games were both held every four years. But starting in 1994, the schedule changed. Now the winter and summer games alternate every two years. Athletes in the next Summer Games—to be held in Beijing, China, Aug. 8-24, 2008—will compete in 302 medal events. The next Winter Games will be held in Vancouver, Canada, in 2010.

Sasha Cohen

2006 WINTER OLYMPIC SPORTS

- Alpine Skiing
- Biathlon
- Bobsled (bobsleigh)
- Cross-country skiing
- Curling
- Freestyle (skiing)
- Figure Skating
- Ice Hockey
- Luge
- Nordic combined
- Short track Speed Skating
- Ski Jumping
- Skeleton
- Snowboarding
- Speed Skating (long track)

PARALYMPICS

The Paralympic Games are the official Olympic Games for athletes with physical, mental, or sensory disabilities. The games got their start in 1948, when Sir Ludwig Guttman organized a competition for World War II veterans with spinal-cord injuries in England. When athletes from the Netherlands joined in 1952, the movement went international.

Olympic-style competition began in Rome in 1961, and the first Winter Paralympics were held in Sweden in 1976. Since 1991, the Paralympics have been held just after Winter and Summer Olympic competition. Following the 2006 Winter Olympics in Turin, Italy, about 590 athletes from more than 40 countries took part in the Paralympic Winter Games at the Turin Olympic venues. The next Summer Paralympics will take place in Beijing, China, in 2008.

OFFICIAL PARALYMPIC SPORTS

Six Competitive Levels: wheelchair, intellectual disabilities, amputees, visual disabilities, cerebral palsy, and other mobility disabilities

Winter: alpine and nordic skiing, ice sledge hockey, wheelchair curling

Summer: archery, athletics, boccia, bowls, cycling, equestrian, football, goalball, judo, powerlifting, sailing, shooting, swimming, table tennis, volleyball, wheelchair basketball, wheelchair dance sport, wheelchair fencing, wheelchair rugby, wheelchair tennis

WEB SITE www.paralympics.org

SPECIAL OLYMPICS

The Special Olympics is the world's largest program of sports training and athletic competition for children and adults with intellectual disabilities. Founded in 1968, Special Olympics has offices in all 50 U.S. states and Washington, D.C., and throughout the world. The organization offers training and competition to nearly 2 million athletes in 150 countries.

The Special Olympics holds World Games every two years. These alternate between summer and winter sports. In winter 2005, Nagano, Japan hosted 1,829 athletes from 80 countries in the 8th Special Olympic World Winter Games. The next World Summer Games are scheduled for October 10-19, 2007, in Shanghai, China. The U.S. planned nationwide games to be held for the first time July 3-8, 2006, in Ames, Iowa.

Auto Racing

NASCAR

Bill France founded the National Association for Stock Car Auto Racing in 1947. "Big Bill" seized on the idea of racing American cars like the kind people drove everyday. The first "Strictly Stock" cars couldn't be modified at all, except for a good engine tuning. Gradually companies started making parts especially for stock car racing—beginning in 1952 with heavy-duty racing tires. Stock cars today are high-tech versions of American-manufactured automobiles.

The first NASCAR championship was staged in 1949. It was originally called Strictly Stock, and got other names after that. Since 2004, the championship has been known as the Nextel Cup. Races in the Nextel Cup series include the Daytona 500, which kicks off the racing season, the Brickyard 400, and the Coca-Cola 600.

PAST NASCAR CHAMPIONS

1980 . . . . . . Dale Earnhardt	1989 . . . . . . Rusty Wallace	1998 . . . . . . Jeff Gordon
1981 . . . . . . Darrell Waltrip	1990 . . . . . . Dale Earnhardt	1999 . . . . . . Dale Jarrett
1982 . . . . . . Darrell Waltrip	1991 . . . . . . Dale Earnhardt	2000 . . . . . . Bobby Labonte
1983 . . . . . . Bobby Allison	1992 . . . . . . Alan Kulwicki	2001 . . . . . . Jeff Gordon
1984 . . . . . . Terry Labonte	1993 . . . . . . Dale Earnhardt	2002 . . . . . . Tony Stewart
1985 . . . . . . Darrell Waltrip	1994 . . . . . . Dale Earnhardt	2003 . . . . . . Matt Kenseth
1986 . . . . . . Dale Earnhardt	1995 . . . . . . Jeff Gordon	2004 . . . . . . Kurt Busch
1987 . . . . . . Dale Earnhardt	1996 . . . . . . Terry Labonte	2005 . . . . . . Tony Stewart
1988 . . . . . . Bill Elliott	1997 . . . . . . Jeff Gordon	

The famous Daytona 500 is a 500-mile race, as the name suggests. But in the history of NASCAR's premier event, four races have fallen short of that mark. In 1965 and 1966, rain shortened the race to 322.5 miles and 495 miles, respectively. Race officials voluntarily shortened the 1974 Daytona to 450 miles due to the 1973-74 oil shortages. The shortest Daytona 500 ever barely made it past the halfway mark. That race was called in 2003 after only 272.5 miles, because of rain.

Indianapolis 500

The first Indianapolis 500 was held in 1911. The race was organized at the Indianapolis Motor Speedway, by a local car dealer named Carl Fisher. Ray Harroun won the first Indy with an average speed of only 74.602 miles per hour. The event was a huge success, and the next year the prize for the winner rose to $20,000—equal to about $400,000 in today's money.

PAST INDY WINNERS

Year	Winner	Speed
1911	Ray Harroun	74.602 mph
1920	Gaston Chevrolet	88.618 mph
1930	Billy Arnold	100.448 mph
1940	Wilbur Shaw	114.277 mph
1950	Johnnie Parsons	124.002 mph
1900	Jim Rathmann	138.707 mph
1970	Al Unser	155.749 mph
1980	Johnny Rutherford	142.862 mph
1990	Arie Luyendyk	185.981 mph*
2000	Juan Montoya	167.607 mph
2001	Helio Castroneves	131.294 mph
2002	Helio Castroneves	166.499 mph
2003	Gil de Ferran	156.291 mph
2004	Buddy Rice	138.518 mph
2005	Dan Wheldon	157.603 mph

* Race record for average lap speed.

All About DANICA PATRICK

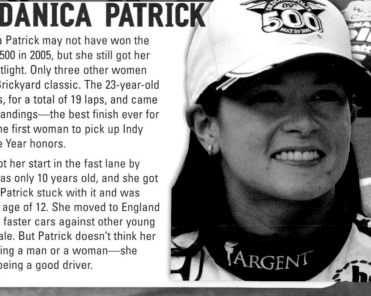

Danica Patrick may not have won the Indianapolis 500 in 2005, but she still got her share of time in the spotlight. Only three other women have ever raced in the Brickyard classic. The 23-year-old held the lead three times, for a total of 19 laps, and came in fourth place in the final standings—the best finish ever for a woman. Patrick became the first woman to pick up Indy Racing League Rookie of the Year honors.

Patrick started small. She got her start in the fast lane by racing go-karts when she was only 10 years old, and she got lapped in her first race. But Patrick stuck with it and was winning go-kart titles by the age of 12. She moved to England when she was 16 to train on faster cars against other young drivers, who were mostly male. But Patrick doesn't think her success should be about being a man or a woman—she wants to be recognized for being a good driver.

BASEBALL

The Chicago White Sox waved goodbye to one of baseball's most infamous losing streaks in the 2005 World Series, beating the Houston Astros in four straight games. The White Sox victory came just one year after the Boston Red Sox snapped another of baseball's most famous losing streaks. 2005 was the first time that the White Sox had won a World Series since 1917. They had lost the World Series in 1919 in what would become known as the "Black Sox" scandal (see next page). Only the Chicago Cubs have gone longer without winning baseball's fall classic.

The 2005 event marked the Houston Astros' first World Series appearance since the franchise joined the National League in 1962. They also became the first team ever to be swept in their World Series debut. White Sox right fielder Jermaine Dye was named the most valuable player (MVP) of the series. He hit .438, with seven hits and three RBIs, including the only run scored in the decisive final game.

2005 MAJOR LEAGUE STANDOUTS

MVP AWARD
NL: Albert Pujols, St. Louis
AL: Alex Rodriguez, New York Yankees

CY YOUNG AWARD (top pitcher)
NL: Chris Carpenter, St. Louis
AL: Bartolo Colon, Los Angeles Angels

ROOKIE OF THE YEAR
NL: Ryan Howard, Philadelphia
AL: Huston Street, Oakland

BATTING CHAMPS
NL: Derrek Lee, Chicago, .335
AL: Michael Young, Texas, .331

HOME RUN LEADERS
NL: Andruw Jones, Atlanta, 51
AL: Alex Rodriguez, New York Yankees, 48

EARNED RUN AVERAGE LEADERS
NL: Roger Clemens, Houston, 1.87
AL: Kevin Millwood, Cleveland, 2.86

COOL FEATS, FACTS, & FIRSTS

▶ Yankees third baseman Alex Rodriguez hit his 400th career home run on June 8, 2005. At only 29 years, 316 days old, "A-Rod" became the youngest player in MLB history to pass that milestone.

▶ Cubs pitcher Greg Maddux claimed his 3,000th career strikeout on July 26, 2005. The 39-year-old became only the 13th pitcher in history to reach that milestone.

▶ Game Three of the 2005 World Series, played Oct. 25, 2005, went longer than any other World Series game in history. The White Sox and Astros battled it out for 5 hours, 41 minutes over 14 innings at Minute Maid Park in Houston, TX. In 1916, the only other World Series game to go to 14 innings lasted only 2 hours, 32 minutes.

Some **Major League** Records*

BATTERS

Most home runs
Career: 755, Hank Aaron (1954-76)
Season: 73, **Barry Bonds** (2001)
Game: 4, by 15 different players

Most hits
Career: 4,256, Pete Rose (1963-86)
Season: 262, **Ichiro Suzuki** (2004)
Game: 7, Rennie Stennett (1975)

Most stolen bases
Career: 1,406, Rickey Henderson (1979-2003)
Season: 130, Rickey Henderson (1982)
Game: 6, Eddie Collins (1912)

PITCHERS

Most strikeouts
Career: 5,714, Nolan Ryan (1966-93)
Season: 383, Nolan Ryan (1973)
Game: 20, **Roger Clemens** (1986, 1996);
      Kerry Wood (1998)

Most wins
Career: 511, Cy Young (1890-1911)
Season: 41, Jack Chesbro (1904)

Most saves
Career: 478, Lee Smith (1980-97)
Season: 57, Bobby Thigpen (1990)

*Through the 2005 season. Players in bold played in 2005. Game stats are for nine-inning games only.

The **BLACK** Sox

"Shoeless" Joe Jackson

Two of baseball's three longest World Series losing streaks came to an end when the Boston Red Sox won the World Series in 2004 and the Chicago White Sox won the crown in 2005. But have you heard of the "Black Sox"?

In 1919, the Chicago White Sox were set to challenge the underdog Cincinnati Reds in a best-of-nine World Series. Favored to win, the White Sox went on to lose the series five games to three, in what would become the biggest scandal in Major League Baseball's history.

A year later, eight White Sox players were accused of plotting with gamblers to intentionally lose the series to the Reds. Fans were suspicious of the match-up from the start. In the first inning of the first game, star Sox pitcher Eddie Cicotte struck Reds leadoff hitter Morrie Raith, and talk of a conspiracy was born.

The men were found not guilty on criminal charges. But those accused—Cicotte, Claude Williams, Charles Gandil, Charles Risberg, George Weaver, Oscar Felsch, Fred McMullin, and "Shoeless" Joe Jackson— were all banned from the game for life. The 1919 lineup has since been nicknamed the "Black Sox" for corrupting the team and the spirit of the World Series.

Baseball Hall of Fame

The National Baseball Hall of Fame and Museum opened in 1939, in Cooperstown, New York. To be eligible for membership, players must be retired from baseball for five years. In 2006, Bruce Sutter was elected to "The Hall" by the traditional vote. A special committee, formed to select African American Hall of Famers from long-overlooked Negro League and pre-Negro League teams, expanded the Class of 2006 to 18 members. The historic group included Effa Manley, the Negro League's Newark Eagles co-owner and first woman elected to Cooperstown. **WEB SITE** www.baseballhalloffame.org

BASKETBALL

Basketball began in 1891 in Springfield, Massachusetts, when Dr. James Naismith invented it, using peach baskets as hoops. At first, each team had nine players instead of five. Big-time pro basketball started in 1949, when the National Basketball Association (NBA) was formed. The Women's National Basketball Association (WNBA) began play in 1997.

Michael Jordan

Great NBA Dynasties

NBA history is full of dynasty teams that set the tone for the league and the sport in general. Here's a look at a few of them—and what made them great.

Boston Celtics (1957-1969) Under the leadership of basketball great Bill Russell, the Boston Celtics dominated the NBA for over a decade, winning 11 championships in 13 years. Legendary head coach Red Auerbach guided the Celtics to eight crowns in a row (1959-66), a feat almost unheard of in any sport. After Auerbach's retirement, future Hall-of-Famer Bill Russell took the reigns and led the team—both on and off the court—as the first African American player-coach in NBA history.

Los Angeles Lakers (1980s) With a starting line-up that included future Hall-of-Famers Kareem Abdul-Jabbar, Earvin "Magic" Johnson, and James Worthy, the "Showtime" Lakers set the pace for the NBA in the 1980s. Between 1980 and 1990, the team gave up only one Pacific Division title (1981), and claimed the NBA championship title in five out of nine Finals appearances.

Chicago Bulls (1991-98) The Bulls appeared at the NBA Finals six times in eight years—and brought a championship home to Chicago each time. Superstar Michael Jordan was the Finals MVP each time, and his two-year "retirement" divided the Bulls' double "three-peat" runs. But even "Air" Jordan couldn't win championships on his own. Without the leadership of Coach Phil Jackson (who went on to guide the L.A. Lakers to three consecutive titles, 2000-02) and teammates like Scottie Pippen, the Bulls could never have claimed their crowns.

Hall of Fame

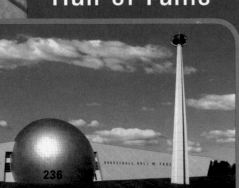

The Naismith Memorial Hall of Fame in Springfield, Massachusetts, was founded to honor great basketball players, coaches, referees, and others important to the history of the game. The class, inducted in September 2006, included NBA stars Charles Barkley, Joe Dumars, and Dominique Wilkins. College coaching legend Geno Auriemma, Big East Commissioner David Gavitt, and Italian National Team coach Sandro Gamba were also enshrined.

WEB SITE *www.hoophall.com*

Some **All-Time** NBA Records*

POINTS

Career: 38,387, Kareem Abdul-Jabbar (1969-89)

Season: 4,029, Wilt Chamberlain (1961-62)

Game: 100, Wilt Chamberlain (1962)

ASSISTS

Career: 15,806, John Stockton (1984-2003)

Season: 1,164 John Stockton (1990-91)

Game: 30, Scott Skiles (1990)

REBOUNDS

Career: 23,924, Wilt Chamberlain (1959-73)

Season: 2,149, Wilt Chamberlain (1960-61)

Game: 55, Wilt Chamberlain (1960)

3-POINTERS

Career: 2,560, Reggie Miller (1987-2005)

Season: 267, Dennis Scott (1996-97)

Game: 12, **Kobe Bryant** (2003)

*Through the 2004-2005 season. Players in bold were active in the 2005-2006 season.

Highlights of the
2005 WNBA Season

Cheryl Ford (right) and Lisa Leslie

Scoring Leader:
Sheryl Swoopes, Houston Comets
Games: 33
Points: 614
Average: 18.6

Rebounding Leader:
Cheryl Ford, Detroit Shock
Games: 33
Rebounds: 322
Average: 9.8

Blocked Shots Leader:
Margo Dydek, Connecticut Sun
Games: 31
Blocks: 71
Average: 2.29

Steals Leader:
Tamika Catchings, Indiana Fever
Games: 34
Steals: 90
Average: 2.65

Assists Leader:
Sue Bird, Seattle Storm
Games: 30
Assists: 176
Average: 5.9

College Basketball

The men's National Collegiate Athletic Association (NCAA) Tournament began in 1939. Today, it is a spectacular 65-team extravaganza. The Final Four weekend, when the semi-finals and finals are played, is one of the most-watched sports competitions in the U.S. The Women's NCAA Tournament began in 1982 and has soared in popularity.

THE 2006 NCAA TOURNAMENT RESULTS

MEN'S FINAL FOUR

SEMI-FINALS:
UCLA 59, LSU 45
Florida 73, George Mason 58

FINAL:
Florida 73, UCLA 57

MOST OUTSTANDING PLAYER:
Joakim Noah, Florida

WOMEN'S FINAL FOUR

SEMI-FINALS:
Maryland 81, North Carolina 70
Duke 64, LSU 45

FINAL:
Maryland 78, Duke 75 (OT)

MOST OUTSTANDING PLAYER:
Laura Harper, Maryland

FOOTBALL

American football began as a college sport. The first game that was like today's football took place between Yale and Harvard in New Haven, Connecticut, on November 13, 1875. The National Football League started in 1922. The rival American Football League began in 1960. The two leagues played the first Super Bowl in 1967. In 1970, the leagues merged as the NFL with an American Football Conference (AFC) and a National Football Conference (AFC).

Super Steelers Sink Seahawks

The Pittsburgh Steelers defeated the Seattle Seahawks on Feb. 5, 2006, 21-10, to clinch Super Bowl XL and their first NFL championship in 25 years. Pittsburgh wide receiver Hines Ward was named the Super Bowl's most valuable player. He caught five passes for 123 yards and one touchdown. The Steelers' Super Bowl victory was the fifth in franchise history. The Dallas Cowboys and San Francisco 49ers are the only other NFL teams to have won that many Super Bowls.

The game was played at Ford Field in Detroit, Michigan, the hometown of Steelers running back Jerome Bettis, who announced his retirement after the game.

2005 NFL LEADERS

RUSHING YARDS: Shaun Alexander, Seattle Seahawks, 1,880
RUSHING TDS: Shaun Alexander, Seattle Seahawks, 27
RECEPTIONS: Larry Fitzgerald, Arizona Cardinals, 103
RECEIVING YARDS: Steve Smith, Carolina Panthers, 1,563
RECEIVING TDS: Marvin Harrison, Indianapolis Colts, 12
Steve Smith, Carolina Panthers, 12
PASSING YARDS: Tom Brady, New England Patriots, 4,110
PASSER RATING: Peyton Manning, Indianapolis Colts, 104.1
PASSING TDS: Carson Palmer, Cincinnati Bengals, 32
INTERCEPTIONS: Ty Law, New York Jets, 10
Deltha O'Neal, Cincinnati Bengals, 10
SACKS: Derrick Burgess, Oakland Raiders, 16

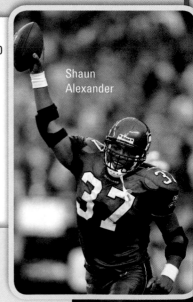

Shaun Alexander

Pro Football Hall of Fame

Football's Hall of Fame in Canton, Ohio, was founded in 1963 by the National Football League to honor outstanding players, coaches, and contributors.

Quarterback Troy Aikman, linebacker Harry Carson, head coach John Madden, quarterback Warren Moon, defensive end Reggie White, and tackle Rayfield Wright were to be inducted in August 2006.

WEB SITE *www.profootballhof.com*

FAMOUS NFL GAMES

THE ICE BOWL

December 31, 1967, NFL Championship, Green Bay, Wisconsin: Green Bay Packers 21, Dallas Cowboys 17.

It was 13 degrees below zero and windy when the game started. 50,000 fans packed the stadium. The Packers, going for their third championship in a row, grabbed an early 14-0 lead, but the cold got to them. Two fumbles in the second half led to a touchdown and a field goal for Dallas. Green Bay was down 17-14, with 4:50 remaining.

Future Hall of Famer Bart Starr led his team down inside the one-yard line. There were 16 seconds left, and the temperature had fallen to –18, and the field was frozen solid. After two running plays went nowhere, Green Bay was out of time-outs. Everyone expected Starr to try a pass. If it failed, the clock would stop, and they could kick a field goal to tie. But Starr took the snap and made his now-famous dive for the touchdown behind guard Jerry Kramer, and the NFL Championship.

THE IMMACULATE RECEPTION

December 23, 1972, AFC Divisional Playoffs, Pittsburgh, Pennsylvania: Pittsburgh Steelers 13, Oakland Raiders 7. Down 7-6, with just over a minute left, the Steelers' Terry Bradshaw fired a pass downfield to halfback John Fuqua, who was hit hard by Raiders defender Jack Tatum just as the ball arrived. It hit one of the players and bounced in the air and, luckily for the Steelers, into the hands of rookie running back Franco Harris. After his "immaculate reception," Harris ran 42 yards for a touchdown with 5 seconds left.

THE MUSIC CITY MIRACLE

January 8, 2000, AFC Wild Card Playoff, Nashville, Tennessee: Tennessee Titans 22, Buffalo Bills 16. After a field goal gave them a 16-15 lead, the Bills kicked off to the Titans with just 16 seconds left in the game. Lorenzo Neal fielded the kick at the Titan 25-yard line, took a step, then handed off to Frank Wycheck. Wycheck ran to his right, stopped, and threw the ball back across the field to a wide open Kevin Dyson. Dyson caught the lateral and with a wall of blockers in front of him, raced 75 yards for a TD and a "miracle" win.

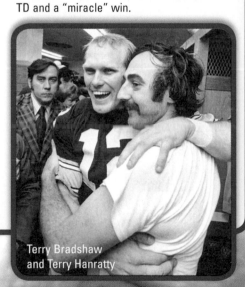

Terry Bradshaw and Terry Hanratty

NFL All-Time Record Holders*

RUSHING YARDS
Career: 18,355, Emmitt Smith (1990-2004)
Season: 2,105, Eric Dickerson (1984)
Game: 295, Jamal Lewis (2003)

RECEIVING YARDS
Career: 22,895, Jerry Rice (1985-2004)
Season: 1,848, Jerry Rice (1995)
Game: 336, Willie Anderson (1985)

PASSING YARDS
Career: 61,361, Dan Marino (1983-99)
Season: 5,084, Dan Marino (1984)
Game: 554, Norm Van Brocklin (1951)

POINTS SCORED
Career: 2,434, Gary Anderson (1982-2003)
Season: 176, Paul Hornung (1960)
Game: 40, Ernie Nevers (1929)

*Through the 2005 season.

COLLEGE FOOTBALL

College football is one of America's most colorful and exciting sports. The National Collegiate Athletic Association (NCAA), founded in 1906, oversees the sport today.

On January 4, 2006, the University of Texas Longhorns beat the USC Trojans in the Rose Bowl, 41-38, winning the national championship. The Longhorns ended the Trojans' two-year reign on top of NCAA Division I.

Unlike college basketball, there is no playoff in college football to determine a single champion. So the best team is determined by polls of sports writers and coaches. Sometimes the polls don't agree. In 2004, USC topped one poll while LSU led in the other. In 2006, both polls named Texas No. 1 (see box).

TOP 5 COLLEGE TEAMS
Chosen by the Associated Press Poll and the Coaches Poll. As of the end of the 2005-06 season.

Rank	AP	Coaches Poll
1	Texas	Texas
2	USC	USC
3	Penn State	Penn State
4	Ohio State	Ohio State
5	West Virginia	LSU

HEISMAN TROPHY

Tailback Reggie Bush of the University of Southern California (USC) was the 2005 winner. The 20-year-old junior received more first place votes than all but one other winner in Heisman history. In 2005, Bush racked up 1,658 rushing yards and averaged 8.9 yards per carry. He also led the NCAA in all-purpose yards, averaging 217.9 per game. Bush's teammate, Trojan QB Matt Leinart, won the prize in 2004 and returned to USC for his senior season in 2005. Bush decided not to follow suit, skipping his senior season to become eligible for the 2006 NFL Draft.

ALL-TIME DIVISION I NCAA LEADERS

RUSHING YARDS
1. 6,397, Ron Dayne, Wisconsin
2. 6,297, Ricky Williams, Texas
3. 6,082, Tony Dorsett, Pittsburgh
4. 6,026, DeAngelo Williams, Memphis
5. 5,598, Charles White, USC

PASSING YARDS
1. 17,072, Timmy Chang, Hawaii
2. 15,031, Ty Detmer, Brigham Young
3. 12,746, Tim Rattay, Louisiana Tech
4. 12,541, Chris Redman, Louisville
5. 12,429, Kliff Kingsbury, Texas Tech

Great Moment in College Football

JANUARY 3, 2003, FIESTA BOWL: OHIO STATE 31, MIAMI (FL) 24 (2 OT). Defending national champ Miami had not lost in 34 straight games. Miami trailed most of the game, then Todd Sievers tied it up at 17 with a field goal in the last regulation-time play. In overtime, Miami scored as Ken Dorsey threw to tight end Kellen Winslow Jr. After an incomplete pass on the 4th down, it seemed that Ohio State had lost. But a pass interference penalty was called on Miami, and three plays later Ohio State quarterback Craig Krenzel scored. In the second overtime, Maurice Clarett scored on a 5-yard run for Ohio State. Miami got to the 1-yard line, but couldn't manage to score. Result: Buckeye championship!

GOLF

Golf began in Scotland as early as the 1400s. The first golf course in the U.S. opened in 1888 in Yonkers, NY. The sport has grown to include both men's and women's professional tours. And millions play just for fun.

The men's tour in the U.S. is run by the Professional Golf Association (PGA). The four major championships (with the year first played) are:

British Open (1860)
United States Open (1895)
PGA Championship (1916)
Masters Tournament (1934)

The women's tour in the U.S. is guided by the Ladies Professional Golf Association (LPGA). The four major championships are:

United States Women's Open (1946)
McDonald's LPGA Championship (1955)
Nabisco Championship (1972)
Women's British Open (1976)

THE ALL-TIME "MAJOR" PLAYERS

These pro golfers have won the most major championships.

MEN
1. Jack Nicklaus, 18
2. Walter Hagan, 11
3. Tiger Woods, 10
4. Ben Hogan, 9
   Gary Player, 9

WOMEN
1. Patty Berg, 15
2. Mickey Wright, 13
3. Louise Suggs, 11
4. Babe Didrikson Zaharias, 10
   Annika Sorenstam, 10

GYMNASTICS

Although the sport goes back to ancient Egypt, modern-day gymnastics began in Europe in the early 1800s. It has been part of the Olympics since 1896. The first World Gymnastic Championships were held in Antwerp, Belgium, in 1903.

Men today compete in the All-Around, High Bar, Parallel Bars, Rings, Vault, Pommel Horse, Floor Exercises, and Team Combined. The women's events are the All-Around, Uneven Parallel Bars, Balance Beam, Floor Exercises, and Team Combined. In rhythmic gymnastics, women compete in All-Around, Rope, Hoop, Ball, Clubs, and Ribbon.

The U.S. excelled in both men's and women's gymnastics at the 2004 Athens Olympics. Women won six medals and the men won three, the most since U.S. gymnasts won 14 medals at the 1984 Olympic Games. Carly Patterson led the women by taking three medals, including a gold in the all-around. The women also won the team silver medal. Paul Hamm won two silvers for the men and a disputed gold in the all-around.

ICE HOCKEY

Ice hockey began in Canada in the mid-1800s. The National Hockey League (NHL) was formed in 1916. In 2006, the NHL had 30 teams—24 in the U.S. and 6 in Canada.

HIGHLIGHTS

Sadly for hockey fans, the 2004-05 NHL season never reached the ice. Team owners and players could not agree on salary caps for players and the season was scrapped. It was the first time a major sport in North America lost an entire season due to a labor dispute.

It took 10 months, but NHL owners and players reached an agreement in July 2005. The league also announced rule changes meant to make the game more fun to watch. The new rules—which were supposed to prevent ties, enhance play, and prevent fighting—went into effect with the beginning of the 2005-06 season on October 5.

SEASON	WINNER	RUNNER-UP
1990-91	Pittsburgh Penguins	Minnesota North Stars
1991-92	Pittsburgh Penguins	Chicago Black Hawks
1992-93	Montreal Canadiens	Los Angeles Kings
1993-94	New York Rangers	Vancouver Canucks
1994-95	New Jersey Devils	Detroit Red Wings
1995-96	Colorado Avalanche	Florida Panthers
1996-97	Detroit Red Wings	Philadelphia Flyers
1997-98	Detroit Red Wings	Washington Capitals
1998-99	Dallas Stars	Buffalo Sabres
1999-2000	New Jersey Devils	Dallas Stars
2000-2001	Colorado Avalanche	New Jersey Devils
2001-2002	Detroit Red Wings	Carolina Hurricanes
2002-2003	New Jersey Devils	Anaheim Mighty Ducks
2003-2004	Tampa Bay Lightning	Calgary Flames

Some All-Time NHL Records*

GOALS SCORED
Career: 894, Wayne Gretzky (1979-99)
Season: 92, Wayne Gretzky (1981-82)
Game: 7, Joe Malone (1920)

POINTS
Career: 2,857, Wayne Gretzky (1979-99)
Season: 215, Wayne Gretzky (1985-86)
Game: 10, Darryl Sittler (1976)

GOALIE WINS
Career: 551, Patrick Roy (1984-2003)
Season: 47, Bernie Parent (1973-74)

GOALIE SHUTOUTS
Career: 103, Terry Sawchuk (1949-70)
Season: 22, George Hainsworth (1928-29)

*Through 2003-04 season

HOCKEY Hall of Fame

The Hockey Hall of Fame in Toronto, Ontario, Canada, was founded in 1943 to honor hockey greats. **WEB SITE** *www.hhof.com*

SOCCER

THE WORLD CUP

Germany was set to become the focus of the sporting world June 9 with the kickoff of the 2006 Men's FIFA World Cup. The month-long tournament is held every four years and remains the world's biggest soccer event. Twelve German cities were to host teams from all over the globe. The championship game was scheduled for July 9 in Berlin.

The U.S. team has played in the last four World Cup tournaments, but before 1990, suffered a 40-year drought when it came to qualifying for the World Cup. To win one of the 32 spots in the tournament, the U.S. has to play a series of matches against other Caribbean, North American and Central American teams.

About 3.2 million tickets were to be sold for the 2006 matches, and more than 1 billion people were expected to watch matches on television. The U.S. team is coached by Bruce Arena and the roster includes Landon Donovan, DaMarcus Beasley, Brian McBride, and Claudio Reyna.

The Women's World Cup is also held every four years. The next one was scheduled for 2007 in China.

MLS MAJOR LEAGUE SOCCER

The L.A. Galaxy claimed its second MLS Cup Championship November 13, 2005, edging out the New England Revolution, 1-0. 90 minutes of regulation play ended in a tied score of 0-0. Midfielder Guillermo (Pando) Ramirez scored the winning (and only) goal in overtime. He was named the MLS Cup MVP. **WEB SITE** *www.mlsnet.com*

Landon Donovan

WHO AM I?

I was born in Ghana on June 2, 1989, and learned to play soccer barefoot. I became a U.S. citizen when I was 13, and began playing MLS soccer in 2004, when I was only 14. My team, D.C. United, won the MLS cup in the first year that I played. I was the youngest person ever to win a national championship on a major U.S. sports team.

Answer: Freddy Adu

TENNIS

Modern tennis began in 1873. It was based on court tennis. In 1877 the first championships were held in Wimbledon, near London. In 1881 the first official U.S. men's championships were held at Newport, Rhode Island. Six years later, the first U.S. women's championships took place, in Philadelphia. The four most important ("grand slam") tournaments today are the Australian Open, the French Open, the All-England (Wimbledon) Championships, and the U.S. Open.

Grand Slam Tournaments
ALL-TIME GRAND SLAM SINGLES WIN

MEN	Australian	French	Wimbledon	U.S.	Total
Pete Sampras (b. 1971)	2	0	7	5	14
Roy Emerson (b. 1936)	6	2	2	2	12
Bjorn Borg (b. 1956)	0	6	5	0	11
Rod Laver (b. 1938)	3	2	4	2	11
Bill Tilden (1893-1953)	*	0	3	7	10
WOMEN					
Margaret Smith-Court (b. 1942)	11	5	3	5	24
Steffi Graf (b. 1969)	4	6	7	5	22
Helen Wills Moody (1905-1998)	*	4	8	7	19
Chris Evert (b. 1954)	2	7	3	6	18
Martina Navratilova (b. 1956)	3	2	9	4	18

Never played in tournament.

Sports Scramble

Unscramble the sports-related words and names below. When you finish, the outlined column of letters will spell out the answer to this riddle.

What is a boxer's favorite drink?

C R A L A M I P P Y S M A G E

N A S H U T H E W I

A R A N S C

G R I L C U N

S R I C H T R E V E

ANSWERS ON PAGES 334-337. FOR MORE PUZZLES GO TO WWW.WORLDALMANACFORKIDS.COM

X GAMES

The X Games were first held in June 1995 in Newport, Rhode Island. Considered the Olympics of action sports, star X Games athletes include skateboarders Paul Rodriguez Jr. and Danny Way Jr., super motocross champion Jeremy McGrath, BMX freestyler Dave Mirra, and snowboarder Shaun White.

2006 Winter X Games About 230 athletes from all over the world competed in the tenth annual Winter X Games, held January 28-31 at Buttermilk Mountain in Aspen/Snowmass, Colorado. Events included Snowboarding, Skiing, SnoCross (snowmobiling), and Moto X (off-road motorcycling). Many athletes who normally would have competed skipped the X Games to stay in top shape for the 2006 Winter Olympics. Snowboarding Olympian Shaun White won his fifth and sixth X Games gold medals, tying the record held by Shaun Palmer. Less than a year after breaking both of his heels and ankles, skier Tanner Hall won his fifth gold in the skiing Superpipe event.

Summer X Games The Summer X Games, held every year since 1995, feature competitions in such events as In-Line Skating, Bike Stunt, Downhill BMX, Moto X, Skateboarding, Surfing, and Wakeboarding. The 12th X Games were set to be held in August 2006 in Los Angeles.

WEB SITE *http://expn.go.com*

did you know? *Skateboarder Danny Way soared into the record books when he jumped over the Great Wall of China on his skateboard in July 2005. What many of the 100 million people watching him on live TV didn't know is that he was performing the fantastic feat on an injured ankle. A month later he went on to win the X Games Big Air competition, even though he still needed a cane to get around.*

X-Fact-ors

BMX rider Dave "Miracle Boy" Mirra holds the record for the most X Games medals, with 20. He won two of those medals at the 2005 Summer X Games, while riding a gold-plated bike.

Jeremy "Twitch" Stenberg landed a 90-foot Moto X backflip—the longest in X Games history—at the 2005 competition.

Shaun White became the first athlete to medal in both Summer and Winter X Games competitions when he nabbed the Skateboard Vert silver medal at the 2005 X Games.

Technology & Computers

How do cops "zap" getaway cars? ➡ page 248

COMPUTER HIGHLIGHTS TIME LINE

1623   Wihelm Schickard built the first machine that could automatically add, subtract, multiply, and divide. He called it a "calculating clock."

1946   The first electronic, programmable, general-purpose computer was invented. It was called ENIAC, for "Electronic Numerical Integrator and Computer."

1967   The Advanced Research Projects Agency (ARPA) allotted money toward creating a computer network. It became ARPAnet, which evolved into the Internet.

1968   The first hypertext system was built by Douglas Engelbart of Stanford Research Institute. Called NLS (oN Line System), the system's design allowed users to move text and data with a mouse (which Engelbart invented in 1963).

1971   The "floppy disk" was introduced by IBM as a means of affordable portable storage.

1975   The Altair 8800 entered the market. It was the first widely sold personal microcomputer.

1975   Microsoft was founded by 20-year-old Bill Gates and 22-year-old Paul Allen. Ten years later, they released the first version of Windows.

1977   The Apple II, Apple's first fully packaged system with a keyboard, was introduced.

1990   The World Wide Web was first launched with one server by British physicist Tim Berners-Lee. He also created Uniform Resource Locators (URLs), the Hypertext Transfer Protocol (HTTP), and Hypertext Markup Language (HTML).

2002   The 1 billionth personal computer was shipped to stores in April, according to research firm Gartner.

COMPUTER TALK

BIT The smallest unit of data.

BLOG Short for "web log." It's a personal journal or diary that people put on a website for others to read.

BOOT To start up a computer.

BROWSER A program to help get around the Internet.

BUG OR GLITCH An error in a program or in the computer.

BYTE An amount of data equal to 8 bits.

CHIP A small piece of silicon holding the circuits used to store and process information.

COOKIE Some websites store information like your password on your computer's hard drive. When you go back to that site later, your browser sends the information (the "cookie") to the website.

DATABASE A large collection of information organized so that it can be retrieved and used in different ways.

DOWNLOAD To transfer information from a host computer to a personal computer through a network connection or modem.

ENCRYPTION The process of changing information into a code to keep others from reading it.

GIG OR GIGABYTE (GB) An amount of information equal to 1,024 megabytes, or (in some situations) 1,000 megabytes.

HTTP Hypertext Transfer Protocol is the method of file exchange used on the World Wide Web.

HTML The abbreviation for HyperText Markup Language, a computer language used to make web pages.

INTERNET A worldwide system of linked computer networks.

K Stands for *kilo*, or "thousand," in Greek. For example, "6K" stands for 6,000 bytes.

MEGABYTE (MB) An amount of information equal to 1,048,516 bytes, or (in some situations) 1 million bytes.

NETWORK A group of computers linked together so that they can share information.

PIXEL The smallest unit of an image on a computer monitor. It can be used to measure the size of an image.

RAM OR RANDOM ACCESS MEMORY Memory your computer uses to open programs and store your work until you save it to a hard drive or disk. Information in RAM disappears when the computer is turned off.

ROM OR READ ONLY MEMORY Memory that contains permanent instructions for the computer and cannot be changed. The information in ROM stays after the computer is turned off.

SPAM Electronic junk mail.

URL OR UNIFORM RESOURCE LOCATOR The technical name for a website address.

VIRUS A program that damages other programs and data. It gets into a computer through the Internet or shared disks.

WI-FI OR WIRELESS FIDELITY Technology that allows people to link to other computers and the Internet from their computers without wires.

The Early Days of Apple

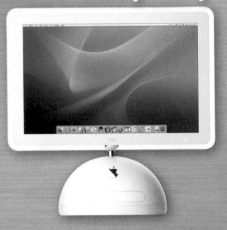

Today, we think of Apple as a company that makes iPods and sells music downloads, as well as making cool computers. But 30 years ago in California's Silicon Valley, the "two Steves"—Steve Jobs and Steve Wozniak—made history when they built the Apple computer in Jobs's garage. At the time, personal computers (PCs) as we know them did not exist. There were large, expensive computers called *mainframes*, but they were used mostly by banks, scientists, and the military, for record-keeping, problem-solving, and statistics. To operate most computer systems, the user had to insert hundreds of paper punch cards containing instructions.

In 1975, the two Steves put all their money together, which was only about $1,300, and Wozniak began building the Apple I—the first PC to use a single circuit board. They began selling these in early 1976, for about $650 each. The Apple I couldn't produce graphics, only text. Since there were no disk drives or CD-ROMs back then, to save and load information, you used an audio cassette deck.

On January 3, 1977, Jobs and Wozniak created the company Apple Computer, Inc., and they released their next model, the Apple II, in April 1977. The Apple II was the first PC that had color graphics. Five years later, the company was worth about $500 million. In 1984, the two whizzes released the Macintosh, which included the first affordable *graphical user interface* (*GUI*), using icons and symbols that are now used on all PCs.

Technology News in . . .

Law

MICROWAVE RADIATION DEVICE

Police chases may seem exciting on television or in the movies, but in real life they can be very dangerous. In order to stop suspects fleeing by car, police use spike strips, which poke holes in the car's tires. This can cause the car to stop, but it can also cause the car to crash.

A new invention uses technology to bring a getaway car to a stop. It is a device that is mounted on a police car and can zap fleeing suspects' cars with microwave radiation. The radiation is mostly harmless to humans but interferes with the getaway car's electronics and onboard computer, stopping the accelerator from working. This new technology was tested by the Los Angeles Police Department and may be introduced soon.

IM (INSTANT MESSAGE) DICTIONARY

BRB Be right back

BTW By the way

CUL or **CUL8R** See you later

GTG Got to go

IDK I don't know

IMHO In my humble opinion

JK Just kidding

LOL Laughing out loud

NE Any

NM Nothing much or Nevermind

NP No problem

OIC Oh I see

OMG Oh my God

PPL People

RL Real life

SRY Sorry

SUP What's up?

THX Thanks

TTFN Ta ta for now

TTYL Talk to you later

UR Your or You're

WTG Way to go

IM chat — File Edit Insert People — Warning Level: 0%

BookofRecordsBoy: Hey, whatz up?!
daWAK gurrl 2007: I'm @ the computer lab.
BookofRecordsBoy: fun fun fun. So, do you wanna do something tonite?
daWAK gurrl 2007: Sure, Let's get some pizza
BookofRecordsBoy: Okay
daWAK gurrl 2007: GTG - I'll IM you when I leave.

TECHTALK

Fill in the blanks to finish the answer to each question.

1. What popular software company is also a fruit, juice, and cider?

☐ ☐ ☐ **L** ☐

2. What type of space exists on the internet?

☐ **Y** ☐ ☐ **S** ☐ ☐ **C** ☐

3. What type of mail can be sent on the computer?

☐ **–M** ☐ ☐ ☐

4. What computer tool is also an animal a cat would enjoy chasing?

☐ ☐ ☐ **S** ☐

5. What can hurt both humans and computers?

V ☐ ☐ ☐ **S** ☐

6. What type of engine helps you find things on the Internet?

S ☐ ☐ ☐ ☐ **H** **E** ☐ ☐ ☐ ☐ **E**

7. What type of top is also the name of a type of computer?

D ☐ ☐ ☐ ☐ ☐ **P**

ANSWERS ON PAGES 334–337. FOR MORE PUZZLES GO TO WWW.WORLDALMANACFORKIDS.COM

Transportation

What city had the first subway in the U.S.? ➡ page 252

Getting from There to Here
A SHORT HISTORY OF TRANSPORTATION

5000 B.C. People harness animal-muscle power. Oxen and donkeys carry heavy loads.

3500 B.C. Egyptians create the first sailboat. Before this, people made rafts or canoes and paddled them with poles or their hands.

983 First locks to raise water level are built on China's Grand Canal. By 1400, a 1,500-mile water highway system was developed.

1450s Portuguese build fast ships with three masts. These plus the compass usher in an age of exploration.

1681 France's 150-mile Canal du Midi connects the Atlantic with the Mediterranean Sea.

5000 B.C.

3500 B.C. In Mesopotamia (modern-day Iraq), vehicles with wheels are invented. But the first wheels are made of heavy wood, and the roads are terrible.

800 Fast, shallow-draft longships make Vikings a powerful force in Europe from 800 to 1100.

Around 1000 Using magnetic compasses, Chinese are able to sail long distances in flat-bottomed ships called junks.

1660s Horse-drawn stagecoaches begin running in France. They stop at "stages" to switch horses and passengers—the first mass transit system.

1730s Stagecoach service begins in the U.S.

1783 In Paris, the Montgolfier brothers fly the first hot air balloon.

1825 The 363-mile Erie Canal connects the Hudson River with Lake Erie, opening up the U.S. frontier and making New York City the top port.

1832 The first U.S. horse-drawn streetcar is driven up and down the Bowery in New York City.

1769 James Watt patents the first successful steam engine.

1807 Robert Fulton patents a highly efficient steamboat.

1830 Inter-city Passenger rail service begins in England with a steam engine built by George Stephenson. It goes about 24 miles an hour.

1839 Kirkpatrick Macmillan of Scotland invents the first pedaled bicycle.

1862 Etienne Lenoir of Belgium builds the first car with an internal-combustion engine.

1869 Transcontinental railroad is completed at Promontory Point, Utah. The Suez Canal opens, saving ships a long trip around Africa.

1887 First practical electric street railway system opens in the U.S. in Richmond, Virginia. Suburbs soon grow around cities as trolley systems let people live farther away from the workplace.

1908 Henry Ford builds the first Model T, a practical car for the general public.

1860s Paddle-wheel steamboats dominate U.S. river travel.

1863 Using steam locomotives, the London subway (known as the "tube") opens.

1873 San Francisco's cable car system begins service.

1897 The first U.S. subway service begins in Boston. New York City follows in 1904.

1903 At Kitty Hawk, North Carolina, the Wright brothers fly the first powered heavier-than-air machine.

1939 The first practical helicopter and first jet plane are invented. The jet flies up to 434 mph. Jet passenger service began in 1952.

1969 U.S. astronauts aboard *Apollo 11* land on the Moon.

1994 Trains cross under the English Channel in the new Channel Tunnel or "Chunnel."

Now

1914 The 50-mile Panama Canal opens, saving ships a nearly 6,000-mile trip around South America.

1964 Shinkansen "bullet train" service (124 mph) begins in Japan.

1976 First supersonic (faster than sound) passenger jet, the Concorde, begins service between New York City and London or Paris.

2004 Millau Viaduct opens in France. With a maximum above-water height of 885 ft., it is the world's highest highway bridge.

Travel

Where can you find Old Faithful? ➡ page 259

In the late 13th century, famed Italian adventurer Marco Polo took a winding 5,600-mile journey overland from Venice, Italy, to Beijing, China. When he returned to Venice, Polo published a chronicle of his travels. The stories were so fantastic that many people didn't believe his tales.

You may not be taking a journey of thousands of miles on your next trip, but the excitement of traveling is the same. People travel for all kinds of reasons, for business, for fun, or to see distant friends and relatives. But whatever the reason people have always had the desire to stretch their legs, explore new places, and have adventures that people may—or may not—believe.

The World's 10 Most-Visited Countries*	The 10 Most-Visited U.S. states*
1. France	1. California
2. Spain	2. Florida
3. U.S.	3. Texas
4. China	4. New York
5. Italy	5. Illinois
6. United Kingdom	6. Nevada
7. Hong Kong	7. Pennsylvania
8. Mexico	8. New Jersey
9. Germany	9. Georgia
10. Austria	10. Virginia
*2004	*2003

World's Five Most-Visited Amusement Parks*

1. Magic Kingdom (Lake Buena Vista, Florida), 15.2 million
2. Disneyland (Anaheim, California), 13.4 million
3. Tokyo Disneyland (Japan), 13.2 million
4. Tokyo Disney Sea (Japan), 12.2 million
5. Disneyland Paris (Marne-La-Vallee, France), 10.2 million

*2004

AMUSEMENT PARKS

The first amusement parks appeared in Europe more than 400 years ago. Attractions included flower gardens, bowling, music, and a few simple rides.

Today's amusement parks are much more impressive. With super-fast roller coasters, parades, shows, and other attractions, amusement parks now have something to amuse just about anyone. Here's a look at some of the most popular amusement parks in the U.S.

▶ Disneyland (Anaheim, California)

Famed animator and cartoonist Walt Disney changed amusement parks forever when Disneyland first opened to the public in 1955. Disney created a fantasy world, with themed sections like "Tomorrowland." The park was immediately successful and remains popular 50 years later. Much of the park has changed, though, with new attractions like Buzz Lightyear Astro Blasters nestled alongside old favorites like Space Mountain and the Matterhorn.

▶ Walt Disney World (Lake Buena Vista, Florida)

Four different theme parks make up Walt Disney World. The Magic Kingdom is a Disneyland-style amusement park. It opened in 1971 and is the most-visited amusement park in the world. Epcot opened in 1982. It consists of two parts. Future World showcases technology with attractions like Mission: Space. The World Showcase features food and attractions distinct to 11 different countries. The other two Disney World theme parks are zoo-themed Animal Kingdom (opened in 1998), and Disney-MGM Studios (1989).

▶ Universal Studios Florida/Islands of Adventure (Orlando, Florida)

Universal Studios opened in 1990 and visitors have been "riding the movies" there ever since. Rides, shows, and other attractions feature favorite movie and TV characters, like Shrek, and take visitors behind the scenes. Islands of Adventure has been open since 1999. The rides and attractions there pay tribute to favorite characters from books and comic books, like Spiderman, the Incredible Hulk, and Dr. Doom.

FABULOUS FACTS

Biggest Park: Walt Disney World, Lake Buena Vista, Florida, 28,000 acres

Most Rides: 68, Cedar Point, Sandusky, Ohio

Most Roller Coasters: 16, Cedar Point, Sandusky, Ohio, ▶ and Six Flags Magic Mountain, Valencia, California

Fastest Roller Coaster: 128 mph, Kingda Ka, Six Flags Great Adventure, Jackson, New Jersey

Tallest Roller Coaster: 456 feet, Kingda Ka, Six Flags Great Adventure, Jackson, New Jersey

255

THE WORLD ALMANAC
ADVENTURER CONTEST

L ast year, *The World Almanac for Kids* invited readers to share stories about their traveling adventures—on road trips or across oceans. It wasn't easy, but we managed to pick just three winners who had amazing adventures to all corners of the globe (and learned something too!).

First Place: J.P. Dhaliwal, 11 years old, Fresno, California
J.P. left his home in California and traveled with his mother, father, and sister to Washington state and Canada. One of the first things that J.P. noticed on his travels was the snow—it doesn't often snow in Fresno. He and his family visited downtown Seattle, Washington, and saw the famous Space Needle monument. They went inside the Space Needle and up 520 feet to the top, where they got amazing views of the whole city. In Canada, J.P. and his family visited Vancouver, British Columbia, where they saw a beautiful church, an aquarium, and a park with huge totem poles. "Visiting other places helps you learn more about the world," said J.P.

Second Place: Joshua Erskine, 7 years old, Vancouver, Washington
Joshua flew halfway around the world to visit Australia, New Zealand, and Fiji. He was in an airplane for 23 hours each way! In Australia, Joshua visited Uluru, a giant rock that, as Joshua says, "appears out of nowhere." Joshua's favorite part of visiting New Zealand was feeding six-foot long eels! The eels sucked meat right out of Joshua's hands. He had to be careful to keep his fingers away from the eels' mouths because eels can clamp onto things and not let go. Joshua enjoyed his adventures Down Under. "I was able to see animals that I would never see at home and meet kids from other parts of the world," Joshua said.

Third Place: Asna Khan, 13 years old, Walnut, California
Asna went all the way to Karachi, Pakistan, on her trip in 2005. She went to Pakistan to visit relatives and had lots of adventures along the way. She even rode a camel, which Asna described as "frightening and also fun at the same time." Asna also spent time at Clifton Beach, which is a little bit different from beaches in the U.S. She saw camels, snake dances, and snake and mongoose fights right on the beach's smooth sand. While stuck in traffic jams, Asna still saw amazing things out her car window—like passersby entertaining people stuck in traffic by making their pet monkeys dance!

ROAD TRIP

Wherever you are, there is likely to be a festival, amusement park, historic site, or national park just a short drive away. A road trip—short or long—can be lots of fun, with plenty of interesting sights along the way.

The first cross-country drive was made in 1903. H. Nelson Jackson and Sewall K. Crocker (and a bulldog named Bud) drove from California to New York in an early car known as a Winton. There were few roads or bridges in the West, and lots of mud everywhere. The whole trip took 63 days and cost $8,000, including the price of the car. In 1909, Alice Huyler Ramsey became the first woman to drive across the U.S. Her trip from New York to San Francisco took 59 days.

By 1930, there were 23 million cars on the road. More than half of American families owned one. Today in the U.S. there are more cars than licensed drivers. People wanted to see things and go places—especially west. The first coast-to-coast highway was the Lincoln Highway, finished by 1930. The most famous highway was Route 66, completed in 1926, connecting Chicago to Los Angeles. Now called "Historic Route 66," it still has billboards and giant statues advertising its famous hotels, attractions, and restaurants.

A ROADSIDE SAMPLER:

Carhenge It's not Stonehenge, the famous English monument, but it looks a little like it. Located in Alliance, Nebraska, Carhenge was built by artist Jim Reinders in 1987, out of 38 vintage automobiles. The cars stand like the ancient stones, in a circle 96 feet in diameter.

Winchester Mystery House ▶ This spooky, sprawling mansion in San Jose, California, has 160 rooms, 950 doors, and 10,000 windows. Staircases lead into ceilings, windows cut into floors, and one door opens onto an 8-foot drop into a kitchen sink.

World's Largest Ball of Twine If string is your thing, check out this nearly 18,000-pound ball of twine in Cawker City, Kansas. It is more than 7 million feet long!

World's Largest Solar System Scale Model This solar system model follows about 40 miles of highway U.S. 1 in northern Maine, from the sun, 50 feet in diameter, at the University of Maine at Presque Isle to tiny Pluto, 1 inch in diameter, mounted on a visitor center wall in Houlton.

NATIONAL PARKS

The world's first national park was Yellowstone, established in 1872. Today, there are 57 national parks, including one in the Virgin Islands and one in American Samoa. The National Park Service oversees 388 areas in all, also including national monuments, battlefields, military parks, historic parks, historic sites, lakeshores, seashores, recreation areas, scenic rivers and trails, and the White House—84.4 million acres all told! For more information, you can write the National Park Service, Department of the Interior, 1849 C Street NW, Washington, D.C. 20240. **WEB SITE** *http://www.nps.gov/parks.html*

YOSEMITE NATIONAL PARK This park, established in 1890, covers 761,266 acres in east-central California. It has the world's largest concentration of granite domes—mountain-like rocks that were created by glaciers millions of years ago. You can see many of them rising thousands of feet above the valley floor. Two of the most famous are Half Dome, which looks smooth and rounded, and El Capitan, which is the biggest single granite rock on earth. Skilled climbers come from all over the world to scale this 3,000-foot-high wall of rock. Yosemite Falls, which drops 2,425 feet, is the highest waterfall in North America. It is actually two waterfalls, called the upper and lower falls, connected by a series of smaller waterfalls. Yosemite also features lakes, meadows, and giant sequoia trees, and is home to bighorn sheep and bears.

GRAND CANYON NATIONAL PARK
This national park, established in 1919, has one of the world's most spectacular landscapes, covering more than a million acres in northwestern Arizona. The canyon is 6,000 feet deep at its deepest point and 15 miles wide at its widest. Most of the 40 identified rock layers that form the canyon's 277-mile-long wall are exposed, offering a detailed look at the Earth's geologic history. The walls display a cross section of the Earth's crust from as far back as two billion years ago. The Colorado River—which carved out the giant canyon—still runs through the park, which is a valuable wildlife preserve with many rare, endangered animals. The pine and fir forests, painted deserts, plateaus, caves, and sandstone canyons offer a wide range of habitats.

PETRIFIED FOREST NATIONAL PARK

In northeast Arizona you'll find one of the world's biggest collections of petrified wood—trees that have turned to stone over millions of years. Some of these fossilized logs are 6 feet in diameter and more than 100 feet long. The Painted Desert is also part of this park. This area of rough "badlands" is dry and filled with canyons and flat-topped rock formations called mesas, from the Spanish word for "table." The rocks of the Painted Desert date back to the Triassic Period of 225 to 195 million years ago. The colorful sandstone and mudstone layers are the result of minerals—iron, manganese, and carbon—that formed in the sediment. At least 16 varieties of lizards and snakes make their home in the park's 93,533 acres. The climate can be extreme there, with violent thunderstorms common in the summer.

MAMMOTH CAVE NATIONAL PARK

Mammoth Cave in south central Kentucky is part of the biggest known cave system in the world. The cave was discovered by pioneers in 1798 and became part of a national park in 1941. There are more than 360 known miles of passageways, with more being discovered each year. The network of caves was created millions of years ago as water dissolved its way through rock. There are narrow tunnels, broad caverns, and giant vertical shafts. The caves are decorated with icicle-shaped mineral formations that hang from the ceiling (*stalactites*) and grow up from the floor (*stalagmites*). Blindfish, eyeless crayfish, colorless spiders, and other rare creatures have adapted to the blackness and isolation of cave life.

YELLOWSTONE NATIONAL PARK

Located mostly in northwestern Wyoming and partly in eastern Idaho and southwestern Montana, Yellowstone is known for its 10,000 hot springs and geysers—more than anyplace else in the world. Old Faithful, the most famous geyser, erupts for about four minutes every one to two hours, shooting 3,700-8,400 gallons of hot water as high as 185 feet. Other geysers include the Giant, which shoots a column of hot water 200 feet high, and the Giantess, which erupts for over four hours at a time, but only about twice a year. There are grizzly bears, wolves, elk, moose, buffalo, deer, beavers, coyotes, antelopes, and 300 species of birds. The use of snowmobiles in the park has been a big controversy. Some people want to ban them because of noise and air pollution; others disagree. They are allowed now, though their use is somewhat limited.

United States

Which state was the last to enter the Union? ➡ page 303

FACTS &FIGURES

AREA 50 states and Washington, D.C.

LAND	3,537,437	square miles
WATER	181,272	square miles
TOTAL	3,718,709	square miles

POPULATION (MID-2006): 298,444,215

CAPITAL: WASHINGTON, D.C.

LARGEST, HIGHEST, AND OTHER STATISTICS

Sears Tower

Largest state:	Alaska (663,267 square miles)
Smallest state:	Rhode Island (1,545 square miles)
Northernmost city:	Barrow, Alaska (71°17′ north latitude)
Southernmost city:	Hilo, Hawaii (19°44′ north latitude)
Easternmost city:	Eastport, Maine (66°59′05″ west longitude)
Westernmost city:	Atka, Alaska (174°12′ west longitude)
Highest settlement:	Climax, Colorado (11,360 feet)
Lowest settlement:	Calipatria, California (184 feet below sea level)
Oldest national park:	Yellowstone National Park (Idaho, Montana, Wyoming), 2,219,791 acres, established 1872
Largest national park:	Wrangell-St. Elias, Alaska (8,323,148 acres)
Longest river system:	Mississippi-Missouri-Red Rock (3,710 miles)
Deepest lake:	Crater Lake, Oregon (1,932 feet)
Highest mountain:	Mount McKinley, Alaska (20,320 feet)
Lowest point:	Death Valley, California (282 feet below sea level)
Tallest building:	Sears Tower, Chicago, Illinois (1,450 feet)
Tallest structure:	TV tower, Blanchard, North Dakota (2,063 feet)
Longest bridge span:	Verrazano-Narrows Bridge, New York (4,260 feet)
Highest bridge:	Royal Gorge, Colorado (1,053 feet above water)

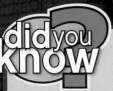
did you know?

Although Eastport, Maine, is the easternmost city in the U.S., the easternmost point is actually Pochnoi Point, Alaska, located in the Aleutian Islands. Pochnoi Point sits west of 180 degrees longitude, at 179 degrees east longitude, making it part of Earth's eastern hemisphere. Alaska also contains the westernmost point in the U.S., which lies on Amatignak Island, also in the Aleutians. It is east of 180 degrees longitude, which puts it in the western hemisphere. The two points are only 63 miles apart!

SYMBOLS OF THE UNITED STATES

THE GREAT SEAL

The Great Seal of the United States shows an American bald eagle with a ribbon in its mouth bearing the Latin words *e pluribus unum* (out of many, one). In its talons are the arrows of war and an olive branch of peace. On the back of the Great Seal is an unfinished pyramid with an eye (the eye of Providence) above it. The seal was approved by Congress on June 20, 1782.

THE FLAG

1777

The flag of the United States has 50 stars (one for each state) and 13 stripes (one for each of the original 13 states). It is unofficially called the "Stars and Stripes."

The first U.S. flag was commissioned by the Second Continental Congress in 1777 but did not exist until 1783, after the American Revolution. Historians are not certain who designed the Stars and Stripes. Many different flags are believed to have been used during the American Revolution.

1795

The flag of 1777 was used until 1795. In that year Congress passed an act ordering that a new flag have 15 stripes, alternate red and white, and 15 stars on a blue field. In 1818, Congress directed that the flag have 13 stripes and that a new star be added for each new state of the Union. The last star was added in 1960 for the state of Hawaii.

1818

There are many customs for flying the flag and treating it with respect. For example, it should not touch the floor and no other flag should be flown above it, except for the UN flag at UN headquarters. When the flag is raised or lowered, or passes in a parade, or during the Pledge of Allegiance, people should face it and stand at attention. Those in military uniform should salute. Others should put their right hand over their heart. The flag is flown at half-staff as a sign of mourning.

PLEDGE OF ALLEGIANCE TO THE FLAG

"I pledge allegiance to the flag of the United States of America and to the republic for which it stands, one nation under God, indivisible, with liberty and justice for all."

THE NATIONAL ANTHEM

"The Star-Spangled Banner" was a poem written in 1814 by Francis Scott Key as he watched British ships bombard Fort McHenry, Maryland, during the War of 1812. It became the National Anthem by an act of Congress in 1931. The music to "The Star-Spangled Banner" was originally a tune called "Anacreon in Heaven."

THE U.S. CONSTITUTION

The Foundation of American Government

The Constitution is the document that created the present government of the United States. It was written in 1787 and went into effect in 1789. It establishes the three branches of the U.S. government — the executive (headed by the president), the legislative (Congress), and the judicial (the Supreme Court and other federal courts). The first 10 amendments to the Constitution (the **Bill of Rights**) explain the basic rights of all American citizens.

You can find the constitution on-line at:

WEB SITE www.house.gov/Constitution/Constitution.html

The Preamble to the Constitution

The Constitution begins with a short statement called the Preamble. The Preamble states that the government of the United States was established by the people.

"We the people of the United States, in order to form a more perfect union, establish justice, insure domestic tranquility, provide for the common defense, promote the general welfare, and secure the blessings of liberty to ourselves and our posterity, do ordain and establish this Constitution for the United States of America."

THE ARTICLES

The original Constitution contained seven articles. The first three articles of the Constitution establish the three branches of the U.S. government.

Article 1, Legislative Branch Creates the Senate and House of Representatives and describes their functions and powers.

Article 2, Executive Branch Creates the office of the President and the Electoral College and lists their powers and responsibilities.

Article 3, Judicial Branch Creates the Supreme Court and gives Congress the power to create lower courts. The powers of the courts and certain crimes are defined.

Article 4, The States Discusses the relationship of the states to one another and to the citizens. Defines the states' powers.

Article 5, Amending the Constitution Describes how the Constitution can be amended (changed).

Article 6, Federal Law Makes the Constitution the supreme law of the land over state laws and constitutions.

Article 7, Ratifying the Constitution Establishes how to ratify (approve) the Constitution.

AMENDMENTS TO THE CONSTITUTION

The writers of the Constitution understood that it might need to be amended, or changed, in the future, but they wanted to be careful and made it hard to change. Article 5 describes how the Constitution can be amended.

In order to take effect, an amendment must be approved by a two-thirds majority in both the House of Representatives and the Senate. It must then be approved (ratified) by three-fourths of the states (38 states). So far, there have been 27 amendments. One of them (the 18th, ratified in 1919) banned the manufacture or sale of liquor. It was canceled by the 21st Amendment, in 1933.

The Bill of Rights: The First Ten Amendments

The first ten amendments were adopted in 1791 and contain the basic freedoms Americans enjoy as a people. These amendments are known as the Bill of Rights.

1. Guarantees freedom of religion, speech, and the press.
2. Guarantees the right to have firearms.
3. Guarantees that soldiers cannot be lodged in private homes unless the owner agrees.
4. Protects people from being searched or having property searched or taken away by the government without reason.
5. Protects rights of people on trial for crimes.
6. Guarantees people accused of crimes the right to a speedy public trial by jury.
7. Guarantees the right to a trial by jury for other kinds of cases.
8. Prohibits "cruel and unusual punishments."
9. Says specific rights listed in the Constitution do not take away rights that may not be listed.
10. Establishes that any powers not given specifically to the federal government belong to states or the people.

Other Important Amendments

13. (1865): Ends slavery in the United States.
14. (1868): Bars states from denying rights to citizens; guarantees equal protection under the law for all citizens.
15. (1870): Guarantees that a person cannot be denied the right to vote because of race or color.
19. (1920): Gives women the right to vote.
22. (1951): Limits the president to two four-year terms of office.
24. (1964): Outlaws the poll tax (a tax people had to pay before they could vote) in federal elections. (The poll tax had been used to keep African Americans in the South from voting.)
25. (1967): Specifies presidential succession; also gives the president the power to appoint a new vice president, if one dies or leaves office in the middle of a term.
26. (1971): Lowers the voting age to 18 from 21.

The Executive Branch

The **executive branch** of the federal government is headed by the president, who enforces the laws passed by Congress and is commander in chief of the U.S. armed forces. It also includes the vice president, people who work for the president or vice president, the major departments of the government, and special agencies. The **cabinet** is made up of the vice president, heads of major departments, and other officials. It meets when the president chooses. The chart at right shows cabinet departments in the order in which they were created. The Department of Homeland Security was created by a law signed in November 2002.

PRESIDENT

VICE PRESIDENT

CABINET DEPARTMENTS

1. State
2. Treasury
3. Defense
4. Justice
5. Interior
6. Agriculture
7. Commerce
8. Labor
9. Housing and Urban Development
10. Transportation
11. Energy
12. Education
13. Health and Human Services
14. Veterans Affairs
15. Homeland Security

HOW LONG DOES THE PRESIDENT SERVE?

The president serves a four-year term, starting on January 20. No president can be elected more than twice, or more than once if he or she had served two years as president filling out the term of a president who left office.

WHAT HAPPENS IF THE PRESIDENT DIES?

If the president dies in office or cannot complete the term, the vice president becomes president. If the president is unable to perform his or her duties, the vice president can become acting president. The next person to become president after the vice president would be the Speaker of the House of Representatives.

The White House has an address on the World Wide Web especially for kids. It is:

WEB SITE http://www.whitehousekids.gov

You can send e-mail to the president at:

EMAIL president@whitehouse.gov

The White House, home of the U.S. president

VOTER TURNOUT IN PRESIDENTIAL ELECTIONS, 1964-2004

(Percent of voting age, 18 and over in 1972 and afterwards, 21 and over in 1964 and 1968.)

Year	Turnout	Year	Turnout
1964	61.4%	1988	50.3%
1968	60.7%	1992	55.2%
1972	55.1%	1996	49.0 %
1976	53.6%	2000	50.3%
1980	52.8%	2004	55.5%
1984	53.3%		

Source: U.S. Census Bureau

Elections

ELECTION 2004
BUSH WINS A
SECOND TERM

On November 2, 2004, President George W. Bush, a Republican, was reelected to another four-year term, defeating Massachusetts Senator John Kerry, a Democrat. President Bush won about 59 million popular votes, or 3 million more than Senator Kerry. But what really mattered was the number of votes he won in the Electoral College (see below). Bush defeated Kerry in 31 states, which gave him 286 electoral votes, 16 more than the 270 he needed to win. Kerry won in 19 states and the District of Columbia, taking in 252 votes.

The map below shows which states Bush won and which states Kerry won. You can see that Kerry did better in the Northeast, the Upper Midwest, and the Far West, while Bush did better in the rest of the country. Only three states, Nevada, Iowa, and New Hampshire supported the candidate of a different party in 2004 than in 2000.

2004 Election
- Won by Bush
- Won by Kerry

The **Electoral College** *State by State*

The Electoral College is not really a college, but a group of people chosen in each state. The writers of the Constitution did not agree on how a president should be selected. Some did not trust ordinary people to make a good choice. So they compromised and agreed to have the Electoral College do it.

The number of electors for each state is equal to the number of senators (2), plus the U.S. House members each state has in Congress. In addition, the District of Columbia has 3 electoral votes. In the early days electors voted for whomever they wanted. In modern times the political parties hold primary elections and conventions to choose candidates for president and vice president. When voters pick candidates of a particular party, they are actually choosing electors from that party. These electors have agreed to vote for their party's candidate, and except in very rare cases this is what they do.

The electors chosen in November meet in state capitals in December. In almost all states, the party that gets the most votes in November wins ALL the electoral votes for the state. In January, the electors' votes are officially opened during a special session of Congress. If no presidential candidate wins a majority of these votes, the House of Representatives chooses the president. This happened in 1800, 1824, and 1877.

Can a candidate who didn't win the most popular votes still win a majority of electoral votes? Yes. That's what happened in 1876, 1888, and again in 2000, when Bush was elected to a first term.

The Legislative Branch

CONGRESS

The Congress of the United States is the legislative branch of the federal government. Congress's major responsibility is to pass the laws that govern the country and determine how money collected in taxes is spent. It is the president's responsibility to enforce the laws. Congress consists of two parts—the Senate and the House of Representatives. ▶

THE SENATE

The Senate has 100 members, two from each state. The Constitution says that the Senate will have equal representation (the same number of representatives) from each state. Thus, small states have the same number of senators as large states. Senators are elected for six-year terms. There is no limit on the number of terms a senator can serve.

The Senate also has the responsibility of approving people the president appoints for certain jobs: for example, cabinet members and Supreme Court justices. The Senate must approve all treaties by at least a two-thirds vote. It also has the responsibility under the Constitution of putting on trial high-ranking federal officials who have been impeached by the House of Representatives.

WEB SITE www.senate.gov

THE HOUSE OF REPRESENTATIVES

▼ The Capitol, where Congress meets

The number of members of the House of Representatives for each state depends on its population according to a recent census. But each state has at least one representative, no matter how small its population. A term lasts two years.

The first House of Representatives in 1789 had 65 members. As the country's population grew, the number of representatives increased. Since the 1910 census, however, the total membership has been kept at 435. After the results of Census 2000 were added up, 8 states gained seats and 10 states lost seats.

WEB SITE www.house.gov

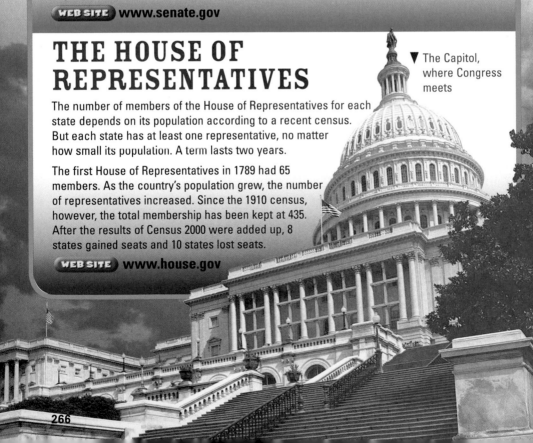

The House of Representatives, by State

Here are the numbers of representatives each state had in 2006, compared with earlier times:

	2006	1995	1975		2006	1995	1975
Alabama	7	7	7	Montana	1	1	2
Alaska	1	1	1	Nebraska	3	3	3
Arizona	8	6	4	Nevada	3	2	1
Arkansas	4	4	4	New Hampshire	2	2	2
California	53	52	43	New Jersey	13	13	15
Colorado	7	6	5	New Mexico	3	3	2
Connecticut	5	6	6	New York	29	31	39
Delaware	1	1	1	North Carolina	13	12	11
Florida	25	23	15	North Dakota	1	1	1
Georgia	13	11	10	Ohio	18	19	23
Hawaii	2	2	2	Oklahoma	5	6	6
Idaho	2	2	2	Oregon	5	5	4
Illinois	19	20	24	Pennsylvania	19	21	25
Indiana	9	10	11	Rhode Island	2	2	2
Iowa	5	5	6	South Carolina	6	6	6
Kansas	4	4	5	South Dakota	1	1	2
Kentucky	6	6	7	Tennessee	9	9	9
Louisiana	7	7	8	Texas	32	30	24
Maine	2	2	2	Utah	3	3	2
Maryland	8	8	8	Vermont	1	1	1
Massachusetts	10	10	12	Virginia	11	11	10
Michigan	15	16	19	Washington	9	9	7
Minnesota	8	8	8	West Virginia	3	3	4
Mississippi	4	5	5	Wisconsin	8	9	9
Missouri	9	9	10	Wyoming	1	1	1

Washington, D.C., Puerto Rico, American Samoa, Guam, and the Virgin Islands each have one nonvoting member of the House of Representatives.

Women in Congress

- As of January 2006, there were 84 women in Congress (70 in the U.S. House of Representatives and 14 in the U.S. Senate). That is more than ever before.

- The first woman elected to the House was Jeannette Rankin (Montana) in 1916.▼ In 1932, Hattie Caraway (Arkansas) was the first woman to be elected to the Senate. Margaret Chase Smith, of Maine, was the first woman elected to both houses of Congress (House in 1940, Senate in 1948).

- New York's Shirley Chisholm became the first African American woman in Congress after being elected to the House in 1968. In 1992, Carol Moseley Braun of Illinois became the first African American woman elected to the Senate.

- In November, 2002, California Representative Nancy Pelosi was selected by her fellow Democrats as their leader in the House of Representatives. This was the highest position in Congress ever held by a woman.

The Judicial Branch

THE SUPREME COURT

The highest court in the United States is the Supreme Court. It has nine justices who are appointed for life by the president with the approval of the Senate. Eight of the nine members are called associate justices. The ninth is the Chief Justice, who presides over the Court's meetings.

WHAT DOES THE SUPREME COURT DO?

The Supreme Court's major responsibilities are to judge cases that involve reviewing federal laws, actions of the president, treaties of the United States, and laws passed by state governments to be sure they do not conflict with the U.S. Constitution. If the Supreme Court finds that a law or action violates the Constitution, the law is struck down.

THE SUPREME COURT'S DECISION IS FINAL.

Most cases must go through other state courts or federal courts before they reach the Supreme Court. The Supreme Court is the final court for a case, and the justices decide which cases they will review. After the Supreme Court hears a case, it may agree or disagree with the decision by a lower court. Each justice has one vote, and the majority rules. When the Supreme Court makes a ruling, its decision is final, so each of the justices has a very important job.

Below are the nine justices who were on the Supreme Court in January 2006. **Back row** (from left to right): Stephen Breyer , Clarence Thomas, Ruth Bader Ginsburg, Samuel Alito. **Front row** (from left to right): Anthony M. Kennedy, John Paul Stevens, Chief Justice John G. Roberts, Antonin Scalia, David H. Souter.

CHANGES AT THE SUPREME COURT

The president chooses new Supreme Court justices, and the U.S. Senate approves them. How does this work?

First, the president nominates the person he wants to be the new Supreme Court justice. Then, over half of the U.S. senators must confirm (approve) the person. New justices joined the court in September 2005 and January 2006.

On July 1, 2005, Associate Justice Sandra Day O'Connor announced that she would retire from the bench as

Supreme Court Justice Samuel Alito Jr. and family with Chief Justice John G. Roberts Jr.

soon as she was replaced. President Bush chose John G. Roberts Jr. to replace her, but on September 3 Chief Justice William Rehnquist died. Bush then asked the Senate to confirm Roberts as Rehnquist's replacement. The Senate voted to do so, 78-22, on September 29. O'Connor's seat was filled later by Samuel Alito Jr. on Jan. 31, 2006, by a vote of 58-42.

John G. Roberts Jr., the new Chief Justice, was born in Buffalo, New York, in 1955, but grew up on the shores of Lake Michigan in Long Beach, Indiana. Roberts always got high grades. He wrestled, pole vaulted, and was captain of the football team but he was also in the choir and drama club. As an adult, he worked for several judges, including William Rehnquist, whom he would later replace. He has also been a lawyer. From 2003 to 2005, he was a judge of the Appeals Court in Washington D.C. He has a wife, Jane, and they have two children, Josephine and Jack.

Samuel Anthony Alito, Jr., the new Associate Justice, was born in Trenton, New Jersey, in 1950. He grew up in nearby Hamilton and was student council president and on the debate team. When he graduated from Princeton University in 1972, his yearbook prediction was that he would "warm a seat on the Supreme Court." He has worked as an attorney and a judge. He has a wife, Martha-Ann, two children, Philip and Laura, and a dog named Zeus.

WHO AM I?

I was born in Baltimore, Maryland, a grandson of a slave. I earned a law degree from Howard University Law School in 1933, and was first in my class. I was a leader in the civil rights movement to end racial segregation. As a lawyer in 1954, I won the Supreme Court case *Brown v. Board of Education*, which ruled that segregation— separating people by race—was against the law. I was the first African American Supreme Court justice, serving from 1967 to 1991.

Answer: Thurgood Marshall

Presidents of the United States

GEORGE WASHINGTON Federalist Party   1789–1797

Born: Feb. 22, 1732, at Wakefield, Westmoreland County, Virginia
Married: Martha Dandridge Custis (1731-1802); no children
Died: Dec. 14, 1799; buried at Mount Vernon, Fairfax County, Virginia
Early Career: Soldier; head of the Virginia militia; commander of the
Continental Army; chairman of Constitutional Convention (1787)

JOHN ADAMS Federalist Party   1797–1801

Born: Oct. 30, 1735, in Braintree (now Quincy), Massachusetts
Married: Abigail Smith (1744-1818); 3 sons, 2 daughters
Died: July 4, 1826; buried in Quincy, Massachusetts
Early Career: Lawyer; delegate to Continental Congress; signer of
the Declaration of Independence; first vice president

THOMAS JEFFERSON Democratic-Republican Party 1801–1809

Born: Apr. 13, 1743, at Shadwell, Albemarle County, Virginia
Married: Martha Wayles Skelton (1748-1782); 1 son, 5 daughters
Died: July 4, 1826; buried at Monticello, Albemarle County, Virginia
Early Career: Lawyer; member of the Continental Congress; author of the
Declaration of Independence; governor of Virginia; first secretary of
state; author of the Virginia Statute on Religious Freedom

JAMES MADISON Democratic-Republican Party   1809-1817

Born: Mar. 16, 1751, at Port Conway, King George County, Virginia
Married: Dolley Payne Todd (1768-1849); no children
Died: June 28, 1836; buried at Montpelier Station, Virginia
Early Career: Member of the Virginia Constitutional Convention (1776);
member of the Continental Congress; major contributor to the U.S.
Constitution; writer of the *Federalist Papers*; secretary of state

JAMES MONROE Democratic-Republican Party   1817–1825

Born: Apr. 28, 1758, in Westmoreland County, Virginia
Married: Elizabeth Kortright (1768-1830); 2 daughters
Died: July 4, 1831; buried in Richmond, Virginia
Early Career: Soldier; lawyer; U.S. senator; governor of Virginia;
secretary of state

JOHN QUINCY ADAMS Democratic-Republican Party 1825–1829

Born: July 11, 1767, in Braintree (now Quincy), Massachusetts
Married: Louisa Catherine Johnson (1775-1852); 3 sons, 1 daughter
Died: Feb. 23, 1848; buried in Quincy, Massachusetts
Early Career: Diplomat; U.S. senator; secretary of state

7 **ANDREW JACKSON** Democratic Party   1829–1837
Born: Mar. 15, 1767, in Waxhaw, South Carolina
Married: Rachel Donelson Robards (1767-1828); 1 son
Died: June 8, 1845; buried in Nashville, Tennessee
Early Career: Lawyer; U.S. representative and senator; soldier in the
   U.S. Army

8 **MARTIN VAN BUREN** Democratic Party   1837–1841
Born: Dec. 5, 1782, at Kinderhook, New York
Married: Hannah Hoes (1783-1819); 4 sons
Died: July 24, 1862; buried at Kinderhook, New York
Early Career: Governor of New York; secretary of state; vice president

9 **WILLIAM HENRY HARRISON** Whig Party   1841
Born: Feb. 9, 1773, at Berkeley, Charles City County, Virginia
Married: Anna Symmes (1775-1864); 6 sons, 4 daughters
Died: Apr. 4, 1841; buried in North Bend, Ohio
Early Career: First governor of Indiana Territory; superintendent of
   Indian affairs; U.S. representative and senator

10 **JOHN TYLER** Whig Party   1841–1845
Born: Mar. 29, 1790, in Greenway, Charles City County, Virginia
Married: Letitia Christian (1790-1842); 3 sons, 5 daughters
   Julia Gardiner (1820-1889); 5 sons, 2 daughters
Died: Jan. 18, 1862; buried in Richmond, Virginia
Early Career: U.S. representative and senator; vice president

11 **JAMES KNOX POLK** Democratic Party   1845–1849
Born: Nov. 2, 1795, in Mecklenburg County, North Carolina
Married: Sarah Childress (1803-1891); no children
Died: June 15, 1849; buried in Nashville, Tennessee
Early Career: U.S. representative; Speaker of the House; governor
   of Tennessee

12 **ZACHARY TAYLOR** Whig Party   1849–1850
Born: Nov. 24, 1784, in Orange County, Virginia
Married: Margaret Smith (1788-1852); 1 son, 5 daughters
Died: July 9, 1850; buried in Louisville, Kentucky
Early Career: General in the U.S. Army

13 **MILLARD FILLMORE** Whig Party   1850–1853
Born: Jan. 7, 1800, in Cayuga County, New York
Married: Abigail Powers (1798-1853); 1 son, 1 daughter
   Caroline Carmichael McIntosh (1813-1881); no children
Died: Mar. 8, 1874; buried in Buffalo, New York
Early Career: Farmer; lawyer; U.S. representative; vice president

FRANKLIN PIERCE Democratic Party — 1853–1857
Born: Nov. 23, 1804, in Hillsboro, New Hampshire
Married: Jane Means Appleton (1806-1863); 3 sons
Died: Oct. 8, 1869; buried in Concord, New Hampshire
Early Career: U.S. representative, senator

JAMES BUCHANAN Democratic Party — 1857–1861
Born: Apr. 23, 1791, Cove Gap, near Mercersburg, Pennsylvania
Married: Never
Died: June 1, 1868, buried in Lancaster, Pennsylvania
Early Career: U.S. representative; secretary of state

ABRAHAM LINCOLN Republican Party — 1861-1865
Born: Feb. 12, 1809, in Hardin County, Kentucky
Married: Mary Todd (1818-1882); 4 sons
Died: Apr. 15, 1865; buried in Springfield, Illinois
Early Career: Lawyer; U.S. representative

ANDREW JOHNSON Democratic Party — 1865–1869
Born: Dec. 29, 1808, in Raleigh, North Carolina
Married: Eliza McCardle (1810-1876); 3 sons, 2 daughters
Died: July 31, 1875; buried in Greeneville, Tennessee
Early Career: Tailor; member of state legislature; U.S. representative;
governor of Tennessee; U.S. senator; vice president

ULYSSES S. GRANT Republican Party — 1869–1877
Born: Apr. 27, 1822, in Point Pleasant, Ohio
Married: Julia Dent (1826-1902); 3 sons, 1 daughter
Died: July 23, 1885; buried in New York City
Early Career: Army officer; commander of Union forces during
Civil War

RUTHERFORD B. HAYES Republican Party — 1877–1881
Born: Oct. 4, 1822, in Delaware, Ohio
Married: Lucy Ware Webb (1831-1889); 5 sons, 2 daughters
Died: Jan. 17, 1893; buried in Fremont, Ohio
Early Career: Lawyer; general in Union Army; U.S. representative;
governor of Ohio

JAMES A. GARFIELD Republican Party — 1881
Born: Nov. 19, 1831, in Orange, Cuyahoga County, Ohio
Married: Lucretia Rudolph (1832-1918); 5 sons, 2 daughters
Died: Sept. 19, 1881; buried in Cleveland, Ohio
Early Career: Teacher; Ohio state senator; general in Union Army;
U.S. representative

21 **CHESTER A. ARTHUR** Republican Party   1881–1885
Born: Oct. 5, 1829, in Fairfield, Vermont
Married: Ellen Lewis Herndon (1837-1880); 2 sons, 1 daughter
Died: Nov. 18, 1886; buried in Albany, New York
Early Career: Teacher; lawyer; vice president

22 **GROVER CLEVELAND** Democratic Party   1885–1889
Born: Mar. 18, 1837, in Caldwell, New Jersey
Married: Frances Folsom (1864-1947); 2 sons, 3 daughters
Died: June 24, 1908; buried in Princeton, New Jersey
Early Career: Lawyer; mayor of Buffalo; governor of New York

23 **BENJAMIN HARRISON** Republican Party   1889-1893
Born: Aug. 20, 1833, in North Bend, Ohio
Married: Caroline Lavinia Scott (1832-1892); 1 son, 1 daughter
    Mary Scott Lord Dimmick (1858-1948); 1 daughter
Died: Mar. 13, 1901; buried in Indianapolis, Indiana
Early Career: Lawyer; general in Union Army; U.S. senator

24 **GROVER CLEVELAND**   1893–1897
See 22, above

25 **WILLIAM MCKINLEY** Republican Party   1897–1901
Born: Jan. 29, 1843, in Niles, Ohio
Married: Ida Saxton (1847-1907); 2 daughters
Died: Sept. 14, 1901; buried in Canton, Ohio
Early Career: Lawyer; U.S. representative; governor of Ohio

26 **THEODORE ROOSEVELT** Republican Party   1901–1909
Born: Oct. 27, 1858, in New York City
Married: Alice Hathaway Lee (1861-1884); 1 daughter
    Edith Kermit Carow (1861-1948); 4 sons, 1 daughter
Died: Jan. 6, 1919; buried in Oyster Bay, New York
Early Career: Assistant secretary of the Navy; cavalry leader in
    Spanish-American War; governor of New York; vice president

27 **WILLIAM HOWARD TAFT** Republican Party   1909–1913
Born: Sept. 15, 1857, in Cincinnati, Ohio
Married: Helen Herron (1861-1943); 2 sons, 1 daughter
Died: Mar. 8, 1930; buried in Arlington National Cemetery, Virginia
Early Career: Reporter; lawyer; judge; secretary of war

28 **WOODROW WILSON** Democratic Party   1913–1921
Born: Dec. 28, 1856, in Staunton, Virginia
Married: Ellen Louise Axson (1860-1914); 3 daughters
    Edith Bolling Galt (1872-1961); no children
Died: Feb. 3, 1924; buried in Washington, D.C.
Early Career: College professor and president; governor of New Jersey

WARREN G. HARDING Republican Party   1921–1923
Born: Nov. 2, 1865, near Corsica (now Blooming Grove), Ohio
Married: Florence Kling De Wolfe (1860-1924); 1 daughter
Died: Aug. 2, 1923; buried in Marion, Ohio
Early Career: Ohio state senator; U.S. senator

CALVIN COOLIDGE Republican Party   1923–1929
Born: July 4, 1872, in Plymouth, Vermont
Married: Grace Anna Goodhue (1879-1957); 2 sons
Died: Jan. 5, 1933; buried in Plymouth, Vermont
Early Career: Massachusetts state legislator; lieutenant governor
        and governor; vice president

HERBERT HOOVER Republican Party   1929-1933
Born: Aug. 10, 1874, in West Branch, Iowa
Married: Lou Henry (1875-1944); 2 sons
Died: Oct. 20, 1964; buried in West Branch, Iowa
Early Career: Mining engineer; secretary of commerce

FRANKLIN DELANO ROOSEVELT Democratic Party 1933–1945
Born: Jan. 30, 1882, in Hyde Park, New York
Married: Anna Eleanor Roosevelt (1884-1962); 4 sons, 1 daughter
Died: Apr. 12, 1945; buried in Hyde Park, New York
Early Career: Lawyer; New York state senator; assistant secretary of
        the Navy; governor of New York

HARRY S. TRUMAN Democratic Party   1945–1953
Born: May 8, 1884, in Lamar, Missouri
Married: Elizabeth Virginia "Bess" Wallace (1885-1982); 1 daughter
Died: Dec. 26, 1972; buried in Independence, Missouri
Early Career: Farmer; haberdasher (ran men's clothing store); judge;
        U.S. senator; vice president

DWIGHT D. EISENHOWER Republican Party   1953–1961
Born: Oct. 14, 1890, in Denison, Texas
Married: Mary "Mamie" Geneva Doud (1896-1979); 2 sons
Died: Mar. 28, 1969; buried in Abilene, Kansas
Early Career: Commander, Allied landing in North Africa and later
        Supreme Allied Commander in Europe during World War II;
        president of Columbia University

JOHN FITZGERALD KENNEDY Democratic Party   1961–1963
Born: May 29, 1917, in Brookline, Massachusetts
Married: Jacqueline Lee Bouvier (1929-1994); 2 sons, 1 daughter
Died: Nov. 22, 1963; buried in Arlington National Cemetery, Virginia
Early Career: U.S. naval commander; U.S. representative and senator

36 LYNDON BAINES JOHNSON Democratic Party 1963–1969
Born: Aug. 27, 1908, near Stonewall, Texas
Married: Claudia "Lady Bird" Alta Taylor (b. 1912); 2 daughters
Died: Jan. 22, 1973; buried in Johnson City, Texas
Early Career: U.S. representative and senator; vice president

37 RICHARD MILHOUS NIXON Republican Party 1969–1974
Born: Jan. 9, 1913, in Yorba Linda, California
Married: Thelma "Pat" Ryan (1912-1993); 2 daughters
Died: Apr. 22, 1994; buried in Yorba Linda, California
Early Career: Lawyer; U.S. representative and senator; vice president

38 GERALD R. FORD Republican Party 1974-1977
Born: July 14, 1913, in Omaha, Nebraska
Married: Elizabeth "Betty" Bloomer (b. 1918); 3 sons, 1 daughter
Early Career: Lawyer; U.S. representative; vice president

39 JIMMY (JAMES EARL) CARTER Democratic Party 1977-1981
Born: Oct. 1, 1924, in Plains, Georgia
Married: Rosalynn Smith (b. 1927); 3 sons, 1 daughter
Early Career: Peanut farmer; Georgia state senator; governor
    of Georgia

40 RONALD REAGAN Republican Party 1981–1989
Born: Feb. 6, 1911, in Tampico, Illinois
Married: Jane Wyman (b. 1914); 1 son, 1 daughter
    Nancy Davis (b. 1923); 1 son, 1 daughter
Died: June 5, 2004; buried in Simi Valley, California
Early Career: Film and television actor; governor of California

41 GEORGE H.W. BUSH Republican Party 1989–1993
Born: June 12, 1924, in Milton, Massachusetts
Married: Barbara Pierce (b. 1925); 4 sons, 2 daughters
Early Career: U.S. Navy pilot; businessman; U.S. representative; U.S.
    ambassador to the UN; CIA director, vice president

42 BILL (WILLIAM JEFFERSON) CLINTON Democratic Party 1993–2001
Born: Aug. 19, 1946, in Hope, Arkansas
Married: Hillary Rodham (b. 1947); 1 daughter
Early Career: College professor; Arkansas state attorney general;
    governor of Arkansas

43 GEORGE W. BUSH Republican Party 2001-
Born: July 6, 1946, in New Haven, Connecticut
Married: Laura Welch (b. 1946); 2 daughters
Early Career: Political adviser; businessman; baseball team owner;
    governor of Texas

MEET THE FIRST LADIES

ABIGAIL ADAMS, wife of John Adams, didn't have much formal education, but she read widely and had strong opinions. The hundreds of letters she wrote to her husband provide a history of life during the Revolutionary era. Besides being the wife of the second U.S. president, she was the mother of the sixth, John Quincy Adams.

ABIGAIL FILLMORE, wife of Millard Fillmore, was a former schoolteacher who started the first library in the White House. After attending the inauguration of her husband's successor, Franklin Pierce, in March 1853, she developed pneumonia, and died several weeks later.

FRANCES CLEVELAND, wife of Grover Cleveland, was the first bride of a president to be married in the White House. With her marriage in 1886, she became the youngest First Lady, at the age of 21. She was known as a delightful hostess. In 1893, she gave birth to Esther Cleveland, the only child ever born to a First Lady in the White House.

EDITH WILSON, second wife of Woodrow Wilson, whose first wife, Ellen, died in the White House. She volunteered in the Red Cross during World War I and, when President Wilson became ill in 1919, helped take care of many presidential duties, earning her the nickname of the "Secret President."

GRACE COOLIDGE, the wife of Calvin Coolidge, graduated from the University of Vermont in 1902, and then became a teacher of the deaf. As First Lady, she continued her support for people with disabilities. An animal lover, she had a pet raccoon named Rebecca in the White House. She had a strong interest in baseball and was a devoted fan of the Boston Red Sox.

ELEANOR ROOSEVELT, wife of Franklin D. Roosevelt, and niece of President Theodore Roosevelt, was an important public figure. She urged her husband to support civil rights and the rights of workers. After his death she served as a delegate to the United Nations. There, she was chairperson of the group that wrote the Universal Declaration of Human Rights.

LAURA BUSH, wife of George W. Bush, was a librarian and teacher. She is interested in books, history, art, and the well-being of children. She and her husband have twin daughters, Jenna and Barbara. Both girls graduated from college in 2004.

United States History

14,000 B.C.– 11,000 B.C.
Paleo-Indians use stone points attached to spears to hunt big **mammoths** in northern parts of North America.

11,000 B.C.
Big mammoths disappear and Paleo-Indians begin to gather **plants** for food.

After A.D. 500
Anasazi peoples in the Southwestern United States live in homes on cliffs, called **cliff dwellings**. Anasazi pottery and dishes are well known for their beautiful patterns.

After A.D. 700
Mississippian Indian people in the Southeastern United States **develop farms** and build burial mounds.

30,000 B.C.– 11,000 B.C.
First people (called **Paleo-Indians**) cross from Siberia to Alaska and begin to move into North America.

9500 B.C.– 1000 B.C.
North American Indians begin using **stone** to grind food and to hunt bison and smaller animals.

1000 B.C.– A.D. 500
Woodland Indians, who lived east of the Mississippi River, bury their dead under large **mounds** of earth (which can still be seen today).

700–1492
Many **different Indian cultures** develop throughout North America.

277

Colonial America
and the American Revolution:
1492–1783

1492
Christopher **Columbus** sails across the Atlantic Ocean and reaches an island in the Bahamas in the Caribbean Sea.

1513
Juan **Ponce de León** explores the Florida coast.

1524
Giovanni da **Verrazano** explores the coast from Carolina north to Nova Scotia, enters New York harbor.

1540
Francisco Vásquez de **Coronado** explores the Southwest.

1565
St. Augustine, Florida, the *first town* established by Europeans in the United States, is founded by the Spanish. Later burned by the English in 1586.

BENJAMIN FRANKLIN (1706-1790)
was a great American leader, printer, scientist, and writer. In 1732, he began publishing a magazine called *Poor Richard's Almanack*. Poor Richard was a make-believe person who gave advice about common sense and honesty. Many of Poor Richard's sayings are still known today. Among the most famous are "God helps them that help themselves" and "Early to bed, early to rise, makes a man healthy, wealthy, and wise."

1634
Maryland is founded as a Catholic colony, with religious freedom for all granted in 1649.

1664
The English seize **New Amsterdam** from the Dutch. The city is renamed New York.

1699
French settlers move into Mississippi and Louisiana.

1732
Benjamin Franklin begins publishing *Poor Richard's Almanack*.

1754-1763
French and Indian War between England and France. The French are defeated and lose their lands in Canada and the American Midwest.

1764-1766
England places taxes on sugar that comes from their North American colonies. England also requires colonists to buy stamps to help pay for royal troops. Colonists protest, and the **Stamp Act** is repealed in 1766.

1607
Jamestown, Virginia, the first English settlement in North America, is founded by Captain John Smith.

1609
Henry Hudson sails into **New York Harbor**, explores the Hudson River. Spaniards settle Santa Fe, New Mexico.

1619
The first African **slaves** are brought to Jamestown. (Slavery is made legal in 1650.)

1620
Pilgrims from England arrive at Plymouth, Massachusetts, on the *Mayflower*.

1626
Peter Minuit buys **Manhattan** island for the Dutch from Manahata Indians for goods worth $24. The island is renamed New Amsterdam.

1630
Boston is founded by Massachusetts colonists led by John Winthrop.

FAMOUS WORDS FROM THE DECLARATION OF INDEPENDENCE, JULY 4, 1776
"We hold these truths to be self-evident, that all men are created equal, that they are endowed by their Creator with certain unalienable rights, that among these are life, liberty, and the pursuit of happiness."

1770
Boston Massacre: English troops fire on a group of people protesting English taxes.

1773
Boston Tea Party: English tea is thrown into the harbor to protest a tax on tea.

1775
Fighting at **Lexington and Concord**, Massachusetts, marks the beginning of the American Revolution.

1776
The Declaration of Independence is approved July 4 by the Continental Congress (made up of representatives from the American colonies).

1781
British General **Charles Cornwallis** surrenders to the Americans at Yorktown, Virginia, ending the fighting in the Revolutionary War.

The New Nation
1784-1900

1784
The first successful daily **newspaper**, the *Pennsylvania Packet & General Advertiser*, is published.

1787
The **Constitutional Convention** meets to write a Constitution for the U.S.

1789
The new **Constitution** is approved by the states. George Washington is chosen as the first president.

1800
The federal government moves to a new capital, **Washington, D.C.**

1803
The U.S. makes the **Louisiana Purchase** from France. The Purchase doubles the area of the U.S.

THE LOUISIANA PURCHASE

WHO ATTENDED THE CONVENTION?

The **Constitutional Convention** met in Philadelphia in the hot summer of 1787. Most of the great founders of America attended. Among those present were George Washington, James Madison, and John Adams. They met to form a new government that would be strong and, at the same time, protect the liberties that were fought for in the American Revolution. The Constitution they created is still the law of the United States.

1836
Texans fighting for independence from Mexico are defeated at the **Alamo**.

1838
Cherokee Indians are forced to move to Oklahoma, along "The **Trail of Tears**."

1844
The **first telegraph** line connects Washington, D.C., and Baltimore.

1846-1848
U.S. war with Mexico: Mexico is defeated, and the United States takes control of the Republic of Texas and of Mexican territories in the West.

1848
The discovery of **gold** in California leads to a "rush" of 80,000 people to the West in search of gold.

1852
Uncle Tom's Cabin is published.

"THE TRAIL OF TEARS"

The **Cherokee Indians** living in Georgia were forced by the government to leave in 1838. They were sent to Oklahoma. On the long march, thousands died because of disease and the cold weather.

UNCLE TOM'S CABIN

Harriet Beecher Stowe's novel about the **suffering of slaves** was an instant bestseller in the North and banned in most of the South. When President Abraham Lincoln met Stowe, he called her "the little lady who started this war" (the Civil War).

1804
Lewis and Clark, with their guide Sacagawea, explore what is now the northwestern United States.

1812-1814
War of 1812 with Great Britain: British forces burn the Capitol and White House. Francis Scott Key writes the words to "The Star-Spangled Banner."

1820
The **Missouri Compromise** bans slavery west of the Mississippi River and north of 36°30′ latitude, except in Missouri.

1823
The **Monroe Doctrine** warns European countries not to interfere in the Americas.

1825
The **Erie Canal** opens, linking New York City with the Great Lakes.

1831
The Liberator, a newspaper opposing slavery, is published in Boston.

1869
The **first railroad** connecting the East and West coasts is completed.

1898
Spanish-American War: The U.S. defeats Spain, gains control of the Philippines, Puerto Rico, and Guam.

1858
Abraham Lincoln and Stephen Douglas **debate about slavery** during their Senate campaign in Illinois.

1860
Abraham **Lincoln** is elected president.

1861
The **Civil War** begins.

1863
President Lincoln issues the **Emancipation Proclamation**, freeing most slaves.

1865
The **Civil War** ends as the South surrenders. President Lincoln is assassinated.

1890
Battle of Wounded Knee is fought in South Dakota—the last major battle between Indians and U.S. troops.

CIVIL WAR DEAD AND WOUNDED
The U.S. **Civil War** between the North and South lasted four years (1861-1865) and resulted in the death or wounding of more than 600,000 people. Little was known at the time about the spread of diseases. As a result, many casualties were also the result of illnesses such as influenza, measles, and infections from battle wounds.

United States Since 1900

WORLD WAR I
In **World War I** the United States fought with Great Britain, France, and Russia (the Allies) against Germany and Austria-Hungary. The Allies won the war in 1918.

1903
The United States begins digging the **Panama Canal**. The canal opens in 1914, connecting the Atlantic and Pacific oceans.

1908
Henry Ford introduces the **Model T** car, priced at $850.

1916
Jeannette Rankin of Montana becomes the first woman elected to Congress.

1917–1918
The United States joins **World War I** on the side of the Allies against Germany.

1927
Charles A. **Lindbergh** becomes the first person to fly alone nonstop across the Atlantic Ocean.

1929
A stock market crash marks the beginning of the **Great Depression**.

1954
The U.S. Supreme Court **forbids racial segregation** in public schools.

SCHOOL SEGREGATION
The U.S. Supreme Court ruled that **separate schools** for black students and white students were **not equal**. The Court said such schools were against the U.S. Constitution. The ruling also applied to other forms of segregation—separation of the races supported by some states.

1963
President John **Kennedy** is assassinated.

1964
Congress passes the **Civil Rights Act**, which outlaws discrimination in voting and jobs.

1965
The United States sends large numbers of soldiers to fight in the **Vietnam War**.

1968
Civil rights leader **Martin Luther King Jr.** is assassinated in Memphis. Senator **Robert F. Kennedy** is assassinated in Los Angeles.

1969
U.S. Astronaut Neil Armstrong becomes the **first person** to walk **on the moon**.

1973
U.S. participation in the **Vietnam War ends**.

THE GREAT DEPRESSION

The stock market crash of October 1929 led to a period of severe hardship for the American people—the **Great Depression**. As many as 25 percent of all workers could not find jobs. The Depression lasted until the early 1940s. The Depression also led to a great change in politics. In 1932, Franklin D. Roosevelt, a Democrat, was elected president. He served as president for 12 years, longer than any other president.

1933

President Franklin D. Roosevelt's **New Deal** increases government help to people hurt by the Depression.

1941

Japan attacks **Pearl Harbor**, Hawaii. The United States enters World War II.

1945

Germany and Japan surrender, **ending World War II**. Japan surrenders after the U.S. drops atomic bombs on Hiroshima and Nagasaki.

1947

Jackie Robinson becomes the **first black baseball player** in the major leagues when he joins the Brooklyn Dodgers.

1950–1953

U.S. armed forces fight in the **Korean War**.

WATERGATE

In June 1972, five men were arrested in the **Watergate** building in Washington, D.C., for trying to bug telephones in the offices of the Democratic National Committee. Some of those arrested worked for the committee to reelect President Richard Nixon. Later it was discovered that Nixon was helping to hide information about the break-in.

1991

The Persian Gulf War: The United States and its allies defeat Iraq.

2000

George W. Bush narrowly defeats Al Gore in a closely fought battle for the presidency.

2004–2005

Bush defeats John Kerry to win a new term. Iraq holds free elections.

1974

President Richard **Nixon resigns** because of the Watergate scandal.

1979

U.S. **hostages are taken in Iran**, beginning a 444-day crisis that ends with their release in 1981.

1981

Sandra Day O'Connor becomes the **first woman** on the U.S. Supreme Court.

1985

U.S. President Ronald Reagan and Soviet leader Mikhail Gorbachev begin working together to **improve relations** between their countries.

1999

After an **impeachment** trial, the Senate finds President Bill Clinton not guilty.

2001

Hijacked jets crashed into the **World Trade Center** and the Pentagon, September 11, killing about 3,000 people.

2003

U.S.-led forces invade Iraq and remove dictator **Saddam Hussein**.

African Americans:
A Timeline

Would you like to learn more about the history of African Americans from the era of slavery to the present? These events and personalities can be a starting point. Can you add some more?

Rev. Dr. Martin Luther King Jr. ▶

1619	─○	First Africans are brought to Virginia as slaves.
1831	─○	Nat Turner starts a **slave revolt** in Virginia that is unsuccessful.
1856-57	─○	**Dred Scott**, a slave, sues to be freed because he had left slave territory, but the Supreme Court denies his claim.
1861-65	─●	The North defeats the South in the brutal Civil War; the **13th Amendment** ends nearly 250 years of slavery. The Ku Klux Klan is founded.
1865-77	─○	Southern blacks play leadership roles in government under **Reconstruction**; the 15th Amendment (1870) gives black men the right to vote.
1896	─●	Supreme Court rules in a case called *Plessy versus Ferguson* that segregation is legal when facilities are **"separate but equal."** Discrimination and violence against blacks increase.
1910	─○	W. E. B. Du Bois (1868–1963) founds National Association for the Advancement of Colored People (NAACP), fighting for equality for blacks.
1920s	─●	African American culture (jazz music, dance, literature) flourishes during the **Harlem Renaissance**.
1954	─○	Supreme Court rules in a case called ***Brown versus Board of Education*** of *Topeka* that school segregation is unconstitutional.
1957	─●	Black students, backed by federal troops, enter segregated Central High School in **Little Rock**, Arkansas.
1955-65	─○	**Malcolm X** (1925–65) emerges as key spokesman for black nationalism.
1963	─●	**Rev. Dr. Martin Luther King Jr.** (1929–68) gives his "I Have a Dream" speech at a march that inspired more than 200,000 people in Washington, D.C.—and many others throughout the nation.
1964	─○	Sweeping **civil rights bill** banning racial discrimination is signed by President Lyndon Johnson.
1965	─●	King leads protest march in **Selma**, Alabama; blacks riot in **Watts** section of Los Angeles.
1967	─○	Gary, Indiana, and Cleveland, Ohio, are first major U.S. cities to elect **black mayors**; Thurgood Marshall (1908–93) becomes first black on the **Supreme Court**.
1995	─●	Hundreds of thousands of black men take part in **"Million Man March"** rally in Washington, D.C., urging responsibility for families and communities.
2001	─○	**Colin Powell** becomes first African American secretary of state.
2005	─●	**Condoleezza Rice** becomes first African American woman secretary of state.

THEY MADE History

These people of color made big contributions to the growth of the United States as a free country.

SOJOURNER TRUTH (1797-1883) was raised as a slave on an estate in upstate New York. Escaping in 1826, she took the name Sojourner Truth. She campaigned against slavery and, later, for women's right to vote.

GEORGE WASHINGTON CARVER (1864-1943) invented nearly 300 products made from peanuts (including types of milk, cheese, flour, ink, soap, and cosmetics) and over 100 products from sweet potatoes. In 1896, he joined the faculty of Alabama's Tuskegee Institute, where he gained an international reputation as an educator.

W.E.B. DU BOIS (1868–1963) was the first black person to earn a doctorate from Harvard University. He helped found the National Association for the Advancement of Colored People (NAACP) and organized meetings that brought together American blacks and Africans. He urged people to see "boauty in black."

MALCOLM X (1925–1965) was a forceful Muslim leader who spoke against injustices toward blacks and promoted the idea of black pride and independence. He was assassinated by rivals in 1965. His life story, *The Autobiography of Malcolm X*, helped make him a hero to many African Americans.

ROSA PARKS (1913–2005) is called the mother of America's civil rights movement. When she refused to give up her bus seat to a white man in 1955, blacks in Montgomery, Alabama, started a boycott of the bus system, which led to desegregation of the city's buses. After her death she became the first woman (and 31st person) in history to lie in honor in the Capitol Rotunda in Washington, D.C.

CESAR CHAVEZ (1927-1993), a Mexican American who was raised in migrant worker camps, started a national farm workers union, the United Farm Workers of America, in 1966. He organized boycotts that eventually made growers agree to better conditions for field workers.

PATSY MINK (1927-2002) was born in Hawaii to Japanese American parents. In 1968 she became the first non-white woman elected to the U.S. House of Representatives. She helped pass the famous 1972 "Title IX" law that required equal rights for women in colleges getting federal funds.

REV. MARTIN LUTHER KING JR. (1929–1968) was the most influential leader of the U.S. civil rights movement from the mid-1950s to his assassination in 1968. In 1964 he received the Nobel Peace Prize. His wife, **CORETTA SCOTT KING** (1927-2006), helped carry on his work.

ANTONIO VILLARAIGOSA (born 1953), a Mexican American, in 2005 became the first Latino mayor of Los Angeles since the 1870s. He is a former labor leader and speaker of the California State Assembly.

ANG LEE (born 1954), born in Taiwan, is a prize-winning Chinese American filmmaker. His best known films include *Crouching Tiger, Hidden Dragon* (2000) and *Hulk* (2003). In 2006 he won an Oscar for his film *Brokeback Mountain*.

OPRAH WINFREY (born 1954) has won many awards as a talk show host, actress, writer, publisher, and film producer. Through Oprah's Angel Network, she has collected millions of dollars to help people in need.

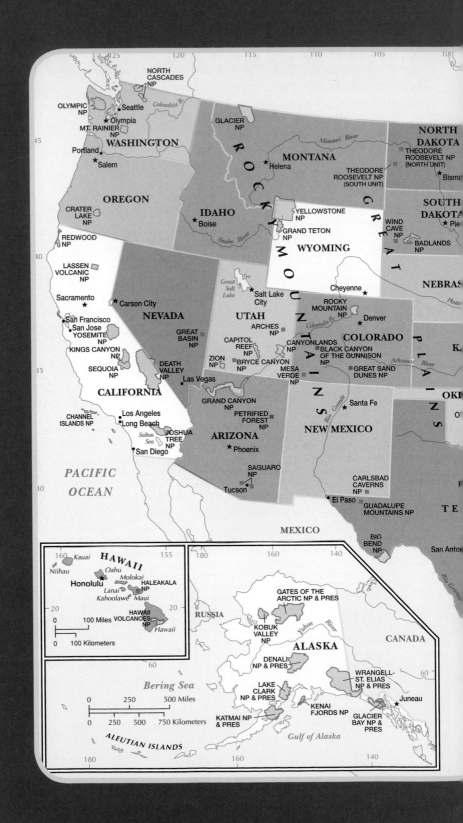

NORTH
CASCADES
NP

OLYMPIC
NP
• Seattle

Columbia R.

GLACIER
NP

Missouri River

NORTH
DAKOTA

★ Olympia
MT. RAINIER
NP

THEODORE
ROOSEVELT NP
(NORTH UNIT)

Portland •

MONTANA

WASHINGTON

Helena ★

THEODORE
ROOSEVELT NP
(SOUTH UNIT)

• Bisma

★ Salem

OREGON

IDAHO

R

• Boise

Snake River

YELLOWSTONE
NP

SOUTH
DAKOTA

CRATER
LAKE
NP

GRAND TETON
NP

WIND
CAVE
NP

★ Pie

REDWOOD
NP

WYOMING

BADLANDS
NP

O

C

LASSEN
VOLCANIC
NP

Great
Salt
Lake

Salt Lake
City

Cheyenne ★

NEBRAS

Sacramento
★

★ Carson City

ROCKY
MOUNTAIN
NP

Platte

Denver •

San Francisco •
San Jose •
YOSEMITE
NP

NEVADA

UTAH

ARCHES
NP

Colorado R.

COLORADO

KA

KINGS CANYON
NP

GREAT
BASIN
NP

CAPITOL
REEF
NP

CANYONLANDS
NP

BLACK CANYON
OF THE GUNNISON

Arkansas

River

ZION
NP

BRYCE CANYON
NP

SEQUOIA
NP

DEATH
VALLEY
NP

MESA
VERDE
NP

GREAT SAND
DUNES NP

OK

CALIFORNIA

• Las Vegas

M

Santa Fe

Rio Grande

★

CHANNEL
ISLANDS NP

Los Angeles •
Long Beach •

GRAND CANYON
NP

PETRIFIED
FOREST
NP

NEW MEXICO

O'

Salton
Sea

JOSHUA
TREE
NP

ARIZONA

• San Diego

★ Phoenix

PACIFIC

SAGUARO
NP

CARLSBAD
CAVERNS
NP

TE

OCEAN

Tucson •

• El Paso

GUADALUPE
MOUNTAINS NP

MEXICO

BIG
BEND
NP

San Anto

Kauai

HAWAII

155

180

160

140

Niihau

Oahu

★

Honolulu

Molokai

HALEAKALA
NP

RUSSIA

GATES OF THE
ARCTIC NP & PRES

Lanai

Maui

Kahoolawe

20

20

KOBUK
VALLEY
NP

Yukon

River

CANADA

HAWAII
VOLCANOES
NP

Hawaii

DENALI
NP & PRES

ALASKA

0   100 Miles

60

WRANGELL-
ST. ELIAS
NP & PRES

60

0   100 Kilometers

Bering Sea

LAKE
CLARK
NP & PRES

0   250   500 Miles

KENAI
FJORDS NP

★ Juneau

GLACIER
BAY NP &
PRES

0   250   500   750 Kilometers

KATMAI NP
& PRES

Gulf of Alaska

ALEUTIAN ISLANDS

180

160

140

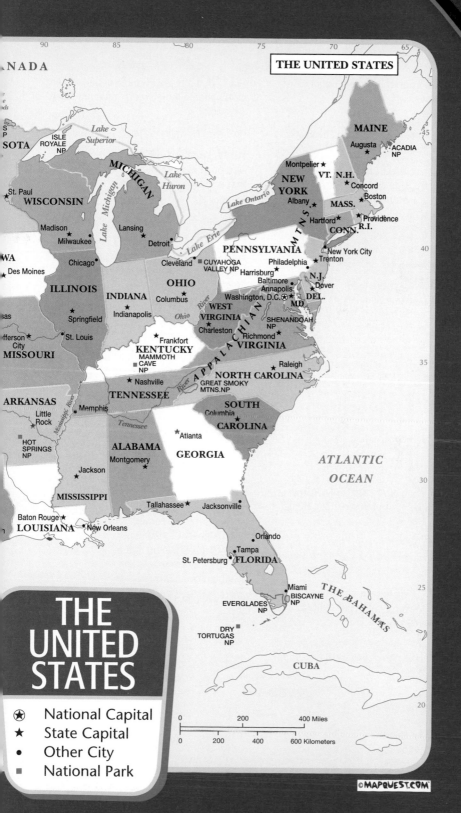

THE UNITED STATES

CANADA

90   85   80   75   70   65

SOTA

ISLE ROYALE NP
Lake Superior
MINNESOTA

MICHIGAN
Lake Huron
Lake Michigan

WISCONSIN
St. Paul
Madison
Milwaukee
Lansing
Detroit

MAINE
Augusta
ACADIA NP
45

Montpelier
VT. N.H.
Concord
Boston

NEW YORK
Albany
Lake Ontario

MASS.
Hartford
Providence
R.I.
CONN.

IOWA
Des Moines
Chicago
Lake Erie

PENNSYLVANIA
Cleveland
CUYAHOGA VALLEY NP
Philadelphia
New York City
Trenton
40

ILLINOIS
INDIANA
OHIO
Columbus
Indianapolis

Harrisburg
Baltimore
Annapolis
Washington, D.C.
MD
N.J.
Dover
DEL.

Springfield
St. Louis
Jefferson City
MISSOURI

Ohio River
WEST VIRGINIA
Charleston

SHENANDOAH NP
Richmond
VIRGINIA

Frankfort
KENTUCKY
MAMMOTH CAVE NP
Nashville

APPALACHIAN MTNS

Raleigh
NORTH CAROLINA
GREAT SMOKY MTNS.NP
35

ARKANSAS
Little Rock
HOT SPRINGS NP
Memphis
TENNESSEE
Tennessee

SOUTH CAROLINA
Columbia

ALABAMA
Montgomery
Jackson
MISSISSIPPI

Atlanta
GEORGIA

ATLANTIC OCEAN
30

Baton Rouge
LOUISIANA
New Orleans
Mississippi River

Tallahassee
Jacksonville

Orlando
Tampa
St. Petersburg
FLORIDA

Miami
BISCAYNE NP
EVERGLADES NP
THE BAHAMAS
25

DRY TORTUGAS NP

CUBA

20

THE UNITED STATES

⊛ National Capital
★ State Capital
• Other City
■ National Park

0   200   400 Miles
0   200   400   600 Kilometers

©MAPQUEST.COM

ALABAMA comes from an Indian word for "tribal town."

ALASKA comes from *alakshak*, the Aleutian (Eskimo) word meaning "peninsula" or "land that is not an island."

ARIZONA comes from a Pima Indian word meaning "little spring place," or the Aztec word *arizuma*, meaning "silver-bearing."

ARKANSAS is a variation of *Quapaw*, the name of an Indian tribe. *Quapaw* means "south wind."

CALIFORNIA is the name of an imaginary island in a Spanish story. It was named by Spanish explorers of Baja California, a part of Mexico.

COLORADO comes from a Spanish word meaning "red." It was first given to the Colorado River because of its reddish color.

Colorado

CONNECTICUT comes from an Algonquin Indian word meaning "long river place."

DELAWARE is named after Lord De La Warr, the English governor of Virginia in colonial times.

FLORIDA, which means "flowery" in Spanish, was named by the explorer Ponce de León, who landed there during Easter.

GEORGIA was named after King George II of England, who granted the right to create a colony there in 1732.

HAWAII probably comes from *Hawaiki*, or *Owhyhee*, the native Polynesian word for "homeland."

IDAHO's name is of uncertain origin, but it may come from a Kiowa Apache name for the Comanche Indians.

Idaho

ILLINOIS is the French version of *Illini*, an Algonquin Indian word meaning "men" or "warriors."

INDIANA means "land of the Indians."

IOWA comes from the name of an American Indian tribe that lived on the land that is now the state.

KANSAS comes from a Sioux Indian word that possibly meant "people of the south wind."

KENTUCKY comes from an Iroquois Indian word, possibly meaning "meadowland."

LOUISIANA, which was first settled by French explorers, was named after King Louis XIV of France.

MAINE means "the mainland." English explorers called it that to distinguish it from islands nearby.

MARYLAND was named after Queen Henrietta Maria, wife of King Charles I of England, who granted the right to establish an English colony there.

MASSACHUSETTS comes from an Indian word meaning "large hill place."

MICHIGAN comes from the Chippewa Indian words *mici gama*, meaning "great water" (referring to Lake Michigan).

MINNESOTA got its name from a Dakota Sioux Indian word meaning "cloudy water" or "sky-tinted water."

Michigan

MISSISSIPPI is probably from Chippewa Indian words meaning "great river" or "gathering of all the waters," or from an Algonquin word, *messipi*.

MISSOURI comes from an Algonquin Indian term meaning "river of the big canoes."

got their names

MONTANA comes from a Latin or Spanish word meaning "mountainous."

Nebraska

NEBRASKA comes from "flat river" or "broad water," an Omaha or Otos Indian name for the Platte River.

NEVADA means "snow-clad" in Spanish. Spanish explorers gave the name to the Sierra Nevada Mountains.

NEW HAMPSHIRE was named by an early settler after his home county of Hampshire, in England.

NEW JERSEY was named for the English Channel island of Jersey.

NEW MEXICO was given its name by 16th-century Spaniards in Mexico.

NEW YORK, first called New Netherland, was renamed for the Duke of York and Albany after the English took it from Dutch settlers.

NORTH CAROLINA, the northern part of the English colony of Carolana, was named for King Charles I.

NORTH DAKOTA comes from a Sioux Indian word meaning "friend" or "ally."

OHIO is the Iroquois Indian word for "good river."

OKLAHOMA comes from a Choctaw Indian word meaning "red man."

OREGON may have come from *Ouaricon-sint,* a name on an old French map that was once given to what is now called the Columbia River. That river runs between Oregon and Washington.

PENNSYLVANIA meaning "Penn's woods," was the name given to the colony founded by William Penn.

RHODE ISLAND may have come from the Dutch "Roode Eylandt" (red island) or may have been named after the Greek island of Rhodes.

SOUTH CAROLINA, the southern part of the English colony of Carolana, was named for King Charles I.

South Dakota

SOUTH DAKOTA comes from a Sioux Indian word meaning "friend" or "ally."

TENNESSEE comes from "Tanasi," the name of Cherokee Indian villages on what is now the Little Tennessee River.

TEXAS comes from a word meaning "friends" or "allies," used by the Spanish to describe some of the American Indians living there.

UTAH comes from a Navajo word meaning "upper" or "higher up."

Utah

VERMONT comes from two French words, *vert* meaning "green" and *mont* meaning "mountain."

VIRGINIA was named in honor of Queen Elizabeth I of England, who was known as the Virgin Queen because she was never married.

WASHINGTON was named after George Washington, the first president of the United States. It is the only state named after a president.

WEST VIRGINIA got its name from the people of western Virginia, who formed their own government during the Civil War.

WISCONSIN comes from a Chippewa name that is believed to mean "grassy place." It was once spelled *Ouisconsin* and *Mesconsing.*

Wyoming

WYOMING comes from Algonquin Indian words that are said to mean "at the big plains," "large prairie place," or "on the great plain."

FACTS
About the
STATES

After every state name is the postal abbreviation. The Area includes both land and water; it is given in square miles (sq. mi.) and square kilometers (sq. km.). Numbers in parentheses after Population, Area, and Entered Union show the state's rank compared with other states. City populations are for mid-2004.

ALABAMA (AL) Heart of Dixie, Camellia State

Birmingham

Montgomery

POPULATION (2005): 4,557,808 (23rd) **AREA:** 52,419 sq. mi. (30th) (135,765 sq. km.) ✿ Camellia ♪Yellowhammer ❊Southern longleaf pine ♫"Alabama" **ENTERED UNION:** December 14, 1819 (22nd) ✪ Montgomery **LARGEST CITIES (WITH POP.):** Birmingham, 233,149; Montgomery, 200,983; Mobile, 192,759; Huntsville, 164,146

⚙clothing and textiles, metal products, transportation equipment, paper, industrial machinery, food products, lumber, coal, oil, natural gas, livestock, peanuts, cotton

WEB SITE *http://www.alabama.gov • http://www.touralabama.org*

did you know? *Built in Birmingham in 1904, a statue of Vulcan stands 56 feet high and is the largest cast iron statue in the world.*

ALASKA (AK) The Last Frontier

Anchorage

Juneau

POPULATION (2005): 663,661 (47th) **AREA:** 663,267 sq. mi. (1st) (1,717,854 sq. km.) ✿Forget-me-not ♪Willow ptarmigan ❊Sitka spruce ♫"Alaska's Flag" **ENTERED UNION:** January 3, 1959 (49th) ✪Juneau **LARGEST CITIES (WITH POP.):** Anchorage, 272,687; Juneau, 31,118; Fairbanks, 30,435

⚙oil, natural gas, fish, food products, lumber and wood products, fur

WEB SITE *http://www.state.ak.us • http://www.travelalaska.com*

did you know? *Alaska is the least densely populated state with 1.1 persons per square mile.*

ARIZONA (AZ) Grand Canyon State

Phoenix

Tucson

POPULATION (2005): 5,939,292 (17th) **AREA:** 113,998 sq. mi. (6th) (295,253 sq. km.) ✿Blossom of the Saguaro cactus ♪Cactus wren ❊Paloverde ♫"Arizona" **ENTERED UNION:** February 14, 1912 (48th) ✪Phoenix **LARGEST CITIES (WITH POP.):** Phoenix, 1,418,041; Tucson, 512,023; Mesa, 437,454; Glendale, 235,591; Chandler, 223,991; Scottsdale, 221,792

⚙electronic equipment, transportation and industrial equipment, instruments, printing and publishing, copper and other metals

WEB SITE *http://www.az.gov • http://www.arizonaguide.com*

did you know? *Cut by the Colorado River, the Grand Canyon has an average depth of 4,000 feet over 277 miles. It is 6,000 feet at its deepest point, and ranges from 1 to 15 miles wide.*

ARKANSAS (AR) Natural State, Razorback State

POPULATION (2005): 2,779,154 (32nd) **AREA:** 53,179 sq. mi. (29th) (137,733 sq. km.) ⚙Apple blossom ♪Mockingbird 🌲Pine ♫"Arkansas" **ENTERED UNION:** June 15, 1836 (25th) ⭐Little Rock **LARGEST CITIES (WITH POP.):** Little Rock, 184,081; Fort Smith, 81,849; Fayetteville, 64,190; North Little Rock, 59,474

⚙food products, paper, electronic equipment, industrial machinery, metal products, lumber and wood products, livestock, soybeans, rice, cotton, natural gas

Little Rock ⭐

WEB SITE http://www.arkansas.gov • http://www.arkansas.com

didyouknow? *The World Championship Duck Calling Contest has been held every Thanksgiving since 1936 in Stuttgart, Arkansas. Competitors are graded on how realistically they quack.*

CALIFORNIA (CA) Golden State

POPULATION (2005): 36,132,147 (1st) **AREA:** 163,696 sq. mi. (3rd) (423,971 sq. km.) ⚙Golden poppy ♪California valley quail 🌲California redwood ♫"I Love You, California" **ENTERED UNION:** September 9, 1850 (31st) ⭐Sacramento **LARGEST CITIES (WITH POP.):** Los Angeles, 3,845,541; San Diego, 1,263,756; San Jose, 904,522; San Francisco, 744,230; Long Beach, 476,564; Fresno, 457,719; Sacramento, 454,330; Oakland, 397,976

⚙transportation and industrial equipment, electronic equipment, oil, natural gas, motion pictures, milk, cattle, fruit, vegetables

⭐Sacramento
San Francisco
Los Angeles
San Diego

WEB SITE http://www.ca.gov • http://www.gocalif.ca.gov

didyouknow? *The highest (Mount Whitney, 14,494 feet) and lowest (Death Valley, -282 feet) points in the "lower 48" states are only about 85 miles apart in California.*

COLORADO (CO) Centennial State

POPULATION (2005): 4,665,177 (22nd) **AREA:** 104,094 sq. mi. (8th) (269,602 sq. km.) ⚙Rocky Mountain columbine ♪Lark bunting 🌲Colorado blue spruce ♫"Where the Columbines Grow" **ENTERED UNION:** August 1, 1876 (38th) ⭐Denver **LARGEST CITIES (WITH POP.):** Denver, 556,835; Colorado Springs, 369,363; Aurora, 291,843; Lakewood, 141,301; Fort Collins, 126,967

⚙instruments and industrial machinery, food products, printing and publishing, metal products, electronic equipment, oil, coal, cattle

⭐ Denver
Colorado Springs

WEB SITE http://www.colorado.gov • http://www.colorado.com

didyouknow? *The Anasazi Indians built entire cities into cliffsides across the American southwest. The settlements built between 1100 and 1300 at Mesa Verde in southwestern Colorado are the largest and best preserved.*

Key: ⚙Flower ♪Bird 🌲Tree ♫Song ⭐Capital ⚙Important Products

CONNECTICUT (CT) Constitution State, Nutmeg State

Hartford

POPULATION (2005): 3,510,297 (29th) **AREA:** 5,543 sq. mi. (48th) (14,356 sq. km.) 🌼Mountain laurel 🐦American robin 🌳White oak 🎵"Yankee Doodle" **ENTERED UNION:** January 9, 1788 (5th) ⭐ Hartford **LARGEST CITIES (WITH POP.):** Bridgeport, 139,910; Hartford, 124,848; New Haven, 124,829; Stamford, 120,226; Waterbury, 108,429

⚙️aircraft parts, helicopters, industrial machinery, metals and metal products, electronic equipment, printing and publishing, medical instruments, chemicals, dairy products, stone

WEB SITE *http://www.ct.gov • http://www.ctbound.org*

did you know? *Many historians believe Connecticut's 1639 constitution was the world's first written constitution and a model for the U.S. Constitution. That's why Connecticut is nicknamed the "Constitution State."*

DELAWARE (DE) First State, Diamond State

Dover
⭐

POPULATION (2005): 843,524 (45th) **AREA:** 2,489 sq. mi. (49th) (6,446 sq. km.) 🌼Peach blossom 🐦Blue hen chicken 🌳American holly 🎵"Our Delaware" **ENTERED UNION:** December 7, 1787 (1st) ⭐Dover **LARGEST CITIES (WITH POP.):** Wilmington, 72,784; Dover, 33,618; Newark, 29,821

⚙️chemicals, transportation equipment, food products, chickens

WEB SITE *http://www.delaware.gov • http://www.visitdelaware.com*

did you know? *The Mason-Dixon line is an L-shaped border that separates Delaware, Pennsylvania, and Maryland. Charles Mason and Jeremiah Dixon drew it in the 1760s to settle a dispute between the colonies. The border is marked to this day with stones about every 1,000 feet.*

FLORIDA (FL) Sunshine State

Tallahassee
⭐
Jacksonville

Miami ●

POPULATION (2005): 17,789,864 (4th) **AREA:** 65,755 sq. mi. (22nd) (170,305 sq. km.) 🌼Orange blossom 🐦Mockingbird 🌳Sabal palmetto palm 🎵"Old Folks at Home" **ENTERED UNION:** March 3, 1845 (27th) ⭐Tallahassee (population, 155,171) **LARGEST CITIES (WITH POP.):** Jacksonville, 777,704; Miami, 379,724; Tampa, 321,772; St. Petersburg, 249,090; Hialeah, 224,522; Orlando, 205,648; Ft. Lauderdale, 164,578

⚙️electronic and transportation equipment, industrial machinery, printing and publishing, food products, citrus fruits, vegetables, livestock, phosphates, fish

WEB SITE *http://www.myflorida.com • http://www.visitflorida.com*

did you know? *The Everglades is a large freshwater marsh that drifts about 110 miles from Lake Okeechobee to Florida Bay. About half of its complex habitat has been preserved as a national park for the more than 500 species of animals and plants that call it home, including endangered crocodiles, panthers, and manatees.*

GEORGIA (GA) Empire State of the South, Peach State

POPULATION (2005): 9,072,576 (9th) **AREA:** 59,425 sq. mi. (24th) (153,910 sq. km.) Cherokee rose Brown thrasher Live oak "Georgia on My Mind" **ENTERED UNION:** January 2, 1788 (4th) Atlanta **LARGEST CITIES (WITH POP.):** Atlanta, 419,122; Augusta, 191,326; Columbus, 182,850; Savannah, 129,808; Athens, 102,744

⚙clothing and textiles, transportation equipment, food products, paper, chickens, peanuts, peaches, clay

WEB SITE *http://www.georgia.gov • http://www.georgia.org*

did you know? *Nearly half of America's peanuts are grown in Georgia.*

Atlanta

HAWAII (HI) Aloha State

POPULATION (2005): 1,275,194 (42nd) **AREA:** 10,931 sq. mi. (43rd) (28,311 sq. km.) Yellow hibiscus Hawaiian goose Kukui "Hawaii Ponoi" **ENTERED UNION:** August 21, 1959 (50th) Honolulu **LARGEST CITIES (WITH POP.):** Honolulu, 377,260; Hilo, 40,759; Kailua, 36,513; Kaneohe, 34,970

⚙food products, pineapples, sugar, printing and publishing, fish, flowers

WEB SITE *http://www.hawaii.gov • http://www.gohawaii.com*

did you know? *The most massive volcano in the world, Mauna Loa ("Long Mountain"), covers half of the island of Hawaii, the "Big" island. About four-fifths of the volcano lies underwater, but its peak reaches 13,681 feet above sea level.*

Honolulu

IDAHO (ID) Gem State

POPULATION (2005): 1,429,096 (39th) **AREA:** 83,570 sq. mi. (14th) (216,445 sq. km.) Syringa Mountain bluebird White pine "Here We Have Idaho" **ENTERED UNION:** July 3, 1890 (43rd) Boise **LARGEST CITIES (WITH POP.):** Boise, 190,122; Nampa, 68,156; Idaho Falls, 52,148; Pocatello, 50,723

⚙potatoes, hay, wheat, cattle, milk, lumber and wood products, food products

WEB SITE *http://www.idaho.gov • http://www.visitid.org*

did you know? *It's estimated that some 300,000 pioneers crossed southern Idaho on the Oregon Trail between 1841 and 1867. At Three Island Park an annual reenactment is held at the famous Snake River crossing.*

Boise

Key: Flower Bird Tree Song Capital Important Products

ILLINOIS
(IL) Prairie State

Chicago

Springfield ⭐

POPULATION (2005): 12,763,371 (5th) **AREA:** 57,914 sq. mi. (25th) (149,997 sq. km.) 🌸Native violet 🐦Cardinal 🌳White oak 🎵"Illinois" **ENTERED UNION:** December 3, 1818 (21st) ⭐ Springfield **LARGEST CITIES (WITH POP.):** Chicago, 2,862,244; Aurora, 166,614; Rockford, 152,452; Naperville, 140,106; Joliet, 129,519; Springfield, 114,738; Peoria, 112,720

⚙️industrial machinery, metals and metal products, printing and publishing, electronic equipment, food products, corn, soybeans, hogs

WEB SITE *http://www.illinois.gov • http://www.enjoyillinois.com*

did you know? *Chicago is the nation's third largest city and home of the 1,450-foot Sears Tower, tallest building in the U.S. The world's first skyscraper, the Home Insurance Building, was built there in 1885.*

INDIANA
(IN) Hoosier State

Indianapolis ⭐

POPULATION (2005): 6,271,973 (15th) **AREA:** 36,418 sq. mi. (38th) (94,322 sq. km.) 🌸Peony 🐦Cardinal 🌳Tulip poplar 🎵"On the Banks of the Wabash, Far Away" **ENTERED UNION:** December 11, 1816 (19th) ⭐Indianapolis **LARGEST CITIES (WITH POP.):** Indianapolis, 784,242; Fort Wayne, 219,351; Evansville, 117,156; South Bend, 105,494; Gary, 99,156

⚙️transportation equipment, electronic equipment, industrial machinery, iron and steel, metal products, corn, soybeans, livestock, coal

WEB SITE *http://www.in.gov • http://www.enjoyindiana.com*

did you know? *The nickname "Hoosier State" became popular in the 1830s, but the origin of the word "hoosier" is not known.*

IOWA
(IA) Hawkeye State

Des Moines ⭐

POPULATION (2005): 2,966,334 (30th) **AREA:** 56,272 sq. mi. (26th) (145,744 sq. km.) 🌸Wild rose 🐦Eastern goldfinch 🌳Oak 🎵"The Song of Iowa" **ENTERED UNION:** December 28, 1846 (29th) ⭐Des Moines **LARGEST CITIES (WITH POP.):** Des Moines, 194,311; Cedar Rapids, 122,206; Davenport, 98,355; Sioux City, 83,680

⚙️corn, soybeans, hogs, cattle, industrial machinery, food products

WEB SITE *http://www.iowa.gov • http://www.traveliowa.com*

did you know? *The eastern and western borders of this state are defined by rivers. The Mississippi River carves out Iowa's eastern border, while the Missouri and Big Sioux rivers form the western border.*

KANSAS (KS) Sunflower State

POPULATION (2005): 2,744,687 (33rd) **AREA:** 82,277 sq. mi. (15th) (213,096 sq. km.) ✿Native sunflower 🐦Western meadowlark 🌲Cottonwood 🎵"Home on the Range" **ENTERED UNION:** January 29, 1861 (34th) ★Topeka **LARGEST CITIES (WITH POP.):** Wichita, 353,823; Overland Park, 162,728; Kansas City, 145,004; Topeka, 121,809

⚙cattle, aircraft and other transportation equipment, industrial machinery, food products, wheat, corn, hay, oil, natural gas

WEB SITE *http:// www.kansas.gov • http://www.travelks.org*

did you know? *The geographic center of the 48 connected U.S. states is near Lebanon, Kansas, near the center of Kansas's northern border.*

KENTUCKY (KY) Bluegrass State

POPULATION (2005): 4,173,405 (26th) **AREA:** 40,409 sq. mi. (37th) (104,659 sq. km.) ✿Goldenrod 🐦Cardinal 🌲Tulip poplar 🎵"My Old Kentucky Home" **ENTERED UNION:** June 1, 1792 (15th) ★Frankfort (population, 27,660) **LARGEST CITIES (WITH POP.)** Louisville, 556,332; Lexington 266,358

⚙coal, industrial machinery, electronic equipment, transportation equipment, metals, tobacco, cattle

WEB SITE *http:// www.kentucky.gov • http://www.kentuckytourism.com*

did you know? *More than 360 miles of natural caves and underground passageways have been mapped under Mammoth Cave National Park. It's the largest network of natural tunnels in the world and might extend up to 1,000 miles.*

LOUISIANA (LA) Pelican State

POPULATION (2005): 4,523,628 (24th) **AREA:** 51,840 sq. mi. (31st) (134,265 sq. km.) ✿Magnolia 🐦Eastern brown pelican 🌲Cypress 🎵"Give Me Louisiana" **ENTERED UNION:** April 30, 1812 (18th) ★Baton Rouge **LARGEST CITIES (WITH POP.):** New Orleans, 462,269; Baton Rouge, 224,097; Shreveport, 198,675; Lafayette, 111,966

⚙natural gas, oil, chemicals, transportation equipment, paper, food products, cotton, fish

WEB SITE *http://www.louisiana.gov • http://www.louisianatravel.com*

did you know? *The Cajun dance music of southwestern Louisiana is a blend of the African, British, Caribbean, French, German-Jewish, Native American, and Spanish cultures that have roots in the area.*

Key: Flower Bird Tree Song Capital ⚙Important Products

MAINE (ME) Pine Tree State

POPULATION (2005): 1,321,505 (40th) **AREA:** 35,385 sq. mi. (39th) (91,647 sq. km.) ✿White pine cone and tassel 🐦Chickadee 🌲Eastern white pine 🎵"State of Maine Song" **ENTERED UNION:** March 15, 1820 (23rd) ⭐ Augusta (population, 18,551) **LARGEST CITIES (WITH POP.):** Portland, 63,905; Lewiston, 35,776; Bangor, 31,595

⚙paper, transportation equipment, wood and wood products, electronic equipment, footwear, clothing, potatoes, milk, eggs, fish, & seafood

Augusta ⭐

WEB SITE *http://www.maine.gov • http://www.visitmaine.com*

didyouknow? *Farmington native Chester Greenwood is credited with inventing earmuffs in 1873 when he was just 15. To honor him, every first Saturday in December, people don their best earmuffs and parade through town.*

MARYLAND (MD) Old Line State, Free State

Baltimore ●

Annapolis ⭐

⭐
Washington, D.C.

POPULATION (2005): 5,600,388 (19th) **AREA:** 12,407 sq. mi. (42nd) (32,134 sq. km.) ✿Black-eyed susan 🐦Baltimore oriole 🌲White oak 🎵"Maryland, My Maryland" **ENTERED UNION:** April 28, 1788 (7th) ⭐Annapolis (population, 36,196) **LARGEST CITIES (WITH POP.):** Baltimore, 636,251; Gaithersburg, 58,091; Rockville, 57,100; Frederick, 57,009; Bowie, 53,840

⚙printing and publishing, food products, transportation equipment, electronic equipment, chickens, soybeans, corn, stone

WEB SITE *http://www.maryland.gov • http://www.mdisfun.org*

didyouknow? *Jousting, the medieval game where two opponents on horseback try to knock the other off with a long pole, is the state sport. But jousting in Maryland involves only one rider, who lances suspended rings.*

MASSACHUSETTS (MA) Bay State, Old Colony

Boston ⭐

POPULATION (2005): 6,398,743 (13th) **AREA:** 10,555 sq. mi. (44th) (27,337 sq. km.) ✿Mayflower 🐦Chickadee 🌲American elm 🎵"All Hail to Massachusetts" **ENTERED UNION:** February 6, 1788 (6th) ⭐Boston **LARGEST CITIES (WITH POP.):** Boston, 569,165; Worcester, 175,966; Springfield, 152,091; Lowell, 103,655; Cambridge, 100,771

⚙ industrial machinery, electronic equipment, instruments, printing and publishing, metal products, fish, flowers and shrubs, cranberries

WEB SITE *http://www.mass.gov • http://www.massvacation.com*

didyouknow? *Massachusetts is a state of many American firsts: college, Harvard, 1636; post office, Boston, 1639; public library, Boston Public Library, 1653; regularly published newspaper, Boston News-Letter, 1704; lighthouse, Boston Harbor, 1716; subway system, Boston, 1898.*

MICHIGAN (MI) Great Lakes State, Wolverine State

POPULATION (2005): 10,120,860 (8th) **AREA:** 96,716 sq. mi. (11th) (250,493 sq. km.) 🌺Apple blossom 🐦Robin 🌲White pine 🎵"Michigan, My Michigan" **ENTERED UNION:** January 26, 1837 (26th) ⭐Lansing **LARGEST CITIES (WITH POP.):** Detroit, 900,198; Grand Rapids, 195,115; Warren, 136,118; Sterling Heights, 127,476; Flint, 119,716; Lansing, 116,941

⚙️automobiles, industrial machinery, metal products, office furniture, plastic products, chemicals, food products, milk, corn, natural gas, iron ore, blueberries

WEB SITE http://www.michigan.gov • http://www.travel.michigan.org

did you know? Detroit, hub of the U.S. auto industry, is called Motor City, or Motown.

Lansing ⭐ Detroit

MINNESOTA (MN) North Star State, Gopher State

POPULATION (2005): 5,132,799 (21st) **AREA:** 86,939 sq. mi. (12th) (225,171 sq. km.) 🌺Pink and white lady's-slipper 🐦Common loon 🌲Red pine 🎵"Hail! Minnesota" **ENTERED UNION:** May 11, 1858 (32nd) ⭐St. Paul **LARGEST CITIES (WITH POP.):** Minneapolis, 373,943; St. Paul, 276,963; Rochester, 93,284; Duluth, 85,556

⚙️industrial machinery, printing and publishing, computers, food products, scientific and medical instruments, milk, hogs, cattle, corn, soybeans, iron ore

WEB SITE http://www.state.mn.us • http://www.exploreminnesota.com

did you know? The "Land of 10,000 Lakes" counts 11,842 lakes bigger than 10 acres within its borders. One out of every six Minnesotans owns a boat, the highest rate of any state.

Minneapolis
St. Paul ⭐

MISSISSIPPI (MS) Magnolia State

POPULATION (2005): 2,921,088 (31st) **AREA:** 48,430 sq. mi. (32nd) (125,433 sq. km.) 🌺Magnolia 🐦Mockingbird 🌲Magnolia 🎵"Go, Mississippi!" **ENTERED UNION:** December 10, 1817 (20th) ⭐Jackson **LARGEST CITIES (WITH POP.):** Jackson, 179,298; Gulfport, 71,851; Biloxi, 50,115

⚙️transportation equipment, furniture, electrical machinery, lumber and wood products, cotton, rice, chickens, cattle

WEB SITE http://www.mississippi.gov • http://www.visitmississippi.org

did you know? Hurricane Katrina flooded Biloxi and Gulfport, Mississippi, with a 20 to 30+ foot storm surge in August 2005. It was the third strongest hurricane to hit the U.S. coast. Hurricane Camille hit Mississippi in August 1969 with record wind speeds averaging 190 mph.

⭐ Jackson

Key: 🌺Flower 🐦Bird 🌲Tree 🎵Song ⭐Capital 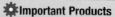⚙️Important Products

MISSOURI

(MO) Show Me State

Kansas City • • **St. Louis**
★ **Jefferson City**

POPULATION (2005): 5,800,310 (18th) **AREA:** 69,704 sq. mi. (21st) (180,533 sq. km.) 🌼Hawthorn 🐦Bluebird 🌳Dogwood 🎵"Missouri Waltz" **ENTERED UNION:** August 10, 1821 (24th) ⭐Jefferson City (population 39,079) **LARGEST CITIES (WITH POP.):** Kansas City, 444,387; St. Louis, 343,279; Springfield, 150,704; Independence, 111,023

⚙transportation equipment, electrical and electronic equipment, printing and publishing, food products, cattle, hogs, milk, soybeans, corn, hay, lead

WEB SITE *http://www.missouri.gov • http://www.missouritourism.org*

did you know? *The "boot heel" in the southeast corner of the state came about at the urging of an influential landowner named John Hardeman Walker. He and other citizens of the area successfully petitioned Congress to be included in the new state.*

MONTANA

(MT) Treasure State

⭐ **Helena**

POPULATION (2005): 935,670 (44th) **AREA:** 147,042 sq. mi. (4th) (380,837 sq. km.) 🌸Bitterroot 🐦Western meadowlark 🌲Ponderosa pine 🎵"Montana" **ENTERED UNION:** November 8, 1889 (41st) ⭐Helena (population, 26,353) **LARGEST CITIES (WITH POP.):** Billings, 96,977; Missoula, 61,790; Great Falls, 56,503; Butte, 32,393

⚙cattle, copper, gold, wheat, barley, wood and paper products

WEB SITE *http://www.mt.gov • http://visitmt.com*

did you know? *The first Tyrannosaurus rex fossil was found in Montana in 1902. The Museum of the Rockies at Montana State University houses the largest collection of dinosaur fossils found in the U.S.*

NEBRASKA

(NE) Cornhusker State

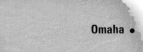

Omaha •

Lincoln ★

POPULATION (2005): 1,758,787 (38th) **AREA:** 77,354 sq. mi. (16th) (200,346 sq. km.) 🌼Goldenrod 🐦Western meadowlark 🌳Cottonwood 🎵"Beautiful Nebraska" **ENTERED UNION:** March 1, 1867 (37th) ⭐Lincoln **LARGEST CITIES (WITH POP.):** Omaha, 409,416; Lincoln, 236,146; Bellevue, 47,347; Grand Island, 44,287

⚙cattle, hogs, milk, corn, soybeans, hay, wheat, sorghum, food products, industrial machinery

WEB SITE *http://www.nebraska.gov • http://www.visitnebraska.org*

did you know? *Arbor Day, the last Friday in April, was first celebrated in Nebraska in 1872, with the planting of more than a million trees.*

NEVADA (NV) Sagebrush State, Battle Born State, Silver State

POPULATION (2005): 2,414,807 (35th) **AREA:** 110,561 sq. mi. (7th) (286,352 sq. km.) ✿Sagebrush ♪Mountain bluebird ⚘Single-leaf piñon, bristlecone pine ♫"Home Means Nevada" **ENTERED UNION:** October 31, 1864 (36th) ✪Carson City (population, 54,311) **LARGEST CITIES (WITH POP.):** Las Vegas, 534,847; Henderson, 224,829; Reno, 197,963

✿Carson City

✿gold, silver, cattle, hay, food products, plastics, chemicals

WEB SITE http://www.nv.gov • http://www.travelnevada.com

didyouknow? The famous "Comstock Lode" silver mine was discovered near Lake Tahoe in 1859. In the mid 1870s it yielded $36 million worth of silver ore a year—over $500 million yearly in 2005 dollars. Nevada still produces 40% of all the silver mined in the U.S.

Las Vegas

NEW HAMPSHIRE (NH) Granite State

POPULATION (2005): 1,309,940 (41st) **AREA:** 9,350 sq. mi. (46th) (24,216 sq. km.) ✿Purple lilac ♪Purple finch ⚘White birch ♫"Old New Hampshire" **ENTERED UNION:** June 21, 1788 (9th) ✪Concord **LARGEST CITIES (WITH POP.):** Manchester, 109,310; Nashua, 87,411; Concord, 42,345

✿industrial machinery, electric and electronic equipment, metal products, plastic products, dairy products, maple syrup and maple sugar

WEB SITE http://www.nh.gov • http://www.visitnh.gov

didyouknow? The strongest gust of wind ever recorded was a 231-mph burst at Mt. Washington in 1934.

Concord ✪

NEW JERSEY (NJ) Garden State

POPULATION (2005): 8,717,925 (10th) **AREA:** 8,721 sq. mi. (47th) (22,587 sq. km.) ✿Purple violet ♪Eastern goldfinch ⚘Red oak ♫none **ENTERED UNION:** December 18, 1787 (3rd) ✪Trenton **LARGEST CITIES (WITH POP.):** Newark, 280,451; Jersey City, 239,079; Paterson, 150,869; Elizabeth, 124,724; Trenton, 85,379

Newark●

✿chemicals, pharmaceuticals/drugs, electronic equipment, nursery and greenhouse products, food products, tomatoes, blueberries, and peaches

WEB SITE http://www.nj.gov • http://www.visitnj.org

✪ **Trenton**

didyouknow? New Jersey has many sports firsts: The first recorded organized baseball game was played in Hoboken in 1846. The first college football game was played between Rutgers and Princeton in New Brunswick in 1869. The first professional basketball game was played in Trenton in 1896.

Key: Flower Bird Tree Song Capital Important Products

NEW MEXICO (NM) Land of Enchantment

Santa Fe
Albuquerque

POPULATION (2005): 1,928,384 (36th) **AREA:** 121,589 sq. mi. (5th) (314,914 sq. km.) ✿Yucca ◗Roadrunner ❀Piñon ♪"O, Fair New Mexico" **ENTERED UNION:** January 6, 1912 (47th) ★Santa Fe **LARGEST CITIES (WITH POP.):** Albuquerque, 484,246; Las Cruces, 79,524; Santa Fe, 68,041; Rio Rancho, 61,953

⚙electronic equipment, foods, machinery, clothing, lumber, transportation equipment, hay, onions, chiles

WEB SITE *http://www.state.nm.us • http://www.newmexico.org*

didyouknow? *Denver, Colorado, may be the "mile high" city at 5,470 feet above sea level, but Albuquerque, New Mexico, is the highest of the 50 largest cities in the U.S. at 6,120 feet.*

NEW YORK (NY) Empire State

Albany
Buffalo
New York City

POPULATION (2005): 19,254,630 (3rd) **AREA:** 54,556 sq. mi. (27th) (141,299 sq. km.) ✿Rose ◗Bluebird ❀Sugar maple ♪"I Love New York" **ENTERED UNION:** July 26, 1788 (11th) ★Albany (population, 93,779) **LARGEST CITIES (WITH POP.):** New York, 8,104,079; Buffalo, 282,864; Rochester, 212,481; Yonkers, 197,126; Syracuse, 143,101

⚙books and magazines, automobile and aircraft parts, toys and sporting goods, electronic equipment, machinery, clothing and textiles, metal products, milk, cattle, hay, apples

WEB SITE *http://www.state.ny.us • http://www.iloveny.com*

didyouknow? *New York City was the first capital of the United States. Congress met there from 1785 to 1790, and George Washington was sworn in as president there on April 30, 1789.*

NORTH CAROLINA (NC) Tar Heel State, Old North State

Raleigh
Charlotte

POPULATION (2005): 8,683,242 (11th) **AREA:** 53,819 sq. mi. (28th) (139,391 sq. km.) ✿Dogwood ◗Cardinal ❀Pine ♪"The Old North State" **ENTERED UNION:** November 21, 1789 (12th) ★Raleigh **LARGEST CITIES (WITH POP.):** Charlotte, 594,359; Raleigh, 326,653; Greensboro, 231,543; Durham, 201,726; Winston-Salem, 191,523

⚙clothing and textiles, tobacco and tobacco products, industrial machinery, electronic equipment, furniture, cotton, soybeans, peanuts

WEB SITE *http://www.nc.gov • http://www.visitnc.com*

didyouknow? *Pepsi-Cola was first sold by Caleb Bradham in New Bern in 1898.*

NORTH DAKOTA (ND) Peace Garden State

POPULATION (2005): 636,677 (48th) **AREA:** 70,700 sq. mi. (19th) (183,112 sq. km.) ✿Wild prairie rose ♫Western meadowlark 🌳American elm 🎵"North Dakota Hymn" **ENTERED UNION:** November 2, 1889 (39th) ⭐Bismarck **LARGEST CITIES (WITH POP.):** Fargo, 91,048; Bismarck, 56,619; Grand Forks, 48,984; Minot, 35,149

⚙wheat, barley, hay, sunflowers, sugar beets, cattle, sand and gravel, food products, farm equipment, high-tech electronics

⭐ Bismarck

WEB SITE http://www.nd.gov • http://www.ndtourism.com

did you know? *The TV tower in Blanchard, North Dakota, is the tallest structure in the world, at 2,063 feet.*

OHIO (OH) Buckeye State

POPULATION (2005): 11,464,042 (7th) **AREA:** 44,825 sq. mi. (34th) (116,096 sq. km.) ✿Scarlet carnation ♫Cardinal 🌳Buckeye 🎵"Beautiful Ohio" **ENTERED UNION:** March 1, 1803 (17th) ⭐Columbus **LARGEST CITIES (WITH POP.):** Columbus, 730,008; Cleveland, 458,684; Cincinnati, 314,154; Toledo, 304,973; Akron, 212,179; Dayton, 160,293

⚙metal and metal products, transportation equipment, industrial machinery, rubber and plastic products, electronic equipment, printing and publishing, chemicals, food products, corn, soybeans, livestock, milk

Cleveland
Columbus ⭐
Cincinnati

WEB SITE http://www.ohio.gov • http://www.discoverohio.com

did you know? *Ohio calls itself the "hall of fame capital of the world" and has halls of fame for pro football, rock and roll, aviation, inventors, Cleveland-style polka, American motorcycles, American classical music, trapshooting, and accounting.*

OKLAHOMA (OK) Sooner State

POPULATION (2005): 3,547,884 (28th) **AREA:** 69,898 sq. mi. (20th) (181,035 sq. km.) ✿Mistletoe ♫Scissor-tailed flycatcher 🌳Redbud 🎵"Oklahoma!" **ENTERED UNION:** November 16, 1907 (46th) ⭐Oklahoma City **LARGEST CITIES (WITH POP.):** Oklahoma City, 528,042; Tulsa, 383,764; Norman, 100,923; Lawton, 88,214; Broken Arrow, 84,399

⚙natural gas, oil, cattle, nonelectrical machinery, transportation equipment, metal products, wheat, hay

Tulsa
⭐ Oklahoma City

WEB SITE http://www.ok.gov • http://www.travelok.com

did you know? *Oklahoma is at the heart of "Tornado Alley" and May is peak tornado time with an average of 20.1 tornadoes hitting the state each May.*

Key: ✿Flower ♫Bird 🌳Tree 🎵Song ⭐Capital ⚙Important Products

OREGON (OR) Beaver State

- Portland
- ⭐ Salem

POPULATION (2005): 3,641,056 (27th) **AREA:** 98,381 sq. mi. (9th) (254,806 sq. km.) 🌸Oregon grape 🐦Western meadowlark 🌲Douglas fir 🎵"Oregon, My Oregon" **ENTERED UNION:** February 14, 1859 (33rd) ⭐Salem **LARGEST CITIES (WITH POP.):** Portland, 533,492; Salem, 146,120; Eugene, 142,681; Gresham, 95,376

⚙️lumber and wood products, electronics and semiconductors, food products, paper, cattle, hay, vegetables, Christmas trees

WEB SITE *http://www.oregon.gov • http://www.traveloregon.com*

did you know? *Oregon's state rock is the thunderegg, an ordinary-looking rock that reveals a wide range of colors when cut and polished. These rocks are found only in areas that have had volcanic activity.*

PENNSYLVANIA (PA) Keystone State

Harrisburg
Pittsburgh ⭐
Philadelphia

POPULATION (2005): 12,429,616 (6th) **AREA:** 46,055 sq. mi. (33rd) (119,282 sq. km.) 🌸Mountain laurel 🐦Ruffed grouse 🌲Hemlock 🎵"Pennsylvania" **ENTERED UNION:** December 12, 1787 (2nd) ⭐Harrisburg (population, 48,540) **LARGEST CITIES (WITH POP.):** Philadelphia, 1,470,151; Pittsburgh, 322,450; Allentown, 106,732; Erie, 103,925

⚙️iron and steel, coal, industrial machinery, printing and publishing, food products, electronic equipment, transportation equipment, stone, clay and glass products

WEB SITE *http://www.state.pa.us • http://www.visitpa.com*

did you know? *An enormous fire has been burning since 1962 in the coal mines below the town of Centralia. Fewer than 20 people remain in the town. Surface temperatures have been measured at over 700°F.*

RHODE ISLAND (RI) Little Rhody, Ocean State

Providence ⭐

POPULATION (2005): 1,076,189 (43rd) **AREA:** 1,545 sq. mi. (50th) (4,002 sq. km.) 🌸Violet 🐦Rhode Island red 🌲Red maple 🎵"Rhode Island" **ENTERED UNION:** May 29, 1790 (13th) ⭐ Providence **LARGEST CITIES (WITH POP.):** Providence, 178,126; Warwick, 87,365; Cranston, 81,986; Pawtucket, 74,330

⚙️costume jewelry, toys, textiles, machinery, electronic equipment, fish

WEB SITE *http://www.ri.gov • http://www.visitrhodeisland.com*

did you know? *At the turn of the last century (1900), Newport was a vacation spot for some of the richest people in America. One of the dozens of summer "cottages" is a 70-room Italian-style palace on a 13-acre ocean-side estate.*

SOUTH CAROLINA (SC) Palmetto State

POPULATION (2005): 4,255,083 (25th) **AREA:** 32,020 sq. mi. (40th) (82,931 sq. km.) Yellow jessamine Carolina wren Palmetto "Carolina" **ENTERED UNION:** May 23, 1788 (8th) Columbia **LARGEST CITIES (WITH POP.):** Columbia, 116,331; Charleston, 104,883; North Charleston, 84,271; Greenville, 56,291

clothing and textiles, chemicals, industrial machinery, metal products, livestock, tobacco, Portland cement

WEB SITE http://www.myscgov.com • http://www.discoversouthcarolina.com

did you know? More battles of the American Revolution were fought in South Carolina than in any other colony. The Civil War began in Charleston harbor, with the first shots fired on Fort Sumter in 1861.

Columbia

SOUTH DAKOTA (SD) Mt. Rushmore State, Coyote State

POPULATION (2005): 775,933 (46th) **AREA:** 77,116 sq. mi. (17th) (199,730 sq. km.) Pasqueflower Chinese ring-necked pheasant Black Hills spruce "Hail, South Dakota" **ENTERED UNION:** November 2, 1889 (40th) Pierre (population, 14,012) **LARGEST CITIES (WITH POP.):** Sioux Falls, 136,695; Rapid City, 61,459; Aberdeen, 24,196

food and food products, machinery, electric and electronic equipment, corn, soybeans

WEB SITE http://www.state.sd.us • http://www.travelsd.com

did you know? The Corn Palace in Mitchell is redecorated every year with themed murals made from corn, grains, and grasses by local artisans. When winter comes, birds and squirrels munch away the exterior.

Pierre

TENNESSEE (TN) Volunteer State

POPULATION (2005): 5,962,959 (16th) **AREA:** 42,143 sq. mi. (36th) (109,150 sq. km.) Iris Mockingbird Tulip poplar "My Homeland, Tennessee"; "When It's Iris Time in Tennessee"; "My Tennessee"; "Tennessee Waltz"; "Rocky Top" **ENTERED UNION:** June 1, 1796 (16th) Nashville **LARGEST CITIES (WITH POP.):** Memphis, 671,929; Nashville, 546,719; Knoxville, 178,118; Chattanooga, 154,853

chemicals, machinery, vehicles, food products, metal products, publishing, electronic equipment, paper products, rubber and plastic products, tobacco

WEB SITE http://www.tennessee.gov • http://www.tnvacation.com

did you know? The top-secret city of Oak Ridge was built for the Manhattan Project, the U.S. government research project (1942-45) that produced the world's first atomic bomb.

Nashville
Memphis

Key: Flower Bird Tree Song 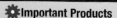Capital Important Products

TEXAS

(TX) Lone Star State

POPULATION (2005): 22,859,968 (2nd) **AREA:** 268,581 sq. mi. (2nd) (695,622 sq. km.) ❀Bluebonnet ⌒Mockingbird ❧Pecan ♪"Texas, Our Texas" **ENTERED UNION:** December 29, 1845 (28th) ⭐Austin **LARGEST CITIES (WITH POP.):** Houston, 2,012,626; San Antonio, 1,236,249; Dallas, 1,210,393; Austin, 681,804; Fort Worth, 603,337; El Paso, 592,099; Arlington, 359,467; Corpus Christi, 281,196

⚙oil, natural gas, cattle, milk, eggs, transportation equipment, chemicals, clothing, industrial machinery, electrical and electronic equipment, cotton, grains

WEB SITE *http://www.tx.gov • http://www.traveltex.com*

did you know? *President George W. Bush grew up in Midland, Texas. He still returns to vacation at his Prairie Chapel Ranch near Crawford, which is known as the "Western White House."*

UTAH

(UT) Beehive State

POPULATION (2005): 2,469,585 (34th) **AREA:** 84,899 sq. mi. (13th) (219,887 sq. km.) ❀Sego lily ⌒Seagull ❧Blue spruce ♪"Utah, This is the Place" **ENTERED UNION:** January 4, 1896 (45th) ⭐Salt Lake City **LARGEST CITIES (WITH POP.):** Salt Lake City, 178,605; West Valley City, 112,678; Provo, 105,410

⚙transportation equipment, medical instruments, electronic parts, food products, steel, copper, cattle, corn, hay, wheat, barley

WEB SITE *http://www.utah.gov • http://www.utah.com*

did you know? *The Mormon Temple in Salt Lake City was built over a 40-year period and completed in 1893. Only members of the Church of Jesus Christ of Latter-day Saints are allowed inside.*

VERMONT

(VT) Green Mountain State

POPULATION (2005): 623,050 (49th) **AREA:** 9,614 sq. mi. (45th) (24,900 sq. km.) ❀Red clover ⌒Hermit thrush ❧Sugar maple ♪"These Green Mountains" **ENTERED UNION:** March 4, 1791 (14th) ⭐Montpelier (population, 8,026) **LARGEST CITIES (WITH POP.):** Burlington, 38,934; Essex Junction, 19,065; Colchester, 17,177; Rutland, 17,080

⚙machine tools, furniture, scales, books, computer parts, foods, dairy products, apples, maple syrup

WEB SITE *http://www.vermont.gov • http://www.vermontvacation.com*

did you know? *Vermont makes more maple syrup than any other state, nearly half a million gallons each year.*

VIRGINIA (VA) Old Dominion

POPULATION (2005): 7,567,465 (12th) **AREA:** 42,774 sq. mi. (35th) (110,784 sq. km.) 🌸Dogwood 🐦Cardinal 🌲Dogwood 🎵"Carry Me Back to Old Virginia"
ENTERED UNION: June 25, 1788 (10th) ⭐Richmond
LARGEST CITIES (WITH POP.): Virginia Beach, 440,098; Norfolk, 237,835; Chesapeake, 214,725; Richmond, 192,494; Arlington, 186,117; Newport News, 181,913

⚙️transportation equipment, textiles, chemicals, printing, machinery, electronic equipment, food products, coal, livestock, tobacco, wood products, furniture

WEB SITE *http://www.virginia.gov • http://www.virginia.org*

didyouknow? *More U.S. presidents were born in this state than in any other, a total of eight, starting with George Washington.*

Alexandria
Richmond ⭐
Norfolk

WASHINGTON (WA) Evergreen State

POPULATION (2005): 6,287,759 (14th) **AREA:** 71,300 sq. mi. (18th) (184,666 sq. km.) 🌸Western rhododendron 🐦Willow goldfinch 🌲Western hemlock 🎵"Washington, My Home" **ENTERED UNION:** November 11, 1889 (42nd) ⭐Olympia (population, 43,519)
LARGEST CITIES (WITH POP.): Seattle, 571,480; Spokane, 196,721; Tacoma, 196,094; Vancouver, 155,053; Bellevue, 116,914

⚙️aircraft, lumber, pulp and paper, machinery, electronics, computer software, aluminum, processed fruits and vegetables

WEB SITE *http://www.access.wa.gov • http://www.experiencewashington.com*

didyouknow? *In 1846, the U.S.–Canada border was "cleaned up" by using a line of latitude, the 49th parallel, as the dividing line. This left the town of Point Roberts, on a 5-square-mile tip of a Canadian peninsula, separated from the U.S. mainland.*

• Seattle
⭐ Olympia

WEST VIRGINIA (WV) Mountain State

POPULATION (2005): 1,816,856 (37th) **AREA:** 24,230 sq. mi. (41st) (62,755 sq. km.) 🌸Big rhododendron 🐦Cardinal 🌲Sugar maple 🎵"The West Virginia Hills"; "This Is My West Virginia"; "West Virginia, My Home Sweet Home" **ENTERED UNION:** June 20, 1863 (35th)
⭐ Charleston **LARGEST CITIES (WITH POP.):** Charleston, 51,684; Huntington, 49,891; Parkersburg, 32,159; Wheeling, 29,891

⚙️coal, natural gas, fabricated metal products, chemicals, automobile parts, aluminum, steel, machinery, cattle, hay, apples, peaches, tobacco

WEB SITE *http://www.wv.gov • http://www.wvtourism.com*

didyouknow? *When Virginia seceded from the U.S. in 1861, the western section refused to leave the union and became the state of West Virginia in 1863.*

⭐ Charleston

Key: 🌸Flower Bird 🌲Tree Song ⭐Capital ⚙️Important Products

WISCONSIN (WI) Badger State

POPULATION (2005): 5,536,201 (20th) **AREA:** 65,498 sq. mi. (23rd) (169,639 sq. km.) 🌼Wood violet 🐦Robin 🌳Sugar maple 🎵"On, Wisconsin!" **ENTERED UNION:** May 29, 1848 (30th) ⭐Madison **LARGEST CITIES (WITH POP.):** Milwaukee, 583,624; Madison, 220,332; Green Bay, 101,100; Kenosha, 93,798; Racine, 80,108

⚙paper products, printing, milk, butter, cheese, foods, food products, motor vehicles and equipment, medical instruments and supplies, plastics, corn, hay, vegetables

WEB SITE *http://www.wi.gov • http://www.travelwisconsin.com*

didyouknow? *The Green Bay Packers have won the most NFL championships of any team (12).*

Madison ⭐
Milwaukee •

WYOMING (WY) Cowboy State

POPULATION (2005): 509,294 (50th) **AREA:** 97,814 sq. mi. (10th) (253,337 sq. km.) 🌸Indian paintbrush 🐦Western meadowlark 🌳Plains cottonwood 🎵"Wyoming" **ENTERED UNION:** July 10, 1890 (44th) ⭐Cheyenne **LARGEST CITIES (WITH POP.):** Cheyenne, 55,362; Casper, 51,240; Laramie, 26,441

⚙ oil, natural gas, petroleum (oil) products, cattle, wheat, beans

WEB SITE *http://www.wyoming.gov*
http://www.wyomingtourism.org

Cheyenne ⭐

didyouknow? *Wyoming is also known as the Equality State and has many firsts for women in America: Women were first given the right to vote while it was still a territory in 1869. Eliza Stewart was the first woman to be part of a grand jury in 1870. Nellie Tayloe Ross became the first female governor in 1925.*

COMMONWEALTH OF PUERTO RICO (PR)

San Juan ⭐

HISTORY: Christopher Columbus landed in Puerto Rico in 1493. Puerto Rico was a Spanish colony for centuries, then was ceded (given) to the United States in 1898 after the Spanish-American War. In 1952, still associated with the United States, Puerto Rico became a commonwealth with its own constitution. **POPULATION (2005):** 3,912,054 **AREA:** 5,324 sq. mi. (13,789 sq. km.) 🌺Maga 🐦Reinita 🌳Ceiba **NATIONAL ANTHEM:** "La Borinqueña" ⭐San Juan **LARGEST CITIES (WITH POP.):** San Juan, 433,733; Bayamón, 224,915; Carolina, 187,337; Ponce, 185,930

⚙chemicals, food products, electronic equipment, clothing and textiles, industrial machinery, coffee, sugarcane, fruit, hogs

WEB SITE *http://www.gobierno.pr • http://www.gotopuertorico.com*

didyouknow? *El Yunque is the only tropical rain forest in the U.S.*

WASHINGTON, D.C.
The Capital of the
UNITED STATES

LAND AREA: 61 square miles **POPULATION (2005):** 550,521
FLOWER: American beauty rose **BIRD:** Wood thrush

WEB SITE http://www.dc.gov • http://www.washington.org

HISTORY Washington, D.C., became the capital of the United States in 1800, when the federal government moved there from Philadelphia. The city of Washington was designed and built to be the capital. It was named after George Washington. Many of its major sights are on the Mall, an open grassy area that runs from the Capitol to the Potomac River.

CAPITOL, which houses the U.S. Congress, is at the east end of the Mall on Capitol Hill. Its dome can be seen from far away.

FRANKLIN DELANO ROOSEVELT MEMORIAL, honoring the 32nd president of the United States, and his wife, Eleanor, was dedicated in 1997. It is outdoors in a parklike setting.

JEFFERSON MEMORIAL, a circular marble building located near the Potomac River. Its design is partly based on one by Thomas Jefferson for the University of Virginia.

KOREAN WAR VETERANS MEMORIAL, dedicated in 1995, is at the west end of the Mall. It shows troops ready for combat.

LINCOLN MEMORIAL, at the west end of the Mall, is built of white marble and styled like a Greek temple. Inside is a large, seated statue of Abraham Lincoln. His Gettysburg Address is carved on a nearby wall.

NATIONAL ARCHIVES, on Constitution Avenue, holds the Declaration of Independence, Constitution, and Bill of Rights.

◄ Jefferson Memorial

NATIONAL WORLD WAR II MEMORIAL, located between the Lincoln Memorial and the Washington Monument at the Mall, honors the 16 million Americans who served during the war. It was dedicated in May 2004.

SMITHSONIAN INSTITUTION has 14 museums, including the new National Museum of the American Indian, the National Air and Space Museum and the Museum of Natural History. The National Zoo is part of the Smithsonian.

U.S. HOLOCAUST MEMORIAL MUSEUM presents the history of the Nazis' murder of more than six million Jews and millions of other people from 1933 to 1945. The exhibit *Daniel's Story* tells the story of the Holocaust from a child's point of view.

WASHINGTON MONUMENT, a white marble pillar, or obelisk, standing on the Mall and rising to over 555 feet. From the top there are wonderful views of the city.

WHITE HOUSE, at 1600 Pennsylvania Avenue, has been the home of every U.S. president except George Washington.

WOMEN IN MILITARY SERVICE FOR AMERICA MEMORIAL, near the entrance to Arlington National Cemetery. It honors the 1.8 million women who have served in the U.S. armed forces.

Volunteering

How can playing the piano be volunteer work? ➡ page 309

Americans Help Out

Does spending your Saturday working in a soup kitchen sound like fun? Well, it is fun! You get to meet new people and help your community. It's true that volunteers don't get paid money, but sometimes feeling like you did a good thing is worth a lot more than a paycheck.

Get Involved

RELIGIOUS GROUPS

Many people volunteer through their religious community. Churches often organize soup kitchens, even homeless shelters. After Hurricane Katrina and Hurricane Rita, United Catholic Charities sent volunteers to the Gulf Coast to help provide food and shelter—as well as hugs and encouragement. They helped over 300,000 people.

SCHOOL GROUPS

Most schools in the United States offer opportunities for their students to volunteer. Some schools sponsor bake sales to raise money for a cause, while others may ask their students to volunteer at a nursing home, where they read or play games with elderly people. In Washington State, some high school students join the Washington Reading Corps and help elementary school students improve their reading. Does your school have any volunteering opportunities? If not, maybe you could start one! Try organizing an after-school food drive or ask your fellow students to donate old winter coats to charities.

NEIGHBORHOOD GROUPS

Many kids' groups and clubs like Boy and Girl Scouts and Campfire participate in neighborhood volunteering projects such as cleaning up a local park or organizing a car wash to raise money for a cause. Maybe you and your friends could spend a Saturday picking up trash around your neighborhood or mowing lawns for elderly people in your community. There are also neighborhood associations that hold monthly meetings. Attend the next one and donate your time and muscle power to an upcoming project.

Volunteering Superstars

STOP THE BOP

After Hurricane Katrina swept through the Gulf Coast, students at Delone Catholic High School in McSherrystown, Pennsylvania, wanted to help the victims. The student council decided to annoy students into donating money. They suggested that the school play Hanson's 1996 hit "MMMBop" before classes began, in-between periods, and nonstop during lunch. They called their idea "Stop the Bop." The ultimate goal was to raise at least $3,000, which could easily be met if every student donated $5. Hanson even joined in the "Stop the Bop" campaign and offered to match the school's funds for Katrina victims. In total, more than $7,000 was raised.

Workers gut a home damaged by Hurricane Katrina

MUSIC THERAPY

◄ Amanda Kaku of Aiea, Hawaii, was four when she started playing the piano to entertain her grandparents. When she was 13, her father contracted a terminal illness. He moved into a hospice, where there was a 24-hour hour care staff. Amanda went to the hospice once a week and played the piano for her father. After he passed away, people at the hospice asked her to continue coming. Now, she spends an hour a week playing songs for the hospice residents and staff. "Many of the patients sit with their eyes closed to listen to the music and feel a little relief from stressful situations," says Amanda.

THANKS FOR HELPING!

In December 2004, the Indian Ocean tsunami killed more than 226,000 people and destroyed hundreds of villages in India, Indonesia, Sri Lanka and other countries.

Companies and nonprofit organizations helped out. These kids in Sri Lanka are having their homes rebuilt by Habitat for Humanity. Part of the money kids spent on last year's *World Almanac for Kids* was donated to Feed the Children.

309

Weather

What does a "front" separate? ➡ page 312

WEIRD WEATHER FACTS

RED RAIN Since ancient times, people have observed storms that brought mysterious red rain. One such storm occurred in southern England in 1968. It left behind a gritty red substance. Upon further study, scientists agreed the red color of the rain was from dust carried all the way from the Sahara desert in Africa.

PINK SNOW From Arctic explorers off Greenland in the 1800s to hikers in California's Sierra Nevada mountains in 2004, many people have come across snow that looks red or pink. Long streaks of this snow, sometimes covering entire mountainsides, have been reported and photographed. It's caused by a microscopic, reddish-colored algae that live only in cold climates.

RAINING FROGS Yes, it can happen. On many occasions, it has been reported that frogs, fish, and other small marine animals have rained down during a storm. This is likely caused by a waterspout or tornado that picks up animals from one spot and drops them down in another.

THE SUMMER THAT NEVER SHOWED
Weather can be affected by other events on Earth. Sometimes, if there is a large volcanic eruption, particles of ash and gases may block the sun in parts of the world, causing colder winters and cooler summers, even in places thousands of miles away. This happened in 1815, when the Tambora volcano erupted in Indonesia, bringing snow and frosts to parts of New England in June, July, and August of the next year.

BIGGEST SNOWFLAKE
The biggest snowflake ever found measured 15 inches across and 8 inches thick. It fell on January 28, 1887, at Fort Keough, Montana.

BALLS OF LIGHTNING Lightning usually strikes in the form of a long bolt from the clouds to the ground or other clouds. Sometimes, lightning can take the form of fiery balls that float to the ground and even enter buildings. These balls often make sizzling noises and give off glowing colors. Scientists think they are made up of heated or electrically charged gases.

RECORD TEMPERATURES BY STATE
(Through 2000)

COLDEST TEMPERATURE

HOTTEST TEMPERATURE

STATE	LOWEST		HIGHEST	
	°F	Latest date	°F	Latest date
Alabama	−27	Jan. 30, 1966	112	Sept. 5, 1925
Alaska	−80	Jan. 23, 1971	100	June 27, 1915
Arizona	−40	Jan. 7, 1971	128	June 29, 1994
Arkansas	−29	Feb. 13, 1905	120	Aug. 10, 1936
California	−45	Jan. 20, 1937	134	July 10, 1913
Colorado	−61	Feb. 1, 1985	118	July 11, 1888
Connecticut	−32	Jan. 22, 1961	106	July 15, 1995
Delaware	−17	Jan. 17, 1893	110	July 21, 1930
Florida	−2	Feb. 13, 1899	109	June 29, 1931
Georgia	−17	Jan. 27, 1940	112	Aug. 20, 1983
Hawaii	12	May 17, 1979	100	Apr. 27, 1931
Idaho	−60	Jan. 18, 1943	118	July 28, 1934
Illinois	−36	Jan. 5, 1999	117	July 14, 1954
Indiana	−36	Jan. 19, 1994	116	July 14, 1936
Iowa	−47	Feb. 3, 1996	118	July 20, 1934
Kansas	−40	Feb. 13, 1905	121	July 24, 1936
Kentucky	−37	Jan. 19, 1994	114	July 28, 1930
Louisiana	−16	Feb. 13, 1899	114	Aug. 10, 1936
Maine	−48	Jan. 19, 1925	105	July 10, 1911
Maryland	−40	Jan. 13, 1912	109	July 10, 1936
Massachusetts	−35	Jan. 12, 1981	107	Aug. 2, 1975
Michigan	−51	Feb. 9, 1934	112	July 13, 1936
Minnesota	−60	Feb. 2, 1996	114	July 6, 1936
Mississippi	−19	Jan. 30, 1966	115	July 29, 1930
Missouri	−40	Feb. 13, 1905	118	July 14, 1954
Montana	−70	Jan. 20, 1954	117	July 5, 1937
Nebraska	−47	Dec. 22, 1989	118	July 24, 1936
Nevada	−50	Jan. 8, 1937	125	June 29, 1994
New Hampshire	−47	Jan. 29, 1934	106	July 4, 1911
New Jersey	−34	Jan. 5, 1904	110	July 10, 1936
New Mexico	−50	Feb. 1, 1951	122	June 27, 1994
New York	−52	Feb. 18, 1979	108	July 22, 1926
North Carolina	−34	Jan. 21, 1985	110	Aug. 21, 1983
North Dakota	−60	Feb. 15, 1936	121	July 6, 1936
Ohio	−39	Feb. 10, 1899	113	July 21, 1934
Oklahoma	−27	Jan. 18, 1930	120	June 27, 1994
Oregon	−54	Feb. 10, 1933	119	Aug. 10, 1898
Pennsylvania	−42	Jan. 5, 1904	111	July 10, 1936
Rhode Island	−25	Feb. 5, 1996	104	Aug. 2, 1975
South Carolina	−19	Jan. 21, 1985	111	June 28, 1954
South Dakota	−58	Feb. 17, 1936	120	July 5, 1936
Tennessee	−32	Dec. 30, 1917	113	Aug. 9, 1930
Texas	−23	Feb. 8, 1933	120	June 28, 1994
Utah	−69	Feb. 1, 1985	117	July 5, 1985
Vermont	−50	Dec. 30, 1933	105	July 4, 1911
Virginia	−30	Jan. 22, 1985	110	July 15, 1954
Washington	−48	Dec. 30, 1968	118	Aug. 5, 1961
West Virginia	−37	Dec. 30, 1917	112	July 10, 1936
Wisconsin	−55	Feb. 4, 1996	114	July 13, 1936
Wyoming	−66	Feb. 9, 1933	115	Aug. 8, 1983

WEATHER WORDS

barometer An instrument that measures atmospheric pressure. Falling pressure means stormy weather, while rising pressure means calm weather.

blizzard A heavy snowstorm with strong winds that, with blowing snow, makes it hard to see.

fog Tiny water droplets that float in the air. It's like a cloud formed at ground level.

freezing rain Water that freezes as it hits the ground.

front Boundary between two air masses.

frost Ice crystals that form on surfaces.

hail Frozen water droplets that keep getting coated with ice until they are heavy enough to fall to the ground as hailstones.

humidity Amount of water vapor (water in the form of a gas) in the air.

meteorologist A person who studies the atmosphere, weather, and weather forecasting.

precipitation Water that falls from clouds as rain, snow, hail, or sleet.

tornado A violently rotating column of air (wind) that forms a funnel. A tornado can suck up and destroy anything in its path, and also cause severe damage from flying debris.

typhoon A hurricane that forms in the western Pacific Ocean.

wind chill A measure of how cold it feels when there is a wind. When it is 35°F and the wind is 15 miles an hour, it will feel like 25°F.

Weather Match

Can you match the terms on the left with the correct meanings on the right?

A. climate

B. arid

C. cumulus

D. atmosphere

E. cirrus

F. tides

G. waterspout

H. barometer

I. humid

J. smog

1. moist air

2. short, wispy clouds

3. long-term weather conditions

4. measures atmospheric pressure

5. widespread air pollution ("smoke and fog")

6. dry

7. layer of gases surrounding Earth

8. big, puffy clouds

9. a tornado that forms over water

10. rise and fall of oceans

ANSWERS ON PAGES 334-337. FOR MORE PUZZLES GO TO WWW.WORLDALMANACFORKIDS.COM

On the Job

Meteorologist

**Carl Arredondo,
Chief Meteorologist at WWL-TV
in New Orleans, Louisiana**

Q: During Hurricane Katrina WWL-TV was the only New Orleans TV station that stayed on air. What was that like?

As Katrina came closer to southeastern Louisiana, we knew it would be either a direct hit or close. Either way it would do a lot of damage. It was very stressful because many people had to evacuate in a short amount of time. Southeastern Louisiana is below sea level and there are a limited amount of escape routes.

Our station staff was working out of a hotel ballroom. I was proud that we were the only ones on the air, but many of us had our homes damaged or destroyed while working. Keeping our minds off of that while trying to give the best coverage was very difficult. My wife, son, and 3 stepchildren stayed with my parents in Texas. Even though they were worried, they could watch me on TV and know I was okay and in a safe place. When we lost telephone service I could still text message on my cell phone.

Q: How did you get interested in meteorology?

I had always been fascinated with the weather. In sixth grade a television meteorologist visited my junior high school in San Antonio, Texas, and I knew I wanted to be a meteorologist. I started working part time at a weather company while still in college.

Q: What is your workday like? Why is your job important?

I know it seems like it's the same weather every day but there's always something different in the atmosphere. It's really important to make sure people know what to do during severe weather. 2006 is going to be another active year with above normal numbers of storms. It never gets boring.

Q: So you never get bored? Come on, something must be boring!

The most boring part is wearing a suit and tie everyday. That's something I wish I could change. That and putting on makeup, which I have to do myself.

Q: What's something that you think kids would find surprising about your job?

That I do all the work myself. I analyze all the graphics that people see and don't see. We talk about computer models on the air but no one sees them. Many people don't realize how much work goes into a daily show. They think the weatherman comes in right before news time, but it's actually a 3-hour process.

Q: What can kids be doing now to get into a career like yours?

You need to study all the math and science you can while in school. You have to do well even when it's not your favorite subject. Math wasn't my favorite subject, but it was something I knew I had to do. I feel very lucky to go to work everyday. There's never a day that I wish I were doing something else.

Weights & Measures

Which is warmer 21° C or 68° F? ➡ page 315

Metrology isn't the study of weather. (That's meteorology.) It is the science of measurement. Almost everything you use every day is measured—either when it is made or when it's sold. Materials for buildings and parts for machines must be measured carefully so they will fit together. Clothes have sizes so you'll know which to choose. Many items sold in a supermarket are priced by weight or by volume.

EARLIEST MEASUREMENTS

The human body was the first "ruler." An "inch" was the width of a thumb; a "hand" was five fingers wide; a "foot" was—you guessed it—the length of a foot! A "cubit" ran from the elbow to the tip of the middle finger (about 20 inches), and a "yard" was the length of a whole arm.

Later, measurements came from daily activities, like plowing. A "furlong" was the distance an ox team could plow before stopping to rest (now we say it is about 220 yards). The trouble with these units was that they were different from person to person, place to place, and ox to ox.

MEASUREMENTS WE USE TODAY

The official system in the U.S. is the customary system (sometimes called the imperial or English system). Scientists and most other countries use the International System of Units (metric system). The Weights and Measures Division of the U.S. National Institute of Standards and Technology (NIST) makes sure that a gallon of milk in California is the same as one in New York. When the NIST was founded in 1901, there were as many as eight different "standard" gallons in the U.S., and four different legal measures of a "foot" in Brooklyn, New York, alone.

ANCIENT MEASURE

1 foot =
length of a person's foot

12 inches

1 yard =
from nose to fingertip

3 feet or 36 inches

1 acre =
land an ox could plow in a day

4,840 square yards

MODERN MEASURE

TAKING TEMPERATURES

There are two main systems for measuring temperature. One is **Fahrenheit** (abbreviated F). The other is **Celsius** (abbreviated C). Another word for Celsius is Centigrade.

Zero degrees (0°) Celsius is equal to 32 degrees (32°) Fahrenheit.

To convert from Celsius to Fahrenheit:

Multiply by 1.8 and add 32.
(°F = 1.8 x °C + 32)

Example: 20° C x 1.8 = 36; 36 + 32 = 68° F

To convert from Fahrenheit to Celsius, reverse the process:

Subtract 32 and divide by 1.8.

Example: 68° F − 32 = 36; 36 / 1.8 = 20° C

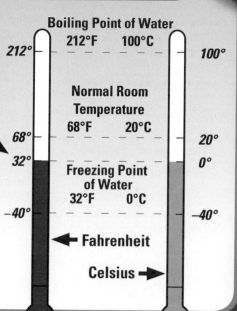

Boiling Point of Water
212°F   100°C

Normal Room Temperature
68°F   20°C

Freezing Point of Water
32°F   0°C

212° — 68° — 32° — −40°

100° — 20° — 0° — −40°

← **Fahrenheit**

Celsius →

F   C

HOTTEST and COLDEST Places in the World

Continent	Highest Temperature	Lowest Temperature
AFRICA	El Azizia, Libya, 136°F (58°C)	Ifrane, Morocco, −11°F (−24°C)
ANTARCTICA	Vanda Station, 59°F (15°C)	Vostok, −129°F (−89°C)
ASIA	Tirat Tsvi, Israel, 129°F (54°C)	Verkhoyansk, Russia, and Oimekon, Russia, −90°F (−68°C)
AUSTRALIA	Cloncurry, Queensland, 128°F (53°C)	Charlotte Pass, New South Wales, −9°F (−23°C)
EUROPE	Seville, Spain, 122°F (50°C)	Ust'Shchugor, Russia, −67°F (−55°C)
NORTH AMERICA	Death Valley, California, 134°F (57°C)	Snag, Yukon Territory, Canada −81°F (−63°C)
SOUTH AMERICA	Rivadavia, Argentina, 120°F (49°C)	Sarmiento, Argentina, −27°F (−33°C)

did you know?

In 2003, scientists at MIT achieved a new record by cooling sodium to half-a-billionth of a degree above absolute zero. That is −459.67°F, or −273.15°C. That's over 300°F colder than any place on Earth.

The METRIC System

The metric system was created in France in 1795. Standardized in 1960 and given the name International System of Units, it is now used in most countries and in scientific works. The system is based on 10, like the decimal counting system. The basic unit for length is the **meter**. The **liter** is a basic unit of volume or capacity, and the **gram** is a basic unit of mass. Related units are made by adding a prefix to the basic unit. The prefixes and their meanings are:

milli-	=	1/1,000
centi-	=	1/100
deci-	=	1/10
deka-	=	10
hecto-	=	100
kilo-	=	1,000

for Example

millimeter (mm) = 1/1,000 of a meter
kilometer (km) = 1,000 meters
milligram (mg) = 1/1,000 of a gram
kilogram (kg) = 1,000 grams

To get a rough idea of measurements in the metric system, it helps to know that a **liter** is a little more than a quart. A **meter** is a little over a yard. A **kilogram** is a little over 2 pounds. And a **kilometer** is just over half a mile.

Homework Help Converting Measurements

From:	Multiply by:	To get:	From:	Multiply by:	To get:
inches	2.5400	centimeters	centimeters	.3937	inches
inches	.0254	meters	centimeters	.0328	feet
feet	30.4800	centimeters	meters	39.3701	inches
feet	.3048	meters	meters	3.2808	feet
yards	.9144	meters	meters	1.0936	yards
miles	1.6093	kilometers	kilometers	.621	miles
square inches	6.4516	square centimeters	square centimeters	.1550	square inches
square feet	.0929	square meters	square meters	10.7639	square feet
square yards	.8361	square meters	square meters	1.1960	square yards
acres	.4047	hectares	hectares	2.4710	acres
cubic inches	16.3871	cubic centimeters	cubic centimeters	.0610	cubic inches
cubic feet	.0283	cubic meters	cubic meters	35.3147	cubic feet
cubic yards	.7646	cubic meters	cubic meters	1.3080	cubic yards
quarts (liquid)	.9464	liters	liters	1.0567	quarts (liquid)
ounces	28.3495	grams	grams	.0353	ounces
pounds	.4536	kilograms	kilograms	2.2046	pounds

LENGTH

The basic unit of **length** in the U.S. system is the **inch**. Length, width, and thickness all use the inch or larger related units.

1 foot (ft.) = 12 inches (in.)

1 yard (yd.) = 3 feet = 36 inches

1 rod (rd.) = 5½ yards

1 furlong (fur.) = 40 rods = 220 yards = 660 feet

1 mile (mi.) (also called statute mile) = 8 furlongs = 1,760 yards = 5,280 feet

1 nautical mile = 6,076.1 feet = 1.15 statute miles

1 league = 3 miles

AREA

Area is used to measure a section of a two-dimensional surface like the floor or a piece of paper. Most area measurements are given in **square units**. Land is measured in **acres**.

1 square foot (sq. ft.) = 144 square inches (sq. in.)

1 square yard (sq. yd.) = 9 square feet = 1,296 square inches

1 square rod (sq. rd.) = 30¼ square yards

1 acre = 160 square rods = 4,840 square yards = 43,560-square feet

1 square mile (sq. mi.) = 640 acres

CAPACITY

Units of **capacity** are used to measure how much of something will fit into a container. **Liquid measure** is used to measure liquids, such as water or gasoline. **Dry measure** is used with large amounts of solid materials, like grain or fruit. Although both liquid and dry measures use the terms "pint" and "quart," they mean different amounts and should not be confused.

Dry Measure

1 quart (qt.) = 2 pints (pt.)

1 peck (pk.) = 8 quarts

1 bushel (bu.) = 4 pecks

Liquid Measure

1 gill = 4 fluid ounces

1 pint (pt.) = 4 gills = 16 ounces

1 quart (qt.) = 2 pints = 32 ounces

1 gallon (gal.) = 4 quarts = 128 ounces

For measuring most U.S. liquids, 1 barrel (bbl.) = 31½ gallons

For measuring oil, 1 barrel (bbl.) = 42 gallons

Cooking Measurements

The measurements used in cooking are based on the **fluid ounce**.

1 teaspoon (tsp.) = ⅙ fluid ounce (fl. oz.)

1 tablespoon (tbsp.) = 3 teaspoons = ½ fluid ounce

1 cup = 16 tablespoons = 8 fluid ounces

1 pint = 2 cups

1 quart = 2 pints

1 gallon = 4 quarts

VOLUME

The amount of space taken up by an object (or the amount of space available within an object) is measured in **volume**. Volume is usually expressed in **cubic units**. If you wanted to buy a room air conditioner and needed to know how much space there was to be cooled, you could measure the room in cubic feet.

1 cubic foot (cu. ft.) – 12 inches x 12 inches x 12 inches = 1,728 cubic inches (cu. in.)

1 cubic yard (cu. yd.) = 27 cubic feet

DEPTH

Some measurements of length are used to measure ocean depth and distance.

1 fathom = 6 feet

1 cable = 120 fathoms = 720 feet

WEIGHT

Although 1 cubic foot of popcorn and 1 cubic foot of rock take up the same amount of space, it wouldn't feel the same if you tried to lift them. We measure heaviness as **weight**. Most objects are measured in **avoirdupois weight** (pronounced a-ver-de-POIZ):

1 dram (dr.) = 27.344 grains (gr.)

1 ounce (oz.) = 16 drams = 437.5 grains

1 pound (lb.) = 16 ounces

1 hundredweight (cwt.) = 100 pounds

1 ton = 2,000 pounds (also called short ton)

World History

Who was the real Lion King? ➡ page 320

Each of the five sections in this chapter tells the history of a major region of the world: the Middle East, Africa, Asia, Europe, or the Americas. Major events from ancient times to the present are described under the headings for each region.

THE ANCIENT MIDDLE EAST

4000–3000 B.C. The world's first cities are built by the Sumerian peoples in Mesopotamia, now southern Iraq. Sumerians develop a kind of writing called cuneiform. Egyptians develop a kind of writing called hieroglyphics.

2700 B.C. Egyptians begin building the great pyramids in the desert.

1792 B.C. Some of the first written laws are created in Babylonia. They are called the Code of Hammurabi.

▲ *Hieroglyphics*

1200 B.C. Hebrew people settle in Canaan in Palestine after escaping from slavery in Egypt. They are led by the prophet Moses.

1000 B.C. King David unites the Hebrews in one strong kingdom.

ANCIENT PALESTINE Palestine was invaded by many different peoples after 1000 B.C., including the Babylonians, Egyptians, Persians, and Romans.

336 B.C. Alexander the Great, King of Macedonia, builds an empire from Egypt to India. ▶

ISLAM: A RELIGION GROWS IN THE MIDDLE EAST 610–632 Around 610, the prophet Muhammad starts to proclaim and teach Islam. This religion spreads from Arabia to all the neighboring regions in the Middle East and North Africa. Its followers are called Muslims.

THE KORAN
The holy book of Islam is the Koran. It was related by Muhammad beginning in 611.

THE SPREAD OF ISLAM ▲ *The Koran*
The Arab armies that went across North Africa brought great change:
• The people who lived there were converted to Islam.
• The Arabic language replaced many local languages as an official language. North Africa is still an Arabic-speaking region today, and Islam is the major faith.

63 B.C. Romans conquer Palestine and make it part of their empire.

Around 4 B.C. Jesus Christ, the founder of the Christian religion, is born in Bethlehem. He is crucified about A.D. 29.

A.D. 632 Muhammad dies. By now, Islam is accepted in Arabia as a religion.

641 Arab Muslims conquer the Persians.

late 600s Islam begins to spread to the west into Africa and Spain.

The pyramids and sphinx at Giza

THE MIDDLE EAST

THE UMAYYAD AND ABBASID DYNASTIES
The Umayyads (661-750) and the Abbasids (750-1256) are the first two Muslim-led dynasties. Both empires stretched across northern Africa and the Middle East into Asia.

711–732 Umayyads invade Europe but are defeated by Frankish leader Charles Martel in France. This defeat halts the spread of Islam into Western Europe.

1071 Muslim Turks conquer Jerusalem.

1095–1291 Europeans try to take back Jerusalem and other parts of the Middle East for Christians during the Crusades.

1300-1900s The Ottoman Turks, who are Muslims, create a huge empire, covering the Middle East, North Africa, and part of Eastern Europe. European countries take over portions of it beginning in the 1800s.

1914-1918 World War I begins in 1914. Most of the Middle East falls under British or French control.

1921 Two new Arab kingdoms are created: Transjordan and Iraq. The French take control of Syria and Lebanon.

1922 Egypt becomes independent from Britain.

JEWS MIGRATE TO PALESTINE
Jews began migrating to Palestine in the 1880s. In 1945, after World War II, many Jews who survived the Holocaust migrated to Palestine.

1948 The state of Israel is created.

THE ARAB-ISRAELI WARS
Arab countries near Israel (Egypt, Iraq, Jordan, Lebanon, and Syria) attack the new country in 1948 but fail to destroy it. Israel and its neighbors fight wars again in 1956, 1967, and 1973. Israel wins each war. In the 1967 war, Israel captures the Sinai Desert from Egypt, the Golan Heights from Syria, and the West Bank from Jordan.

1979 Egypt and Israel sign a peace treaty. Israel returns the Sinai to Egypt.

THE MIDDLE EAST AND OIL
About 20% of the oil we use to drive cars, heat homes, and run machines comes from the Middle East. Many countries rely on oil imports from the region, which has more than half the world's crude oil reserves.

The 1990s and 2000s

• In 1991, the U.S. and its allies go to war with Iraq after Iraq invades Kuwait. Iraq is defeated and signs a peace agreement but is accused of violating it. In 2003, the U.S., Britain, and other allies invade Iraq and remove the regime of Saddam Hussein. Free elections are held and a democratic government is formed, but violence there continues.

• Tensions between Israel and the Palestinians increases. In 2005, Israel pulls out from Gaza. In 2006, elections in the West Bank and Gaza bring Hamas, an organization that has historically been dedicated to eliminating the state of Israel, to power.

Dome of the Rock and the Western Wall, Jerusalem ▶

ANCIENT AFRICA

ANCIENT AFRICA

In ancient times, northern Africa was dominated by the Egyptians, Greeks, and Romans. However, we know very little about the lives of ancient Africans south of the Sahara Desert. They did not have written languages. What we learn about them comes from weapons, tools, and other items from their civilization.

2000 B.C. The Nubian Kingdom of Kush, rich with gold, ivory, and jewels, arises south of Egypt. It is a major center of art, learning, and trade until around A.D. 350.

1000 B.C. Bantu-speaking people around Cameroon begin an 1,800-year expansion into much of eastern and southern Africa.

500 B.C. Carthage, an empire centered in Tunisia, becomes rich and powerful through trading. Its ports span the African coast of the Mediterranean Sea. Rome defeats Carthage and its most famous leader, Hannibal, during the second Punic War (218-201 B.C.).

• The Nok in Nigeria are the earliest users of iron for tools and weapons south of the Sahara Desert. They are also known for their terracotta ◀ sculptures.

• The Christian Kingdom of Aksum in northern Ethiopia becomes a wealthy trading center on the Red Sea for treasures like ivory. It makes its own coins and monuments, many of which survive today.

By A.D.700 Ghana, the first known empire south of the Sahara Desert, takes power through trade around the upper Senegal and Niger Rivers. Its Mande people control the trade in gold from nearby mines to Arabs in the north.

By 900 Arab Muslim merchants bring Islam to the Bantu speakers along the east coast of Africa, creating the Swahili language and culture. Traders in Kenya and Tanzania export ivory, slaves, perfumes, and gold to Asia.

1054-1145 Islamic Berbers unite into the Almoravid Kingdom centered at Marrakech, Morocco. They spread into Ghana and southern Spain.

1230-1400s A Mande prince named Sundiata (the "Lion King") forms the Mali Kingdom where Ghana once stood. Timbuktu becomes its main city.

1250-1400s Great Zimbabwe becomes the largest settlement (12,000-20,000 Bantu-speaking people) in southern Africa.

1464-1591 As Mali loses power, Songhai rises to become the third and final great empire of western Africa.

1481 Portugal sets up the first permanent European trading post south of the Sahara Desert at Elmina, Ghana. Slaves, in addition to gold and ivory, are soon exported.

1483-1665 Kongo, the most powerful kingdom on central Africa's west coast, provides thousands of slaves each year for Portugal. Portugal's colony Angola overtakes the Kongo in 1665.

Niger River, Mali

AFRICA

1650-1810 Slave trading peaks across the "Slave Coast" from eastern Ghana to western Nigeria as competing African states sell tens of thousands of captured foes each year to competing European traders.

THE AFRICAN SLAVE TRADE

African slaves were taken to the Caribbean to harvest sugar on European plantations. Later, slaves were taken to South America and the United States. The ships from Africa were overcrowded and diseased. About 20% of the slaves died during the long journey.

1652 The Dutch East India Company sets up a supply camp in southern Africa at the Cape of Good Hope (later Cape Town). Dutch settlers and French Protestants called Huguenots establish Cape Colony. Their descendants are known as the Boers or Afrikaners and develop a distinct language and culture.

1792 Freed slaves, mostly from Britain and the Americas, found Freetown in Sierra Leone.

1803 Denmark is the first European country to ban slave trading. Britain follows in 1807, the U.S. in 1808. Most European nations ban the trade by 1820, but illegal trading continues for decades.

1814 Britain purchases the Dutch South African colony at Cape Town. British colonists arrive after 1820.

1816-28 The Zulus, ruled by the chieftain Shaka, dominate eastern South Africa.

1835-43 The "Great Trek" (march) of the Boers away from British Cape Town.

1884-85 European nations meet in Berlin and agree to divide control of Africa. No African states are invited to the agreements. The "Scramble for Africa" lasts until World War I. Only Ethiopia and Liberia remain independent.

1899-1902 Great Britain and the Boers fight in South Africa in the Boer War. The Boers accept British rule but are allowed a role in government.

1948 The white Afrikaner-dominated South African government creates the policy of apartheid ("apartness"), the total separation of races. Blacks are banned from many restaurants, theaters, schools, and jobs. Apartheid sparks protests, many of which ended in bloodshed.

1957 Ghana gains independence from Britain, becoming the first territory in Africa below the Sahara to regain freedom from European rule. Over the next 20 years, the rest of Africa would gain independence.

1990-94 South Africa abolishes its policy of apartheid. In 1994, Nelson Mandela becomes South Africa's first black president. ▶

1994 Fighting between Hutu and Tutsi ethnic groups in Rwanda leads to the massacre of more than 500,000 civilians.

1998-2004 Fighting in the Democratic Republic of the Congo involves 9 nations. About 4 million die, mostly from starvation and disease. While the war is officially over by 2003, fighting continues.

◀ **2006** Ellen Johnson-Sirleaf becomes president of Liberia, Africa's first elected female leader.

ANCIENT ASIA

3500 B.C. People settle in the Indus River Valley of India and Pakistan and the Yellow River Valley of China.

2500 B.C. Cities of Mohenjo-Daro and Harappa in Pakistan become centers of trade and farming.

Around 1523 B.C. Shang peoples in China build walled towns and use a kind of writing based on pictures. This writing develops into the writing Chinese people use today.

衣
貽
夷

Around 1050 B.C. Chou peoples in China overthrow the Shang and control large territories.

563 B.C. Siddhartha Gautama is born in India. He becomes known as the Buddha—the "Enlightened One"—and is the founder of the Buddhist religion ◄ (Buddhism).

551 B.C. The Chinese philosopher Confucius is born. His teachings—especially the rules about how people should treat each other—spread throughout China and are still followed today.

320–232 B.C.
- Northern India is united under the emperor Chandragupta Maurya.
- Asoka, emperor of India, sends Buddhist missionaries throughout southern Asia to spread the Buddhist religion.

221 B.C. The Chinese begin building the Great Wall. Its main section is more than 2,000 miles long and is meant to keep invading peoples out.

202 B.C. The Han people of China win control of all of China.

A.D. 320 The Gupta Empire controls northern India. The Guptas, who are Hindus, drive the Buddhist religion out of India. They are well known for their many advances in mathematics and medicine.

618 The Tang dynasty begins in China. The Tang dynasty is well known for music, poetry, and painting. They export silk and porcelains as far away as Africa.

The Silk Road Around 100 B.C., only the Chinese knew how to make silk. To get this light, comfortable material, Europeans sent fortunes in glass, gold, jade, and other items to China. The exchanges between Europeans and Chinese created one of the greatest trading routes in history—the Silk Road. Chinese inventions such as paper and gunpowder were also spread via the Silk Road. Europeans found out how to make silk around A.D. 500, but trade continued until about 1400.

960 The Northern Sung dynasty in China makes advances in banking and paper money. China's population of 50 million doubles over 200 years, thanks to improved ways of farming that lead to greater food production.

The Great Wall of China ▶

ASIA

1000 The Samurai, a warrior people, become powerful in Japan. They live by a code of honor known as *Bushido*.

1180 The Khmer Empire in Cambodia becomes widely known for its beautiful temples.

1206 The Mongol leader Genghis Khan creates an empire that stretches from China to India, Russia, and Eastern Europe.

1264 Kublai Khan, grandson of Genghis Khan, rules China as emperor from his new capital at Beijing.

1368 The Ming dynasty comes to power in China. The Ming drive the Mongols out of the country.

1526 The Mughal Empire in India begins under Babur. The Mughals are Muslims who invade and conquer India.

1644 The Ming dynasty in China is overthrown by the Manchu peoples.

1839 The Opium War takes place in China between the Chinese and the British. The British and other Western powers want to control trade in Asia. The Chinese want the British to stop selling opium to the Chinese. Britain wins the war in 1842.

1858 The French begin to take control of Indochina (Southeast Asia).

1868 In Japan, Emperor Meiji comes to power. Western ideas begin to influence the Japanese.

Statutes from Angkor Wat temple, Cambodia ▼

THE JAPANESE IN ASIA Japan became a powerful country during the early 20th century. In the 1930s, Japan began to invade some of its neighbors. In 1941, the United States and Japan went to war after Japan attacked the U.S. Navy at Pearl Harbor, Hawaii.

1945 Japan is defeated in World War II after the U.S. drops atomic bombs on the Japanese cities of Hiroshima and Nagasaki.

1947 India and Pakistan become independent from Great Britain.

1949 China comes under the rule of the Communists led by Mao Zedong. The Communist government abolishes private property and takes over all businesses.

1950–1953 THE KOREAN WAR North Korea, a Communist country, invades South Korea. The U.S. and other nations join to fight the invasion. China joins North Korea. The fighting ends in 1953. Neither side wins.

1954–1975 THE VIETNAM WAR The French are defeated in Indochina in 1954 by Vietnamese nationalists. The U.S. sends troops in 1965 to fight on the side of South Vietnam against the Communists in the North. The U.S. withdraws in 1973. In 1975, South Vietnam is taken over by North Vietnam.

1989 Chinese students protest for democracy, but the protests are crushed by the army in Beijing's Tiananmen Square.

The 1990s Britain returns Hong Kong to China (1997). China builds its economy, but does not allow democracy.

The 2000s U.S.-led military action overthrows the Taliban regime in Afghanistan (2001) and seeks to root out terrorists there. North Korea admits it has been developing nuclear weapons, and Iran is believed to be developing them.

A powerful earthquake in the Indian Ocean in December 2004 sets off huge waves (tsunamis) that kill more than 226,000 people in Indonesia, Sri Lanka, and other countries.

ANCIENT EUROPE

4000 B.C. People in many parts of Europe start building monuments out of large stones called megaliths. Examples can still be seen today, including Stonehenge in England.

2500 B.C.–1200 B.C.

The Minoans and the Mycenaeans

- People on the island of Crete (Minoans) in the Mediterranean Sea built great palaces and became sailors and traders.
- People in the city of Mycenae in Greece built stone walls and a great palace.
- Mycenaean people invaded Crete and destroyed the power of the Minoans.

THE TROJAN WAR

The Trojan War was a conflict between invading Greeks and the people of Troas (Troy) in Southwestern Turkey around 1200 B.C. Although little is known today about the real war, it has become a part of Greek poetry and mythology (see pages 136-137). According to a famous legend, a group of Greek soldiers hid inside a huge wooden horse. The horse was pulled into the city of Troy. Then the soldiers jumped out of the horse and conquered Troy.

900-600 B.C. Celtic peoples in Northern Europe settle on farms and in villages and learn to mine for iron ore.

600 B.C. Etruscan peoples take over most of Italy. They build many cities and become traders.

Temple of Athena Nike ▼

SOME ACHIEVEMENTS OF THE GREEKS

The early Greeks were responsible for:

- The first governments that were elected by people. Greeks invented democratic government.

▲ *Socrates*

- Great poets such as Homer, who composed the *Iliad*, a long poem about the Trojan War, and the *Odyssey*, an epic poem about the travels of Odysseus.
- Great thinkers such as Socrates, Plato, and Aristotle.
- Great architecture, like the Parthenon and the Temple of Athena Nike on the Acropolis in Athens (see below).

431 B.C. The Peloponnesian Wars begin between the Greek cities of Athens and Sparta. The wars end in 404 B.C. when Sparta wins.

338 B.C. King Philip II of Macedonia in northern Greece conquers all the cities of Greece.

336 B.C. Philip's son Alexander the Great becomes king. He conquers lands and makes an empire from the Mediterranean Sea to India. For the next 300 years, Greek culture dominates this vast area.

The Parthenon

ANCIENT EUROPE

264 B.C.–A.D. 476
THE ROMAN EMPIRE

The city of Rome in Italy begins to expand and capture surrounding lands. The Romans gradually build a great empire and control all of the Mediterranean region. At its height, the Roman Empire includes Western Europe, Greece, Egypt, and much of the Middle East. It lasts until A.D. 476.

ROMAN ACHIEVEMENTS

- Roman law. Many of our laws are based on Roman law.
- Great roads to connect their huge empire. The Appian Way, south of Rome, is a Roman road that is still in use today.
- Aqueducts to bring water to the people in large cities.
- Great sculpture. Roman statues can still be seen in Europe.
- Great architecture. The Colosseum, which still stands in Rome today, is an example of great Roman architecture.
- Great writers, such as the poet Virgil, who wrote the *Aeneid*.

49 B.C. A civil war breaks out that destroys Rome's republican form of government.

45 B.C. Julius Caesar becomes the sole ruler of Rome but is murdered one year later by rivals.

27 B.C. Octavian becomes the first emperor of Rome. He takes the name Augustus. A peaceful period of almost 200 years begins.

The Temple of Saturn, Rome

THE CHRISTIAN FAITH Christians believe that Jesus Christ is the Son of God. The history and beliefs of Christianity are found in the New Testament of the Bible. Christianity spread slowly throughout the Roman Empire. The Romans tried to stop the new religion and persecuted the Christians. They were forced to hold their services in hiding, and some were crucified. Eventually, more and more Romans became Christian.

▲ *A painting of Jesus Christ*

THE BYZANTINE EMPIRE, centered in modern-day Turkey, was the eastern half of the old Roman Empire. Byzantine rulers extended their power into western Europe; the Byzantine Emperor Justinian ruled parts of Spain, North Africa, and Italy. Constantinople (now Istanbul, Turkey) became the capital of the Byzantine Empire in A.D. 330.

313 The Roman Emperor Constantine gives full rights to Christians. He eventually becomes a Christian himself.

410 The Visigoths and other barbarian tribes from northern Europe invade the Roman Empire and begin to take over its lands.

476 The last Roman emperor, Romulus Augustus, is overthrown.

768 Charlemagne becomes king of the Franks in northern Europe. He rules a kingdom that includes parts of France, Germany, and northern Italy.

800 Feudalism becomes important in Europe. Feudalism means that poor farmers are allowed to farm a lord's land in return for certain services to the lord.

▼ *The Colosseum, Rome*

EUROPE

896 Magyar peoples found Hungary.

800s–900s Viking warriors and traders from Scandinavia begin to move into the British Isles, France, and parts of the Mediterranean.

Viking helmet ▼

989 The Russian state of Kiev becomes Christian.

1066 William of Normandy, a Frenchman, successfully invades England and makes himself king. He is known as William the Conqueror.

1096–1291 THE CRUSADES In 1096, Christian European kings and nobles sent a series of armies to the Middle East to try to capture Jerusalem from the Muslims. Between 1096 and 1291 there were about ten Crusades. The Europeans briefly captured Jerusalem, but in the end, the Crusades did not succeed in their aim.

One result of the Crusades was that trade increased greatly between the Middle East and Europe.

1215 THE MAGNA CARTA The Magna Carta was a document agreed to by King John of England and the English nobility. The English king agreed that he did not have absolute power and had to obey the laws of the land. The Magna Carta was an important step toward democracy.

1290 The Ottoman Empire begins. It is controlled by Turkish Muslims who conquer lands in the eastern Mediterranean and the Middle East.

Ottoman Palace ▶

1337–1453 WAR AND PLAGUE IN EUROPE

- The Hundred Years' War (1337) begins in Europe between France and England. The war lasts until 1453 when France wins.

- The bubonic plague (Black Death) begins in Europe (1348). As much as one third of the whole population of Europe dies from this deadly disease, caused by the bite of infected fleas.

1453 The Ottoman Turks capture the city of Constantinople and rename it Istanbul.

1517 THE REFORMATION The Reformation led to the breakup of the Christian church into Protestant and Roman Catholic branches in Europe. It started when the German priest Martin Luther opposed some teachings of the Church. He broke away from the pope (the leader of the Catholic church) and had many followers.

1534 King Henry VIII of England breaks away from the Roman Catholic church. He names himself head of the English (Anglican) church.

1558 The reign of King Henry's daughter Elizabeth I begins in England. During her long rule, England's power grows.

▲ *Queen Elizabeth*

1588 The Spanish Armada (fleet of warships) is defeated by the English navy as Spain tries to invade England.

EUROPE

1600s The Ottoman Turks expand their empire through most of eastern and central Europe.

1618 Much of Europe is destroyed in the Thirty Years' War, which ends in 1648.

1642 The English civil war begins. King Charles I fights against the forces of the Parliament (legislature). The king's forces are defeated, and he is executed in 1649. But his son, Charles II, returns as king in 1660.

1762 Catherine the Great becomes the Empress of Russia. She allows some religious freedom and extends the Russian Empire.

1789 **THE FRENCH REVOLUTION** The French Revolution ended the rule of kings in France and led to democracy there. At first, however, there were wars, much bloodshed, and times when dictators took control. Many people were executed. King Louis XVI and Queen Marie Antoinette were overthrown in the Revolution, and both were executed in 1793.

1799 Napoleon Bonaparte, an army officer, becomes dictator of France. Under his rule, France conquers most of Europe by 1812.

1815 Napoleon's forces are defeated by the British and German armies at Waterloo (in Belgium). Napoleon is exiled to a remote island and dies there in 1821.

1848 Revolutions break out in countries of Europe. People force their rulers to make more democratic changes.

1914–1918 **WORLD WAR I IN EUROPE** At the start of World War I in Europe, Germany, Austria-Hungary and the Ottoman Empire opposed England, France, Russia, and, later, the U.S. (the Allies). The Allies win in 1918.

1917 The czar is overthrown in the Russian Revolution. The Bolsheviks (Communists) under Vladimir Lenin take control. Millions are starved, sent to labor camps, or executed under Joseph Stalin (1929-1953).

THE RISE OF HITLER Adolf Hitler became dictator of Germany in 1933. He joined forces with rulers in Italy and Japan to form the Axis powers. In World War II (1939-1945), the Axis powers were defeated by the Allies—Great Britain, the Soviet Union, and the U.S. During his rule, Hitler's Nazis killed millions of Jews and other people in what we now call the Holocaust.

▲ *Italy's Benito Mussolini and Adolf Hitler*

1945 The Cold War begins. It is a long period of tension between the United States and the Soviet Union. Both countries build up their armies and make nuclear weapons but do not go to war directly against each other.

The 1990s Communist governments in Eastern Europe are replaced by democratic ones. Divided Germany becomes one nation, and the Soviet Union breaks up. The European Union (EU) takes steps toward European unity. The North Atlantic Treaty Organization (NATO) bombs Yugoslavia in an effort to protect Albanians driven out of the Kosovo region.

2002 The euro becomes the single currency in 12 European Union nations.

◄ *Napoleon Bonaparte*

THE AMERICAS

10,000-8000 B.C. People in North and South America gather plants for food and hunt animals using stone-pointed spears.

Around 3000 B.C. People in Central America begin farming, growing corn and beans for food.

1500 B.C. Mayan people in Central America begin to live in small villages.

500 B.C. People in North America begin to hunt buffalo to use for meat and for clothing.

100 B.C. The city of Teotihuacán is founded in Mexico. It becomes the center of a huge empire extending from central Mexico to Guatemala. Teotihuacán contains many large pyramids and temples.

A.D. 150 Mayan people in Guatemala build many centers for religious ceremonies. They create a calendar and learn mathematics and astronomy.

900 Toltec warriors in Mexico begin to invade lands of Mayan people. Mayans leave their old cities and move to the Yucatan Peninsula of Mexico.

1000 Native Americans in the southwestern United States begin to live in settlements called pueblos. They learn to farm.

1325 Mexican Indians known as Aztecs create the huge city of Tenochtitlán and rule a large empire in Mexico. They are warriors who practice human sacrifice.

1492 Christopher Columbus sails from Europe across the Atlantic Ocean and lands in the Bahamas, in the Caribbean Sea. This marked the first step toward the founding of European settlements in the Americas.

1500 Portuguese explorers reach Brazil and claim it for Portugal.

1519 Spanish conqueror Hernán Cortés travels into the Aztec Empire in search of gold. The Aztecs are defeated in 1521 by Cortés. The Spanish take control of Mexico. ▶

WHY DID THE SPANISH WIN?

How did the Spanish defeat the powerful Aztec Empire in such a short time? One reason is that the Spanish had better weapons. Another is that many Aztecs died from diseases brought to the New World by the Spanish. The Aztecs had never had these illnesses before, and so did not have immunity to them. Also, many neighboring Indians hated the Aztecs as conquerors and helped the Spanish to defeat them.

1534 Jacques Cartier of France explores Canada.

1583 The first English colony in Canada is set up in Newfoundland.

1607 English colonists led by Captain John Smith settle in Jamestown, Virginia. Virginia was the oldest of the Thirteen Colonies that turned into the United States.

1619 First African slaves arrive in English-controlled America.

1682 The French explorer René Robert Cavelier, sieur de La Salle, sails down the Mississippi River. The area is named Louisiana after the French King Louis XIV.

Mayan pyramid, Yucatan Peninsula, Mexico

THE AMERICAS

EUROPEAN COLONIES By 1700, most of the Americas are under the control of Europeans:

Spain: Florida, southwestern United States, Mexico, Central America, western South America.

Portugal: eastern South America.

France: central United States, parts of Canada.

England: eastern U.S., parts of Canada.

Holland: eastern U.S., West Indies, eastern South America.

1700s European colonies in North and South America grow in population and wealth.

1775-1783
AMERICAN REVOLUTION The American Revolution begins in 1775 when the first shot is fired in Lexington, Massachusetts. The thirteen original British colonies in North America become independent under the Treaty of Paris, signed in 1783.

SIMÓN BOLÍVAR: LIBERATOR OF SOUTH AMERICA In 1810, Simón Bolívar began a revolt against Spain. He fought against the Spanish and in 1924 became president of the independent country of Greater Colombia. As a result of his leadership, ten South American countries became independent from Spain by 1830. ▶

1810-1910 MEXICO'S REVOLUTION In 1846, Mexico and the United States go to war. Mexico loses parts of the Southwest and California to the U.S. A revolution in 1910 overthrows Porfirio Díaz.

Becoming Independent

Most countries of Latin America gained independence from Spain in the early 1800s. Others weren't liberated until much later.

COUNTRY	YEAR OF INDEPENDENCE
Argentina	1816
Bolivia	1825
Brazil	1822[1]
Chile	1818
Colombia	1819
Ecuador	1822
Guyana	1966[2]
Mexico	1821
Paraguay	1811
Peru	1824
Suriname	1975[3]
Uruguay	1825
Venezuela	1821

[1] From Portugal. [2] From Britain. [3] From the Netherlands.

1867 The Canadian provinces are united as the Dominion of Canada.

1898 **THE SPANISH-AMERICAN WAR** Spain and the U.S. fight a brief war in 1898. Spain loses its colonies Cuba, Puerto Rico, and the Philippines.

U.S. POWER IN THE 1900s During the 1900s, the U.S. strongly influenced affairs in the Americas. The U.S. sent troops to various countries, including Mexico (1914; 1916–1917), Nicaragua (1912–1933), Haiti (1915–1934; 1994–1995), and Panama (1989). In 1962, the U.S. went on alert when the Soviet Union put missiles on Cuba.

1994 The North American Free Trade Agreement (NAFTA) is signed to increase trade between the U.S., Canada, and Mexico.

2001 Radical Muslim terrorists crash planes into U.S. targets, killing about 3,000 people; the U.S. launches a "war on terrorism."

2003 U.S.-led forces invade Iraq and overthrow the regime of Saddam Hussein.

THEN & NOW
FROM 2006

10 Years ago–1996

Then: Bill Clinton was reelected to a second term as president of the U.S.

Now: Since leaving office in 2001, President Clinton has written a best-selling book and worked hard to promote aid for victims of the Indian Ocean tsunami. His wife, Hillary Rodham Clinton, is a U.S. senator.

Then: Astronaut Shannon Lucid lived in space for 188 days in a row, setting a record for U.S. astronauts.

Now: The U.S. record for a single mission is now 196 days, reached by astronauts Carl Walz and Dan Bursch in 2002.

50 Years ago–1956

Then: Montgomery, Alabama, city buses were desegregated, after a year-long bus boycott, organized by Reverend Martin Luther King Jr. The boycott started after a black woman named Rosa Parks refused to give up her seat.

Now: Reverend Martin Luther King Jr. is a national hero whose birth is celebrated as a holiday every year in January. Rosa Parks was honored in the Capitol Rotunda after she died in 2005 at the age of 92.

Then: A new federal minimum wage of $1 an hour, up from 75 cents, went into effect.

Now: Since 1997 the minimum wage in the U.S. has been $5.15 an hour.

Then: In Game 5 of the World Series, Yankee Don Larsen pitched the first-ever perfect World Series game.

Now: As of summer 2006, no World Series pitcher has equaled Larsen's achievement.

100 Years ago–1906

Then: A massive earthquake hit San Francisco on April 18. The quake and rapidly spreading fires killed more than 3,000 people and destroyed much of the city.

Now: The city was rapidly rebuilt. The beautiful San Francisco metropolitan area is home to more than four million people.

Then: Brothers Will Keith and John Harvey Kellogg began marketing a cereal they invented, called cornflakes.

Now: Kellogg Company sells about $10 billion worth of food products every year, from Frosted Flakes and Rice Krispies to cookies and Pop Tarts.

300 Years ago–1706

In 2006 America celebrated the 300th birthday of Benjamin Franklin, a printer, almanac publisher, writer, diplomat, inventor, and scientist who was one of the country's founding fathers. Franklin started working at the age of 10, but became a big success and retired at the age of 48.

THEN & NOW FROM 2007

10 years ago–1997

Then: Diana, the Princess of Wales and former wife of Britain's Prince Charles, died in a car crash in Paris. She was survived by their two young sons, Prince William (then 15 years old) and Prince Harry (then 12).

Now: Prince Charles is married to Camilla Parker-Bowles. As of spring 2006, Prince William was studying to be a military officer and Prince Harry had just completed training at the same military school.

Then: Madeleine Albright was sworn in as the first-ever woman secretary of state and the highest ranking woman in the U.S. government. ▶

Now: Condoleezza Rice is now secretary of state, the second woman ever to hold that post.

50 Years ago–1957

Then: The Soviet Union successfully launched *Sputnik*, the world's first artificial satellite, beating the U.S. in the space race and raising concerns that the U.S. was not doing enough to train future scientists.

Now: The U.S. passed the Soviet Union in the space race, even landing humans on the Moon, and the Soviet Union itself has collapsed. But there still are serious concerns over U.S. science and math education.

◀ **Then:** President Dwight Eisenhower sent federal troops to enforce a court order and escort nine black students into a former all-white high school in Little Rock, Arkansas. The governor had used state National Guardsmen to block them, and there were fears for the students' safety because of angry mobs.

Now: The high school is a National Historic Site and known as one of the state's best schools.

100 Years ago–1907

Then: President Theodore Roosevelt sent a fleet of 16 battleships (the "Great White Fleet") to tour the world and show off American power combined with a desire for peace. This project reflected one of Roosevelt's favorite mottos: "Speak softly, but carry a big stick."

Now: The United States is the world's only superpower, but is engaged in an ongoing "war on terrorism."

400 Years ago–1607

In May 1607 a group of about 100 colonists on three ships landed in a marshy area on the coast of Virginia. They started "Jamestown," the first permanent English settlement in America. The colonists had to deal with food shortages, disease, fires, and Indian raids, but the settlement lasted for about 100 years. Jamestown has been restored and is now part of the Colonial National Historic Park in Virginia.

WOMEN IN HISTORY

The following women played important roles in shaping some of history's biggest events.

CLEOPATRA (69-30 B.C.), queen of Egypt famous for her association with Roman leaders Julius Caesar and Mark Antony. After her father's death, Cleopatra, at the age of about 17, and her 12-year-old brother Ptolemy jointly ruled and, by custom, were forced to marry each other. A few years later, she was sent away, but came back to rule when Caesar defeated her enemies. For a time, she lived with Caesar in Rome until his assassination in 44 B.C. She later went back to Egypt, where she met and married Antony.

JOAN OF ARC (1412-1431), heroine and patron saint of France, known as the Maid of Orléans. She led French troops to a big victory over the English in the Battle of Orléans (1429), a turning point in the Hundred Years' War. Joan believed she was guided by voices from God, and she dressed like a male warrior. In 1431 she was burned at the stake as a heretic. The Catholic Church later declared her innocent, and she was made a saint in 1920. She is the subject of many monuments, paintings, and works of literature.

▼ SOJOURNER TRUTH

(c. 1797-1883), abolitionist and women's rights activist (born Isabella Baumfree). She was raised as a slave on an estate in upstate New York. She escaped in 1826. In 1843, she became a traveling preacher and took the name Sojourner Truth. She traveled widely, speaking out against slavery and for women's rights. Her famous speech, "Ain't I a Woman?" was about how women were as smart and strong as men.

ELIZABETH CADY STANTON

(1815-1902), social reformer and leader of the women's rights movement. Along with Lucretia Mott, she organized the first women's rights convention (1848), and won passage of a resolution demanding voting rights for women. She was president of the National Woman Suffrage Association, which she and Susan B. Anthony founded in 1869.

Elizabeth Cady Stanton & Susan B. Anthony

SUSAN B. ANTHONY (1820-1906),

social reformer who, with Elizabeth Cady Stanton, led the struggle for women's rights. She was a lifelong campaigner for women's suffrage, but died 14 years before the adoption of the 19th Amendment, which allowed women to vote. She opposed the use of liquor and worked to free slaves. In 1979, the U.S. Mint issued the Susan B. Anthony dollar coin in her honor.

FLORENCE NIGHTINGALE

(1820-1910), British nurse and founder of modern nursing. She was a superintendent of female nurses during the Crimean War in Turkey, where she trained nurses and helped set up field hospitals, saving many lives. In 1860 she founded the first professional nursing school, at Saint Thomas' Hospital in London. In 1907, she became the first woman to receive the British Order of Merit. ▶

JULIETTE GORDON LOW (1860-1927), founder of the Girl Scouts of the USA. In 1912, a year after meeting Boy Scouts founder Sir Robert Baden-Powell in England, she organized the first Girl Guides troop in the U.S. It had 18 members. The name of the group was changed to Girl Scouts in 1913. She devoted the rest of her life to working with the Girl Scouts. Today there are nearly 4 million Girl Scouts in the United States.

◄ **GOLDA MEIR** (1898-1978), Israeli prime minister (1969-1974). She was born in Kiev, Russia, but she and her family emigrated to the U.S. when she was a child. In 1921, she and her husband moved to Palestine (now Israel). She was a signer of Israel's declaration of independence and held several government posts. She came out of retirement at the age of 71 to become prime minister. Her government was known for its open-door policy, which encouraged Soviet Jews to come to Israel.

BETTY FRIEDAN (1921-2006), American feminist leader whose book *The Feminine Mystique* (1963) challenged the idea that women could be happy only as wives and mothers. She was a co-founder (1966) and the first president (1966-1970) of the National Organization for Women (NOW), which seeks equal rights for women. ▶

VALENTINA TERESHKOVA (born 1937), Russian cosmonaut and the first woman in space. During her 3-day spaceflight in June 1963 aboard the *Vostok 6*, she orbited Earth 48 times. Five months later, she married cosmonaut Andrian Nikolayev. In 1964, she gave birth to a daughter, the first child born to parents who had both flown in space.

BILLIE JEAN KING (born 1943), American tennis player who became a symbol for women's equality. King won 12 Grand Slam singles titles. But her most famous victory may have been in the 1973 "Battle of the Sexes" match, when she beat male player Bobby Riggs in 3 straight sets. King helped start the first successful women's pro tennis tour in 1970. In 1971 she became the first woman athlete to win more than $100,000 in one season.

▲ **DR. MAE JEMISON** (born 1956) was the first African American woman to go into space. She flew on the 1992 space shuttle *Endeavour* as a science mission specialist. She was born in Decatur, Alabama, and grew up in Chicago. Dr. Jemison is a medical doctor who also has degrees in chemical engineering and African and African American studies.

Answers

Books

RECORD-BREAKING BOOKS, PAGE 42

Book with Most One-Day Sales: *Harry Potter and the Half-Blood Prince*; Bestselling Book of All Time: The Bible; Biggest Library in the World: Library of Congress

HOW WELL DO YOU KNOW HARRY POTTER? PAGE 43

1. Himself with his family; 2.The girl's toilet occupied by Moaning Myrtle; 3. A stag; 4. Ireland; 5. Neville Longbottom; 6.Professor Snape

Buildings, PAGE 53

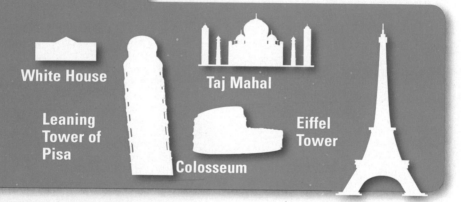

White House

Leaning Tower of Pisa

Taj Mahal

Colosseum

Eiffel Tower

Environment

PAGE 63

1-B.Solar power; 2-D. Hydroelectric power; 3-A. Wind power; 4-C. Geothermal energy

Language

JOKES AND RIDDLES, PAGE 114-115

1. The third man is bald; 2. A baseball team; 3. The milkman was the only person who was not female; 4. It had a virus; 5. By Norse code; 6. A glove; 7. Because there are no pupils to see; 8. A devil of a time; 9. "You go on ahead, and I'll just hang around."; 10. A firequacker; 11. Hide and speak; 12. A bed; 13. He wanted to make a clean getaway; 14. The Mississippi River; 15. Every morning you'll rise and shine; 16. Fry-day; 17. It gives a little wine; 18. aRRRgh; 19. Firecrackers; 20. "Put it on my bill."; 21. He thought it was a high school; 22. Pilgrims; 23. Because there were so many knights; 24. He got tired of the hole business; 25. Fingernails; 26. A coffin; 27. Neither, they both weigh a pound; 28. A daughter; 29. It was an empty water glass; 30. A candle; 31. An apple a day keeps the doctor away; 32. Nine; 33. It gets wet; 34. A mountain with hiccups; 35. Because it has four A's and one B.

WORD CONNECT, PAGE 115

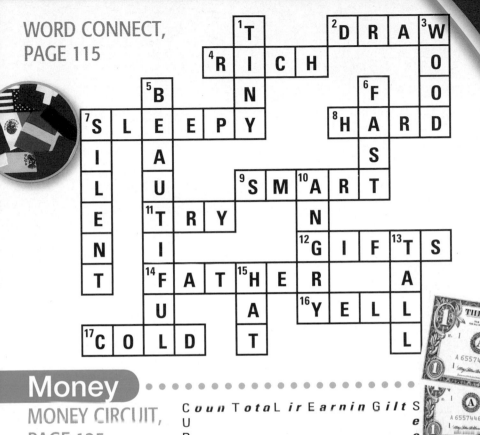

Crossword solution:

- 1 (down) T
- 2 (across) DRAW, 3 (down) WOOD
- 4 (across) RICH
- TINY
- 5 (down) BEAUTIFUL
- 6 (down) FAST
- 7 (across) SLEEPY, 7 (down) SILENT
- 8 (across) HARD
- 9 (across) SMART, 10 (down) ARNT
- 11 (across) TRY, 11 (down) TITUF
- 12 (across) GIFTS, 13 (down) TALL
- 14 (across) FATHER, 15 (down) HEAT
- 16 (across) YELL
- 17 (across) COLD

Money

MONEY CIRCUIT, PAGE 125

C **oun** T **ota**L **ir E a** r **nin** G **il**t S
U   e
R   c
R   u
E   r
N   i
C   t
Y **eno** M u S **nao** L e k c **i** N e Y

Movies & TV

MOVIE MATCH, PAGE 129

1. A red headed girl + Bald headed dad = *Annie*; 2. A wild animal + Ice queen = *The Chronicles of Narnia*; 3. Midwestern girl + Evil green sorceress = *The Wizard of Oz*; 4. Large sea-dwelling mammal + Wannabe chief of the tribe = *Whale Rider*; 5. Mysterious recluse + Two curious kids = *To Kill a Mockingbird*

Answers

Numbers

FUN WITH NUMBERS, PAGE 189

1. Derek would earn $4,160 over 10 years; Aisha would earn $10.7 million in 30 days. 2. All of them. 3. Three. Two of them will have to be one color. 4. She could have a double chocolate, a double vanilla, a vanilla and chocolate, a chocolate and strawberry, a vanilla and strawberry, or a double strawberry double-scoop cone.

SUDOKU, PAGE 189

Puzzle answers are in red.

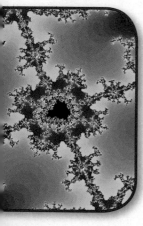

2	6	5	1	9	8	3	4	7
7	8	4	2	5	3	1	6	9
3	9	1	4	7	6	2	8	5
4	5	3	7	2	9	8	1	6
9	1	6	3	8	5	7	2	4
8	7	2	6	1	4	9	5	3
1	4	8	5	3	7	6	9	2
5	3	9	8	6	2	4	7	1
6	2	7	9	4	1	5	3	8

Prizes and Contests

ANOTHER WAY OF SAYING IT, PAGE 201

1. Music Group: Green Day; 2. Song: "Wake Me Up When September Ends;" 3. TV Show: *Drake and Josh*; 4. Athlete: Lance Armstrong; 5. Cartoon: *SpongeBob Squarepants*

Science

WHO DISCOVERED WHAT? PAGE 207

1. microorganisms; 2. gravity; 3. oxygen; 4. electricity; 5. X-rays.

WORD SEARCH, PAGE 217

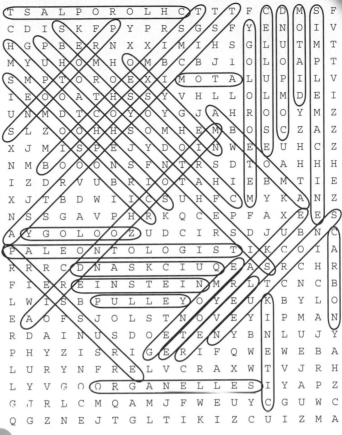

```
T S A L P O R O L H C T T T F C D M S F
C D I S K F P Y P R S G S F Y E N O I V
H G P B E R N X X I M I H S G L U T M T
M Y U H O X H O M B C B J I O O A P T T
S M P T O R O E X I M O T A L U P I L V
I E O O A T H S S Y V H L L O L M D E I
U N M D T C O Y O Y G J A H R O O Y M Z
S L Z O O H H S O M H E M B O S C Z A Z
X J M I S P E J Y D O I N W E U H C A Z
N M B O O O N S F N T R S D T O A H H H
I Z D R V U B R I O T A H I E B M T I E
X J T B D W I I C S U H F C M Y K A N Z
N S S G A V P H R K Q C E P F A X E E S
A Y G O L O O Z U D C I R S D J U B N C
P A L E O N T O L O G I S T I K C O I A
R R R C D N A S K C I U Q E A S R C H R
F I E R E I N S T E I N M R L T C N C B
L W I S B P U L L E Y O Y E U K B Y L O
E A O F S J O L S T N O V E Y I P M A N
R D A I N U S D O E T E N Y B N L U J Y
P H Y Z I S R I G E R I F Q W E W E B A
L U R Y N F R E L V C R A X W T V J R H
L Y V G O R G A N E L L E S I Y A P Z
G J R L C M Q A M J F W E U Y C G U W C
Q G Z N E J T G L T I K I Z C U I Z M A
```

Sports • • • • • • • • • • • • • • • •

SPORTS SCRAMBLE, PAGE 244

C R A L A M I P P Y   S M A G E: **PARALYMPIC GAMES**
N A S H U   T H E W I: **SHAUN WHITE**
A R A N S C: **NASCAR**
G R I L C U N: **CURLING**
S R I C H   T R E V E: **CHRIS EVERT**

Technology • • • • • • • • • •

TECH TALK, PAGE 249

1. Apple; 2. Cyberspace; 3. E-mail; 4. Mouse; 5. Virus; 6. Search engine; 7. Desktop.

Weather • • • • • • • • • • •

WEATHER MATCH, PAGE 312

A-3. long-term weather conditions; B-6. dry; C.-8. big, puffy clouds; D-7. layer of gases surrounding Earth; E-2. short, wispy clouds; F.-10. rise and fall of oceans; G-9. tornado that forms over water; H-4. measures atmospheric pressure; I-1. moist air; J-5. widespread air pollution ("smoke and fog").

INDEX

A

Academy Awards 8, 9, 126, 285
Accidents *See* Disasters
Acid rain 66
Adams, Abigail 270, 276
Adams, John 270, 280
Adams, John Quincy 270
Afghanistan 154
  earthquake 58
  map 150
  war and aftermath
    (2001-) 120, 323
Africa
  facts about 85
  history 82, 320–321
  map 152–153
African Americans
  historic events 279, 281, 284
  historic figures 19, 216, 282, 284, 285, 332, 333
  Kwanzaa 101
Aging process 88
Airplanes *See* Aviation
Air pollution 27, 66–67
Alabama
  facts about 290
  map 287
  origin of name 288
Alamo 280
Alaska
  facts about 290
  map 286
  origin of name 288
Albania 154
  map 149
Alcohol 96
Alexander, Shaun 17, 238
Algeria 154
  map 152
Alito, Samuel 18, 268, 269
Aly and A.J. 13
Amazing Race, The (TV show) 7
Amendments to U.S. Constitution 263, 284

American Camp Association 54
American Idol (TV show) 7, 13, 132
American Indians *See* Native Americans
American Museum of Natural History 130
American Revolution (1775-1783) 118, 279, 329
Amish (religious group) 205
Amoebas 213
Amphibians 23
Amusement parks 254, 255
Ancient civilizations
  Africa 320
  Americas 328
  Asia 322
  calendars 100
  Europe 324–325
  Middle East 318
  weights and measures 314
Andorra 154
  map 148
Angola 154
  map 153
Animals 20–31
  classifying 22
  endangered species 27
  fastest/largest/smallest 24
  Goodall research 216
  life span 25
  names for adults/babies 25
  names of groups 26
  pandas 18, 27
  pets 26
  time line for 21
  waste from 63, 72
Antarctica 85
  map 147
Anthony, Susan B. 332
Antietam, battle of (1862) 118
Antigua and Barbuda 154
  map 145
Apple Computer Inc. 248
Arctic Ocean 85
Argentina 155
  map 147

Arizona
  facts about 290
  map 286
  national parks 258, 259
  origin of name 288
Arkansas
  facts about 291
  map 287
  origin of name 288
Armenia 155
  earthquake 58
  map 150
Armstrong, Neil 282
Art 32–35
  kids' contest 198
  museums 130
  portrait drawing 35
Arthropods 23
Arthur, Chester A. 273
Asia
  facts about 85
  history 82, 322–323
  map 150–151
Asteroids 221
Astronauts 225, 253, 282, 333
Astronomy *See* Space
Atlantic Ocean 85
Australia
  energy production 62
  facts about 85, 155
  map 142
  Sydney Opera House 51
  Tasmanian devils 29
Austria 155
  map 148
  tourism 254
Automobiles
  biodiesel fuel 63
  family games 79
  Model T Ford 252, 282
  police chases 248
  road trips 257
  safety measures 96
Auto racing 11, 232–233
Aviation 108, 252–253
  disasters 60
  ear popping on planes 214

Awards *See* Prizes and
          contests
Azerbaijan 155
   map 150
Aztecs 227, 328

B

Bachelet, Michelle 140
Bahamas, The 155
   map 145
Bahrain 156
   map 150
Ballet 135, 183
Balloons & ballooning 251
Bangladesh 156
   map 151
Barbados 156
   map 145
Barbie dolls 76
Baseball 16, 215, 228,
          234–235
   integration of (1947) 283
Basketball 10, 17, 228,
          236–237
Belarus 156
   map 149
Belgium 156
   map 148
Belize 156
   map 145
Bell, Alexander Graham 108
Benin 156
   map 152
Bhagavad Gita 203
Bhutan 156
   map 151
Bible 202, 325
Bicycles and bicycle riding
          228, 251
Big Dipper 227
Billionaires 125
Bill of Rights, U.S. 263
Biodiversity 23
Biology *See* Life science
Biomass energy 65
Biomes 70–71
Birds 23
Birthdays of celebrities
          36–39
Black Americans *See*
          African Americans
Black Eyed Peas (music
          group) 12
Black holes 216, 221

Blaine, David 116
Bloom, Orlando 8
Boer War (1899) 321
Bolívar, Simón 329
Bolivia 157
   map 146
Books 42–47
   awards 42
   bookmaking 47
   children's authors 42, 46
   quiz 43
Boomerangs 76
Bosnia and Herzegovina 157
   map 148
Boston Tea Party 279
Botswana 157
   map 153
Bowling 228
Bradshaw, Terry 239
Brazil 157
   energy consumption 62
   map 146
Breakdancing 135
Bridges 52
Brownstones (painting) 33
Brunei 157
   map 151
Buchanan, James 272
Buddhism 202, 322
   holy days 205
Bugs *See* Insects
Buildings 48–53, 260
   puzzle 53
Bulgaria 157
   map 149
Bureau of Engraving and
          Printing, U.S. 123
Burj Al Arab Hotel (Dubai) 51
Burkina Faso 157
   map 152
Burping 93
Burundi 157
   map 153
Bush, George H.W. 275
Bush, George W. 18, 265,
          275, 283
Bush, Laura 275, 276
Bush, Reggie 240
Byzantine Empire 325

C

Cabinet of the United States
          264
Calendars 100

California
   Chavez/Villaraigosa
          achievements 285
   earthquakes 58
   facts about 280, 291
   map 286
   origin of name 288
   tourism 130, 254, 255, 257,
          258
Calories 90, 91
Cambodia 158
   map 151
Cameroon 158
   map 152
Camping 54–55
Canada 158
   energy production/
          consumption 62
   immigrants from 195
   map 144
   national holiday 100
Cancer, Tropic of 84
Cape Verde 158
Capitals
   of nations 154–177
   of states 290–306
Capitol, U.S. 307
Capricorn, Tropic of 84
Card tricks 117
Cars *See* Automobiles
Carter, Jimmy (James Earl)
          196, 275
Carver, George Washington
          216, 285
Caspian Sea 80
Celebrities
   birthdays 36–39
   faces and places in the
          news 6–17
Cells (biology) 212
Celsius (centigrade)
          temperature 315
Census, U.S. 192–194
Central African Republic 158
   map 152
Central America 145,
          328–329
Chad 158
   map 152
Challenger disaster (1986)
          225
Chanukah *See* Hanukkah
Chavez, Cesar 285
Cheek, Joey 18

Chemical elements 208–209
Cherokee Indians 280
Cherry pit spitting 201
Children
    around the world 178–179
    authors for 42, 46
    charity event 18
    contests for 198–199, 256
    favorite sports 228
    Kids' Choice Awards 197,
        201
    museums 130, 131
    weight problems 91
Chile 158
    earthquake 58
    map 147
    woman leader 140
China 158
    armed forces 120
    earthquake 58
    energy production/
        consumption 62
    Great Wall 17, 62, 245, 322
    immigrants from 185
    map 151
    most widely spoken
        language 110
    New Year 100
    tallest buildings 49
    tourism 254
Cholesterol 90
Christianity 202, 205
    history 318, 325, 326
    holy days 204
Christmas 98, 99, 204
Circulatory system 92
Cities
    largest in United States
        182, 290–306
    largest in world 191
    national capitals 154–177
    state capitals 290–306
    with tallest buildings 49,
        260
Civil rights movement 19,
    282, 284, 285
Civil War, U.S. 118, 280, 281,
    284
Clark, William 82, 83, 281
Cleopatra 332
Cleveland, Frances 273, 276
Cleveland, Grover 273

Clinton, Bill (William
    Jefferson) 275, 283
Clothing See Fashion
Coast Guard, U.S. 121
College sports
    basketball 237
    football 240
Colombia 159
    immigrants from 195
    map 146
    volcanic eruption 59
Colorado
    facts about 291
    map 286
    origin of name 288
Colors 34
Color wheel 34
Columbia disaster (2003) 225
Columbus, Christopher 82,
    83, 278
Columbus Day 99
Comets 221, 224, 226
Comoros 159
    map 153
Compounds, chemical 209
Computers 246–249
    instant messaging 249
    Internet 107
    puzzle 249
    terminology 247
    time line 246
Congo, Democratic Republic
    of the 159
    map 153
Congo, Republic of the 159
    map 153
Congress, U.S. 266–267, 285
Connecticut
    facts about 292
    map 287
    origin of name 288
    tourist attraction 51
Constitution, U.S. 262–263,
    268, 280
Constitutional Convention
    280
Contests See Prizes and
    contests
Continents
    drift of 87
    facts about 85
    hottest and coldest places
        315
    maps 142–153, 155

Cook, James 82, 83
Coolidge, Calvin 274
Coolidge, Grace 274, 276
Copernicus, Nicolaus 216
Cornelius, Nathan 199
Coronado, Vásquez de 278
Cosmonauts 225
Costa Rica 159
    map 145
Côte d'Ivoire (Ivory Coast)
    159
    map 152
Countries See Nations
Cousteau, Jacques 83
Cow chip throwing 201
Crayola crayons 76
Crazy Horse 183
Croatia 159
    map 148
Crusades (1096-1291) 326
Cuba 159
    immigrants from 195
    map 145
Curie, Marie 216
Curling 229
Currency See Money
Cyprus 160
    map 150
Czech Republic 160
    map 148

D

Dams 53, 64
Darwin, Charles 216
Davis, Shani 14
Daytona 500 232
Death, leading causes of 96
Declaration of Independence
    279
Deep Impact (space probe)
    226
Delaware
    facts about 292
    map 287
    origin of name 288
Democracy 140
Denmark 160
    map 148
Depression, economic 283
Deserts 71, 80
De Soto, Hernando 82
Diatoms 213
Dice 78
Digestive system 92, 93

Disasters 56-61
  earthquakes 58
  tsunami 59
Disneyland (California/
        France/Japan) 254,
        255
Diwali (Hindu festival) 100
Djibouti 160
  map 152
DNA 212
Dogs 26, 30, 31, 184
Dollar bills 123, 124
Dolphins 30
Dominica 160
  map 145
Dominican Republic 160
  immigrants from 195
  map 145
Donovan, Landon 16, 243
Drinking 96
Du Bois, W.E.B. 284, 285

E

Earth 222
  earthquake production 58
  hemispheres of 84
  latitude and longitude 84
  science 206
  seasons 220
  structure of the 58, 86, 208
Earthquakes 50, 58
East Timor See Timor Leste
Echoes 214, 215
Eclipses 219
Ecuador 160
  map 146
Edison, Thomas 108
Efron, Zac 13
Egypt 160
  calendar 100
  Cleopatra 332
  King Tut 32
  longest river 80
  map 152
Einstein, Albert 216
Eisenhower, Dwight D. 274
Election Day 99
Elections 264, 265
Electoral College 265
Elements, chemical 208–209
Elevators 50
El Salvador 161
  immigrants from 195
  map 145

Emancipation Proclamation
        281
Endangered species 27
Endocrine system 92
Energy 62–65, 210
England See United Kingdom
English language 112–113
Entertainment
    Kids' Choice Awards 197
    movies and TV 6–9, 13,
        126–129
Environment 62–73
    air pollution 66–67
    biodiversity 23
    garbage and recycling
        72–73
    puzzle 63
    water pollution 69
Equator 84
Equatorial Guinea 161
    map 153
Erie Canal 281
Eritrea 161
    map 152
Estonia 161
    map 149
Etch a Sketch 76
Ethiopia 161
    map 152
Euro (European currency)
        327
Europe 85
    history 82, 324–327
    map 148–149
Everybody Hates Chris (TV
        show) 6
Evolution 21, 216
Executive branch, U.S. 262,
        264
Exercise 91
Exploratorium 130
Explorers 82, 83, 278–279, 328
Explosions 60
Eyesight 94

F

Faces and places in the
        news 6–19
Fahrenheit temperature 315
Fall (season) 220
Family trees 41
Farting 93
Fashion 74–75
Fat, dietary 90
Father's Day 98, 99

Federer, Roger 16
Fermat's Last Theorem 188
Fiji 161
    map 143
Fillmore, Abigail 271, 276
Fillmore, Millard 271
Films See Movies
Finland 161
    map 149
Fires 60
First ladies 270–276
Fish 23
Flags
    of nations of world
        154–177
    of United States 177, 261
Floods 61
Florida
    facts about 278, 292
    map 287
    origin of name 288
    tourism 254, 255
Food
    nutrients, calories and
        fat 90
    pyramid 89
    recycling 73
Football 17, 228, 230–240
Ford, Gerald R. 275
Ford, Henry 282
Forests 70
Fossil fuels 62, 64
Fourth of July 98, 99
France 161
    energy consumption 62
    highway bridge 253
    Joan of Arc profile 332
    map 148
    tourism 130, 254
Franklin, Benjamin 108, 278,
        330
Franklin Delano Roosevelt
        Memorial 307
French and Indian War 278
French Revolution 327
Friedan, Betty 333
Fungi 213

G

Gabon 162
    map 153
Galaxies 221
Gambia, The 162
    map 152

Games and toys 76–79
  classic toys 76
  family car games 79
  Scrabble 200
  video games 77
Garbage 72–73
Garfield, James A. 272
Genealogy 41
Generations 40
Genes 212
Geography 80–87
  contest 199
  continents and oceans
    85, 206
  explorers 82
  globe 84
  largest/smallest countries
    190
  reading a map 81
Geometry 186–187
Georgia (nation) 162
  map 150
Georgia (state)
  facts about 280, 293
  map 287
  origin of name 288
  tourism 254
Geothermal energy 65
Germany 162
  energy consumption 62
  map 148
  tourism 254
  woman leader 140
Ghana 162
  map 152
Gila monsters 29
Girl Scouts 333
Glass House (Connecticut)
  51
Global warming 67
Globe 84
Gold rush 280
Golf 241
Goodall, Jane 216
Gorbachev, Mikhail 283
Gordon, Jeff 11
Gore, Al 283
Government, forms of 140
Grammar 103
Grand Canyon National Park
  258
Grand Coulee Dam 53
Grandparents' Day 99
Grant, Ulysses S. 272

Grass and grasslands 63, 71
Gravity 215
Great Britain *See* United
  Kingdom
Great Depression 282, 283
Great Seal of United States
  261
Great Wall of China 17, 245,
  322
Greece 162
  ancient history 324
  Greek language 113
  map 149
  mythology 136–137, 227
Greenhouse effect 67, 70
Greenland 80, 144
Greenwich meridian 84
Grenada 162
  map 145
Guatemala 162
  children from 178
  immigrants from 195
  map 145
Guggenheim Museum
  (Spain) 51
Guinea 163
  map 152
Guinea-Bissau 163
  map 152
Guyana 163
  map 146
Gymnastics 241

H

Haiti 163
  map 145
Halley's Comet 221
Halloween 98, 99
Halls of Fame
  baseball 235
  basketball 236
  football 238
  hockey 242
Hanratty, Terry 239
Hanukkah 98, 99
Harding, Warren G. 274
Harlem Renaissance 285
Harrison, Benjamin 273
Harrison, William Henry 271
Harry Potter (fictional
  character) 43
Hawaii
  facts about 293
  hula dancing 135

  map 286
  Mink, Patsy 285
  origin of name 288
Hawking, Stephen 216
Hayes, Rutherford B. 272
Health 88–97
  aging process 88
  exercise 91
  human body 92–93
  medical museums 131
  nutrition 89–90
  sensory perception 94–95
Hearing 94, 214, 215
Heart, human 92
Heisman Trophy 240
Hemispheres of Earth 84
Henry, Beulah 108
Henson, Matthew 83
High School Musical (TV
  movie) 13
Hiking 228
Hillary, Sir Edmund 83
Hinduism 203, 322
  holy days and festivals
    100, 205
Hip-hop
  breakdancing 135
  fashions 75
Hitler, Adolf 327
Hockey *See* Ice hockey;
  Underwater hockey
Holidays 98–101
  odd holidays 101
  religious holy days
    204–205
Holocaust Memorial
  Museum, U.S. 307
Homework help 102–107
  geometry 186
  Internet research 107
  multiplication 185
  taking tests 102
  writing skills 104–106
Honduras 163
  map 145
Hong Kong 254
Hoover, Herbert 274
Hoover Dam 53, 64
Houdini, Harry 116
House of Representatives,
  U.S. 266–267
Hudson, Henry 279
Hula 135
Human body 92–93

Human Genome Project 212
Hungary 163
  map 148
Hurricanes 56
Hussein, Saddam 120, 283
Hutchinson, Vanessa Anne 13

I

Ice hockey 242
Iceland 163
  map 148
Idaho
  facts about 293
  map 286
  origin of name 288
Idioms 112
Illinois
  facts about 294
  map 287
  origin of name 288
  tourism 254
Immigration 195
Immune system 93
Incinerators 72
Inclined planes 211
Independence Day 98, 99
India 163
  armed forces 120
  earthquakes 58
  energy consumption 62
  immigrants from 195
  map 150
Indiana
  facts about 294
  map 287
  origin of name 288
Indianapolis 500 233
Indian Ocean 59, 85
Indonesia 164
  map 151
  volcanic eruptions 59
Insects 22
Instant messaging 249
Instruments, musical 134
Internet 43, 107
Inventions 108–109
Invertebrates, types of 22
Iowa
  facts about 294
  map 287
  origin of name 288
Iran 120, 164
  earthquakes 58
  energy production 62

hostage crisis 283
  map 150
Iraq 164
  Iraq War (2003-) 19, 120,
    283, 319
  map 150
  Persian Gulf War (1991)
    119
Ireland 164
  map 148
Islam 203, 318
  holy days 204
Island, biggest 80
Islands of Adventure
    (Florida) 255
Israel 164
  history 319
  map 150
  Meir profile 333
Italy 164
  map 148
  tourism 254
  Turin Winter Olympics
    (2006) 14–15, 230
  volcanic eruption 59

J

Jackson, Andrew 271
Jamaica 164, 195
  map 145
James, LeBron 10
Jamestown 279, 331
Japan 164, 283, 323
  Baseball Classic win 16
  earthquake 58
  energy consumption 62
  map 151
  tourist attractions 254
  volcanic eruption 59
Jefferson, Thomas 270, 307
Jefferson Memorial 307
Jemison, Dr. Mae 333
Jerusalem 326
Jews and Judaism 203
  ancient Hebrews 318
  Holocaust impact 119, 307
  holy days 98, 99, 204
  museums 307
  Palestine migration 319
Joan of Arc 332
Job profiles
  Coast Guard trainer 121
  dog trainer 31

meteorologist 313
  nurse 97
Joggling 229
Johnson, Andrew 272
Johnson, Lyndon Baines
    275, 284
Johnson-Sirleaf, Ellen 140
Jokes 114–115
Jordan 165
  children from 178
  map 150
Joseph, Chief 183
Judaism See Jews and
    Judaism
Judicial branch, U.S. 262,
    268–269
Jupiter (planet)
  exploration of 224
  facts about 222, 223

K

Kansas
  facts about 295
  map 286
  origin of name 288
  tourist attraction 257
Kashyap, Anurag 199
Kass, Daniel 15
Katrina, Hurricane 56, 61,
    308-309, 313
Kazakhstan 165
  map 150
Kennedy, John Fitzgerald
    274, 282
Kennedy, Robert F. 282
Kentucky
  facts about 295
  map 287
  national park 259
  origin of name 288
Kenya 165
  map 153
Kepler, Johannes 216
Kerry, John 265, 283
Key, Francis Scott 118
Kidneys 92
Kids' Choice Awards 197, 201
King, Billie Jean 333
King, Coretta Scott 285
King Jr., Rev. Martin Luther
    98, 99, 196, 282, 284,
    285
Kingsley, Mary Henrietta 83
Kiribati 165
  map 143

Kites 200
Klassen, Cindy 15
Knightley, Keira 8
Koran 203, 318
Korea, North *See* North
        Korea
Korea, South *See* South
        Korea
Korean War 119, 283, 307,
        323
Korean War Veterans
        Memorial 307
Kuwait 165
  map 150
Kwanzaa 99
Kyrgyzstan 165
  map 150

L

Labor Day 98, 99
Lakes 80, 260
Landfills 72
Language 110–115
  early writing 318
  foreign words 111
  grammar 103
  idioms 112
  jokes and riddles 114–115
  languages spoken in
        United States 110
  major world languages
        110
  names of the months 100
  new words 112
  official languages of
        nations 154–177
  puzzle 115
  writing skills 104–106, 198
Laos 166
  map 151
Latimer, Lewis 108
Latin (language) 113
Latitude 84
Latvia 166
  map 149
Lava 59
Lawrence, Jacob 33
League of Nations 118–119
Lebanon 166
  map 150
Lee, Ang 285
Legislative branch, U.S.
        266–267
LEGO bricks 76

Leonardo da Vinci 33
Lesotho 166
  map 153
Levers 211
Lewis, Meriwether 82, 83,
        281
Liberia 140, 166
  map 152
Libya 166
  map 152
Liechtenstein 166
  map 148
Life science 206, 212–213
Light 65, 210, 214
Lightning 96, 108, 210, 226,
        310
Lin, Maya 33
Lincoln, Abraham 272, 280,
        281, 307
Lincoln Memorial 307
Lindbergh, Charles 282
Literature *See* Books
Lithuania 166
  map 149
Little League 228
Lizards 29
Longitude 84
Looking back from 2006 and
        2007 330–331
Louisiana
  facts about 295
  map 287
  origin of name 288
Louisiana Purchase 280
Louvre (museum) 130
Low, Juliette Gordon 333
Lunar eclipses 219
Luxembourg 167
  map 148

M

Macedonia 167
  map 149
Machines 211
Madagascar 167
  map 153
Madison, James 270, 280
Magic 116–117
Magic Kingdom (Florida) 254
Magma 59
Magna Carta 326
Maine
  facts about 296
  map 287

  origin of name 288
  tourist attraction 257
Maine (U.S. battleship) 118
Malawi 167
  map 153
Malaysia 167
  map 151
Malcolm X 284, 285
Maldives 167
  map 150
Mali 167
  map 152
Malta 167
  map 148
Mammals 23
Mammoth Cave National
        Park 259
Mancuso, Julia 14
Maps
  of continents and nations
        142–153
  plates of Earth 58
  reading of 81
  of United States 145,
        286–287
Marco Polo 82, 83, 254
Mars (planet)
  exploration of 224
  facts about 222, 223
Marshall, Thurgood 284
Marshall Islands 168
  map 143
Martin Luther King Jr. Day
        98, 99
Maryland
  facts about 278, 296
  map 287
  origin of name 288
Massachusetts
  facts about 279, 296
  map 287
  origin of name 288
Matchbox cars 76
Mathematics *See* Numbers
Mauritania 168
  map 152
Mauritius 168
McKinley, William 273
Measurements *See* Weights
        and measures
Meir, Golda 333
Memorial Day 99
Mercator projection 84

Mercury (planet)
  exploration of 224
  facts about 222, 223
Meridians of Earth 84
Merkel, Angela 140
Meteoroids 221
Meteorology 312, 313
Metric system 314, 316
Mexican War (1846-1848)
  118, 280
Mexico 168
  Cinco de Mayo 100
  energy production 62
  history 328–329
  immigrants from 195
  map 145
  tourism 254
  volcanic eruption 59
Michigan
  facts about 297
  map 287
  origin of name 288
Microbes 213
Micronesia 168
  map 143
Microwave radiation 248
Middle East
  history 318–319
  map 150
Military 118–121
Milky Way 221
Minerals 90
Mink, Patsy 285
Minnesota
  facts about 297
  map 287
  origin of name 288
Mint, U.S. 123
Minuit, Peter 279
Mirra, Dave 245
Mississippi
  facts about 297
  map 287
  origin of name 288
Missouri
  facts about 298
  map 287
  origin of name 288
Missouri Compromise 281
Moldova 168
  map 149
Monaco 168
  map 148

Mona Lisa (painting) 33
Monarchy 140
Money 122–125
  national currencies
    154–177
  puzzle 125
  richest people 125
Mongolia 168
  map 151
Monroe, James 270
Monroe Doctrine 281
Montana
  facts about 298
  map 286
  origin of name 289
Montenegro See Serbia and
    Montenegro
Moon
  facts about 219, 282
  lunar eclipses 219
Morocco 168
  map 152
Mother's Day 98, 99
Mountains 71, 80, 85, 260
Mount Everest 80, 83, 85
Movies and TV 126–129
  Kids' Choice Awards 197
  personalities 6–9, 13, 285
  popular TV shows 127, 132
  quiz 129
Mozambique 169
  map 153
Multiplication 185
Muscular system 93
Museums 51, 130–131
  holocaust 307
Music and dance 132–135
  dance forms 135
  instruments of orchestra
    134
  Kids' Choice Awards 197
  music therapy 309
  personalities 12–13
  "Stop the Bop" campaign
    309
  Sydney Opera House 51
  top albums of 2005 132
Mussolini, Benito 327
Myanmar 120, 169
  map 151
Mythology 136–139, 227

N

Names, popular given 40
Namibia 169
  map 153
Napoleon Bonaparte 327
NASCAR 11, 232
National anthem, U.S. 261
National parks, U.S. 258–
    259, 260
National World War II
    Memorial 307
National Zoo (Washington,
    D.C.) 18
Nations 140–179
  currency and exchange
    rates 154–177
  energy producers and
    users 62
  immigration 195
  languages 110, 154–177
  maps 142–153, 286–287
  population 190–191
Native Americans 180–183
  Aztec culture 227
  cultural areas 181
  facts about 277, 280, 281,
    328
  famous figures 183, 285
  U.S. census 182
Natural resources See
    Energy
Nauru 169
  map 143
Nebraska
  facts about 298
  map 286
  origin of name 289
  tourist attraction 257
Nebulas 221
Nepal 169
  map 150
  tallest mountain 80
Neptune (planet)
  exploration of 224
  facts about 223
Nervous system 92
Netherlands, The 169
  map 148
Nevada
  facts about 299
  map 286
  origin of name 289
  tourism 254

New Deal 283
New Hampshire
  facts about 299
  map 287
  origin of name 289
New Horizons (spacecraft)
  226
New Jersey
  facts about 299
  map 287
  origin of name 289
  tourism 254
New Mexico
  facts about 300
  map 286
  origin of name 289
Newspapers 43
Newton, Sir Isaac 207, 216
New Year's Day 98, 99
New York (state)
  facts about 279, 300
  map 287
  origin of name 289
  tourism 254
New York City
  holiday celebrations 98
  population 192
  tourist attractions 130
  World Trade Center attack
    49, 283
New Zealand 169
  map 143
Nicaragua 169
  map 145
Nickelodeon Kids' Choice
    Awards 197, 201
Niger 170
  map 152
Nigeria 170
  map 152
Nightingale, Florence 332
Nile River 80
Nixon, Richard Milhous 275,
  283
Nobel Prizes 196, 216
Norse mythology 138
North America
  facts about 85
  history 82, 277, 328–329
  map 144–145
North Carolina
  facts about 300

map 287
origin of name 289
North Dakota
  facts about 301
  map 286
  origin of name 289
North Korea 119, 120, 165
  map 151
Norway 170
  map 148
Nuclear energy 60, 64
Numbers 184–189
  multiplication 185
  puzzles 189
Nursing 97, 332
Nutrition 89–90

O

Oceans 71, 85, 142–153, 214,
  215
O'Connor, Sandra Day 269,
  283
Octopush (underwater
    hockey) 229
Oh, Sadaharu 16
Ohio
  facts about 301
  map 287
  origin of name 289
Oil (fuel) 319
Oklahoma
  facts about 301
  map 286
  origin of name 289
Olympics 14–15, 18, 230
  Paralympics/Special
    Olympics 231
Oman 170
  map 150
Opium War (1839) 323
Orchestra, instruments of
  134
Oregon
  facts about 302
  map 286
  origin of name 289
Outer space *See* Space
Ozone layer 66

P

Pacific Islands map 143
Pacific Ocean 85
Painting 32–33

Pakistan 120, 170
  earthquake 58
  map 150
Palau 170
  map 143
Paleo-Indians 277
Paleontology *See* Science
Palestine 318, 319
Panama 170
  map 145
Panama Canal 282
Pandas, Giant 18, 27
Papua New Guinea 170
  map 143
Paraguay 171
  map 147
Paralympics 231
Parks 258–259, 260
Parks, Rosa 19, 285
Pascal's triangle 188
Patrick, Danica 233
Pennsylvania
  facts about 302
  map 287
  origin of name 289
  tourism 254
Persian Gulf War (1991) 119,
  283, 319
Peru 171
  earthquake 58
  map 146
Petrified Forest National
    Park 259
Pets 20, 26
Philippines 171
  immigrants from 195
  map 151
  volcanic eruption 59
Photosynthesis 214
Photography 32
Physical science 206,
  210–211
Physical scientists 216
Pi (mathematical constant)
  186
Pierce, Franklin 272
Piercing 75
Pig farms 72
*Pirates of the Caribbean:
    Dead Man's Chest*
    (movie) 8
Planes *See* Aviation
Planets 218, 222–224, 226
Plants 23, 70–71, 214
Plastic 209

Pledge of Allegiance 261
Pleiades 227
Pluto (planet) 223, 226
Poland 171
 immigrants from 195
 map 149
Polar bears 28
Polk, James Knox 271
Polygons and polyhedrons
 187
Ponce de León, Juan 278
Population 190–195
 of cities 191, 192
 immigrants 195
 of nations 154–177,
  190–191
 of United States 192–195
Portugal 171
 map 148
Postal abbreviations 290–
 306
Powell, Colin 284
Prefixes 113
Presidents' Day 99
Presidents of United States
 cabinet departments 264
 death and succession 264
 election of 264, 265
 facts about 270–276
 term of office 264
Prime numbers 184
Prizes and contests 42,
 196–201, 256
 puzzle 201
Probability 78
Proteins 90
Puerto Rico 145, 306
Pulleys 211
Puzzles and quizzes
 answers to 334–337
 buildings 53
 computers 249
 energy 63
 Harry Potter 43
 money 125
 movies 129
 numbers 189
 prizes and contests 201
 riddles 114–115
 science 207, 217
 sports 244
 synonyms 115
 weather 312

Q

Qatar 171
 map 150
Quicksand 214

R

Railroads See Trains
Rain 310, 312
Rainbows 215
Rain forests 70
Rankin, Jeanette 282
Reagan, Ronald 275, 283
Recycling 73
Reference books 45
Reformation 326
Rehnquist, William 269
Religion 202–205
 major holy days 204–205
Reproductive system 93
Reptiles 23
Respiratory system 92
Revolutionary War See
  American Revolution
Rhode Island
 facts about 302
 map 287
 origin of name 289
Rice, Condoleezza 284
Riddles 114–115
Right to Play (charity) 18
Ring of Fire 59
Rivers 80, 260
Roberts, John G. 18, 268, 269
Robinson, Jackie 283
Rock, Chris 6
Rocks 86
Roethlisberger, Ben 17
Roller coasters 255
Romania 171
 children from 179
 map 149
Rome, ancient 325
 Latin 113
 mythology 136–137
Roosevelt, Eleanor 274, 276
Roosevelt, Franklin Delano
 274, 283, 307
Roosevelt, Theodore 196,
 273
Rotten sneaker contest 200
Russia 171
 armed forces 120
 energy production/
  consumption 62

maps 144, 149, 150–151
 space exploration 225
Rwanda 172
 map 153

S

Sacagawea (Shoshone
 woman) 183
Sahara Desert 80
Saint Kitts and Nevis 172
 map 145
Saint Lucia 172
 map 145
Saint Vincent and the
 Grenadines 172
 map 145
Samoa 172
 map 143
San Marino 172
 map 148
Santa Anna, Anonio López
 de 118
Sao Tomé and Príncipe 172
 map 153
Satellites 221
Saturn (planet)
 exploration of 224
 facts about 222
 lightning storm 226
Saudi Arabia 172
 energy production 62
 map 150
School segregation 282
Science 206–217
 branches of 206
 chemical elements
  208–209
 classroom experiments
  209, 213
 famous scientists 216
 kids' contest 198
 museums 130
 puzzles 207, 217
 questions and answers
  214–215
Scientific method 207
Scooter riding 228
Scrabble 200
Screws 211
Scuba diving 215
Sculpture 32, 33, 201
Seasons 220
Senate, U.S. 266

Senegal 172
  map 152
Sensory perception 94–95
September 11, 2001 terrorist
      attacks 49, 283
Septuplets 40
Serbia and Montenegro 173
  map 149
Sereno, Paul 216
Settlers of Catan (game) 78
Seychelles 173
Ships 250–253
  disasters 61
Sierra Leone 173
  map 152
Sight See Eyesight
Signs and symbols
  chemical elements
      208–209
  on maps 81
  U.S. emblems 261
Silk Road 322
Silly Putty 76
Singapore 173
  map 151
Skateboarding 17, 228, 245
Skating 14–15, 18, 228, 230
Skiing 14, 230
Skyscrapers 48–50
Slave trade 279, 281, 321
Slovakia 173
  map 148
Slovenia 173
  map 148
Smell, sense of 95
Smithsonian Institution 130,
      200, 307
Smog 66
Smoking 96
Snakes 20, 30
Sneaker contest, rotten 200
Snow 201, 310, 312
Snowboarding 15, 230
Soccer 16, 77, 228, 243
Social science 206
Softball 228
Sojourner Truth 285, 332
Solar eclipses 219
Solar system 218
  unmanned missions 224
Solomon Islands 173
  map 143
Somalia 173
  map 152
Sound 210, 214, 215

South Africa 174
  map 153
South America
  facts about 85
  history 328–329
  map 146–147
South Carolina
  facts about 303
  map 287
  origin of name 289
South Dakota
  facts about 303
  map 286
  origin of name 289
South Korea 119, 120, 165
  children from 179
  immigrants from 195
  map 151
Soviet Union See Russia
Space 218–227
  astronauts/cosmonauts in
      225, 253, 282, 333
  Columbia disaster 225
  eclipses 219
  famous scientists 216
  unmanned probes 224
Spain 174, 278
  map 148
  tourism 51, 254
Spanish-American War
      (1898) 118, 281, 329
Special Olympics 231
Spelling Bee, National 199
Sports 228–245
  auto racing 232-233
  baseball 16, 228, 234–235
  basketball 17, 236–237
  football 17, 238–240
  golf 241
  gymnastics 241
  ice hockey 242
  Olympics 14–15, 18, 230
  Paralympics/Special
      Olympics 231
  puzzle 244
  soccer 16, 243
  tennis 16, 244
  X Games 17, 245
Spring (season) 220
Sprouse, Dylan and Cole 6
Sri Lanka 174, 309
  map 150

Stanton, Elizabeth Cady 332
Starry Night, The (painting)
      33
Stars
  galaxies 221
  Pleiades/Big Dipper 227
  sun as star 218
Stars (people) See Faces
      and Places in the
      News
"Star-Spangled Banner"
      118, 261, 281
States of United States
  Electoral College votes
      265
  facts about 260, 290–306
  national parks 258–259
  origins of names 288–289
  population of 192–193, 195
  quarters 123
  record temperatures 311
  representation in U.S.
      House 267
Stefani, Gwen 133
Stenberg, Jeremy 245
Stock car racing 232
Storms 56–57, 61
Stowe, Harriet Beecher 280
Sudan 174
  longest river 80
  map 152
Suffixes 113
Suite Life of Zack and Cody,
      The (TV show) 6
Summer 220
Sun
  distance from planets
      222–223
  light and energy from 65,
      214, 215
  solar eclipses 219
  as star 218
Super Bowl 17, 238
Supreme Court, U.S. 18,
      268–269, 283
  historic rulings 282, 284
Suriname 174
  map 146
Swaziland 174
  map 153
Sweden 174
  map 148
Switzerland 174
  map 148

Sydney Opera House (Australia) 51
Symbols *See* Signs and symbols
Synonyms 115
Syria 175
  map 150

T

Taft, William Howard 273
Taiwan 175
  map 151
  tallest building 49
Tajikistan 175
  map 150
Tallchief, Maria 183
Tanzania 175
  map 153
Tasmanian devils 29
Taste, sense of 95
Taylor, Zachary 271
Technology 246–249
Teddy bears 76
Telegraph 280
Telephones *See* Cell phones
Television *See* Movies and TV
Tempel 1 (comet) 226
Temperature 311, 315
Ten Commandments 318
Tennessee
  facts about 303
  map 287
  origin of name 289
Tennis 16, 244, 333
Tereshkova, Valentina 333
Terrorism *See* September 11, 2001 terrorist attacks
Texas
  facts about 304
  map 286
  Mexican War fought over 118
  origin of name 289
  tourism 254
Thailand 175
  map 151
Thanksgiving 99
Thorpe, Jim 183
Tibet 80
Tidal waves *See* Tsunami
Timor-Leste (East Timor) 175
  map 151

Togo 175
  map 152
Tonga 175
  map 143
Torah 203
Tornadoes 57, 312
Totalitarianism 140
Totem poles 182
Touch, sense of 95
Tourism *See* Travel
Toys *See* Games and toys
"Trail of Tears" 280
Trains 251–253, 281
  disasters 60
Transcontinental railroad 252
Transportation 250–253
Travel 254–259
Trees 70, 71
  Christmas 98
Trinidad and Tobago 175
  map 146
Tripitaka 202
Trojan War 324
Tropics 84
Truman, Harry S. 274
Truth, Sojourner 285, 332
Tsunami 59, 309
Tundra 71
Tunisia 176
  map 152
Turkey 120, 176
  earthquake 58
  map 150
Turkmenistan 176
  map 150
Tutankhamen (King Tut) 32
Tuvalu 176
  map 143
Tyler, John 271

U

Uganda 176
  map 153
Ukraine 176
  map 149
Uncle Tom's Cabin (book) 280
Underwater hockey 229
Underwood, Carrie 13
United Arab Emirates 51, 176
  map 150

United Kingdom (Great Britain) 176
  children from 179
  energy production/consumption 62
  immigrants from 195
  map 148
  Nightingale profile 332
  tourism 254
  at war with America 118, 279, 281
United Nations 141
United States 177, 260–307
  capital of 307
  Constitution 262–263
  earthquakes 58
  elections 264, 265
  energy production/consumption 62
  flag 177, 261
  history time line 277–283
  immigrants 195
  languages spoken 110
  largest cities 192
  legal holidays 99
  maps 145, 286–287
  motto 261
  national anthem 261
  national parks 258–259
  national symbols 261
  paper money and coins 122–124
  population 192–195, 260
  presidents 270–275
  revenues and expenditures 122
  space exploration 224–226
  states, facts about 288–289, 290–306
  tourism 254, 255, 257–259
  volcanic eruption 59
  wars and military 118–121
Universal Studios (Florida) 255
Uranus (planet)
  exploration of 224
  facts about 223
Urinary system 93
Ursa Major *See* Big Dipper
Uruguay 177
  map 147
Usher (Usher Raymond) 133

Utah
facts about 304
map 286
origin of name 289
Uzbekistan 177
map 150

V

Valentine's Day 99
Van Buren, Martin 271
Van Gogh, Vincent 33
Vanuatu 177
map 143
Vatican City 177
map 148
Venezuela 177
highest waterfall 80
map 146
Venus (planet)
exploration of 224
facts about 222, 223
Vermont
facts about 304
map 287
origin of name 289
Verrazano, Giovanni da 278
Vertebrates, types of 22
Veterans Day 98, 99
Vice presidents of the United
States
in presidential succession
264
who became president
270–275
Videos and video games 77,
197
Vietnam 177
immigrants from 195
map 151
Vietnam Veterans Memorial
33
Vietnam War 119, 282, 323
Villaraigosa, Antonio 285
Virginia
facts about 284, 305
map 287
origin of name 289
tourism 254
Vision See Eyesight
Vitamins 90
Volcanoes 59, 310
Volleyball 228
Volunteering 308–309
Voting 264, 265

W

Walking 228
*Wallace and Gromit: The
Curse of the Were-
Rabbit* (movie) 8
Walt Disney World (Florida)
255
War of 1812 118, 281
Washington (state)
facts about 305
map 286
origin of name 289
Washington, D.C. 18, 130,
131, 280, 284, 307
Washington, George 118,
270, 280, 307
Washington Monument 307
Water
energy from 64
hydrological cycle 68
pollution 27, 69
use and conservation
68–69
Waterfalls 80
Watergate scandal 283
Way, Danny 17, 245
Weather 310–313
hottest and coldest places
315
quiz 312
temperatures 311, 315
Wedges 211
Weights and measures
314–317
West Virginia
facts about 305
map 287
origin of name 289
Wetlands 69
Whales 27
Wheels and axles 211
White, Shaun 15, 245
White House 264, 307
Wilson, Edith 273, 276
Wilson, Woodrow 118, 273
Wind energy 65
Winfrey, Oprah 285
Winter 220
Winthrop, John 279
Wisconsin
facts about 306
map 287
origin of name 289

Witherspoon, Reese 9
Women
in Congress 267
government leaders 140
historic figures 285,
332–333
military service memorial
307
WNBA 237
Woods, Tiger 241
Words See Language
World Almanac Adventurer
contest 256
World Baseball Classic 16
World Cup 16, 243
World history 318–333
Africa 320–321
Americas 328–329
Asia 322–323
Europe 324–327
Middle East 318–319
World Series 234, 235
World Trade Center (New
York City) 49, 283
World War I (1914-1918) 119,
282, 327
World War II (1939-1945) 74,
119, 283, 307, 323, 327
Wright, Wilbur and Orville 108
Wyoming
facts about 306
map 286
national park 259
origin of name 289

X

Xena (solar system object)
223
X Games 17, 245

Y

Yellowstone National Park
259
Yemen 177
map 150
Yosemite National Park 258
Yo-yos 76
Yugoslavia See Serbia and
Montenegro

Z

Zambia 177
map 153
Zimbabwe 177
map 153

Illustration and Photo Credits

Front Cover: Background, Getty Images; Girl Jumping, Jupiter Images; Boy, Corbis. **Back Cover**: Reese Witherspoon, AP/Wide World Photos; Harry Houdini, LOC P&P Rep. #LC-USZ62-112419. **3**: Reese Witherspoon, AP/Wide World Photos. **6**: Suite Life of Zack and Cody, The Disney Channel/Photofest; Everybody Hates Chris, UPN/Photofest. **7**: American Idol, MARIO ANZOUNI/Reuters/Landov; The Amazing Race, CBS/Landov. **8**: Pirates of the Caribbean, Peter Mountain Copyright: ©Disney Enterprises, Inc. and Jerry Bruckheimer, Inc, All rights reserved; Wallace & Gromit, DreamWorks/Photofest. **9**: Reese Witherspoon, AP/Wide World Photos. **10**: LeBron James, AP/Wide World Photos. **11**: Jeff Gordon, AP/Wide World Photos; #24 Car, Kevin Kane/WireImage.com. **12**: The Black Eyed Peas, AP/Wide World Photos. **13**: Aly and AJ, Carrie Underwood, AP/Wide World Photos; High School Musical, Disney Channel. **14**: Julia Mancuso & Shani Davis, AP/Wide World Photos. **15**: Shaun White, FRANCO DEBERNARDI/EPA /Landov; Cindy Klassen, AP/Wide World Photos. **16**: Donovan & Oh, AP/Wide World Photos. **17**: Way, AP/Wide World Photos; Rothlisberger, GARY C. CASKEY/EPA/Landov. **18**: Cheek, AP/Wide World Photos; Bush, SHAWN THEW/EPA/Landov; Pandas, REUTERS/Shealah Craighead/HO/Landov . **19**: Soldiers, U.S. Navy photo by Photographer's Mate 1st Class Alan D. Monyelle; Parks, AP/Wide World Photos; Booking photo, AP/Wide World Photos. **20**: Hamster and snake, AP World Wide Photos/MUTSUGORO OKOKU ZOO. **27**: Panda, Whale, Photos.com. **28**: Bear, Fritz Polking/Peter Arnold. Inc.; Paw, Dan Guravich/Corbis; Teeth, Flip Nicklin/Minden Pictures. **30**: Python Pete, AP/Wide World Photos; Dophin and soldier, U.S. Navy photo by Photographer's Mate 1st Class Brien Aho. **33**: *Brownstones*, Courtesy of Clark Atlanta University Art Galleries. **35**: © Evan Schwartz. **36**: Robinson, Library of Congress Serial and Government Publications Division, Rep. #LC-USZC4-6144 DLC; Darwin, LOC P&P Rep. #LC-USZ61-104; Witherspoon, AP/Wide World Photos. **37**: Jefferson, LOC P&P Rep. #LC-USZ62-8195; Ride, NASA; Williams, AP/Wide World Photos. **38**: Radcliffe, AP/Wide World Photos; Neil Armstrong, NASA; Duff, Mike Lee/Landov. **39**: Nagra, AP/Wide World Photos; Damon, AP/Wide World Photos; Beethoven, LOC P&P Rep. #LC-USZ62-29499. **41**: Thomas Family, Ogden, UT (1924), Courtesy of Edward A. Thomas. **42**: Small Steps, Used by permission of Dell Publishing, a division of Random House, Inc.; Rosa, Courtesy of Henry Holt and Co. **44**: Flush, Used by permission of Alfred A. Knopf, an imprint of Random House Children's Books, a division of Random House, Inc.; Book without Words, Hyperion Books for Children; Spider Spins a Story © 1997 by Jill Maxx. All rights reserved. Used by permission from Rising Moon. **45**: The Penderwicks, Used by permission of Alfred A. Knopf, an imprint of Random House Children's Books, a division of Random House, Inc.; TINTIN, Copyright © renewed 1982 by Casterman. Reprinted by permission of Little, Brown and Company (Inc.); FAREWELL TO MANZANAR by Jeanne Wakatsuki and James D. Houston. Copyright © 2002. Reprinted by permission of Houghton Mifflin Company. All rights reserved; Egyptology, Courtesy of Candlewick Press. **46**: Paolini, AP/Wide World Photos; Paterson, © Samantha Loomis Paterson. **49**: Taipei Financial Centre, AP/Wide World Photos. **50**: Home Insurance Building, Courtesy of Frances Loeb Library, Graduate School of Design, Harvard University. **51**: Bilbao, Allan Jaworski; Burj Al Arab Hotel, Courtesy of Jumeirah International; Johnson's Glass House, Ron Blunt. **53**: Millau Viaduct, JEAN-PHILIPPE ARLES/Reuters /Landov. **54**: Boys, Camp Sea Gull, Arapahoe, NC; Camp John Marc, Camp John Marc, Dallas, TX. **55**: Courtesy of Circus Smirkus. **57**: Tornado, NOAA Photo Library, NOAA Central Library; OAR/ERL/National Severe Storms Laboratory (NSSL). **61**: Johnstown, Pa. Flood, LOC P&P Rep. #LC-USZ62-60962. **74**: Tuxedo, LOC P&P Rep. **75**: Women at work, LOC P&P Rep. #LC-DIG-FSAC-1A35341. **75**: Disco, Frank A. Cezus/Getty Images; LL COOL J, WENN/Landov. **76**: Crayons, © 2006 Binney & Smith. **77**: Sid Meier's Civilization IV, Courtesy of Fixaris Games. **78**: Settlers, Mayfair Games, Inc. **82**: Cook, LOC P&P Rep. #LC-USZ62-25351. **83**: Henson, LOC P&P Rep. #LC-USZC4-7503. **86**: © Dale Williams. **108**: Edison, LOC P&P Rep. #LC-DIG-CWPBH-04044; Bell, LOC P&P Rep #LC-USZ62-104276. **116**: Houdini, LOC Item in McManus-Young Collection. **116**: Blaine, AP/Wide World Photos. **117**: © Aram A. Schvey. **118**: Key, LOC P&P Rep. #LC-USZC4-6200; Antietam, LOC P&P Rep. #LC-USZC4-1768; MAINE, LOC P&P Rep. #LC-USZ62-65547. **119**: Wilson, LOC P&P Rep. #LC-USZ62-107577; Omaha Beach, National Archives; My Tho, Vietnam. U.S. Archive; war planes, USAF. **120**: Aeriel Vehicle, U.S. Marine Corps photo by Cpl. Paul Leicht; Troops, Photo Courtesy of the U.S. Army. **121**: BMC Andrew Fabbo. **123**: Quarters, U.S. Mint. **125**: Bill Gates, Courtesy of Microsoft Corporation. **126**: Disney, Hulton Archive/Getty Images. **127**: Pennington, ABC/Photofest; Shrek 2, Dream Works Pictures. **128**: Lavagirl and Sharkboy, Dimension Films/Photofest; Toy Story, Walt Disney Pictures/Photofest. **129**: Narnia, Walt Disney Pictures/Photofest **130**: Grasshopper, AP/Wide World Photos; Louvre, AP/Wide World Photos. **131**: Skulls, Photo by Don Spiro Courtesy, Mütter Museum, College of Physicians of Philadelphia. **132**: Destiny's Child, Clarkson, AP/Wide World Photos. **133**: Usher, FRED PROUSER/Reuters/Landov; Stefani, AP/Wide World Photos. **135**: Maya Park, ballet positions, Zoë Kashner; Worm, Devin Wagner; Hula, © James R. Keenley. **139**: Poseidon, © Hans Andersen. **140**: Bachelet, AP/Wide World Photos; Merkel, UN Photo/X; Sirleaf-Johnson, UN Photo/Mark Garten. **154-177**: Flags, Mapquest. **179**: Romanian Kids, © Aram A. Schvey; South Korea, AP/Wide World Photos. **180**: Totem, © Edward A. Thomas. **182**: Totem, © Edward A. Thomas. **183**: Jim Thorpe, Cumberland County Historical Society; Chief Joseph, LOC P&P Rep. #LC-USZ61-2088; Sacagawea, Golden Dollar Obverse © 1999 U.S. Mint All Rights Reserved. **184**: Dog, Photo by Timothy J. Pennings. **195**: Immigrants, LOC P&P Rep. #LC-B201-5202-13. **196**: Wiesel, Boston University; ElBaradei, Dean Calma/IAEA. **197**: Lohan, Noel Hines/Landov; Black, AP/Wide World Photos. **198**: Exploravision, Jacqueline Malonson/JAX Photography; Warhol, REUTERS/Chip Fast/Landov. **200**: Kids with Kite, Photos.com. **205**: Amish, AP/Wide World Photos. **210**: Oscilloscope display, © Loren Winters/Visuals Unlimited; Light, © Michael Meyerhofer. **211**: Axe, Pulley, & See Saw, Photos.com. **213**: Mould on bread, Stephan Goerlich/dpa/Landov. **213**: Amoeba, © Wim van Egmond/Visuals Unlimited; Anton Van Leeuwenhoek, Image © History of Science Collections, University of Oklahoma Libraries. **214**: Ear, Photos.com. **215**: Scuba, Photos.com. **216**: Kepler, Image © History of Science Collections, University of Oklahoma Libraries; George Washington Carver, LOC P&P Rep. #LC-J601-302. **220**: Planet Earth Seasons, Argosy Publishing. **221**: NGC 4414 Galaxy & Comet Hale-Bopp, NASA. **224**: Mariner 2, Mars Odyssey, & Cassini spacecraft's view of Saturn lightning, NASA. **226**: New Horizons & Deep Impact, NASA. **227**: The Plaeades, Hubble. **229**: White & Underwater Hockey Team, AP/Wide World Photos. **230**: Cohen, AP/Wide World Photos. **231**: Storey, TONY GENTILE/Reuters/Landov; Swimmers Special Olympics, Courtesy of Special Olympics. **232**: Stewart, AP/Wide World Photos. **233**: Patrick, AP/Wide World Photos. **234**: Chicago White Sox, AP/Wide World Photos. **235**: Shoeless Joe Jackson, LOC P&P Rep. #LC-USZ62-28948. **236**: Jordan, Mike Blake/Reuters/Landov; Basketball Hall of Fame, Naismith Memorial Basketball Hall of Fame. **237**: Ford, AP/Wide World Photos. **238**: Alexander, AP/Wide World Photos. **239**: Bradshaw, AP/Wide World Photos. **240**: Reggie Bush, AP/Wide World Photos. **241**: Woods, AP/Wide World Photos. **243**: Donovan Major League Soccer. **245**: Adu, AP/Wide World Photos. **245**: Way & Mirra, AP/Wide World Photos. **248**: iMac, Apple Computer, Inc. **252**: Wright Brothers plane, LOC P&P Rep. #LC-USZ62-5155A. **253**: Millau Viaduct, JEAN-PHILIPPE ARLES/Reuters/Landov. **255**: Twister, Courtesy of Cedar Point. **257**: Winchester Mystery House, Winchester Mystery House, San Jose, CA. **259**: Mammoth Cave National Park, National Park Service. **267**: Jeannette Rankin LOC P&P Rep. #LC-DIG-GGBAIN-23837. **268**: Justices of the U.S. Supreme Court, LARRY DOWNING/Reuters /Landov. **269**: Alito & Roberts, WENN/Carrie Devorah/Landov; Thurgood Marshall, LOC P&P Rep. #LC-U9-1027B-11. **270-274**: Washintgon, Adams, Jefferson, Madison, Monroe, Adams, Jackson, Harrison, Tyler, Pierce, Buchanan, Johnson, Hayes, Arthur, Harrison, McKinley, Roosevelt, Wilson, Harding, Hoover, Roosevelt, Eisenhower © 1967 by Dover Publications. **271-275**: Van Buren, Polk, Taylor, Fillmore, Lincoln, Grant, Garfield, Cleveland, Taft, Coolidge, Truman, Kennedy, Nixon, LOC P&P. **275**: Johnson, Lyndon B. Johnson Library; Ford, Courtesy of Gerald R. Ford Museum; Carter, Courtesy of Jimmy Carter Library; Reagan, Courtesy of Ronald Reagan Library; George H.W. Bush, Official White House Photograph; Bill Clinton, Courtesy of the White House; George W. Bush, Eric Draper-The White House. **276**: Abigail Adams, LOC P&P Rep. #LC-USZ62-10016; Abigail Fillmore, Photo courtesy of the Millard Fillmore House Museum, East Aurora, New York; Frances Cleveland, LOC P&P Rep. #LC-USZ62-25797; Edith Wilson, LOC P&P Rep. #LC-USZ62-25808; Grace Coolidge, LOC P&P Rep. #LC-USZ62-100816; Eleanor Roosevelt, LOC P&P Rep. #LC-USZ62-25812; Laura Bush, Eric Draper—The White House. **284**: Martin Luther King, Lyndon B. Johnson Library. **285**: Malcolm X, LOC P&P Rep. #LC-DIG-PPMSC-01274. **285**: Patsy Mink, Time Life Pictures/Getty Images. **309**: College students, Marvin Nauman/FEMA photo; Kaku, The Prudential Spirit of Community Awards; Habitat for Humanity, Mia Toschi. **314**: Edward A. Thomas, Timothy Bryk. **318**: Hieroglyphics, © Edward A. Thomas; Alexander the Great, LOC P&P Rep. #LC-USZ62-40088. **321**: Gambari with Sirleaf-Johnson, UN Photo/Mark Garten. **327**: Hitler and Mussolini, National Archives. **328**: Cortes, LOC P&P Rep. #LC-USZ62-47764. **330**: Bill Clinton, Courtesy of the White House; San Francisco earthquake, LOC P&P Rep. #LC-USZ62-123117. **331**: Little Rock school, UPI/Landov; Albright, U.S. State Department. **332**: Truth, LOC P&P Rep. #LC-USZ62-119343; Stanton & Anthony, LOC P&P Rep. #LC-USZ62-83145; Nightingale, LOC P&P Rep. #LC-USZ62-5877. **333**: Meir, LOC P&P Rep. #LC-U9-27286-5; Jemison, NASA; Friedan, LOC P&P Rep. #LC-USZ62-115884.